BETWEEN ETHICS
AND
AESTHETICS

SUNY series in Aesthetics and the Philosophy of Art
Mary C. Rawlinson, Editor

BETWEEN ETHICS
AND
AESTHETICS
Crossing the Boundaries

Edited By

Dorota Glowacka
and
Stephen Boos

State University
of
New York Press

Published by
State University of New York Press, Albany

© 2002 State University of New York

For information, address State University of New York Press,
90 State Street, Suite 700, Albany, NY 12207

Production by Michael Haggett
Marketing by Patrick Durocher

Library of Congress Cataloging-in-Publication Data

Between ethics and aesthetics : crossing the boundaries / edited by Dorota
Glowacka and Stephen Boos.
     p. cm.—(SUNY series in aesthetics and the philosophy of art)
    Includes bibliographical references and index.
    ISBN 0-7914-5195-X (alk. paper)—ISBN 0-7914-5196-8 (pbk. : alk.
paper)
    1. Aesthetics.   2. Ethics.   3. Art—Moral and ethical aspects.   I.
Glowacka, Dorota, 1960–   II. Boos, Stephen, 1953–   III. Series.

BH39 .B425 2002
111'.85—dc21   2001049301

10 9 8 7 6 5 4 3 2 1

CONTENTS

ACKNOWLEDGMENTS

The editors of this book gratefully acknowledge the diligence, cooperation, and enthusiasm of all the contributors.

We also want to thank our friends and colleagues at the University of King's College for their unceasing encouragement and support. Special thanks to Dr. Colin Starnes, the President, and to the Research and Travel Committee of the University of King's College Faculty, for financial support during the preparation of the manuscript. We are grateful to Joy Loder and Stephanie Boudreau for typing parts of the manuscript and to Sharon Brown and Pat Dixon for their help with the endless little tasks. Many thanks to Steve McCullough for his work on the index. We would also like to thank the editors at SUNY Press for their assistance and valuable editorial suggestions.

We owe a great deal to our families, who have patiently endured our busy weekends. To Zbyszek, Maga, and Jerome and to Carmel, Alexander, and Daniel—our biggest thanks.

LIST OF ILLUSTRATIONS

Dorota Glowacka and Stephen Boos

The quarrel between philosophy and art, beauty and morality, art and politics, and aesthetics and ethics in Western culture is symbolized in Plato's *Republic* by the denigration and expulsion of poets from the polis. Poetry, Plato's Socrates says, misrepresents gods, heroes, and the truth. The symbolic return of the exiled poets is found in Aristotle's rehabilitation of mimesis and his defense of the moral and epistemological value of art. According to Aristotle, tragedy is not only concerned with universal truth, but its cathartic effect makes better citizens. Since antiquity, the dispute between art and ethics has assumed at least two principal forms: art is either regarded as subservient to ethical, religious, and philosophical spheres or, as in Nietzsche and Heidegger, it constitutes an autonomous, self-sufficient aesthetic realm lying beyond good and evil, a sphere beyond political, social, and ethical concerns.

If, in classical antiquity, the forms of art and religion are indistinguishable, in the High Middle Ages, art becomes the handmaiden of religion. The medieval poet is still religious but acknowledges the limitations of his craft, as does Dante in the *Divine Comedy*, by pointing to a religious sphere lying beyond his imaginative and poetic grasp. In the Renaissance period, alongside a developing secularism and worldliness, art initiates the process of liberating itself from religion. Art is no longer merely subservient to either philosophy or religion but comes to possess an irreducible and unique status. The emergence of an autonomous, self-sufficient realm of the aesthetic is quickly followed, particularly in the eighteenth century, by the establishment of the modern science of aesthetics. Although A.G. Baumgarten, in his *Aesthetica*, is perhaps the first to characterize the aesthetic as a perceptual knowledge mediate between theoretical and practical knowledge, it is Kant who, in his *Critique of Judgment*, best articulates the problematic nature of the relationship between beauty and the realm of truth and moral goodness. According to Kant, aesthetic judgment is not only distinct from understanding and reason but also forms a bridge between the concepts of nature and freedom. Kant elevates aesthetic judgment above the realm of the merely empirical and emphasizes its reliance on the free play of the faculties of imagination and understanding, unbounded by the determinate concepts of either theoretical or practical reason. At the same time, the aesthetic experience of the sublime is thought by Kant to awaken in us a feeling of our supersensible destination (i.e., the idea of the morally good). This link between the sublime and a higher good, between aesthetics and morality, remains incomplete in Kant, since the concurrence between beauty and morality, as Kant says, works only by analogy, in the manner of "as if."

The primacy of aesthetics over theoretical and ethical life is explicit in the aesthetic theories of many nineteenth-century philosophers and artists. Friedrich Schiller, writing shortly after the French Revolution, argues that aesthetic education alone enables humanity to make the transition from nature to moral and political freedom. Friedrich Schlegel, on the other hand, writes about the need for a new mythology, the most artful of all works of art, which will be forged out of the depths of the modern spirit of idealism. Arthur Schopenhauer regards visual works of art as representations of the Ideas and music as the direct expression of a metaphysical Will.

The metaphysically privileged role assigned to art and aesthetics over morality and ethics is perhaps most pronounced in the philosophical theory of Friedrich Nietzsche. In *The Birth of Tragedy*, Nietzsche writes that art and not morality is the truly metaphysical activity of mankind, and that the existence of the world can be legitimated only on aesthetic grounds. Martin Heidegger and Theodor Adorno, on the other hand, regard art as a way of overcoming the inherent limitations of modern technological society. Heidegger conceives the fine arts as a form of aletheia, a way of "revealing," which can "save" us from the twofold danger of modern technology, whereas Adorno, for whom genuine works of art are unintelligible wholes, turns to the avant-garde for the critique of advanced capitalist society.

According to traditional views, therefore, ethics and aesthetics are either autonomous and separate from each other or one is subservient to the other. The chapters in *Between Ethics and Aesthetics: Crossing the Boundaries* question the legitimacy of these well established formulations and insist on the need to rethink the existing definitions of aesthetics and ethics and the relations between them. Contemporary ethical philosophers have increasingly recognized the heterogeneity inherent in ethics, which is irreducible to the totalizing claims of any given system of thought.

Perhaps one of the strongest indicators of these changing trends in contemporary thought is the growing interest, among scholars from various disciplines, in the work of Emmanuel Levinas. Against traditional formulations of ethics as a normative project grounded in the primacy of the I, Levinas defines the ethical as a moral responsibility for the well-being of the Other. According to Levinas, the very notions of subjectivity, consciousness, and freedom already presuppose an infinite, nondischargeable debt to the Other. For Levinas, Western representational paradigms are the project of an egological, imperial subject, while aesthetics, traditionally understood as producing a likeness of the Other, colludes in the appropriation of Otherness by the same. Levinas himself has never attempted to redefine aesthetics within the parameters of the Other, yet his critique has precipitated various searches for a possibility of an "other" aesthetics, capable of accommodating radical alterity without reducing it to the measure of the same. Poststructuralist thinkers such as Jean-François Lyotard, Jean-Luc Nancy, Maurice Blanchot, and Jacques Derrida, often directly influenced by Levinas' "ethics of ethics," have searched for ways to articulate the exteriority that transcends thought itself and therefore remains nonrepresentable. Also, as shown by several authors in this book, some of the most powerful explorations of the possibilities to accord visibility and voice to Otherness that eludes Western representational practices have recently taken place within feminist theory, in the works of authors such as Luce Irigaray, Gayatri Spivak, Drucilla Cornell and bell hooks.

The concern for the connection—and divide—between ethics and aesthetics is one of the most important issues in contemporary theoretical debates. This book has been conceived as a forum for the presentation of current discussion on ethics and aesthetics but also as a site where traditional formulations of these notions are being contested. In the editors' view, the questions arising from modernity's crisis of representation necessitate an ongoing, interdisciplinary discussion about the intersections of ethics and aesthetics. To this end, *Between Ethics and Aesthetics* promotes a plurality of approaches from disciplines such as philosophy, literary theory, social and political thought, postcolonial theory, women's studies, cultural studies, theology, art history, and Holocaust studies. These polyvalent voices converse and converge but just as often resist one another. Such a structure is designed to set in motion interpretive practices that challenge the very notion of disciplinarity and discrete disciplinary boundaries. As a result, the discursive register of the essays is broad, including specialized theoretical discussions, close readings of literary texts and analyses of artworks, and personal statements and narratives by artists and other people involved in the processes of artistic production and promotion of the arts. It is our hope that this infringement on the principle of congruity, consistency, and decorum will spur further discussions about the applicability of current philosophical debates on ethics and aesthetics to concrete artistic and literary practices.

The book is divided into four thematic sections, each of which explores the boundaries between ethics and aesthetics from a particular angle, asking questions about the relations between philosophical reflection and art, aesthetics and the thought of the Other, aesthetics and politics, and ethics and artistic practice, respectively.

The chapters in Part 1, "Rethinking Ethics and Aesthetics: Between Philosophy and Art," return to the works of Kant, Schiller, and Hegel and reconsider central issues of aesthetics such as the conjunction between beauty and morality versus the disinterestedness of aesthetic judgment, the relation between philosophy and art and thus the very possibility of aesthetics, and, importantly, the immanently gendered nature of philosophical reflection on ethics and aesthetics. In the first chapter, "Rethinking the Aesthetic: Kant, Schiller, and Hegel," Stephen Boos examines the history of modern aesthetics and argues that the modern aesthetic sensibility should be viewed as the reconciling synthesis of practical and theoretical life, duty and inclination, and reason and feeling. Kant, Boos claims, acknowledges the mediating role of the aesthetic in the system of reason but tends to emphasize the separation of aesthetics from ethics. It is Schiller, rather, who establishes the primacy of aesthetics in intellectual and practical life. Following Schiller, Hegel elevates the aesthetic into the realm of religion and philosophy. Art and philosophy, Hegel asserts, both engage in acts of reconciling the highest oppositions and contradictions in human existence, although philosophy is "higher" than art in this endeavor. In a deconstructive gesture, Boos locates in Hegel's reflection on aesthetics, specifically in the famous discussion of *Antigone*, a moment when the task of art is not reconciliation and synthesis of opposites but exposition of contradiction and paradox.

While Boos claims that the task of *Antigone* may be to expose contradiction and paradox at the core of the polis, Tina Chanter, in Chapter 2, "Looking at Hegel's Antigone through Irigaray's Speculum," argues that Luce Irigaray's reading of Hegel enables us to see in the mythical character of Antigone a new ethics of sexual difference that would no longer regard her as a political outlaw but instead acknowledge the ethical legitimacy of her actions. Hegel's identification of women with nature prejudices his view that Antigone lacks an ethical spirit, despite the action she takes on behalf of her brother. Chanter, following Irigaray, uproots Hegel's assumptions about women and shows that they depend on the view of female biology, which is in itself embedded in cultural stereotypes about women's passivity and lack of political efficacy. The feminist dismantling of the Hegelian topos of Woman prepares the way for a revised conception of civil rights that takes account of sexual difference.

A challenge to the dominant view of the separation between ethics and aesthetics in Kant's philosophy, as discussed in Boos' chapter, is offered in Rodolphe Gasché's reflection on a link between the judgments of the beautiful and the sublime, and the morally good—in Kant's *Critique of Judgment*. In Chapter 3, "Linking Onto Disinterestedness, or the Moral Law in Kant's *Critique of Judgment*, Gasché argues that the act of negating the sensible in judgments of the beautiful and the sublime opens a space within the aesthetic for a possible relation with moral feeling, a relation that is more explicit in the sublime. The disengagement from the sensible, Gasché points out, causes reason to take an intellectual interest in the sublime, although such interest does not affect the purity of aesthetic judgment. In other words, Kant preserves the separation between ethics and aesthetics but also allows the transition from aesthetics to ethics.

Although in Chapter 4, "Gesture and Commentary," Jean-François Lyotard also returns to Kant, his elaboration of the sublime in particular, he wonders about the very possibility of aesthetics in the wake of philosophy's recent awareness of its own limitations in relation to art. Lyotard argues for an aesthetics of feeling, which breaks with Hegel's subordination of art to philosophy. Lyotard confirms that color, volume, tone, and line, which comprise the work of art as its gestures in time/space/matter, demand philosophical commentary, yet the perceptible singularity of a work of art renders it impenetrable to thought. Lyotard proposes that not only should philosophy relinquish its claim to dominance over art but also that, in order to comment competently on the gestures of art, it should first acknowledge and confront its own "gesticulation."

Part 2, "Aesthetics and the Question of the Other," takes up the issue of thematizing alterity in discourse and explores the possibilities of imagining the Other in ways that do not reduce heterogeneity to the measure of the same. This engagement with the problematic of radical alterity has been inspired by the ethical philosophy of Emmanuel Levinas and his critique of traditional aesthetics as injurious to the Other. The chapters in this section look toward ethics as a way of addressing the crisis of representation, although they do so in different contexts of philosophy, literary theory, theology, and feminist theory.

Richard Kearney, in "Levinas and the Ethics of Imagining," Chapter 5, investigates Levinas' claim that a solution to the modern crisis of representation, precipitated by the resurgence of the Other, can be found in ethics. Levinas' argument for the hegemony of the ethical imposes a view of poetics subordinated to ethics, in which the role of imagination in acts of representation appears to be suppressed. However, by examining Levinas' own readings of Proust, Célan, Blanchot, and Agnon, Kearney proposes that Levinas' distrust of images is not directed against imagination as such; on the contrary, it necessitates an "other" poetics or a poetics that is answerable to the Other.

Dorota Glowacka, in Chapter 6, "Disappearing Traces: Emmanuel Levinas, Ida Fink's Literary Testimony, and Holocaust Art," situates Kearney's diagnosis that Levinas' writings open up a possibility of new aesthetic practices in the context of Holocaust literature and art. Glowacka argues that reconceptualizing aesthetics in terms of bearing witness to the Other is particularly relevant to aesthetic practices that have been inspired by the Holocaust. Drawing on Levinas' articulation of the experience of absolute alterity as a trace—a nonphenomenal event that underlies all thematization of Otherness in language or image—she refers to these works as "the art of disappearing traces." Glowacka illustrates her

argument with examples from literary testimony by Ida Fink, an Israeli writer of
Polish origin, and from contemporary Holocaust art.

Unlike Kearney's and Glowacka's theoretical analyses, Martin Rumscheidt, in "Poetry, Theology, and Ethics: A Study in Paul Célan," Chapter 7,
offers a personal reflection from a German-Canadian theological perspective.
He proposes a provocative thesis that perhaps theology's either distancing itself from aesthetics or subjugating aesthetic concerns to the task of the
Church's tutelage has been detrimental for its capacity to provide an ethics for
human subjects. Rumscheidt resumes Glowacka's inquiry into the possibility
of ethics and aesthetics in the wake of the Holocaust and relates it to the
question about the possibility of post–Auschwitz theology. He contends that
Auschwitz exposed the dangers of separation between the domains of aesthetics, politics, and religion, and he argues for a need to integrate aesthetics
("poetry") into theology if it is to be reborn "after Auschwitz." Yet for Rumscheidt, who calls himself "a child of Nazi Germany," the success of such an
undertaking hinges on the need to reexamine Christianity's representations of
its "other"—the Jew. Rumscheidt wrestles with the aporetic task of nonappropriative refiguring of the Jew in the Christian context through a reading of
Paul Célan's poem *Death Fugue*.

Finally, Marjorie Stone, in "Between Ethics and Anguish: Feminist Ethics,
Feminist Aesthetics, and Representations of Infanticide in 'The Runaway Slave
at Pilgrim's Point' and *Beloved*," Chapter 8, brings the discussion on the relations
between ethics and aesthetics to bear upon the issue of articulating black female
experience, specifically in relation to representations of infanticide by white
anti-slavery and black writers from the nineteenth century to the present. The
author is concerned with aesthetic practices that allow for the "othering" of anguish in ways that may divorce it from the context of ethics altogether, yet she
also takes issue with the assumption that art is incapable of expressing the "limit
experience" of human anguish. Stone proposes, therefore, a strategic substitution
of "anguish" for aesthetics in the phrase "between ethics and aesthetics" and argues that in order to adequately address the above concerns, it is imperative for
literary criticism to search for new ways of integrating feminist ethics (with its
contentious insistence on "the real") and feminist aesthetics (supposedly confined to "the representational").

Emmanuel Levinas points out, in *Totality and Infinity*, that the ethical relation between the I and the Other does not obtain in the void: the intersub-
jective space in which the advent of the Other is announced is also the space of
others; it constitutes a community.[1] Part 3 of this book explores this dimension
by looking at the conjunction of aesthetics and politics.

In Chapter 9, "Feminine Writing, Metaphor, and Myth," Drucilla Cornell
defends the role of myth in feminist theory and argues that the process of figuration and remythologization *allows*, rather than *prohibits*, the feminist project
to be both ethical and politically efficacious. Deconstructing the divide be-

tween imagination, in its mythical and utopian dimension, and the social and political reality of women's lives, Cornell demonstrates that myths have always been a touchstone of feminine identification. Whether in Kristeva's "mythology" of the mother, Cicoux's engagement of mythical figures, or Irigaray's writing of the feminine through mimesis, the myth has been an irreducible presence in feminist theory. Such reinterpretations of mythical figures are expressions of the utopia beyond patriarchy and gender hierarchy, although this does not have to involve an appeal to essentialism (and here Cornell distinguishes her project from Gayatri Spivak's "strategic essentializing"). A necessarily aesthetic dimension of remythologizing the feminine, therefore, does not result in replacing the political with the aesthetic. On the other hand, the supposed dangers of reinstating the myths of the feminine stem from an essentialist desire for a universal human subject (such as de Beauvoir's repudiation of the myth of femininity as the male fantasy of Woman as Other). Cornell also responds to the charge that the recourse to myth obscures feminine specificity and the diversity of lives of actual women through the discussion of Toni Morrison's reliance on the myth of Medea (*Beloved*) to articulate the very difference of the Afro-American mother's situation.

In Chapter 10, "Aesthetics and Politics," renowned Marxist critic Terry Eagleton explores the meaning and possibility of "political aesthetics"—the term often thought to be contradictory, since aesthetics has its genesis precisely in its opposition to the political realm. Every society, Eagleton asserts, creates a quasi-sacred place for itself, over and above the political, in which it becomes aware of its fundamental values; in modern times, this place has been called aesthetics or literature. The politicization of the aesthetic is hotly contested in contemporary philosophical circles, because it was first constructed as a refuge from the ravages of capitalism (although, as Eagleton notes, it was also the birthplace of a post–bourgeois political ideal of humanity). Eagleton considers two different senses of the aestheticization of politics: postmodernism and socialism. The postmodern solution to the structural contradiction in which advanced capitalism finds itself is, in his view, unacceptable, because it seeks to deconstruct the existing superstructure while retaining the material basis of capitalism. Socialism, on the other hand, believes that the material conditions for the aestheticization of politics have yet to be constructed. In the latter context, Eagleton proposes that literature, in conjunction with theory, may harbor a potential for political aesthetics, although it has not constituted one yet.

In distinction to Eagleton, Victor Li, in Chapter 11, "An Ethics of the Name: Rethinking Globalization," draws on the deconstructive and postmodern theories of Jacques Derrida, Jean-François Lyotard, Kenneth Burke, Pierre Bourdieu, and Slavoj Žižek in order to draw a connection between political economy and aesthetic culture and to argue for an "ethics of the name" that can be linked to practical and political issues in the world. He explores a possibility of such ethics through a critical analysis of the term *globalization*, which itself has a kind of aesthetic or shaping quality that, in a sublime fashion, seeks to be self-determining and equal only to itself and is thus unable to account for radical difference that always exceeds "the name." It is also symptomatic of the economic and instrumental rationality that forecloses diverse, open-ended forms of inquiry. The aesthetic of globalization, therefore, must face up to an ethical demand, in a Levinasian sense, issuing from alterity that cannot be reduced to the same. Li's deconstructive reading is strategic: it opens globalization's hegemony to dispute and rearticulation and posits a task of searching for "names" that would resist the vision of a globe completely saturated by capital.

Krzysztof Ziarek, in Chapter 12, "The Social Figure of Art: Heidegger and Adorno on the Paradoxical Autonomy of Artworks," provides a philosophical framework for discussions about the social and political role of art. In the author's view, explanations of the social significance of art in terms of cultural production, social effects, or aesthetic ideology are no longer sufficient. In an attempt to address art "after aesthetics," Ziarek turns to the aesthetic theories of Adorno and Heidegger. While Adorno insists on the radical social significance of the formal figuration in modern art, defending it against the naive misconceptions of social aesthetic, Heidegger takes the discussion of art beyond the notion of form and representation and examines it as an active event. Through these readings, Ziarek proposes that art's relevance and critical potential reside in what he calls "the social figure of art." By opening up a certain mode of knowing, the figure of art understood as occurrence acquires historical and social significance, challenging the very parameters of the rationality that organizes social-cultural discourse. The figure of art does not in itself produce revolutionary counter-forces, but it inflects the dynamic between the forces already in existence: it is this inflection that has significant political and ethical implications. Looking at the work of Samuel Beckett, Marcel Duchamp, and dadaists, Ziarek argues that the avant-garde in particular emphasizes the "figural" force of art that allows for contestation and poetic transformation of reality.

Importantly, David MacFadyen, in Chapter 13, "Politics, Aesthetics, and Ethics in Joseph Brodsky's Poem *On the Death of Zhukov*," provides a specific example of politicizing aesthetics through a reading of Nobel Prize laureate Joseph Brodsky's eulogy on the death of Marshall Zhukov. The poem, lauding the hero of the Soviet Union and stylized in the tradition of the Soviet pathos, marks a strange hiatus in the career of the dissident poet, twice exiled from his country. MacFadyen seeks the answer to the enigma of Brodsky's apparent embracing of the Soviet ethos by scrutinizing the poet's complex relationship to the entire Soviet aesthetics and to the ideology that underwrites it. Zhukov, in Brodsky's poetic embodiment, becomes a potent challenge to the rhetoric of

Soviet propaganda. Brodsky's use of the Soviet aesthetics becomes subversive when the tropes that serve to cement ideology are deconstructed and employed as the means of resisting the totalitarian discourse. MacFadyen's chapter is thus an implicit critique of Eagleton's foregrounding of the socialist context as the privileged site of the radical transformation of art.

While continuing to ask questions about the political relevance and transformative potential of art, Part 4, "Toward an Ethical Art Practice?" offers the reader an opportunity to hear the voices of contemporary artists and art critics. In Chapter 14, "Beauty and the Beast," Alex Colville, a well-known Canadian painter and a recipient of the Order of Canada, reflects on the interrelations of ethics and aesthetics. Quoting a number of prominent Western artists and thinkers, Colville insists on the need to reconsider the modernist notion of art's autonomy and to conceive of beauty and truth, of culture and politics, as inseparably intertwined in the work of art.

Elizabeth Edwards, in Chapter 15, "The Banal Profound and the Profoundly Banal: Andy Warhol," offers a provocative intervention into the statements that insist on the integration of ethics and aesthetics. Given the recent "return to ethics" in contemporary theory, Edwards questions whether "the autonomy of art" was ever really possible, or whether such a possibility is merely an anxious prelude to a massive recuperation of art by ethics. Confronting certain current ethicizing theories of art, Lyotard's theory of the sublime in particular, the author argues that the notion of banality, as developed in the specific historical moment of the early 1960s, resists assimilation into either ethics or aesthetics. Particularly in Andy Warhol's art, banality is not removed from the subject matter; rather, it is rendered available for aesthetic pleasure. Edwards calls for a restitution of "mere enjoyment" in the experience of art, the term debased by aesthetics since Kant, as a counterweight to the ethical claim of contemporary art theories that often efface a historically specific gesture of pop art.

Unlike Edwards' theory-oriented art criticism, Chapter 16, "Short Circuit: The Story of An Exhibition That Provoked Unforeseen Consequences," is a personal narrative by Susan Gibson Garvey, the curator of Dalhousie University Art Gallery in Halifax and a practicing artist herself. It describes her experiences during an exhibition of contemporary activist art entitled *No Laughing Matter*, which was put together by New York's Independent Curators Incorporated. The exhibits in the show commented, often ironically, upon a number of controversial social issues. Unexpectedly for the organizers, one of the exhibits, the work by Carrie May Weems, which makes provocative statements about racial stereotyping, spurred powerful adverse reactions from the local black community. The incident became a divisive issue at the university and in the community at large and almost resulted in the closing of the art gallery. Although painful for the parties involved, the debacle raised important questions about the role and perception of activist art, as well as the place of a university art gallery in the community. Gibson Garvey herself ponders the social implications of works of art, which challenge the autonomy of the gallery as the space for the unencumbered contemplation of art.

The last chapter in this book, "Other Tongues: Language and Hybridity in Recent Canadian Video Art," raises a similar question about the role and efficacy of socially engaged art practice in the context of video art. The author, Marusya Bociurkiw, a new-generation video artist and art curator, reflects on the work of six Canadian video filmmakers (Cathy Sisler, Shani Mootoo, Nelson Henricks, Philip Napier, Ruth Cuthand, and Elizabeth MacKenzie), whose works are actively engaged in contesting hegemonic cultural politics. For all of them, the search for a cinematic language of difference in video art mirrors the quest for a new subaltern language and an alternative cultural identity. Some of the fragile homes for difference the artists have located are the immigrant, postcolonial voices, gay and lesbian languages of the body, and the suppressed languages of the First Nations. Bociurkiw also examines the critical apparatus that has been, at times, marked by dualistic categories and thus has given insufficient voice to cultural difference. Combining the elements of queer and postcolonial theory, she questions the notion of a separate category for the Other as itself entrenched in the exploitative logic of the West and calls for experimentation in video art that would allow it to voice marginalized identities.

The work we are presenting here taps into present intellectual currents; its predecessors include *Ethics/Aesthetics: Postmodern Positions*, [2] which elaborates on the dilemmas of postmodernism in the context of literature, popular culture, and theory such as Lacanian psychoanalysis or Foucault's theories of power; a special 1995 issue of *L'Esprit créateur*, "Beyond Aesthetics?" which focuses on the challenge that the need to redefine aesthetics poses for philosophy, Hegelianism in particular; a 1996 collection of mostly literary criticism, *Ethics and Aesthetics: The Moral Turn of Postmodernism*,[3] published in Heidelberg, Germany, with limited circulation in North America; and a special 1999 issue of *PMLA*, devoted to ethics and literary study. [4] Also of relevance are the volumes published by Stanford University Press in the series *Meridian: Crossing Aesthetics*, although their context is specifically philosophical and theoretical.

Although in recent years several individual studies investigating the relation between ethics and aesthetics have also appeared, considering the vast body of works that focuses on *either* ethics and aesthetics, almost exclusively within the confines of particular disciplines, [5] there is a further need to explore the interrelations between the two in contemporary contexts. This book has been conceived in the belief that an interdisciplinary approach is the most promising framework for such an investigation.

NOTES

1. Emmanuel Levinas, "The Other and the Others," *Totality and Infinity*, trans. Alphonso Lingis (Pittsburgh: Duquesne University Press, 1969), 212–14.

2. Robert Merrill, ed., *Ethics/Aesthetics: Postmodern Positions* (Washington, D.C.: Maisonneuve Press, 1988).

3. Gerhard Hoffmann and Alfred Hornung, eds. *Ethics and Aesthetics: The Moral Turn of Postmodernism* (Heidelberg: C. Winter, 1996).

4. See *PMLA* Vol. 114, No. 1 (January 1999). Derek Attridge's excellent essay, "Truth, Literature, Ethics: Relating to the Other" (*PMLA*, 20–31) is of particular relevance to this volume.

5. See, for example, Wayne Booth, *The Company We Keep: An Ethics of Fiction* (Chicago: University of Chicago Press, 1988), J. Hillis Miller, *The Ethics of Reading: Kant, de Man, Eliot, Trollope, James, and Benjamin* (New York: Columbia University Press, 1987), Christopher Norris, *Truth and the Ethics of Criticism* (Manchester: Manchester University Press, 1994), Tobin Siebers, *The Ethics of Criticism* (Ithaca, N.Y.: Cornell University Press, 1988), Adam Zachary Newton, *Narrative Ethics* (Cambridge: Harvard University Press, 1995), and Jill Robbins, *Altered Readings: Levinas and Literature* (Chicago: University of Chicago Press, 1999).

PART I

Rethinking Ethics and Aesthetics:
Between Philosophy and Art

CHAPTER 1

Rethinking the Aesthetic: Kant, Schiller, and Hegel

Stephen Boos

The attempt to rethink the relationship between the ethical and the aesthetic requires a return to Kant, Schiller, and Hegel, since it is largely through their efforts that the modern notion of the aesthetic as the reconciling unity of spirit and nature, duty and inclination, and reason and feeling was first invented. Kant grasps the notion of the aesthetic as the unity of theoretical and practical reason but is unable, in the end, to surmount the limitations of the Understanding that plunges modern culture into two worlds, the world of spirit and the world of nature. Schiller, on the other hand, recognizes the aesthetic as the way out of this cultural crisis, since he regards the aesthetic as the unity of spirit and nature, of duty and inclination, a unity that escapes the Understanding. Finally, Hegel recognizes in the aesthetic, as Schiller understands it, the reawakening of philosophy and Reason itself, which shares art's attempt to resolve the oppositions and fragmentations of modern culture. It is precisely this attempt to reconcile or resolve contradiction and opposition in both its philosophical and artistic forms that has been called into question more recently by those who see in it the universalizing tendencies of modernity. Rethinking the aesthetic therefore involves rethinking the task that Schiller and Hegel assigned to art and philosophy. Is the task of art and philosophy to reconcile contradiction and opposition, or to set them free?

Modern aesthetics, the study of art, its nature, effects, and place in human life, is a fairly new discipline. It was initiated in the middle of the eighteenth century by A.G. Baumgarten who, in his work *Aesthetica*, investigates a form of knowledge that is mediate between practical and theoretical knowledge. Baumgarten was interested in a mode of knowledge in which wholes or ideas are neither recognized for their practical purposes nor broken down into their component parts by science or knowledge, but instead contemplated in all of their sensible and indivisible appearance for the sake of the insight and delight that such contemplation yields. This third realm of perceptual knowledge, lying between practical and theoretical knowledge, is the realm of aesthetics.

Hegel acknowledges the debt of modern aesthetics to both Kant and Schiller. Kant, he says, initiated the proper understanding of the notion of the aesthetic, although he was unable to complete it. In the *Critique of Judgment*, Kant does delimit the realm of aesthetic judgment by distinguishing it from the theoretical and practical uses of reason and elevating aesthetics, as well as art and beauty, from the capricious realm of the merely pleasant and agreeable into the realm of subjective universality. Kant's account, I shall argue, recognizes the need for the aesthetic, for a mediating ground between theoretical and practical reason, but is resigned to the view that the notion of the beautiful is indeterminate, that is, is not determinable by concepts but refers to the feeling of the subject. The aesthetic therefore remains distinct from the ethical in Kant, in spite of the contrary view implied by the mediating role that he assigns to the aesthetic.

It is a philosophical poet, Friedrich Schiller, whom Hegel regards as working through the inadequacies of Kant's theory. According to Schiller, the realm of the aesthetic is one in which the oppositions and contradictions belonging to theoretical and practical reason are annulled. This is the notion of beauty and the aesthetic as the unity of universal and particular, duty and inclination, reason and feeling, and spirit and nature. Schiller takes the bolder step, which he thinks is implicit in Kant's *Critique of Judgment* itself, of attributing a central place to art and the aesthetics of beauty in both theoretical and practical life. In the *Letters on the Aesthetic Education of Man*, Schiller claims that education by art and beauty is the mutual formation of the rational and the sensuous impulses. Kant is unable to surmount the opposition and separation between the rational and sensuous sides of human experience. Schiller, on the other hand, seeks to show how this opposition is overcome in and through the aesthetic. It is through art and beauty, the aesthetic, that the unity of the rational and sensuous sides of human existence, which for Kant remains a mere "ought" or "demand," manifests itself. In Schiller, the aesthetic takes precedence over the ethical in the sense that it calls for the mutual formation of reason and feeling or duty and inclination. Schiller seeks to recover or restore the sense of the beautiful in ethical and intellectual life.

Hegel accepts Schiller's view of the aesthetic as the reconciling unity of spirit and nature, duty and inclination, and reason and feeling. Hegel calls this reconciling unity of opposition the Idea and its adequate sensuous shape in art the Ideal. Art, according to Hegel, belongs to the realm of absolute spirit, that is, it is its task to find a way out of these contradictions and oppositions by showing that neither the one side nor the other of these oppositions is true,

that truth lies only in their reconciliation and mediation, and that this reconciliation is not a mere "ought" or "demand" but is accomplished in the here and
now. The truth or Idea is not something that lies "beyond" this world, it is not
itself a mere "ought," but it discloses itself through art, religion, and philosophy. This means that in art spirit has to do with itself, or comes to self-
consciousness, by giving itself an idealized sensuous form or pure appearance.
Kant recognizes that the aesthetic transcends the abstractions of the Understanding but restricts it to the realm of subjective universality. Hegel, on the
other hand, elevates art into the realm of truth, a realm which it shares with
philosophy, and which therefore makes aesthetics, the philosophy of art, possible. It is because they belong to the same realm that art and philosophy can
no longer be regarded as opposed, even if Hegel claims that philosophy is
"higher" than art. In Hegel, the aesthetic offers a necessary correction of the
modern intellect and its moral worldview, although it is itself surpassed by
philosophy in this endeavor.

JUDGMENT OF THE BEAUTIFUL: KANT

In this first section, I argue that although Kant recognizes both the need for
and the place of the aesthetic in his system, his account emphasizes the distinction between the aesthetic and the ethical. Kant elevates aesthetics from the
realm of the merely agreeable into the realm of subjective universality, but he
falls short of the realm of truth. I begin by providing a brief outline of the first
two *Critiques*, the *Critique of Pure Reason* and the *Critique of Practical Reason*,
before turning to the *Critique of Judgment*.[1] As we shall see, Kant distinguishes
aesthetic judgments from theoretical knowledge on the one hand and from
mere subjective judgments of the agreeable and disagreeable on the other hand.
Kant does not regard aesthetic judgments as theoretical judgments, since
knowledge proper, according to Kant, is restricted to the phenomenal realm of
the Understanding. Aesthetic judgments are noncognitive matters of taste or
feeling in spite of their claim to universal validity.

The central contribution of Kant was to establish the autonomy of aesthetic judgment as distinct from both theoretical and practical (moral) knowledge. Aesthetic judgments are noncognitive (nontheoretical) universally valid
judgments. Kant undertakes an architectonic survey of the uses and limitations
of reason in its intellectual and practical life in the first two critiques. In the
Critique of Pure Reason, he lays down the limits of reason in its theoretical use.
The *Critique* limits theoretical knowledge to the phenomenal world, the world
of appearances, with the consequence that we can know nothing about things
in themselves. The categories of the Understanding, by means of which we
both constitute and come to know experience, categories such as causality, substance, and so on, also are limited in their application to the realm of possible

experience. The concepts we use in thinking about what may lie beyond the world of possible experience are called ideas of reason. Reason here attempts to regulate rather than constitute our experience of objects. It cannot use its ideas, for example, the unifying idea of a world in itself, independent of experience, to constitute its objects and so give rise to or result in theoretical knowledge. The world as it is in itself is for us a world we think but do not know. Our desire to unify our experiences by reason is so great, however, that reason easily strays beyond the bounds of possible knowledge and becomes embroiled in various antinomies or contradictions. We cannot "know" the supersensible objects in themselves, a God, or even ourselves as subjects in ourselves. All we can do is postulate such ideas.

In the *Critique of Practical Reason*, Kant examines the limits of reason in relation to moral life. In its practical role, reason imposes obligations on us and carries them out in freedom from natural necessity. Theoretical knowledge is knowledge of what is the case. Practical knowledge is cognition of what ought to be the case. We are, Kant claims, conscious of ourselves as operating under a moral law. That law commands us to fulfill our duty without regard for our natural inclinations. Kant calls this moral law the categorical imperative.[2] The first formulation is: Act only on that maxim or subjective principle of your will, which you could will at the same time that it should become a universal law. Moral life assumes that we can indeed act independently of natural causes, otherwise it would be meaningless to blame or praise people for their actions. If all of our actions are causally determined, and we cannot act otherwise, then the moral life, which assumes that we can choose and act otherwise, is not possible. This is our noumenal freedom of will—freedom not only from causality but freedom to be self-legislating. There are three postulates assumed by our moral experience—the existence of God, freedom of the will, and the immortality of the soul. These are postulates of reason; we assume them to be the case, without theoretical proof, since without them the moral life is not possible.

The *Critique of Judgment* was envisioned by Kant himself as constituting the unity of the other two critiques, that is, as the unity of theoretical and practical reason. It sets out to decide what justification, if any, is possible for aesthetic judgments, above all, judgments of taste, and for teleological judgments. How, if at all, Kant asks, is it possible to judge something in nature or art as beautiful on the basis of something very subjective, a feeling of pleasure, and yet demand for our judgment a universal assent?[3]

According to Kant, one's apprehension of x as beautiful is not the detection of some property in x. It is, rather, the awareness that x causes some feeling in oneself. The paradigm for Kant's analysis of aesthetic judgments is the judgment, "The rose I am looking at is beautiful." Although the predicate suggests that beauty is a property, this is not the case. Beauty is nothing in itself, apart from a relation to the subject's feeling. So far, beauty is indistinguishable from secondary properties such as blue and sweet. Hence, Kant concludes, it is the feeling of the beautiful that must be examined in order to account for the judgment's claim to universal validity. A judgment of taste is not a theoretical claim. It is not a logical judgment but an aesthetic one, by which Kant means a judgment whose basis is subjective. On the other hand, an aesthetic judgment is not simply a matter of the agreeable, since it makes a claim to universality. When I claim that x is beautiful, I am not simply claiming that *I* feel that it is beautiful but making a claim that is valid for others as well. The feeling of the beautiful has a universal dimension that my liking of chocolate ice cream does not. How are aesthetic judgments possible? How can a noncognitive, nontheoretical judgment have universal validity?

In the first section of the *Critique of Judgment*, Kant explicates aesthetic judgments by reference to four "moments." The first aspect of aesthetic judgments is their disinterestedness. Kant distinguishes judgments about beauty from our judgments about the agreeable or pleasant on the one hand and from judgments about the good on the other hand. If we have an interest in an object on behalf of some sensuous need, or a desire for its possession and use, then the object is not important to us on its own account but because of our needs and interests. In the aesthetic relation, on the other hand, the pleasure or delight we take in the object is disinterested. We remain indifferent to the existence of the thing and do not seek to possess it to satisfy exterior interests. Kant connects the disinterested pleasure in the aesthetic relation with the judging of the form of the object. It is disinterested in the sense that my relation to the object, when it is purely aesthetic, is closer to contemplation or appreciation of the pure appearance of the object. Kant also distinguishes the disinterested pleasure of aesthetic judgments from judgments about the intrinsic and extrinsic goodness of things. Our practical judgments about the goodness of things always assume a determinate concept. If I claim that x is good, it is because I have in mind some concept of what it is good for and so do not appreciate the thing as it simply appears without regard to its utility or instrumental value. My judgment that x is good is subsumed under a concept of good. So, in judging that this hammer is good, I make a judgment that presupposes a definite notion of what constitutes a good hammer (one whose head is made of steel, rather than of some other material, if I am driving in nails).

The second aspect of aesthetic judgments concerns the way in which the beautiful pleases universally without a concept. The person who makes a claim that an object is beautiful makes a claim that he or she thinks has universal validity. We also speak of beauty as if it were an attribute of objects, but we are mistaken. Beauty is not a property of objects. It follows, on Kant's account, that the universality in aesthetic judgments cannot arise from a category of the Understanding. The universality in aesthetic claims is subjective and not objective, as in the case of our knowledge claims. When we judge an object as beautiful rather than merely pleasant, one judges not only for oneself but for everyone else, that is, one judges with a universal voice, yet one does so without a concept, that is, without a category of the Understanding. To make this demand is to presuppose that the taste and feeling by which we make the judgment is common to everyone and hence implies a *sensus communis*, a "common sense." The good or the right in our practical judgments is subsumed under universal concepts, and the action counts as good if it corresponds with these concepts. The beautiful invokes a universal pleasure without any such correspondence with a concept or purpose. The subjective universality in an aesthetic judgment refers to nothing other than the state of mind in the free play of the imagination and the Understanding. It is this sensation, the sensation of the harmony of our cognitive faculties, or of cognition in general, which is brought about by our apprehension of the object that we impute to every other person.

The third moment of aesthetic judgment concerns the purposiveness of an object, insofar as this is perceived in it without any representation of a purpose. It is the pure form, considered independently of any external or internal purpose, that distinguishes an aesthetic relation to an object from either utility or perfection (goodness). To regard something as beautiful is to cease to ask, "What is it for?" The determining ground of a judgment of beauty is not a concept or purpose but the feeling of the harmony of our faculties in the free play of the Understanding and imagination that the form of the object brings about. The pure aesthetic judgment depends upon the recognition of an inner finality of form, freed from purpose.

The final moment or aspect of the beautiful is that it is recognized as the object of a necessary delight. The necessity that is present in an aesthetic judgment is not derived from concepts of the Understanding, nor from a consensus based on experience. The principle upon which the necessity is based is, Kant claims, a common sense. It is the taste of a *sensus communis* by which we judge certain forms as to whether they have such purposiveness without a purpose.

Kant's aesthetics is preoccupied with the task of showing how aesthetic judgments are possible. They are to be understood as neither theoretical nor practical, and yet they are not reducible to matters of the merely agreeable or disagreeable. In this sense, beauty is closer to truth and goodness than to the merely agreeable and disagreeable. Nevertheless, pure aesthetic judgments are not cognitive but noncognitive. Beauty refers to a feeling in the subject and not the concept of an object. Kant's aesthetics, in spite of its contribution to the liberation of aesthetic judgment, remains caught within the web of the modern intellect for which the reconciliation of the opposition and struggle between reason and feeling, duty and inclination, and so on is either not possible or is present as a mere "demand" or "ought."

THE PRIMACY OF THE AESTHETIC: SCHILLER

In his lectures on fine art, Hegel credits Schiller (1759–1805) for advancing beyond the standpoint of the Kantian philosophy, with its duty for duty's sake, and its formless intellectualism, which apprehends nature and actuality, sense and feeling, as just a barrier and limitation.[4] Schiller therefore sees the aesthetic as the way out of the dilemma into which we are plunged by modern culture. Indeed, according to Schiller, the aesthetics of beauty makes possible the free development, the mutual formation of our rational and sensuous natures. In his *On the Aesthetic Education of Man*, written in the wake of the French Revolution, Schiller considers the relationship between art and politics and proposes the view that art can play a crucial role in facilitating the continuous transformation of the natural political state into the modern rational State.[5] Schiller claims that each individual carries within himself or herself an ideal of humanity which it is the task of the individual to strive to realize in his or her own existence. This ideal is represented by the State, the political community in which all human beings endeavor to unite themselves. There are two ways in which the individual in time might harmonize with this ideal. On the one hand, the State, as the embodiment of ethics, law, and intelligence, might impose itself by simply cancelling individuality. On the other hand, the individual in time might become the State, elevating himself or herself to the ideal of humanity (*AE*, 31–32).

Reason, Schiller asserts, demands unity and universality and concordance with the law and the universal. Nature, on the other hand, demands multiplicity and individuality. Each, he thinks, places equal demands upon us. It therefore follows that something is lacking in our education if the rational or moral can only assert itself through the renunciation of the natural, and if the State is only able to attain unity and universality by suppressing variety and difference. The State, Schiller argues, must recognize the universal and the particular, the rational and sensuous sides of its individuals, and in making itself moral and rational, it must not destroy nature. In other words, we need to find a way of reconciling the demands of reason, unity and universality with the demands of nature, multiplicity, and particularity. Schiller proposes the aesthetic education of character as the solution to the political problems of modernity.

Aesthetic education is to bring about the demand for the mediation and reconciliation between reason and nature, the universal and the particular, and so on. Aesthetic education proceeds by rationalizing nature and naturalizing reason: that is, by forming inclination and sensuousness so that they become rational in themselves, and similarly by enabling reason and the intellect to emerge from their abstraction to become natural. The beautiful is declared by Schiller to be the mutual formation of the sensuous and rational.

In the course of the general argument of the *Letters*, Schiller presents a transcendental psychological account of beauty and the aesthetic itself (*AE*,

64–72). There are, he says, two basic drives within human existence that appear to be opposed and irreconcilable: the sensuous and the formal. The sensuous impulse arises out of our physical existence or sensuous life, the body, and is concerned with temporality, our being within time, which is in a continual process of becoming and alterity. The formal impulse, on the other hand, which stems from our rational nature, aims at universality and necessity. Reason, in its self-legislating role, both judges and acts for the entire species for all time. "We are no longer individuals, but species; the judgment of all spirits is expressed by our own, the choice of all hearts is represented by our action" (*AE*, 67).

It would appear that there is an insurmountable antagonism at the core of human existence. The belief in the necessary and radical opposition between the sensuous and formal impulses is the basic premise of Kantian ethics. But once we accept that premise, we are compelled to subordinate the sensuous impulse to the rational for the sake of preserving unity and universality. The result of such subordination is uniformity rather than harmony. The sensual impulse is repressed but not reconciled. Ethical life becomes an endless struggle of reason subordinating natural inclination. Schiller challenges the basic premise of Kantianism. The formal and sensuous impulses are not by nature opposed to one another. Each has its proper sphere, and each is equally valid. It is only when one impulse encroaches on the sphere of the other in an exclusive, one-sided manner that opposition results. It is the task of culture and aesthetic education in particular, Schiller claims, to prevent these two impulses and their respective spheres from encroaching on one another. It does this by allowing the development of both impulses and bringing about their mutual subordination and coordination. The result is harmony rather than uniformity in thinking and willing.

Schiller calls the transcendental disposition in which the two impulses are engaged in this reciprocal action the play impulse as well as the aesthetic state. The sense impulse requires time and variation. The formal impulse requires the extinction of time and no variation. The play impulse would aim "at the extinction of time within time and the reconciliation of becoming with absolute being, of variation with identity" (*AE*, 74). The object of the sensuous impulse is life. The object of the formal impulse is shape or form, as it is grasped by the intellect. The object of the play impulse is living shape or beauty, understood in the broadest and most general sense.

Schiller thinks that the aesthetic disposition, which lies midway between the demands of reason and nature, is a state in which the opposition between the formal and sensuous impulses cancels itself out without destroying the impulses themselves. It therefore makes possible the transition from the sensuous drive, which comes first in time, to the moral and rational. The aesthetic facilitates the transition from the sensuous to the moral and rational. Without this facilitation there is the subordination of the sensuous to reason or of reason to the sensuous but not harmony. The aesthetic, according to Schiller, enables the ethical and the sensuous to fulfill themselves without encroaching on one another. Indeed, Schiller makes a further claim. The aesthetic, if permitted, results in a kind of grace in intellectual and ethical life that is otherwise missing.

RECONCILIATION IN ART AND PHILOSOPHY: HEGEL

Hegel, I claimed earlier on, accepts Schiller's notion of the aesthetic as the unity of spirit and nature, of universality and particularity, and of duty and inclination. If knowledge and ethics set the bounds of Kant's aesthetics, and if the aesthetic, according to Schiller, is the mutual formation of intellectual and sensuous life, then it is philosophy, for Hegel, which demonstrates the autonomy of the aesthetic while also recognizing its limitations. Art, according to Hegel, is autonomous; it has its end and aim in itself and is not reducible to the aim of moral instruction. It does not serve but surpasses the modern intellect, for which the aesthetic remains unintelligible. And yet, as Hegel understands it, art proper is only the first form of absolute spirit, followed by religion and philosophy.

I begin by clarifying Hegel's claim that art is a form of absolute spirit, and in particular his view that it is the sensuous presentation of the Idea. Hegel concludes his discussion of the aims of art by claiming that it is its vocation "to unveil the truth in the form of sensuous artistic configuration . . . and so to have its end and aim in itself, in this very setting forth and unveiling" (*A*, 55). Art, like philosophy, is one of the means that cancels and reduces to unity the abstract oppositions of the modern intellect. Following Schiller, Hegel discerns a crisis in modern culture which, he adds, has been present throughout history in less acute forms. The modern intellect, which Hegel refers to elsewhere as the Understanding—it is the same intellect which Wordsworth derides in his poetry, and which underlies the Kantian philosophy—has divided us into two worlds that contradict one another. On the one hand, we are imprisoned in the everyday world of reality and temporality, living the insatiable life of sensuality and carried away by natural impulses and passions. On the other hand, the individual elevates himself or herself to the realm of thought and freedom, engages in self-legislating acts of will, and produces purely formal universal moral laws and duties. Such acts, Hegel adds, do violence to nature and its diversity by stripping it of life and individuality. Since, as Schiller recognized, both reason and nature place equal demands upon us, humanity is tossed back and forth between these two worlds and is unable to find satisfaction in either one.

Hegel assigns the task of overcoming this crisis in modernity to philosophy. "It becomes the task of philosophy to supersede the oppositions, i.e. to show that neither the one alternative in its abstraction, nor the other in the like one-sidedness, possesses truth, but that they are both self-dissolving; that truth lies only in the reconciliation and mediation of both, and that this mediation is no mere demand, but what is absolutely accomplished and is ever self-accomplishing" (*A*, 56). He attributes this same act of reconciliation and mediation to art. Art, therefore, is akin to philosophy.

Art is the sensuous presentation of the Idea, and the Idea, as I have stated, is alone what is actual and true according to Hegel. Before I turn to an example of what Hegel means by the sensuous presentation of the Idea, further clarification of the genesis of art out of human need is called for if we are to avoid thinking of the realm of absolute spirit as discontinuous with the realm of finite spirit, and so accuse Hegel of reintroducing a view of the divine as radically other. Hegel thinks that art arises in response to our need to find a final resolution to the central contradictions arising out of our lives as finite human beings. Even freedom in a genuine rational state, in which the will realizes itself, is one-sided and restricted. Consciousness must therefore go beyond the state to find a higher sanction. This higher realm in which we seek the final resolution of the contradictions and oppositions in our finite lives is what Hegel refers to as the realm of absolute spirit. The highest truth, the Idea, is the resolution of the highest opposition and contradiction. In it, the opposition between freedom and necessity, spirit and nature, knowledge and its object, and law and impulse is overcome. Philosophy shows that neither freedom by itself in isolation from necessity nor necessity from freedom is true. What is true is the harmony and unity of freedom and necessity, and the truth, for Hegel, is present in the here and now. It is in relation to this higher realm that Hegel thinks we should consider art (*A*, 101–105).

Art first accomplishes this higher vocation as the *Kunstreligion* of classical Greece. Classical sculpture is the attainment of the Ideal, the sensuous embodiment of the Idea, the moment of the perfect interpretation of spirit and nature, and it captures what Schiller means by the living shape of beauty and what Hegel means by the sensuous appearance of the Idea. Sculpture is the center of the arts of the beautiful in Hegel's account. Classical Greek tragedy, on the other hand, sets these sculptures in motion. Sophocles' *Antigone* conveys, in terms of our poetic imagination rather than in the external medium of stone, the harmony or unity of the spiritual and natural. The central conflict of *Antigone* involves the collision between the state, that is, ethical life in its spiritual universality, and the family, that is, natural ethical life. Hegel says the following about the play:

> Creon, the King, had issued, as head of the state, the strict command that the son Oedipus, who had risen against Thebes as an enemy of his country, was to be refused the honour of burial. This command contains an essential justification, provision for the welfare of the entire city. But Antigone is animated by an equally ethical power, her holy love for her brother, whom she cannot

leave unburied, a prey of the birds. Not to fulfill the duty of burial would be against family piety, and therefore she transgresses Creon's command. (*A*, 221)

Since the spiritual aspect of an individual, in this case political obligation, and the natural element, associated with family piety, are mutually dependent, the hero who exclusively identifies herself with one side of the ethical substance denies something equally essential, and so brings about her downfall.

> Antigone lives under the political authority of Creon (the present King); she is herself the daughter of a King (Oedipus) and the fiancee of Haemon (Creon's son), so that she ought to pay obedience to the royal command. But Creon too, as father and husband, should have respected the sacred tie of blood and not ordered anything against its pious observance. So there is immanent in both Antigone and Creon something that in their own way they attack, so that they are gripped and shattered by something intrinsic to their own actual being. Antigone suffers death before enjoying the bridal dance, but Creon too is punished by the voluntary deaths of his son and his wife, incurred, the one on account of Antigone's fate, the other because of Haemon's death. (*A*, 1217)

According to Hegel's conception of the Ideal, the *Antigone* communicates a poetic vision of an affirmative reconciliation of the colliding ethical powers by showing that each side is necessary to the existence of the other. The divine makes its appearance as the necessary unity of the family and the state.

This reading reflects Hegel's view that art, like religion and philosophy, takes the divine as its highest subject matter. Indeed, Greek religion, according to Hegel, is a religion of art. Furthermore, art enjoys a resurrection of its highest vocation as religious romantic art and later on, I would argue, as philosophical art. In any case, it is Hegel's contention that art, like philosophy and religion, seeks to reconcile the highest oppositions and contradictions that plague human consciousness. Hegel also claims that philosophy is better able to accomplish in the modern world what art accomplished in the world of antiquity. This is not to say that art is dead but only that those days in which art afforded either the highest or the only form of reconciliation are in the past.

I began by claiming that rethinking the aesthetic involves rethinking the task that Schiller and Hegel assign to both art and philosophy. The crucial task of art and philosophy, according to Hegel, is to bring about reconciliation, the reconciliation between spirit and nature, freedom and necessity, universality and particularity, duty and inclination, and so on. It is precisely this view of art's vocation and the aesthetic that has been called into question. It is no longer so obvious that it is the task of art to seek reconciliation, even if we agree with Hegel that this has been its task in the past. Indeed, it would appear that art has ceased to believe in its ability to provide such absolute reconciliations but instead now devotes its energies to exposing the paradoxes and contradictions in the attempt of philosophy to provide such absolute syntheses. In this sense, art may have attained a self-consciousness that philosophy still lacks.

Instead of turning to examples of contemporary art to support this claim about the self-consciousness of art, I end by appealing to *Antigone* and *Oedipus Rex* (*A*, 1217–18). According to Hegel, Antigone and Creon represent equally valid ethical powers whose truth is the unity or harmony of both sides. Is this really the case? I do not think so. Antigone and Creon are not equal to one another in terms of ethical right. Creon acts in a demonstrably tyrannical fashion, blinded by a narrow sense of power and a lack of foresight. He can hardly be said to be acting in the interests of the state. Antigone, on the other hand, acts with the firm determination and heroism of one who has divine right on her side, knowingly and willingly, going to her death. Unfortunately, for Creon, knowledge of the ethical rightness of Antigone comes too late to alter what has happened. Antigone, in this sense, exposes the hypocrisy and self-contradiction in Creon's rule. Her defiance calls into question his claim to know the good of the polis. Sophocles exposes contradiction and dissolution at the heart of an apparently reconciled and justified state of affairs. Hegel would agree that the action of the play allows contradiction and opposition to develop to its extreme, but he thinks that it results in the self-consciousness of an underlying unity or harmony of ethical powers. If, on the other hand, Antigone and Creon are not regarded as representing equally justified ethical powers, then one might argue that Creon comes to an awareness of the self-contradictory nature of action.

The significance of irony in Sophocles is better demonstrated in *Oedipus Rex*. According to the Hegelian reading, *Oedipus Rex* is about the conflict between ignorance and knowledge, the unconscious and the conscious, prophecy and enlightenment, or perhaps even the family and the state, as well as its resolution. I would not omit the Hegelian approach but think that it overlooks other aspects of the play. In particular, it underplays the standpoint of irony. *Oedipus Rex* is deeply ironical in the sense that in the act of fleeing his fate, Oedipus actually fulfils it. Irony is the awareness of the essentially paradoxical nature of human action and self-consciousness. According to this view, it is not the task of art to reconcile such paradoxes but to present and expose them.

NOTES

1. See the translator's Introduction in I. Kant, *Critique of Judgment*, trans. W. S. Pluhar (Indianapolis: Hackett, 1987), for a useful overview of the three *Critiques*. Also see S. Körner, *Kant* (Harmondsworth: Penguin, 1979).

2. I. Kant, *Fundamental Principles of the Metaphysics of Morals,* trans. T. Abbot (New York: Bobbs-Merrill, 1949), 38.

3. I. Kant, *Critique of Judgment,* trans. J. H. Bernard (New York: Hafner, 1951). Hereafter cited as *CJ.*

4. G.W.F. Hegel, *Aesthetics: Lectures on Fine Art,* trans. T. M. Knox (Oxford: Clarendon, 1975), 61. Hereafter cited in the text as *A.*

5. F. Schiller, *On the Aesthetic Education of Man,* trans. R. Snell (New York: Ungar, 1965). Hereafter cited in the text as *AE.*

CHAPTER 2

Looking at Hegel's Antigone through Irigaray's Speculum

Tina Chanter

THE ETERNAL IRONY OF THE COMMUNITY

For Hegel, the relationship between family and state is both necessary and hierarchically arranged in terms of the relation between parts and whole. Similarly, the relationship between the sexes is ordered according to the same schema, the female representing the family and the male representing the state. According to the same structured series of oppositions that repeatedly emerge—female/male, night/day, inner/outer, natural/political—the family is the site of potentiality for the individual to develop into a fully fledged communal being. Male, of course, since the female is tied up with the family from the beginning. In a negative movement, the individual departs from his familial grounding in the organic life, supported by the mother, and moves on out into the public sphere, the realm in which his individuality acquires a higher, universal, communal significance. The family thus does its part for the whole community by letting the individual go, by remaining eternally a site of possibility, by allowing the individual to realize the true potentiality that exists for him in the shape of the external world in its universal form.

It is tempting to read the relationship between, on the one hand, the part and the whole, and, on the other hand, potentiality and actuality, as relationships that fit snugly together, go neatly hand in hand with one another. It may appear that the human or communal is identified with the male ethic,

Tina Chanter, excerpt from "Looking at Hegel's Antigone through Irigaray's Speculum," in *Ethics of Eros: Irigaray's Rewriting of the Philosophers* (New York: Routledge, 1995), 108–26. Reprinted with permission of the author and the publisher.

and the divine or familial is identified with the female ethic, as if the balance of power were indisputable and straightforward. But Hegel warns against this. "Now, although human right has for its content and power the actual ethical substance that is conscious of itself, i.e., the entire nation, while the *divine* right and law has for its content and power the individual who is beyond the real world, yet he is not without power."[1] Hegel expands this judgment in paragraph 455, where he emphasizes the need to see the relationship between the state and the family as a relationship between the whole and its parts, and where he reflects upon the purpose of war. The "superior law" of the community, which is individuated in the form of government, allows "the Family to expand into its constituent members, and to give to each part an enduring being and a being-for-self on its own" (*PhS*, 272; *PhG*, 323–24). While allowing such developments, the powers of government cannot afford to let its individual members and local organizations forget the higher purpose of their existence, or the protection afforded them by the state as a whole. "Spirit is at the same time the power of the whole, which brings these parts together again into a negative unity, giving them the feeling of their lack of independence, and keeping them aware that they have their life only in the whole" (*PhS*, 272; *PhG*, 324). In a passage that is crucial for the present discussion Hegel comments upon the role of war, which is of course the occasion of Polynices' death:

> The Spirit of universal assembly and association is the simple and negative essence of those systems which tend to isolate themselves. In order not to let them become rooted and set in this isolation, thereby breaking up the whole and letting the (communal) spirit evaporate, government has from time to time to shake them to their core by war.[2] By this means the government upsets their established order, and violates their right to independence, while the individuals who, absorbed in their own way of life, break loose from the whole and strive after the inviolable independence and security of the person, are made to feel in the task laid on them their lord and master, death. Spirit, by thus throwing into the melting-pot the stable existence of these systems, checks their tendency to fall away from the ethical order, and to be submerged in a [merely] natural existence; and it preserves and raises conscious self into freedom and its own power. The negative essence shows itself to be the real power of the community and the force of its self-preservation. The community therefore possesses the truth and the confirmation of its power in the essence of the Divine Law and in the realm of the nether world. (*PhS*, 272–73; *PhG*, 324)

Hegel's reference to death as the real master in the master-slave relationship is of particular interest to us, given the way in which that relation serves as a paradigm for Beauvoir's attempt to configure the relationship between male and female. By his reasoning in this passage Hegel establishes that war is conducted not solely for purposes of defense, nor merely for concerns extrinsic to the state's internal structure, such as its contingent relations with other states. It is also a necessary means of imposing internal civic order. War is the means by which the community safeguards the unity of its members and protects its members from dissolving their communal bonds into individual and partial motives, which disregard the unity of the whole. When Hegel states that "the negative essence shows itself to be the real power of the community and the force of its self-preservation," he acknowledges that it is the individual who poses the most serious threat to the preservation of equilibrium in the state. In doing so, he echoes the sentiment of Creon's words when he declares that it would be better to be beaten by a man than by a woman—for, as we saw, women are cast as guardians of the family, roles in which their action consists of representing the family in the form of the individual. Men, on the other hand, direct their activity toward the communal spirit of the whole, acting on behalf of the interests of the state. Sophocles writes:

> If men live decently it is because
>   discipline saves their very lives for them.
> So I must guard the men who yield to order,
>   not let myself be beaten by a woman.
> Better, if it must happen, that a man
>   should overset me.
> I won't be called weaker than womankind.[3]

In his fear of being beaten by a woman, Creon admits to the danger inherent in the individual's capacity to wreak havoc within the community.[4] Hegel finds in the fear to which Creon gives expression "the everlasting irony [in the life] of the community" (*PhS*, 288; *PhG*, 340).[5] While there is no question that the law of the community, human order, and male rule remains "superior" in Hegel's eyes, the threat posed by the divine law is manifest in the individual's action on behalf of the family, and it is embodied in the female figure of Antigone. In response to this threat, government, says Hegel, deems it necessary to go to war. Confronted by the power of its women, and fearing for its safety, government goes so far as to put the (male) members of its community at risk before the (male) members of another. A strange turn of events indeed. How could such a reversal have taken place?

In acknowledging the threat of womankind as the impetus behind war, Hegel reverses the logic that one might have expected. Instead of simply castigating women in their role of helpless and powerless victims, the weaker sex in need of protection from the stronger sex—their male counterparts, who go off and fight wars on behalf of the community—Hegel suggests exactly the opposite. The exigency of war results from the government's need to prevent the members of its community from collapsing into divisive and self-interested conflicts that ignore their own wider interests as members who belong to a state. Hegel thereby acknowledges in a backhanded way the extent of the power of women, while nonetheless insisting that their motives do not transcend the unconscious, natural, familial bonds that circumscribe them from the start.

We are confronted with a scenario in which men go to war ostensibly for the protection of the whole state, but in fact in order to preempt the internal dissension that would break out were it not for the threat of war—which, if it is not entirely artificial and imaginary, is still a fabrication. This synthetic threat may pass itself off as having to do with outside invaders, but in fact has just as much to do with tensions internal to the city-state. To the extent that individuals believe in the external threat of war, they do indeed stand in need of protection from it. At the same time, however, it is their own individuality from which they are being protected. This is the myth that wards off the ridicule and laughter of the women, in the face of which the state could not hold up, were the threat not contained. Women, it seems, must be protected from themselves, otherwise they would forget to act in unison, as a whole. It is in their own best interests that they be confined to their proper spheres, and even if that means confining them to an underground cave, burying them alive, then so be it. What would happen, after all, should they be inadvertently let loose, given free rein, allowed to deliver their laughter in full-bodied hilarity? What would happen if their ridicule of the state were openly condoned, acknowledged, conceded, recognized?

WOMAN'S PLACE IN THE DIALECTIC
OF NATURE AND HISTORY

In reading Sophocles' dramatization of tragic conflict within the body politic, in what ways, if any, will Hegel have transcended, surpassed, or redefined the relations between men and women as represented by the oppositional mutuality he establishes between male and female body parts? How far will Hegel's understanding of Sophocles' *Antigone* be governed by the views he espouses about sexual difference in the *Philosophy of Nature*? To what extent will his interpretation of the drama he judges to be "the most magnificent and satisfying work of art,"[6] at least from the point of view of its resolution of the tragic "'pathos' of a specific individual" (*AFA*, vol. 2, 1217), rearticulate his preconception that the female sex is essentially inactive, undeveloped, and undifferentiated, a mere imitation of its male counterpart, and an inadequate one at that? This question can be recast in a way that addresses more directly the question of sexual difference. Is Hegel guilty of that familiar fault that seems to characterize so much of the tradition of Western philosophy, whereby woman is equated with, confined to, conflated with nature? Implicit in this question about woman's equation with nature is, of course, another question, or rather another aspect of the same question, the question of whether, in her very equivalence to what we call natural, woman is excluded from culture, which accordingly remains the privileged domain of man.

By extending this train of thought to Irigaray, I want to ask a second question, one that is still more pertinent to a debate that has dominated feminist theory for some time now. Before passing on to Irigaray, however, let me note the following: to move straight to this second question is to act as if there were no difference between, on the one hand, posing a question about the role of nature in Irigaray's commentary on Hegel's discussion of Antigone and, on the other hand, questioning the relationship Hegel establishes between women and nature. By including Irigaray within the compass of the first question, as if her inclusion in its orbit were unproblematic, I am only delaying a confrontation that will not tolerate being put off for very long, one whose return can be predicted with certainty: the question of sexual difference. This strategic delay gives me the opportunity to note a further, and perhaps still more intransigent, although not unrelated, difficulty in the procedure I have begun to employ.

A moment ago, in raising the question of women's relation to nature in Hegel, I spoke of an implied contrast between nature and culture. This contrasting pair of opposites is never very far from the surface of Hegel's meditation on Antigone, a meditation orchestrated by a series of now-familiar oppositions to which the distinction between nature and culture is no foreigner—singular and universal, family and state, human and divine, female and male, passive and active, night and day.[7] In fact, it is in opposing the forces of nature that the conflict between Antigone and Creon finds its ultimate resolution in justice, according to Hegel. The wrong that Creon inflicts on Polynices by disallowing his burial consists in leaving him at the mercy of the power of nature, which makes him into a "mere thing" (*PhS*, 278; *PhG*, 329). Hegel says, "The wrong which can be inflicted on the individual in the ethical realm is simply this, that something merely *happens* to him" (*PhS*, 277–78; *PhG*, 329). Antigone's achievement is to make concrete the "enduring reality" of Polynices' blood and thereby prove that he "still lives on in the household" (*PhG*, 277; *PhS*, 329). By burying Polynices against Creon's wishes, Antigone transforms "what has simply *happened*" into a "*work deliberately done*, in order that the mere being of the wrong, its ultimate form, may also be something *willed* and thus something agreeable" (*PhS*, 278; *PhG*, 330).

If, unlike Creon, Antigone remains circumscribed by the family, in another way her destiny is not so distant from Creon's. Even if they are in no position to realize it themselves, Antigone and Creon are united in their opposition against the power of nature. Both seek, and both fail, to overcome natural forces, albeit in different ways. Yet at the same time, Hegel sees Antigone herself as no more than an instrument of nature, as the vessel through which Polynices' death is transformed from something merely natural into something willed, deliberate, human. Antigone, in Hegel's account, as a mere woman, is relegated to the realm of the merely natural. She does not transcend nature but merely submits to it, by playing out the role allotted to her by her sex, as guardian of the family. If, early in Hegel's reading, in the section on "The Ethical World: Human and Divine Law: Man and Woman," Antigone submits to nature, by the time we reach the end of the next section, "Ethical Action: Human and Divine Knowledge: Guilt and Destiny," we find Creon too submitting to nature. The overriding force of nature—the magnificence of which the chorus has sung (A, 332–75) and which Heidegger, among others, makes so central to his understanding of the play—is nowhere more apparent than in the closing pages of this section.[8] The full consequences of the destruction and vengeance that have been unleashed during the action of the play take their toll. Not only does Antigone's sex prove to be subject to natural powers, so too does Creon's. The whole community, to the extent that it is not free of nature's power, experiences an ethical crisis.[9] A community that sought to preserve itself by dishonoring a traitor finds itself the victim of hostile powers that "rise up" and destroy it (PhS, 287; PhG, 339). True to the movement of Hegelian philosophy, insofar as it privileges the whole, human law must engulf the "separatism" of the "independent families presided over by womankind" (PhS, 287–88; PhG, 340). The body politic tries to maintain itself by "consuming and absorbing"—the language of ingestion is not lost on Irigaray[10]—the wayward nature of woman. In its very attempt to digest, to assimilate, and in this process of incorporation, to outlaw, the "purely private pleasures and enjoyments" (PhS, 288; PhG, 340) that are embodied by women, the political community nonetheless finds itself subject to the body it wants to banish. It is brought down, laid to waste, demolished by that which it most wants to deny, but on which it discovers itself wholly dependent. The irony lies in the fact that it is precisely the same power through which woman makes a mockery of the state to which in the end the state must appeal. For all the "earnest wisdom" (PhS, 288; PhG, 340) that sets it apart from contingent individuality, from the personal and private life of the family, government nonetheless must find a way of appeasing the natural forces that rule women, the blood ties that have such an ancient heritage and such intransigent defenders as Antigone. For in the resources of the family, says Hegel, the state "finds its weapons" (PhG, 288; PhS, 341). To the extent that Antigone's position is consistently associated with the "power of youth," the state, in the figure of Creon, learns that it must foster the very individuality that it attempted to crush.[11] The livelihood of the state depends on that which threatens it, namely "raw and irresponsible youth" (PhS, 288; PhG, 341). Hegel expresses this contradiction in a sentence that could almost have been written by Foucault, when he says, "The community . . . can only maintain itself by suppressing this spirit of individualism, and because it is an essential moment, all the same creates it and, moreover, creates it by its repressive attitude towards it as a hostile principle" (*PhS*, 288; *PhG*, 341).[12] The state confronts its failure in its attempt to suppress what it must revive—namely, the spirit of individualism. This is because it was nothing more than the physical prowess of Eteocles, with a measure of good luck thrown in, that determined the success of the state and the survival of the community. If the only thing standing between the survival of the state and its defeat is the strength of its soldiers and mere chance, then the state owes its existence to causes that are not purely human but rather inhuman, natural, and uncontrollable. Hegel says, "Because the existence of ethical life rests on strength and luck, the *decision is already made* that its downfall has come" (*PhS*, 289; *PhG*, 341). The fact that nature has played a part in the preservation of the state and in its ability to withstand a traitorous attack reveals its instability. In Hegel's words, "The germ of destruction inherent in the beautiful harmony and tranquil equilibrium of the ethical spirit itself" is revealed (*PhS*, 289; *PhG*, 342). For all of its civilized government and culture, the *polis* is still subject to the hazardous and indiscriminate laws of nature, still answerable to the gods of the old order. The very performance of tragedies enacts the struggle between nature and culture, but however eloquently Sophocles can portray this conflict, neither he nor his audiences can eliminate the threat of nature. The natural laws of physical strength destroy any hope of the permanent, peaceful coexistence of the two opposing moments of ethical consciousness. If the state insists on the sacrifice of bodily enjoyment to the good of the whole, the desires of the body prove finally to be irrepressible.

How, then, does Irigaray situate Hegel's celebration of Antigone, "that noblest of figures that ever appeared on earth?"[13] It is not by a direct challenge to Hegel, nor by attempting to overthrow his authority as an interpreter of Greek tragedy. She does not merely posit an alternative reading of the *Antigone*, nor mount a defense of the drama on the grounds that Hegel fails to appreciate the complexity of the play. Had she wanted simply to challenge his authority, she might have pointed to a wealth of detail that Hegel overlooked in his urgency to compress the various aspects of Sophocles' tragedy into a framework that may be fluid in some respects but is rigid in its overall movement, allowing him to underplay some features of the text at the expense of others—producing, for example, a unity in the figure of Antigone that is belied by the diverse motives she reveals in Sophocles' text.[14] But Irigaray resists a head-on confrontation with Hegel, accepting, in general terms, the reading of Sophocles' *Antigone* that Hegel advances. She works within his terms of reference, reproducing the structured oppositions that lead Antigone along the narrow and constricting passage that begins with her decision to perform the burial of her brother and ends in her death. While she follows the same path as Hegel, Irigaray also makes ambiguous the borders that define this passage of confinement, casting it in an ironic light, bringing into question the hierarchy of the oppositions supporting it, reproducing them but adding a new dimension to them, giving them a new angle, reading the text with a new twist. She replicates the moves that Hegel produces, but at the same time she steps back from the scheme he endorses—acting the part of Hegel's Antigone, perhaps.

What are we to make of Irigaray's unearthing, uprooting, and transplanting the "eternal irony of the community" into another discourse? Upgrading a phrase that Hegel uses almost in passing, taking it up as the title of her commentary on Hegel in *Speculum*, Irigaray might be upbraided for celebrating, with Hegel, the status of women as marginal—which is indisputably how they appear in Hegel's text, despite the nobility he extols in the figure of Antigone. However much she disengages from his project or reverses his intentions, does she not also signal his authority?

Does Irigaray not incriminate herself as a party to Hegel's identification of women with nature, the unconscious, the indeterminate—dragging us down, with Antigone, into the netherworld, entombing us with her, so that we too are destined to be walled up in her underground cave? In doing so does she not refuse to acknowledge women's proper existence beyond the nether regions, equating us with the body rather than the mind, with feeling rather than reason, with intuition rather than knowledge? Does she not risk holding us captive with Antigone, who only partakes in the public domain through her association with her brother? In short, does not Irigaray do women a disservice by reinscribing sexual difference, by embracing the time-honored distinctions between body and mind, passivity and activity, the natural and the political, the private and the public? Does she not thereby inscribe or mark, reinscribe or re-mark, the female ethic as somehow less than, and answerable to, the politics of men? Perhaps I can best respond to these questions by returning to Irigaray's Hegelian Antigone and, along the way, recording the divergence between Irigaray's approach and a number of other contemporary attempts to grapple with the difficulties Hegel presents for feminism.

ANTIGONE'S EVASION

By burying her brother, Antigone not only acts in accordance with her familial duty, she knowingly defies the king's authority by ignoring Creon's injunction that no one is to bury Polynices because of his attack on Thebes. Antigone fulfils her responsibility to the law she represents, and she does so in full knowledge of the law she thereby violates—Creon's law, the man's law, the law of the state, the law according to the human conventions established by the ruler of the *polis*. She knows what she is doing. The fact that she is aware of Creon's law but does not recognize it makes her all the more ethical—and all the more guilty—in Hegel's eyes. According to Hegel, ethical consciousness and guilt go hand in hand. "The ethical consciousness is more complete, its guilt more inexcusable, if it knows *beforehand* the law and the power which it opposes, if it takes them to be violence and wrong, to be ethical merely by accident, and, like Antigone, knowingly commits the crime" (*PhS,* 284; *PhG,* 336).[15] Unlike Oedipus, who was unaware of transgressing the law of incest until after the fact, Antigone knows the law that she opposes from the start. "Oedipus," says Hegel in the *Aesthetics,* "has killed his father; he has married his mother and begotten children in this incestuous alliance; and yet he has been involved in these most evil crimes without either knowing or willing them" (*AFA,* vol. 2, 1214). Because Oedipus is unconscious of what he has done, "without having willed it" (ibid.), the tragedy of the collision in *Oedipus Rex* and *Oedipus Colonus* is of a more formal type than what Sophocles demonstrates in *Antigone,* or what Aeschylus develops in *The Seven Against Thebes.* In Hegel's view:

> The chief conflict treated most beautifully by Sophocles, with Aeschylus as his predecessor, is that between the state, i.e., ethical life in its *spiritual* universality, and the family, i.e. *natural,* ethical life. These are the clearest powers that are presented in tragedy, because the full reality of ethical existence consists in harmony between these two spheres and in absence of discord between what an agent has actually to do in one and what he has to do in the other. (*AFA,* vol. 2, 1213)

Antigone thus enacts, in the most determined way, the familial ethic dictated by her sex, and at the same time, by the very same token, by the very same act, she disrupts the meaning of the sacred law that she nevertheless follows to the letter. As Mills says, "Hegel misses what is most significant: Antigone must enter the political realm, the realm of second nature, in order to defy it on behalf of the family; the realm of first nature. In so doing Antigone transcends Hegel's analysis of the 'law of woman' as 'natural ethical life' and becomes a particular self."[16] For Knox too, "Antigone's defiance of the polis is a political as well as a religious action. [17]

What prevents Hegel from seeing Antigone's act as a political intervention? In terms of the structure that pervades his thinking, the answer is simple: women and politics do not go together. Women, by nature, are not political beings. The political sphere—the human sphere—is by definition the realm of self-conscious action, but self-conscious ethics is not for Antigone. As a woman, she is confined to the realm of the family, governed by divine providence. If it is easy to discern the structure by which Antigone is excluded from the human, self-conscious life of the state, but representative of the divine, unconscious bonds of the family, it is much less simple to see how and why this structure came into play in the first place. What is clear is that Antigone epitomizes the tragic figure for Hegel, in that she knows full well that her action will be judged criminal by the human law. She does not consider that the authority of the human law is higher than that of the law that she recognizes—namely, the divine law—but she is prepared to accept the punishment of her denial. While refusing to acknowledge that, for her, the human law is superior to the divine law, at the same time she acknowledges that, for the rulers of the *polis*, the human law is superior. As a consequence of her refusal to compromise, she accepts the punishment meted out to her by the leader of a community which she does not recognize as the highest court of law. She is willing to die, and yet she herself does not recognize Creon's word as final. For Hegel, this means that she fails to attain the ethicality of her act.

Rather than launch prematurely into a feminist reclamation of the heroic nobility of Antigone's act by turning it into what Gellrich calls "an encomium of female rebellion and kinship bonds," or in the words of the same critic, by interpreting the play as a "defense of political authority and governmental controls of individualistic extremism" (*TT*, 46), let me try to avoid both alternatives and remain for the moment within the question that has served as a guide thus far. If, in burying Polynices, Antigone acts in full awareness of the consequences of her action, in what sense does she remain unconscious of the ethical content of her act? How can she both know what she is doing and remain unconscious of its ethicality?

One critic responds to the problem of "Hegel's complex and contradictory discussion of the role of women" by declaring that the "ad hoc nature of his logic becomes nonsensical."[18] Benjamin Barber reaches this conclusion because Hegel's logic "draws inferences from nature that nature cannot support," because "its technical portrait of anatomical nature is badly flawed," and "above all because it contradicts everything Hegel otherwise tells us about dialectic and the relations dialectic conceives between nature and spirit" (*SPH*, 17). While Barber's article has the merit of admitting the problematic status of women in Hegel's philosophy, his discussion is too vague to advance the debate much beyond an evasion of the problem, by blanket dismissals of Hegel's logic. His view is that Hegelian dialectics is supposed to supersede nature, and that its failure to transmute women's naturalness into spirit provides evidence of the inadequacy of Hegel's method in general.[19] Barber does not do justice to Hegel's concept of nature, which is no simple, fixed, or stable entity. As Seyla Benhabib observes, Hegel's political philosophy can be seen in terms of the constant transformation that nature undergoes:

> *Geist* which emerges from nature, transforms nature into a second world; this "second nature" comprises the human, historical world of tradition, institutions, laws, and practices (*objektiver Geist*), as well as the self-reflection of knowing and acting subjects upon objective spirit, which is embodied in works of art, religion, and philosophy (*absoluter Geist*).[20]

Benhabib goes on to ask if Hegel's concept of *Geist* permits him to "transcend the 'naturalistic' basis of gender conceptions in the modern period, such as to place the relation between the sexes in the social, symbolic, historical, and cultural world?" (*HWI*, 132). Benhabib challenges Hegel's portrayal of women without losing sight of the extent to which, in Hegel, nature is always available for reworking. No doubt the success of Benhabib's challenge to Hegel resides in part in her refusal to underestimate Hegel's sophistication. While I hope that the present discussion also manages to avoid underestimating Hegel, my interest in Hegel's relation to feminism has a different orientation, one that it gains from the recent development in feminist theory that casts doubt upon the sex/gender distinction that Benhabib's question to Hegel appears to take for granted.

We have already seen that while the distinction between sex and gender cannot simply be abandoned, the adequacy with which some feminists conceptualize it is currently being questioned by a growing body of feminist criticism [. . .]. By focusing our attention on Hegel's understanding of female anatomy as an inferior version of the male sex, Irigaray suggests that Hegel does not simply reduce women to biology. Rather, he reads the feminine ethic back into his account of the sexual body, reading the organism according to the circumscribed ethical action that has been allotted to women in advance of any inquiry into their bodily existence. According to Hegel, Antigone is not conscious of the ethicality of her act, because she is answerable to the implicit, inner, divine realm of family kinship, the dark subcontinent of emotions, feelings, passions, and pleasures, the undercurrents that the state seeks to subdue, its underbelly. These inner depths in the hidden recesses of the body will rise up and destroy those in power, precisely because the latter assume absolute rights over the incomprehensible forces of the underworld. Inasmuch as humans presume themselves to be able to overcome any other force, they will experience their downfall. Antigone's death proves to be the occasion for such a catastrophe, unleashing the subterranean powers of a primeval world, governed by timeless laws that devour the ethical spirit from within.[21] Through her love for her brother, Antigone destroys Creon. Taking Haemon and Eurydice with her in death, she accomplishes the destruction of Creon's family. Her action not only leaves Creon's spirit broken but brings the ethical spirit of his community down with him. Creon stands in sharp contrast to both Antigone and Haemon, neither of whom deviates from their intentions. Whereas Creon regards Haemon's vow to kill himself, if Antigone is punished by death, a mere threat, it is Creon's own declarations that prove to be empty, not his son's.

The youthful dedication of Antigone to her brother, and that of Haemon to Antigone, makes a mockery of Creon's firm belief in the iron rule of discipline. Creon underestimates the strength of family bonds and is made to pay for his error through the loss of his own family. Death and destruction prove to be his undoing. The death of his only son and the subsequent death of his wife show Creon that the powers invested in a political leader are not so great and all encompassing that they can overcome the ties that bind Antigone to Polynices, Haemon to Antigone, and Eurydice to Haemon. The clash between *physis* and *nomos*, the personal and the political, individual and universal, family and state, divine and human, between the old gods and the new, youth and age, inner and outer, implicit and explicit, unconscious and conscious, night and day, pleasure and discipline, and, finally, female and male is brought to a head in a confrontation between nature and culture. How far is man's struggle against nature also his struggle against woman? How much is Hegel's treatment of Antigone a meditation on the need to tame her wild spirit, to calm her unruly disposition, or to balance the spontaneity of her actions by the neutralizing influence of the community?

Tragedy, for Hegel, results in the collapse of the ethical ideal into a world of warring forces in which nature triumphs over the tranquility of the city and in which conscious human action gives way to unconscious, unknowable, incalculable forces. In this respect, it is not Creon's action (which overreaches itself in its attempt at complete mastery) but Antigone's that allows the Hegelian dialectic to proceed. In raising the possibility that Hegel might be guilty of aligning women with nature, it is as if we—those of us who have witnessed repeatedly that alignment—knew in advance what it might mean to perform it. It is as if the very terms themselves, women as much as nature, were not, at least in some ways, up for question. If the terms *women* and *nature* are to a limited extent and in some moments in question for Hegel, they are all the more so for Irigaray. By naming the immensely problematic split between nature and culture, as if I hoped to explain by it something in Hegel's treatment of women in his discussion of the figure Antigone, I undertake a difficult task. I am in danger of taking for granted the explanatory force of this fundamental pair of opposites—nature/culture—in referring women and men to either side of the divide, as if that simple referral could illuminate once and for all the content and meaning of the difference between the sexes—as if the first pair of opposites could serve as some kind of stable ground for the second, as if the concepts of nature and culture were easily defined, separated, segregated from one another, as if they were not interminably, irrevocably bound up with one another, as if their meaning were self-evident and their independence incontestable.

To say that Hegel simply decided to equate women to nature not only misconstrues the inextricability of nature and culture, it also misstates the problem by implicating him in women's history of subordination, as if it were his personal responsibility. Neither Hegel nor any other single individual can have simply decided, by fiat or with one blow, to circumscribe women in nature once and for all. How far Hegel can be held responsible for taking his place in a long tradition that has institutionalized women's inferiority over and over again and in what ways this might be said to be true are not questions that tolerate quick answers. Nevertheless, it remains the case that Hegel's alignment of women with nature—however unstable both of these categories are rendered at times in his thinking—is so far entrenched in a tradition that inscribes and reinscribes women as inferior that it is difficult to read his texts against the grain of that tradition. But that is precisely what Irigaray helps us do. The questions Irigaray brings to Hegel and to the philosophical tradition for which he stands (and what better choice than Hegel—a thinker who attempted to think the history of philosophy and to incorporate it into his own system) fall outside of the tradition that Hegel assumes. Precisely because Hegel's confrontation with the tradition of philosophy was so dazzlingly comprehensive, because he took the history of philosophy so seriously, we can learn from rereading Hegel—if we allow ourselves to do so without being blind to the prejudices of his time, nor to his conviction that he stood at the pinnacle of philosophical thought. Irigaray shows not only that Hegel assumes in advance that Antigone is prohibited from properly ethical action, but that he does so by reading her failure to act as if it were inscribed in her body. Being a woman is enough to disqualify her from doing anything that is not already circumscribed by her body—which Hegel reads as passive. Hegel sets up the female body as the ground of Antigone's inactivity, assuming that her apolitical nature stems from her anatomy. But his very description of female anatomy is already permeated by the principle that Antigone, as a woman whose sphere of ethical action is circumscribed by the family, cannot act. This assumption is brought under critical scrutiny by Irigaray, who sees Hegel's construction of the female body as a continuation of a long-established belief that is not so much a function of biology as it is the result of the conviction that femininity is by definition passive, inactive, and ineffectual. Irigaray shows how Hegel's comprehension of female anatomy is infused with the cultural assumptions and ethical imperatives that he prescribes for and imputes to women. By demonstrating the extent to which Hegel's account of women's "nature" is bound up—in what she calls (as we just saw) "an amazing vicious circle" (*SO*, 233; *SA*, 277)—with Hegel's cultural prescriptions for women, Irigaray destabilizes what Hegel takes to be the rock and foundation of his cultural prescription of women's roles, namely, the "natural" function of women's bodies.

Nancy Tuana demonstrates the implausibility of conceiving of the sex/gender divide in terms of such a rigid dichotomy, preferring to see the distinction as "interactionist."[22] She explains traditional accounts of sex and gender and the need to overcome the metaphysical tendency to posit absolute binary oppositions by referring to what she calls the "fabric metaphor" (*RNN*, 83). The relation between sex and gender, as it is often understood, can be compared to the way in which the vertical threads of the warp cross and interweave with the horizontal threads of the woof in a piece of fabric. The vertical threads represent the genetic factors, while the horizontal strands represent the environmental factors that determine any given characteristic or trait. This model, according to Tuana, does not adequately conceptualize the interactive relation between genes and environment, or between sex and gender, insofar as it continues to conceive of the two contributing factors as inherently separable from one another. Tuana says that the fabric model

> does serve to emphasize the mutual intertwining of genes and environment but models it in such a way that each remains a separate mechanism unaffected by the process of their intertwining. The threads of the warp are separate and discrete from those of the woof, a model that precludes the possibility of a dynamic interaction. . . .This relationship cannot be treated as additive. One cannot parse out the contributions of genes, of the developmental environment, of culture, etc., and sum the results. To do so restricts the range of relationships possible and leads one to adopt a simplistic nature/nurture dichotomous thinking. (*RNN*, 83–84)

Tuana makes clear the complexity of the relation between nature and nurture and, by extension of her argument, the complexity of the relation between sex and gender. She emphasizes the importance of going beyond a merely "additive" understanding of the relationship between nature and nurture. While this model marks an advance over the traditional separation of nature from culture, it falls short of understanding the sense in which there is a *dynamic interaction* between nature and nurture to the extent that this image still retains the idea that nature is "a distinct and separate . . . *mechanism* from the *mechanism* of nurture" (*RNN*, 81). What is needed, in Tuana's view, are models of "dynamic interaction" (*RNN*, 81), or "frameworks which enable us to see biological and cultural adaptation as interdependent" (*RNN*, 84–85).

If one concedes that biology and culture have a mutually interactive relationship, then their impact on one another would extend to our ideas of what counts as biology and what counts as culture. What constitutes biology as a discipline is influenced by cultural developments, including technological advances, and what counts as culture is similarly affected by biological determinants—which in turn are comprised, in part, of cultural influences. If one understands the relation of gender to sex as genuinely inextricable, as Tuana suggests, it becomes more difficult than it might seem initially (perhaps even impossible) to separate those aspects of traits that are due to gender from those due to sex. The categories themselves impinge on one another, overlapping in ways that will always be shifting, contingent, and not entirely transparent to us. Another way of stating the same point in more general terms is that we always define the relationship between sex and gender from a cultural standpoint. The fact that we cannot help but identify culture and nature from within a given culture does not mean that culture is always the more influential of the pair but rather that culture and nature are bound up with and implicated in one another in ways that are not reducible to quantitative analysis. The result is that feminine and masculine traits cannot be simply attributed either to sex or gender. The very concepts of sex and gender not only resist easy or stable definitions, but their instability also puts into question the applicability of the causal model of reasoning to which attributions of particular traits to sex or gender tend to appeal. To return to the fabric metaphor, neither set of threads is static and unchanging. Each is affected by the presence of the other in ways that make it impossible to ever completely isolate one from the other. It is not just that nature and culture interact at each node at which they intersect with one another, but that after each such interaction, what counts as culture and what counts as nature will themselves be changed by that interaction. Of course, even this way of conceptualizing the relation between culture and nature remains inadequate insofar as no node of interaction could be properly isolated from its context (*RNN,* 81). What we call nature can never be definitely separated from what we call culture.

In his "Remarks on Antigone," Friedrich Hölderlin says: "It is a great resource of the secretly working soul that at the highest state of consciousness, it evades consciousness."[23] In this chapter I have been concerned with the meaning of that evasion, with its consequences for Hegel's Antigone as a woman and with Irigaray's appropriation of and rethinking of these consequences in *Speculum.* Antigone's fate, her tragedy, is contained in the aspect of her existence that assigns her to her sex. The entire tragic consequences of her action are entailed by the simplicity with which she adheres to her female nature, by which she denies herself the only opportunity available to her to realize her full potential as a woman, namely, motherhood. In this lies the nobility and greatness for which Hegel congratulates her, insisting nonetheless that she lacks the ethical spirit that would confirm her understanding of community. Having followed the rationale of Hegel's reading of the figure of Antigone, we are in a better position to judge the wisdom of Irigaray's refiguring of Sophocles' Antigone as a call to create a new ethics of sexual difference.

It is necessary, according to Irigaray, to "renew the line of feminine genealogy" in order to render possible a new ethics of sexual difference.[24] Such an ethics would no longer cast Antigone as an outlaw—an "anarchist" (*TD,* 103–04) whose actions amount merely to insubordination, or to a violation of the state's decree.[25] Rather, it would acknowledge the validity of her actions, which issue from a set of laws other than those represented by Creon: respect for the order of the cosmos, the terrestrial order, maternal genealogy, the engendering of life, and respect for the gods and for the rights of burial (*TD,*

82–83, 84). Antigone's burial of Polynices is only seen as a disruption of the state by those who possess full citizenship, that is, by men who are able to exercise their civil and political rights.

In the same way that Creon paid no heed to the laws that governed Antigone's action, Irigaray thinks that contemporary civil codes continue to ignore the specific rights and duties of women. To the extent that this is true, Irigaray characterizes the laws that organize society—which is still largely managed by men (*TD*, 85)—as uncivil.[26] These laws are regulated, according to Irigaray, by the fascination with the "infinite subtleties" involved in the "manufacture, commerce and possession of goods" (*TD*, 85). Among the incivilities permitted by a society governed by the commerce of goods, Irigaray includes the disregard of the natural environment—"of nature, the sun and the earth, water and air" (*TD*, 87); a lack of respect for the "genealogy of women," which consists in an idealization of virginity on the one hand and the violence of incest and rape on the other hand (*TD*, 87–88); and the abuse of images of women in pornography and advertising (*TD*, 88).[27]

Because the civil and political rights that men enjoy are permeated with a lack of respect for women, Irigaray does not think that it is possible to effectively extend these civil rights to women without revising our conception of what constitutes such rights. What is needed is a reconceptualization of the civic sphere, so that the supposedly neutral (but in fact masculine biased) social and political rights and duties that have traditionally defined this sphere are specified further in terms of rights and duties pertaining to sexual difference. Practically, in addition to endorsing the civil rights of women (*TD*, 96), this entails making visible the unwritten, unacknowledged, secret laws that have characterized relations among women (*TD*, 94). In other words, it is necessary to create a symbolic order for women that will not only subtend their civil rights but will also call for a new conception of the civic realm, one that takes account of sexual identity. Unless some attempt is made to formulate the rights and duties specific to women, any success feminism has in securing equality for women will tend to confer privileges upon women as if they were token men. Moreover, it will tend to operate in line with the prejudices that structure the various hierarchies that patriarchy embraces. To the extent that feminist efforts to secure equality with men fail to systematically subject the patriarchal system to critique, they will perpetuate the exclusionary practices in which patriarchy engages—confirming, for example, its norms of racial discrimination and compulsory heterosexuality. The possibility of articulating an ethic of sexual difference is bound up with the need to insist on recognizing the validity of the specific rights and duties of specific groups distinct from their identity as defined by the social whole. Insofar as this project appeals to the importance of specifying multiple ways of existing in a society, it opens the way for an ethics that extends beyond sexual difference.

NOTES

1. Georg W. F. Hegel, *Phenomenology of Spirit*, trans. A.V. Miller (Oxford: Clarendon Press, 1979). 271. Hereafter cited as *PhS*; *Phänomenologie des Geistes*, ed. J. Hoffmeiser (Hamburg: Felix Meiner), 323. Hereafter cited as *PhG*.

2. As Derrida observes, "Intermittence—jerking rhythm—is an essential rule. If there were only war, the community's natural being-there would be destroyed." Jacques Derrida, *Glas*, trans. John Leavy Jr. and Richard Rand (Lincoln: University of Nebraska Press, 1986), 147. *Glas* (Paris: Editions Galilée, 1974), 166.

3. Sophocles, *Antigone*, trans. Elizabeth Wycoff. In *Sophocles I*, ed. David Grene and Richmond Latimore. *The Complete Greek Tragedies* (Chicago: University of Chicago Press, 1954), 674–80. Hereafer cited as *A*. For further reference to women as the weaker sex in *Antigone*, see *A*, 61–63, 484–85, 578–79, 740–41, 746, and 756. There is also an important association between youth and womanhood, which Hegel notices and develops, on which I will comment later.

4. Creon not only makes repeated reference to Antigone's sex, as if he regards her refusal to obey him as a test of his male strength (see *A*, 484 and 525), his sensitivity to the fact that it is a woman who challenges his authority is highlighted when he insults the son of Haemon by calling him "weaker than a woman!" (*A*, 749) and a "woman's slave" (*A*, 756).

5. Hegel says that "Womankind—the everlasting irony [in the life] of the community—changes by intrigue the universal end of the government into a private end, transforms its universal activity into a work of some particular individual, and perverts the universal property of the state into a possession and ornament of the Family. . . . In general, she maintains that it is the power of youth that really counts: the mother who bore him, that of the brother as being one in whom the sister finds man on a level of equality, that of the youth as being one through whom the daughter, freed from her dependence [on the family] obtains the enjoyment and dignity of wifehood. The community, however, can only maintain itself by suppressing this spirit of individualism, and, because it is an essential moment, all the same creates it and, moreover, creates it by its repressive attitude towards it as a hostile principle" (*PhS*, 288, *PhG*, 340–41).

6. Georg W. F. Hegel, *Aesthetics: Lectures on Fine Art*. 3 vols, trans. T. M. Knox (Oxford: Clarendon Press, 1974), vol. 2, 1218. Hereafter cited as *AFA*.

7. Szondi argues that the conflict between nature and art is central not only to Holderlin's and Schelling's conception of tragedy but also to Hegel's, although Hegel gives it a different emphasis. Szondi says, "The conflict between inorganic law and living individuality, between the universal and the particular, is thus not illuminated: it is dynamically surpassed and absorbed into the heart of the notion of identity." Peter Szondi, "The Notion of the Tragic in Schelling, Hölderlin, and Hegel," *On Textual Understanding and Other Essays*, trans. Harvey Mendelsohn. *Theory and History of Literature*, vol. 15 (Minneapolis: Minnesota University Press, 1986).

8. Martin Heidegger, *Introduction to Metaphysics*, trans. Ralph Manheim (New Haven: Yale University Press, 1987), 146-65. *Einführung in die Metaphysik* (Tübingen: Niemeyer, 1953), 112–26. Also see Victor Ehrenberg, *Sophocles and Perycles* (Oxford: Basil Blackwell, 1954), 61–66.

9. Flay says, the "overarching presupposition of unity is evidenced not only in the reflection that the polis is one, but even more concretely and reflexively embodied in the conservative view of the chorus in the plays to which Hegel directs us." Joseph C. Flay, *Hegel's Quest for Certainty* (Albany: State University of New York, 1984), 166–67. He adds that the chorus "as the unity of the polis is there to speak for the ethical substance" (169).

10. Luce Irigaray, *Speculum of the Other Woman*, trans. Gillian C. Gill (Ithaca, N.Y.: Cornell University Press), 220. Hereafter cited as *SO*; *Speculum de l'autre femme* (Paris: Editions Minuit, 1974), 274. Hereafter cited as *SA*.

11. To follow up the theme of youth in *Antigone*, see *A*, 216, 681, 719, 726, 728, 735, and 1034.

12. Foucault says of sex, "One had to speak of it as of a thing to be not simply condemned or tolerated but managed, inserted into systems of utility, regulated for the greater good of all, made to function according to an optimum." Michel Foucault, *History of Sexuality*, vol. 1, trans. Robert Hurley (Harmondsworth, Middlesex: Penguin, 1984), 24. It is in the sense in which Foucault thinks of the discourse of sexuality as being produced in the age of repression that is analogous to the way in which Hegel sees the "spirit of individualism" as not only being subject to suppression but also as being created by that suppression in the first place.

13. Georg W. F. Hegel, *Hegel's Lectures on the History of Philosophy*, vol. I, ed. and trans. E. S. Haldane (London: Routledge & Kegan Paul, 1955), 441.

14. Gellrich comments that Antigone's "character disseminates in directions that are not contained with or controlled by the moral claim to which Hegel maintains she adheres in burying her brother." Michelle Gellrich, *Tragedy and Theory: The Problem of Conflict Since Aristotle* (Princeton, N.J.: Princeton University Press, 1988), 53. Hereafter cited as *TT*.

15. Consider how Hegel can maintain without contradiction both that Antigone embodies ethical consciousness par excellence and that, since she violates the law of the state knowingly, her "guilt is more inexcusable" than it would have been had she buried her brother in ignorance of Creon's edict. How can Antigone's act of defiance be at one and the same time the supreme representation of ethical consciousness, in the Hegelian sense, and nevertheless implicate her as inexcusably guilty? We should not make the mistake of imposing on the figure of Antigone our contemporary idea of character. Recall that in his account of the concrete development of dramatic poetry, Hegel makes a point of differentiating between the "modern use of the term" character and the "individual pathos" of the heroic figure. If we cannot make sense of the heroic figure of Greek tragedy by simply imputing to it modern notions of character, neither can we reduce it to merely abstract moral principles. Hegel says, "They occupy a vital central position between both, because they are firm figures who simply are what they are, without any inner conflict, without any hesitating recognition of someone else's 'pathos,' and therefore (the opposite of our contemporary 'irony') lofty, absolutely determined individuals, although this determinacy of theirs is based on and is representative of a particular ethical power" *(AFA*, vol. 2, 1209-10).

16. Patricia Jagentowitz Mills, *Woman, Nature, and Psyche* (New Haven, Conn.: Yale University Press), 27.

17. Bernard Knox, *The Heroic Temper: Studies in Sophoclean Tragedy* (Berkeley: University of California Press, 1983), 75. Hereafter cited as *HT*. Knox shows that the terms in which Antigone speaks of her "loyalty to blood relationship" are "exactly the terms a citizen would use of his loyalty to the *polis*, in political terms, in fact. . . .This loyalty of hers is in fact a political loyalty not only because the particular circumstances force her to choose between family and *polis*, but also because historically the strong, indissoluble tie of blood relationship had in earlier times, through the *genē*, the 'clans,' been the dominating factor in the citizen's social and political environment. It was much older than the *polis*, and in democratic Athens still showed on every side signs of its continued power as a rival and even a potential danger to the newer civil institutions and forms of organization" (76).

18. Benjamin Barber, "Spirit Phoenix and History's Owl or the Incoherence of Dialectics in Hegel's account of Women." *Political Theory*, vol. 16, no. 1 (February 1988): 5–28. Hereafter cited as *SPH*.

19. Barber says that Hegel "restores Antigone and the female race to the bondage of history . . . harking back to the very physical nature that dialectics supersede" (*SPH*, 12). Barber elaborates a few pages later. "Although everywhere else in his work both the youthful and the senatorial Hegel proclaim the dialectical preeminence of spirit over nature, with women, nature is given preeminence over spirit. When he remarks that the differences in the physical characteristics of the sexes has a rational basis that endow them with intellectual and ethical significance, Hegel blithely stands the dialectic on its head, giving it (as Marx was to do two decades later) a material base. So that to maintain the special position of women, Hegel is forced into a kind of proto-materialism in which the dog of spirit get wagged by the tail of nature" (*SPH*, 17). See *The Philosophy of Right*, trans. and ed. T. M. Knox (Oxford: Clarendon Press, 1945), para. 165.

20. Seyla Benhabib, "On Hegel, Women, and Irony," *Feminist Interpretations of Political Theory*, eds. Mary Lyndon Shanley and Carole Pateman (Oxford: Polity Press in association with Basil Blackwell, 1991), 132. Reprinted in Benhabib, *Situating the Self: Gender, Community, and Postmodernism in Contemporary Ethics* (New York: Routledge, 1992), 242–59; see esp. 245. Hereafter cited as *HWI*.

21. On Antigone's wild nature, or her identification with untamable, unthinkable dimensions, see Charles Segal, "*Antigone: Death and Love, Hades and Dionysus*," *Oxford Readings in Greek Tragedy*, ed. Erich Segal (Oxford: Oxford University Press, 1983), 170–71. Previously published in Charles Segal, *Tragedy of Civilization: An Interpretation of Sophocles* (Cambridge: Oxford University Press, 1981).

22. Nancy Tuana, "Re-fusing Nature/Nurture," *Hypatia Born* (Bloomington: Indiana University Press, 1990), 86. Hereafter cited as *RNN*.

23. Friedrich Hölderlin, "Remarks on Antigone," *Essays and Letters on Theory*, ed. T. Pfau (Albany: State University of New York Press, 1988), 111. See Szondi's "The Notion of the Tragic in Schelling, Hölderlin, and Hegel" for a discussion of Hegel's understanding of tragic conflict as the contradiction of "inorganic law and living individuality" (49–50). Szondi's essay shows the proximity between Hölderlin's understanding of tragedy in terms of the paradox that subsists in man's place in relation to nature, "a place which not only indicates that he is her servant, but which also reveals nature's dependence on man" (46). For Hölderlin, as Szondi says, the dialectic of tragedy is one

"in which the strong can appear by itself only as weakness and requires something weak in order that its strength may appear" (47). We have seen how close this understanding of tragedy is to Hegel's own conception of it, as represented in his discussion of the *Antigone* in the *Phenomenology of Spirit*. Women, as the eternal irony of the community, constitute the weak link in the community. The strength of the community can only appear through its suppression of the spirit of individuality that women represent.

For an interesting discussion of Hölderlin's and Heidegger's understanding of Antigone and Oedipus, see Christopher Fynsk, *Heidegger: Thought and Historicity* (Ithaca, N.Y.: Cornell University Press, 1986), 174–229.

24. Luce Irigaray, *Le temps de la* différance (Paris: Librarie Général Française, 1989), 120–21. Hereafter cited as *TD*.

25. Antigone is regarded by the chorus as "*autonomos*" (*A*, 821). Knox says this is "a word which is generally applied to cities—'independent, living under their own laws'— but is here applied, in a bold figure of speech which contains the essence of the play's conflict, to an individual—she 'lives by her own law'" (*HT*, 66).

26. Irigaray rejects the assumption of the "patriarchal" society—that men are "civil" and women are "uncivil"—and emphasizes instead the ways in which patriarchal society is itself lacking in civility, enumerating the ways in which it pays no respect to women (*TD*, 85–92). It is noteworthy that the chorus says of Antigone, "The girl is bitter. She's her father's child" (*A*, 471), or, as Lacan says, "She is *homos*. We translate that as best we can by 'inflexible.' It literally means something uncivilized, something raw. Jacques Lacan, *The Seminar of Jacques Lacan*, Book VII, ed. Jacques-Alain Miller (New York: W.W. Norton, 1992), 263.

27. See also Luce Irigaray, *Sexes and Genealogies*, trans. Gillian C. Gill (New York: Columbia University Press, 1993), 5; *Sexes et Parentés* (Paris: Minuit, 1987), 17–18

CHAPTER 3

Linking Onto Disinterestedness, or the Moral Law in Kant's Critique of Judgment

Rodolphe Gasché

About to engage the beautiful arts in *Critique of Judgment*, in a work whose analysis of beauty has been based essentially, if not exclusively, on the beautiful of nature, Kant recalls that for a judgment of taste to be pure, that is, to be such a judgment in the first place, a judgment "must have no interest [whatsoever] *as its determining ground*" (138).[1] The beautiful arts are not to be exempted from this basic requirement for pure judgments of taste established in the "Analytic of the Beautiful" if the judgment thereupon is to be a pure judgment concerning their beauty. As Kant argued at the beginning of the Third Critique, in terms of quality, that is, in terms of what distinguishes it from other (aesthetic) judgments, a judgment of taste must be disinterested, or in other words, entirely free of any satisfaction deriving from the representation of the existence of the object that is judged.[2] "Such satisfaction always [having] reference to the faculty of desire, either as its determining ground or as necessarily connected with its determining ground" (38), a pure judgment of taste must be free of the senses' and the will's partiality toward the existence of objects that cause the respective pleasures of the sensibly pleasant and the morally good. A pure judgment of taste, in contrast, comes into being only when all such concernment with the existence of the object is excluded, and when that which is judged beautiful (rather than pleasant or good) pleases independently of "whether anything depends or can depend on the existence of the thing, either for myself or for any one else" (38). Undoubtedly, a judgment of the senses and a moral judgment are both aesthetic judgments, because both derive pleasure from their object. But the satisfactions involved are intimately tied to the existence and the continued desirability of the object. Distinct from them is the pure aesthetic judgment, or judgment of taste. For it to be possible at all, that is, for it to derive satisfaction from the fact that a thing for which one has no concept (or any use) still has the mere form of an object, this condition of disinterestedness in the existence of the object must obtain. Otherwise, the judgment will be either a judgment of the senses or a moral judgment, but certainly not a pure aesthetic judgment. With "disinterestedness," Kant manages to exhibit a category of aesthetic judgments that, rather than being grounded on the pleasure from the existence of the object, finds satisfaction with the possibility that a thing for which no concept is available has nonetheless the form of an object and consequently meets the minimal conditions of cognizability, namely, representability. Within the broad domain of aesthetic judgments, the judgments based on a disinterested pleasure carve out a sphere of judgments that in distinction from judgments of the senses are not private and incommunicable but that are not universal either, because they would then rest, as with moral judgments, on the pre-given and universally shared concept of the good. "Disinterestedness" is the index, within the general domain of aesthetic judgments, of one particular area of judgments that can lay claim to universality without any pre-given concepts, because disinterested pleasure stems from the discovery that the objects under consideration have form, more precisely, the mere form of an object, rather than no form (and thus refusing representation). Since the pleasure in question concerns the very possibility of cognition when it is faced with objects for which the understanding cannot provide concepts, it can safely be assumed that anyone, in principle, could enter into agreement with such a judgment. Disinterestedness is thus constitutive of pure aesthetic judgments as judgments that establish the possibility that certain things are objects, and that secure in this manner the possibility of cognition for these objects. Disinterestedness is the condition under which a very specific, if not singular, kind of epistemological accomplishment comes to light, and it is with it, and with it alone, that Kant's aesthetics is concerned.

Kant's reminder that this condition of disinterestedness for aesthetic judgment on the beautiful remains fully valid and is not to be rescinded in the course of his analysis of the beautiful arts becomes all the more crucial as this analysis also explores a possible relation between the beautiful and the morally good. Indeed, one of the more persisting and enduring misunderstandings of Kant's aesthetics is the belief that disinterestedness in judgments of beauty roundly excludes any possible linkage of beauty to the morally good. Such a relation of the beautiful of art to the morally good, to a concept that is at our disposal insofar as we are rational beings, and that we cannot but wish, and will, to have reality, suggests interest. Even though interest can be attributed to all powers of the mind, the morally good warrants interest because interest itself is intimately, and essentially, tied to the faculty of reason as a faculty of principles.[3] The question concerning a possible interest in the beautiful that guides, perhaps even motivates, Kant's discussion of the beautiful arts is thus one of the beautiful's moral and rational relevance. By attending to the beautiful of the arts, and to this question of a possible interest in their beauty, Kant's aesthetics of the beautiful would thus seem to take a turn from what numerous commentators consider a frivolous concern with mere form to more serious or substantial issues. What further seems to support such a view is that in addition to this turn, Kant also admits to a connection of the moral to the beautiful of nature. Although the mere form at stake in a pure disinterested judgment of taste is found pleasurable, because it signifies that the object is attuned to the powers of cognition and is thus not at all a frivolous concern, the introduction of the question of interest suggests a kind of turning point, or hinge, in Kant's thinking about the beautiful. What are the reasons for having the question of interest return after everything that has been established with regard to disinterestedness as being essential to the pure judgment of the beautiful? Has Kant relaxed his standards? Has he abandoned all interest in pure judgments of taste and then turned to the aesthetic judgments in the morally good which, because they presuppose concepts, are impure judgments of taste? What are the precise reasons for broaching the question of interest at the moment Kant resorts to the analysis of artificial beauty? And finally, given Kant's reminder that the principles set forth by the "Analytic of the Beautiful" are not to be rescinded when considering the beautiful arts, how does interest link on to disinterestedness? What kind of form does their articulation take? These are among the questions that we will have to ask at this undoubtedly crucial juncture of Kant's text.

Before seeking an answer to these questions, we need to point out that the theme of interest brought up in the chapters concerning artificial beauty (and seemingly for the first time in relation to beauty) had already been at issue in Kant's discussion of the sublime. Notwithstanding Kant's broaching this issue in the "General Remark upon the Exposition of the Aesthetical Reflective Judgment," almost exclusively with respect to the sublime, a discussion of this chapter should enable us to understand better what Kant means by interest, and how it is linked onto disinterested judgments of taste. Furthermore, since it is certainly not by accident that the question of an interest in the sublime is made to precede its thematization with respect to the beautiful, we can also expect this chapter to provide some hints about why the interest in the beautiful could only be properly discussed in the wake of what has been established about the interest in the sublime.

Returning one more time to the different kinds of feeling that are the grounds of determination of aesthetical judgments, and in reference to which an object, or its representation, is classified as either pleasant, beautiful, sublime, or good, Kant remarks:

The *absolutely good*, subjectively judged according to the feeling that it inspires (the object of the moral feeling), as capable of determining the powers of the subject through the representation of an *absolutely compelling* law, is specially distinguished by the *modality* of a necessity that rests *a priori* upon concepts. This necessity involves, not merely a *claim*, but a *command* for the assent of everyone and belongs in itself to the pure intellectual rather than to the aesthetical judgment, and is by a determinant and not a mere reflective judgment ascribed, not to nature, but to freedom. (107)

It follows from all of this that the pleasure inspired by the morally good cannot be part of an investigation into the pure aesthetical reflective judgments. The satisfaction in the good should be singled out from the sphere of the investigation of judgments of taste in the same way as the feeling of the pleasant, not because it is based on a judgment of the senses as is the latter, but because it rests on an intellectual judgment. Yet while the judgment of taste bars all "natural combination with the feeling of the pleasant" (107), its relation to the satisfaction with the morally good is more complex. Indeed, as Kant argues, even though the judgment of the absolutely good is clearly a determinant judgment by which the idea of the good is ascribed to the subject, the "*modification of [the subject's] state*" to which this determination *can* give rise—one which consists in the subject's feeling of "*hindrances* in sensibility and at the same time [of] its superiority to them by their subjugation"—shows the moral feeling to be "cognate [*verwandt*] to the aesthetical judgment and its formal conditions" (107). Thanks to this formal resemblance to the aesthetic judgment, the moral feeling can even "serve to represent [*vorstellig zu machen*] the conformity to law of action from duty as aesthetical, i.e. as sublime or even as beautiful, without losing purity" (107). In short, although the pleasure in the good is the result of an intellectual determination of the will—an intellectual pleasure, as it were, no doubt entirely distinct from the pleasure of the senses, but also from that of the beautiful and the sublime—the need to overcome hindrances of sensibility in the process of intellectual determination of the will, and whose successful effectuation induces a sense of superiority in the subject, also predisposes moral feeling to serve as an aesthetical representation of moral action. Moral feeling as a satisfaction in the absolutely good thus seems to warrant inclusion in the Kantian aesthetics. At the same time, it is necessary to emphasize the modalities of this recognition. If the moral feeling does not lose its intellectual purity in this process, in short, if no confusion whatsoever takes place between the feeling that derives from the subject's intellectual determination and the feeling that predisposes it as an aesthetical representation of the morally good, it is basically for two reasons. First, the moral feeling's capability for aesthetical representation is (only) added to the subjective judgment about the absolutely good. Second, only a formal similarity, or isomorphism, between the modification of the subject's state by the moral law and what obtains in the aesthetical judgment of the sublime and the beautiful explains this feeling's ability to serve as an aesthetical representation. In no way is the moral feeling itself positively to be confused with an aesthetical representation of the absolutely good. Only because the moral feeling can lead to a modification of the subject's state akin to what obtains in the judgment of the sublime and the beautiful can this feeling, in addition to what it is, also assume the function of rendering aesthetically the law present. If the moral feeling's aesthetic credentials have thus been acknowledged, the aesthetic function of moral feeling is, nonetheless, an indirect, oblique, if not also contingent, possibility, since it is based on a feeling that the subject *can* have in addition to the feeling that the morally good produces in him or her. It is therefore a rather intricate and precarious possibility.

Kant has thus made room for an aesthetic function of moral feeling in conformity with the principles of the power of judgment. Undoubtedly, the ways in which one has to understand such aesthetical representation, if Kant's claim that the purely intellectual does not warrant any sensible presentation is not to be contradicted, remain to be seen. We will return to this question in the context of Kant's discussion of whether something such as intellectual beauty or sublimity is conceivable. For the time being, I note that by thus acknowledging an aesthetical representation of the morally good, Kant has implicitly opened up the question of a possible relation of the beautiful and the sublime to the moral law. If the moral law allows for an aesthetical representation in which it can be represented either as sublime or even as beautiful, the question inevitably arises concerning the sublime's and the beautiful's commerce with the morally good. From the start, however, it must be kept in mind that the possibility of a sublime or even beautiful representation of the morally good does in no way imply that, by nature, or as such the sublime or the beautiful, would necessarily be aesthetical representations of the moral law. In conformity with what has been established throughout the analytics of the beautiful and the sublime, Kant does not renege on the distinctions between the different kinds of pleasure when he returns to this question at the beginning of the "General Remark." They are distinct kinds of satisfactions not to be lumped together. The moral feeling's aesthetic achievement is to be kept rigorously separate from the aesthetic accomplishments of, especially, the beautiful and the sublime. Nevertheless, it needs to be remarked that the four kinds of satisfactions listed by the "General Remark" are classified according to the four judgmental moments involved in the judgments upon both the beautiful and the sublime. The pleasant is made intelligible by quantity; the beautiful requires a representation of quality; the sublime consists only in a relation; and the moral feeling is of the order of a modality. Undoubtedly, the reason for resorting to this classification is, first, to separate the four pleasures as sharply as possible. The absolutely compelling law involved in moral feeling severs it entirely from all the other kinds of satisfactions. But since it is possible to graft onto the moral feeling a modification of the subject that resembles the one found in the sublime and the beautiful, the question becomes whether in spite of their difference from moral feeling the beautiful and the sublime do not also in turn allow for the addition of a relation to the morally good. Before further exploring this line of thought, let me stress one more time that what makes it possible for the moral feeling to become an aesthetical representation of the moral law is the formal structure that it has in common with the sublime and the beautiful, when this feeling is associated with the feeling of hindrances of sensibility and their respective overcoming by the powers of the subject. This formal structure is the hinge between the feeling of morality and the other pleasures relevant for judgments of taste. It connects both types of feeling in the mode of an addition. But not only does the aesthetical representation of moral laws derive from formal likeness (which causes such representation to be of the order of an addition), any possible relation of aesthetical feelings such as those of the beautiful and the sublime to the absolutely good must rest on a similar formality. Furthermore, such a relation can only have the nature of an appendage. It follows that for a correct understanding of how the morally good can be linked onto pure aesthetical judgments, it is imperative to pinpoint the exact reasons that cause both to be formally similar to one another.

What possible relation then can the feelings of the beautiful and the sublime have to the morally good? The definition in the "Analytic of the Aesthetical Judgment" of the beautiful, and to some extent of the sublime as well, is far from being suggestive in this respect. No wonder that after having put the fourfold distinction of the aesthetically relevant pleasures into place, Kant proceeds in the "General Remark" to a subtle redefinition of beauty and sublimity:

> The *beautiful* is what pleases in the mere judgment (and therefore not by the medium of sensation in accordance with a concept of the understanding). It follows at once from this that it must please apart from all interest. The *sublime* is what pleases immediately through its opposition to the interest of sense. (107)

Thus recast, the difference between the beautiful and the sublime rests on the different fate to which they subject the sensible. As we shall see hereafter, this redefinition is necessary for attaching the question of interest to disinterested judgments of taste. In any case, in the beautiful, the sensible is felt to be subjectively purposive for contemplative understanding in general. Since no definite purpose intervenes in such a judgment, the sensible is "reduced" to the mere form that is beneficial for the powers of cognition. It is a disinterested judgment in that the sensible is stripped here of all appeal to the senses (and to the definite concepts of cognition). The sublime, in contrast, is characterized by a total resistance to the sensible, and such resistance is felt to be subjectively purposive in terms of practical reason. A judgment about the sublime is thus even more disinterested than the one upon the beautiful. Radically turning away from the sensible, it subjectively predisposes the mind for the ideas of reason. Both treatments of sensibility in these judgments, says Kant, "are purposive in reference to the moral feeling. The beautiful prepares us to love disinterestingly something, even nature itself; the sublime prepares us to esteem something highly even in opposition to our own (sensible) interest" (108). Despite the difference between the two pure aesthetic reflective judgments, the way they deal with the sensible opens the space in both for a relation with moral feeling. More precisely, Kant describes them as judgments that prepare the subject for moral feeling. The reason for these aesthetic judgments' anticipatory evocation of moral feeling rests with the status they allot to the sensible. These judgments treat the sensible in a way similar to what obtains in moral judgments. In other words, what makes these judgments upon the beautiful and the sublime intimations of moral feeling is nothing less than their disinterestedness. To the extent that the judgments upon the beautiful are witness to a disinterested love in that which is a prime object of sensible interest—nature—and that judgments upon the sublime estimate that the sacrifice of all interest is purposive for higher considerations, they anticipate that other kind of disposition of the mind: the disposition for ideas, or purely intellectual (i.e., moral) judgment. Although entirely distinct from moral feeling, the disinterestedness constitutive of both judgments of taste predisposes them to relate to moral feelings in a mode of relating that Kant calls preparatory. This means that without such disinterestedness, they could not assume this preliminary role at all. Furthermore, by giving up on disinterestedness, in other words, by lacking a formal analogy to intellectual judgments, the aesthetical judgment would also fail to provoke any (moral) interest.

Before we can engage the issue of how reason can take an interest in disinterested judgments of taste, we need to deepen our understanding of how such judgments of taste "prepare" us for moral judgment. Although the beautiful is also said to be purposive in reference to the moral feeling, the feeling of the sublime, and even more narrowly, the sublime in its dynamical aspect, realizes this possibility most properly. In the sublime, Kant recalls, "the unattainability of nature [is] regarded as a presentation of ideas" (108). When faced with an object, or spectacle, of nature that we fail to comprehend cognitively even though we "extend our empirical faculty (mathematically or dynamically) . . . reason infallibly intervenes [*so tritt unausbleiblich die Vernunft hinzu*], as the faculty expressing the independence of absolute totality, and generates the unsuccessful effort of the mind to make the representation of the senses adequate to these [ideas]" (108). Undoubtedly, reason's intervention in judgments of the sublime makes these judgments prepare us for moral feeling. But how are we to understand this intervention? Does it not at first suggest that reason has been absent from the imagination's attempt to comprehend nature in its totality by extending itself? Furthermore, if reason infallibly supervenes when nature becomes unattainable to the imagination, is it a power very different from the sensible power of the imagination? In the encounter with the empirical faculty, reason's intervention consists of adding itself to the imagination. This addition takes place only after the imagination has extended itself and yet has failed to comprehend nature aesthetically. At that moment, the addition becomes infallible. But if reason has not been involved per se, and is a faculty of an entirely different kind, how can it add itself to the imagination in the first place? How are we to think its arrival, and in what way is it present in the sublime?

Kant specifies that at the very moment when the imagination fails to discover, by its extension, an aesthetical fundamental measure for the whole of nature, reason intervenes in the shape of the idea of the supersensible. As the imagination becomes deprived of its aesthetic comprehending powers in front of a sublime object, or spectacle of nature, the *thought* of a supersensible measure or standard forces itself upon this faculty. Although even nature in its totality could not serve to present objectively this idea, Kant holds that the aesthetically unattainable nature can be construed as its presentation. If reason infallibly joins the empirical faculty in its quandary, it does not add itself from the outside, as it were, to the imagination's doings. Instead, the imagination itself is led to do something out of the ordinary, namely, to conceive of a supersensible idea, something that can only be thought, and thereby becomes aware of its own supersensible determination or destination. It is thus not the heterogeneous faculty of reason itself that intervenes in the imagination's perplexing situation, but rather it is reason in the form of the imagination's realization (and actualization) of the thought of a destination, or determination, as distinct from that which the imagination will incur in its usual employment. Clearly, the imagination itself begins to conceive of the supersensible idea, and hence of its own supersensible potential. It alone arrives at the realization that there is a higher standard for comprehending infinitely unbounded nature, without knowing exactly what this standard consists of, and it alone realizes the existence of such a standard in its unsuccessful comprehension of nature. Indeed, the very judgment that the incomprehensible phenomenon of nature is subjectively purposive—hence, sublime—does not come about without a sense of a higher destination of the mind. Kant writes:

> But this idea of the supersensible, which we can no further determine—so that we cannot *know* but only *think* nature as its presentation—is awakened in us by means of an object whose aesthetical appreciation strains the imagination to its utmost bounds, whether of extension (mathematical) or of its might over the mind (dynamical). And this judgment is based upon a feeling

of the mind's destination, which entirely surpasses the realm of the former (i.e. upon the moral feeling), in respect of which the representation of the object is judged as subjectively purposive. In fact, a feeling of the sublime in nature cannot well be thought without combining therewith a mental disposition which is akin to the moral. (108–109)

Yet even though the judgment upon the sublime is not possible without the feeling of a destination of the mind that is different from its involvement with nature, this is not yet the supersensible destination of which the moral feeling is the expression. If the mental disposition present in the aesthetical judgments upon the sublime resembles the moral feeling, it does so to the extent of having all of the formal characteristics of the moral feeling, but without itself being properly one. The prime characteristics of this feeling immanent to the aesthetic judgment—a feeling that forms the basis of judging the representation of nature that unseats the imagination as subjectively purposive—are spelled out in the following passage:

> And although the immediate pleasure in the beautiful of nature likewise presupposes and cultivates a certain *liberality* in our mental attitude, i.e. a satisfaction independent of mere sensible enjoyment, yet freedom is thus represented as in *play* rather than in that law-directed *occupation* which is the genuine characteristic of human morality, in which reason must exercise dominion [*Gewalt*] over sensibility. But in aesthetic judgments upon the sublime this dominion is represented as exercised by the imagination, regarded as an instrument of reason. (109)

What makes the aesthetic judgments of either the beautiful or the sublime resemble the moral disposition is that in both a certain freedom with respect to the sensible has been gained. In the judgment upon the sublime, however, the sensible is disowned altogether in the name of a felt higher destination of the mind. As we have seen, this treatment of the sensible constitutes the aesthetic judgment's disinterestedness. Moreover, this negative relation to the sensible (and to existence) opens up within the aesthetic judgment a dimension that is not unlike the one that constitutes moral feeling. It is in the judgment upon the sublime, in particular, that this similarity is the greatest. But in this latter aesthetic judgment, it is not reason itself that resists, and rejects, sensibility. Rather, the imagination is the agent of this exclusion of the sensible. As a result, Kant can say that the imagination can here be represented as a proxy of reason. From the perspective of morality, the imagination certainly operates in the sublime judgment like an instrument of reason. But since reason is not present as such, that is, present in a determined way, in the aesthetic judgment, the imagination does not draw on the faculty in question. It acts alone. Rather than abdicating to reason, the highest sensible faculty acquires an autonomy of sorts by depriving itself (violently) of what makes it a sensible faculty. It contracts a self for itself and turns itself into a faculty with an identity of its own.[4] Yet although the self-sacrifice of what characterizes the imagination in its usual, empirical employment bestows upon it "an extension and a might greater than it sacrifices," Kant adds that "the ground of [this extension and might] is concealed from itself" (109). While the imagination *feels* the deprivation, it does not *know* what purpose it is for. But if the negative satisfaction that characterizes the feeling of the sublime is judged subjectively purposive in view of an undetermined higher destination and determination of the mind, the sublime feeling is still not yet a moral feeling. Indeed, precisely, because it is sublime, this feeling is not moral. The expansion of the imagination, and the might it feels to have acquired by the sacrifice of the law that determines its ordinary, empirical employment, is an empty extension and might. But, in fact, this extension has carved out within it the space—a depression, of sorts—necessary for receiving, or for being filled with, moral ideas. In sum, as the case of the aesthetic judgment upon the sublime demonstrates in a privileged fashion, the fate incurred by sensibility—in the case of the sublime, which also includes the imagination's own fate as a sensible faculty—causes the aesthetic feeling to have the formal characteristics analogous to those of moral feeling. Given that the imagination deprives itself of its sensible nature in the immanent feeling of a higher destination and determination of the mind without knowing what the latter's ground is, no determined concept operates in the aesthetic judgment in question. Consequently, there is nothing moral in predicating sublimity. Nonetheless, by making room for a higher determination of the mind by surrendering all standards of the senses (though it remains undetermined what that determination may be), the aesthetic feeling of the sublime acquires a formal resemblance to the moral judgment. Yet, however formal, the resemblance of the aesthetic judgment upon the sublime attracts the attention of reason. The formal nature of the disinterested judgment of taste compels reason to step forward and, in principle, to take an interest in the aesthetic feeling of the sublime. From everything we have seen, this is an interest that arises solely because of what the judgment of taste is capable of achieving when it remains radically disinterested.

But before explicitly broaching the topic of the interest reason brings to the sublime, a further remark on the distinct way in which reason bears on the aesthetic judgment of the sublime is certainly appropriate. In the course of a discussion of how the resistance, by certain affects, of nature within us—a discussion that, rather than being transcendental, has the flavor of Kant's precritical and empirical *Observations on the Beautiful and the Sublime*[5]—permits one to classify them as sublime, Kant admits that such resistance against everything sensible in the sublime makes it a quite abstract mode of representation. And yet, he writes:

We need not fear that the feeling of the sublime will lose by so abstract [*eine dergleichen abgezogene*] a mode of presentation—which is quite negative in respect of what is sensible—for the imagination, although it finds nothing beyond the sensible to which it can attach itself, yet feels itself unbounded by this removal of its limitations; and thus that very abstraction [*Absonderung*] is a presentation of the Infinite, which can be nothing but a mere negative presentation, but which yet expands the soul. (115)

As previously seen, the very elimination of all sensible, hence intuitable, presentation in the sublime enables the imagination to enter into a relation of sorts to the purely intellectual. The above passage permits one to grasp with greater accuracy how the imagination's bracketing of the sensible propels reason to join it, what "reason" means in this context, and hence of how the relation between the imagination and reason that characterizes the sublime (and that distinguishes it from the beautiful, in which the imagination relates to the understanding) is to be thought. Indeed, the imagination's resistance to the sensible (and its interests) is achieved through a separation by which it sets itself apart and cuts itself off [*Absonderung*] from everything sensible. Having thus become severed from the sensible, including from itself as a sensible faculty, the imagination allows reason to join and add itself to it. But it is not reason itself that moves toward the imagination. Rather, by isolating itself from the sensible, the imagination has subjected itself to an operation formally similar to that which reason demands. By cutting all relation to the sensible, a possible relation of the imagination to reason thus opens up in judgments upon the sublime. In sum, if the imagination and reason are in a subjectively purposive relation in the sublime, this relation is merely for the self-severing of the imagination from the sensible, by which it becomes unbounded (denaturalized, as it were), and thus, as Kant states, the merely negative presentation of the intellectual power. Schematically speaking, the relation between the imagination and reason in the sublime is one in which a severing of the relation to the sensible has changed the nature of the imagination to the point of formal similarity to reason. Consequently, reason can be said to have linked onto the imagination's doings, not in the sense that reason itself would have become involved, but in that the imagination's resistance to the sensible is rational.[6] Reason can, therefore, also be seen to take an interest in the imagination's activity in judgments upon the sublime.

The question of interest first emerges in the "General Remark" in the context of another one of Kant's powerful reminders that the Third Critique's transcendental investigation of aesthetical judgments is restricted to the analysis of pure aesthetical reflective judgments, in other words, to aesthetical judgments free of definite concepts. Following a discussion of the strict conditions under which alone the sight of the starry sky, the ocean, or the human figure can give rise to an aesthetical judgment, rather than to a judgment of the senses, or a teleological judgment, Kant concludes that if the judgment is determined by sensation or a concept of the understanding, "it may be conformable to law, [but] cannot be the act of a *free* judgment" (111). But a free judgment such as the aesthetical judgment must also be free of intellectual concepts, that is, concepts of reason, or ideas. No determined concept of reason is to serve as its ground. Kant thus objects to the use of notions such as "intellectual beauty or sublimity" also on the grounds that the intellectual itself bars all positive commerce with the realm of the aesthetical. He writes:

> [A]lthough both [intellectual beauty or sublimity], as objects of an intellectual (moral) satisfaction, are so far compatible with aesthetic satisfaction, that they *rest* upon no interest, yet they are difficult to unite with it because they are meant to *produce* an interest. This, if its presentation is to harmonize with the satisfaction in the aesthetical judgment, could only arise by means of a sensible interest that we combine with it in the presentation; and thus damage would be done to the intellectual purposiveness, and it would lose its purity. (111)

The morally good is something that pleases in and for itself in that it is purposive in itself. Purely intellectual satisfaction in the good is therefore as disinterested as the aesthetic satisfaction in the beautiful or sublime. However, because in a judgment upon the good "there is always involved the concept of a purpose, and consequently the relation of reason to the (at least possible) volition, and thus a satisfaction in the *presence* of an object or an action," a judgment upon the good always involves some kind of interest (41). Now by its intellectual (or moral) quality, intellectual beauty and sublimity are bound to produce interest. As a consequence, such beauty could not be pure. Furthermore, if such beauty were to allow for an aesthetic satisfaction, the interest to be produced by the intellectual and moral would necessarily belong to the order of the senses. Under these circumstances, however, the purity of the intellectual or moral would therefore be compromised. The notion of intellectual beauty or sublimity is thus thoroughly self-contradictory. But Kant's refutation of such a notion is not merely negative. Indeed, by implication, the argument that something (such as the morally good) that is bound to produce interest cannot lend itself to a direct aesthetical presentation without contaminating the latter's aesthetical nature already suggests the possibility of an indirect presentation that would harmonize with the satisfaction in the aesthetical judgment, in that this satisfaction would combine with a nonsensible interest. Such a configuration would preserve full aesthetic satisfaction. In a nutshell, it is advanced here that, aesthetically speaking, the interest produced by the morally good can only be a nonsensible interest if the judgment is to remain an aesthetic one. Kant announces here as well that if reason is to take an interest in the beautiful and the sublime, it can also only be an intellectual interest. This is then also the point where one begins to understand the full impact of Kant's reformulation in the "General Remark," however subtle, of beauty and sublimity in terms of the fate incurred by the sensible in their respective representations. This redefinition clears the space for the introduction of an interest that is not sensible and that can be added on to aesthetic representation without damaging its constitutive disinterestedness.

As previously seen, Kant had admitted moral feeling's aesthetic compatibility. Such compatibility, we recall, arises exclusively from the subject's negative relation to sensibility in the process of the intellectual determination of the will. The feeling associated with the subject's overcoming of hindrances in the order of sensibility enables the modification of the subject's state to become an aesthetical representation of the absolute law. Thus if the morally good is to be judged aesthetically, this can be achieved solely by the sacrifice that it demands of sensibility. From the perspective of sensibility, the moral law is adverse to the interest of sensibility. In fact, as Kant contends, the moral law "makes itself aesthetically known to us through sacrifices" (111). The satisfaction in aesthetical judgments about the morally good is also only "negative, i.e. against this interest [of sensibility], but regarded from the intellectual side it is positive and combined with an interest" (112). Based upon everything seen, this latter interest derives from nothing less than the deprivation of the interest of the senses. From the viewpoint of morality, the intellectual interest stems from the sacrifice of all sensible interest in the aesthetical representation (of the moral law). This is the (only) sense that the expression of an interest in the disinterested can have. Yet the aesthetical presentation of the moral law remains an aesthetical presentation. It consists in the (intuitable) presentation of the (self-)violation of the sensible. But, at the same time, the sensible's retreat is also ("positively") a presentation of the moral law, since the interest that the latter cannot but produce is, as a result of the sacrifice of the interest of the senses, inevitably a nonsensible interest rather than a sensible one. No loss of purity occurs here, neither of the aesthetical nor of the intellectual. The aesthetical remains intact, in that it is only the indirect presentation of the law, whereas the interest that combines with the latter's presentation has become intellectual.

A natural consequence of this integrity of the aesthetical and the intellectual is "that the intellectual, in itself purposive, (moral) good, aesthetically judged, must be represented as sublime rather than beautiful" (112). The feeling of the sublime is a feeling in which sensibility is sacrificed, but which is also combined with a certain pleasure, because this sacrifice is testimony to a higher power in us. Because of the sublime's intransigency with respect to the sensible, it is the preferred mode for aesthetically judging the morally good. But there is another even more essential reason for this preference. Given that in a sublime representation a radical evacuation of everything sensible opens up the possible reference to the unconditionally good, the sublime is a judgment that (though still aesthetical) deprives itself almost entirely of anything aesthetic. In sum, within the spectrum of the aesthetical reflective judgments, the judgment upon the sublime is also a kind of judgment that even sacrifices itself as an *aesthetical* reflective judgment, to be able to accommodate the moral law. It is barely an aesthetical reflective judgment anymore. Let us not forget, however, that in the sublime the mind discovers merely that it has an additional suprasensible destination. In the sublime feeling, no positive reference to reason in any determined sense takes place. But the discovery of the mind's intellectual destination and determination at the expense of the sensible enables the sublime to serve also as an aesthetical representation of the morally good (even though such representation can be aesthetical only on the condition that no definite ideas of the good are involved). In principle, such a judgement can therefore also cause interest.

With this reformulation of the sublime, I return to Kant's analysis of the beautiful arts and their potential for being morally relevant. But prior to taking on Kant's discussion, it needs to be recalled that although the "General Remark" did not categorically exclude the beautiful from having a possible relation (for formal reasons) to the morally good, the sublime was recognized as the privileged representation where such a relation could be found aesthetically. It is thus within the shadow of what has been established so far about the sublime that the question of an interest in pure judgments upon the beautiful needs to be approached. Granted that the beautiful too can cause interest, it is quite significant that Kant, as we will be able to verify, accords the beautiful of nature a privilege in this respect.[7] In contrast, only a rather slim portion of man-made art—the art of genius—is capable of sustaining a moral interest. As is evident from the chapters here under discussion (41 and 42), the beautiful of nature meets Kant's approval, because the judgments about such beauty are disinterested and thus have the potential of being immediately interesting. The purpose of Kant's elaboration on the arts is precisely to find whether art, or one kind of art, is compatible with disinterested judgments, and as a result disposed to provoke interest.

Kant opens his inquiry into a possible interest from a moral point of view in the beautiful by arguing that because the pure aesthetical judgment excludes all interest as its determining ground, it does not follow "that, after it has been given as a pure aesthetical judgment, no interest can be combined with it" (138–39). How is one to understand such posteriority? What kind of relation does it suggest if it only comes after disinterested beauty has been judgmentally established and if, furthermore, the interest that is to be combined with this beauty—an interest in the disinterested—is not to take place at the expense of the constituting disinterestedness? Since a pure judgment of taste in itself is entirely disinterested, any interest must be of the nature of a post hoc addition that does not compromise the purity of a judgment which, as we have previously seen, rests on a certain isolated activity of the faculties involved. The interest to be combined with such a judgment can, therefore, only be "indirect, i.e. taste must first of all be represented as combined with something else, in order that we may unite with the satisfaction of mere reflection upon an object a *pleasure in its existence* (as that wherein all interest consists)" (139). What are these manifestly exterior concerns that could invite one to take an interest in the beautiful? Kant distinguishes two kinds of such concerns that can connect with the judgment upon the beautiful. One is empirical, namely, the "inclination proper to human nature" to socialize, and the other, "intellectual, [namely] the property of the will of being capable of *a priori* determination by reason. Both these involve a satisfaction in the presence of an object and so can lay the foundation for an interest in what has by itself pleased without reference to any interest whatsoever" (139). Given the transcendental sweep of Kant's inquiry into how the disinterested beautiful can become the object of an interest, I will linger only briefly on the empirical concern with the existence of beautiful things. Since feelings are private and singular, the unique ability to communicate a feeling such as the pleasure associated with the beautiful explains the human interest for the beautiful, in that human beings have a natural propensity toward society. In essence, the interest that human beings can connect with taste derives from the latter's furthering of this anthropological inclination. It is an interest, Kant suggests, that arises within society as a *means* to advance communication, which is thus not only indirect but also mediate and consequently empirical. As a transcendental investigation, however, the Third Critique has the task of exploring a possibly more fundamental way in which beauty and interest can combine, in a relation that remains indirect but is also immediate. Of course, there is the interest in the charms that nature bestows upon its beautiful forms. This is an interest that, indeed, is immediate, but it is also empirical. But in the framework of a transcendental inquiry, only the question of an interest which "may have a reference, although only indirectly, to the judgment of taste *a priori*" (140) will be of importance.

The empirical interest taken in the beautiful is primarily social and directed toward furthering social life. In contrast, a possible indirect interest in the beautiful that would also be immediate and *a priori*, and which Kant calls intellectual, would have to arise in solitary contemplation. Whereas the connoisseur of art looks at beautiful objects on display not only as a human being intent on sharing his or her pleasure with others but also as one who judges these objects as objects of art, hence, in view of a concept available to all, the solitary spectator and judge of the beautiful figure of a wild flower in which he or she takes interest, has no such mediate design of communicating such observations to others. Moreover, the spectator looks at this beautiful object with his or her own eyes alone. Indeed, deprived of all universally shared concepts and reduced to its minimal facultative abilities, the solitary mind is disposed beneficially for the contemplation in aesthetical reflective judgments of forms in which, subsequently, it can take an intellectual interest. I note that this emphasis on solitary contemplation of natural beauty—the only one to cause an immediate interest—for arousing an interest in its existence (in addition to what obtains in the disinterested judgment of taste) signals an analogy to the sublime, which is also the "object" of solitary contemplation. In fact, certain conditions of self-isolation (i.e., the cutting of all of the natural ties to the human others) are sublime. In the final part of the "General Remark," after having distinguished several states of mind, especially enthusiasm and apathy, as affects that demonstrate a power to resist sensibility, and that consequently can be judged sublime, Kant brings up an even more extreme form of affective resistance against the sensible. He writes: "*Separation* [*Absonderung*] *from all society* is regarded as sublime [as well] if it rests upon ideas that overlook all sensible interest. To be sufficient for oneself, and consequently to have no need of society, without flying from it, is something bordering on the sublime, as is any dispensing with wants" (116). With "separation from all society," Kant does not only evoke a sublime affect that completes his taxonomy of sublime states of mind but also one that is interesting for exclusively intellectual reasons. Whereas beautiful and sublime satisfactions (resting on disinterested judgments) provoke an interest because of their general communicability, and which hence is empirical, "separation from all society" opens the possibility of a sublime affect that is interesting precisely because it refuses such communicability and in the same breath the empirical interest that comes with the latter. The interest that such a state of mind incites is indeed immediate. Complete isolation from society is a sublime affect, because it testifies to intellectual concerns that override even this last residue of the sensible that is sociability and communicability. The interest taken in such a sublime has no mediate reasons. It attaches itself to this extreme form of a sublime affect on merely intellectual or moral grounds. A case in point is sadness exclusively due to moral ideas. It is a sadness of individuals, who for moral reasons alone, rather than on the basis of misanthropy or anthropophoby, have renounced society and the need for communication. With this possibility of a state of mind that is so extreme that no empirical interest can attach itself to it, but which is found immediately interesting, the "General Remark" sets the stage for a discussion of a nonempirical interest in the beautiful. Of course, that this possibility is discussed by Kant with reference to the sublime is no accident. The concern with existence, or more precisely with a moral interest, arises primarily in the "presence" of the faculty of reason. It involves an intellectual judgment. Whereas only the imagination and the understanding are in play in the pure judgment upon the beautiful, the imagination refers already to reason in judgments upon the sublime.

Before I proceed with the analysis of a possible indirect and immediate interest in the beautiful, let me determine, as precisely as possible, what exactly it is that Kant seeks to accomplish, otherwise we will not be in a position to assess the stakes of the inquiry as a whole. Kant asks whether there is an *a priori indirect relation*—a relation, consequently, made possible by the very nature of the disinterested judgment—between pure taste and a concern with existence. It is a paradoxical question that inquires into the possibility of appending [*angehängt*] an interest to "taste, taken in its purity," which is not mediate, hence, not empirical, but which already inheres in the disinterested judgment itself without jeopardizing its disinterestedness. Such an a priori appendix made possible by pure taste, and on the condition that taste remains pure, or entirely disinterested, is to be found in the intellectual interest that can be combined with pure judgments of taste. Kant spells out the stakes of his inquiry, saying that "if an interest should be detected as bound up with this form [that is, indirectly, but in a priori fashion], taste would detect for our faculty of judging a means of passing from sense enjoyment to moral feeling; and so not only would we be better guided in employing taste purposively, but there would be thus presented a link in the chain of human faculties *a priori*, on which all legislation must depend" (140). The demonstration of an indirect, but a priori appendable interest in pure beauty and taste would allow one to argue that pure, disinterested beauty plays an intermediary and mediating role between charm and moral feeling, or more generally between nature and freedom. But it is also clear, from what we have established so far, that for a judgment about the beautiful to have moral interest, it must remain fully disinterested, and hence entirely distinct from a judgment about the good. Given that all other feelings of pleasure and displeasure are linked to interest, the sole pleasure found in disinterested judgments concerning the mere form of objects reveals that nature (feeling) and reason are capable of agreement. Disinterestedness on the level of the senses—a possibility realized solely in the case of entirely pure judgments of taste—is the provision under which alone a relation between the beautiful and ethics is conceivable. At this point, one can no longer overlook the fact that the rigorous sorting out of the pure judgments of taste from judgments of the senses and the morally good is the very condition under which the aesthetic judgment upon the beautiful can at all assume a kind of mediating role and eventually serve as a symbol of morality.

The indirect interest capable of combining with disinterested beauty, sought by Kant to support the idea of an agreement in principle between nature and freedom, cannot be a mediate interest. Beauty is not to be a means for the satisfaction of some need or desire if it is to have an affinity to the morally good. The interest to be taken in the beautiful must therefore be immediate. Yet, as Kant is quick to remark, the beautiful of art does not meet this requirement. Only the beautiful of nature fulfills this condition. Kant opens his discussion "Of the Intellectual Interest in the Beautiful" by "admit[ting] at once that the interest in the *beautiful of art* (under which I include the artificial use of natural beauties for adornment and so for vanity) furnishes no proof whatever of a disposition attached to the morally good or even inclined thereto" (141). The beautiful of art thus seems to bar all intellectual interest. Undoubtedly, Kant's reasons are at first only empirical, since he only takes note of the fact that those who are connoisseurs in taste are rarely of good moral character. But as we shall see, there are more fundamental reasons, reasons owing to art qua art, that prevent one from taking an intellectual interest in artificial beauty. First, however, the privilege that Kant accords to natural beauty with respect to moral feeling needs to be highlighted. He writes:

> If a man who has taste enough to judge the products of beautiful art with the greatest accuracy and refinement willingly leaves a chamber where are to be found those beauties that minister to vanity or to any social joys and turns to the beautiful in nature to find, as it were, delight for his spirit in a train of thought that he can never completely evolve [*den er sich nie völlig entwickeln kann*], we will regard this choice of his with veneration [*Hochachtung*] and attribute to him a beautiful soul, to which no connoisseur or lover [of art] can lay claim on account of the interest he takes in his [artistic] objects (142).

From the perspective of the mere judgment of taste, there is no difference between beautiful objects of nature and of art. What alone counts for such a judgment is whether the object has form. Hence no consideration of superiority obtains here. But at the very moment interest is taken in the beautiful, only the forms of nature would seem to guarantee the immediacy of this interest, and thus its intellectual nature. Although the passage just quoted serves only to emphasize the high esteem and great respect that we bestow upon one who escapes from the beautiful social world of the art lovers to contemplate in solitude the beauties of nature (thereby revealing a cultivated moral inclination that deserves respect), an analysis of the delight that one's spirit discovers in such contemplation brings to the fore the reasons for the superiority of natural over artificial beauty.

The contemplation [*Beschauung*] of nature in which the good soul takes an immediate interest solely concerns the beauty of its forms. Kant tells his reader that, "[I]t is to be remembered, however, that I speak here strictly of beautiful *forms* of nature, and I set aside the *charms* that she is wont to combine so abundantly with them, because, though the interest in the latter is indeed immediate, it is only empirical" (141). The intellectual interest in the beautiful of nature is immediate only if it is connected to the forms of nature. Considering Kant's understanding of form, this restriction is not surprising. Natural form alone reveals an aspect of nature that is a priori desirable. Indeed, whenever the mind in disinterested judgments of taste is capable of sensing form in objects of nature that the understanding is incapable of recognizing, nature displays its suitability to cognition. The mind attaches an immediate interest to perceived natural form, or the beautiful of nature, because this form indicates nature's adequateness to our faculties of cognition. It is only natural, one may say, for the mind to take an interest in such form, and for it to thus desire, in an immediate fashion, the presence (existence) of form in nature. One is reminded here of Kant's statement in the "General Remark," that "the beautiful prepares us to love disinterestingly something, even nature itself," and that on this basis (on the grounds of the bracketed interest in the sensible), the beautiful is a feeling "purposive in reference to the moral feeling" (108). But the interest experienced by the mind when faced with beautiful form in nature is not moral interest itself. According to Kant, however, it is at least "favorable to the moral feeling" (141). The feeling, Kant says, is "akin to the moral feeling [*der Verwandschaft nach*]" (143), because what is at stake in it is nature's susceptibility to the precepts of freedom. But Kant adds as well that, "He who takes such an interest in the beauties of nature can do so only insofar as he previously has firmly established his interest in the morally good" (143). In other words, and not unlike what had already been established in the "General Remark" about our disposition toward the sublime, to be able to take an active interest in natural beauty, one must have judged (disinterestedly) the mere forms of the maxims of reason on their own merit and developed an interest in their practical realization and presence. Apart from pure disinterested judgments concerning the suitability of mere natural forms to cognition in general, a moral formation [*Ausbildung*], not unlike the culture necessary for making judgments on the sublime, is required if one is also to manifest a concern with natural forms' existence. On this condition alone is it possible to develop "without any clear, subtle, and premeditated reflection . . . a similar immediate interest in the objects of the former [aesthetical judgment], as in those of the latter [moral judgment]" (143). But for reasons analogous to those that obtain in the case of the sublime, the need for the moral cultivation in question makes such immediate interest in the beautiful a rare commodity. It is an uncommon, if not exceptional, mental disposition.

A further condition for the interest in natural beauty to be immediate, Kant observes, is that [t]his thought "must accompany our intuition and reflection on beauty, viz., that nature has produced it; on this alone is based the immediate interest that we take in it. Otherwise there remains a mere judgment of taste, either devoid of all interest, or bound up with a mediate interest" (142). The famous Kantian examples of the artificial flowers and of the mischievous boy who knew how to imitate the song of the nightingale bring home this point. They are unable to provoke any such interest, because nature must be seen to produce these beautiful forms as signs not only of its nonadversity to human cognition but also, on the contrary, of its active self-offering to a disinterested representation (and hence, in the final resort, to cognition). Only when

nature is viewed to produce its beautiful forms in accordance with rules beneficial for cognition in general does it incite interest. As Kant remarks, the faculty of the intellectual judgment (reason)—apart from taking an interest in the
mere forms of practical maxims which themselves please immediately (as instances of the good) without this judgment being based on any interest whatsoever—is also interested

> that the ideas (for which in moral feeling it arouses an immediate interest)
> should have objective reality, i.e. that nature should at least show a trace or
> give an indication [*eine Spur zeige, oder einen Wink gebe*] that it contains in it-
> self a ground for assuming a regular agreement [*gesetzmäßige Übereinstim-
> mung*] of its products with our entirely disinterested satisfaction (which we
> recognize *a priori* as a law for everyone, without being able to base it upon
> proofs). Hence reason must take an interest in every expression on the part of
> nature of an agreement of this kind. Consequently, the mind cannot ponder
> upon the beauty of nature without finding itself at the same time interested
> therein. (143)

Such immediate interest in the forms of nature arises only on the condition
that they are perceived as active hints by nature of its pliability to reason. Nature's beautiful forms must present themselves as expressions of its suitability to
reason, as nature's way of speaking to us, and for us to attach an interest in what
in itself pleases in a disinterested fashion. As Kant observes, the beautiful forms
of nature are "that cipher [*Chiffreschrift*] through which nature speaks to us fig-
uratively" (143). Only if the mere natural forms that we judge purposive in disinterested pleasure, and beneficial to cognition in general (hence beautiful), are
also perceived as the characters, or ciphers through which nature announces to
us that its products are intended for us, does reason have a stake in these forms'
existence. For indeed the existence of these forms is proof of the objective realization in nature of what is so different from it: the ideas, the exigencies, or
precepts of reason.

At this point, it is certainly appropriate to confront a possible, indeed, quite
common misunderstanding in Kant criticism. The interest taken in natural
beauty is easily misunderstood as resulting from the moral ideas themselves that
are associated with such beauty, or that are supposed to inhere in the latter. But
if this were the case, the judgment regarding natural beauty would no longer
be a judgment of taste. Further, the interest in the beautiful would be merely
mediate (as would be the case if something such as intellectual beauty were
conceivable). The question that Kant addresses in chapters 41 and 42 of the
Critique of Judgment concerns an interest in disinterested judgments of taste. If
natural beauty is superior to artificial beauty, it is because natural beauty pleases
in and by itself, rather than "by means of its purpose," as in the case of artificial

beauty (144). The interest provoked by natural beauty is not caused by the moral idea itself that can be found associated with it. Although the beauty of an object of nature interests us insofar as it is attached to a moral idea, it is not this idea itself that is decisive. Kant makes it amply clear that it is not the fact that a moral idea is associated with a natural beauty that makes it immediately interesting, but instead it is "the character [of this beauty] as such in virtue of which it is qualified for such an association, and which therefore intrinsically belongs to it [*sondern die Beschaffenheit derselben an sich selbst, dass sie sich zu einer solchen Beigesellung qualifiziert, die ihr also innerlich zukommt, interessiert unmittelbar*]" (144, trans. modified). Natural beauty attracts only our interest, because internally, in and by itself, it qualifies for the appendage in question. The interest in the beauty of nature arises merely by its capacity for the indirect and a priori moral appendix, and in no way by the moral ideas themselves. Even though the beautiful pleases without any consideration of existence whatsoever, and by its form alone, it incites an interest, because it manifests an a priori disposition (a structural potentiality) of nonadversity, or rather, of a susceptibility to an indirect moral addendum. This potential for an a priori appendix renders natural beauty superior to the beautiful of art. Kant concludes:

> It is easy to explain why the satisfaction in the pure aesthetical judgment in the case of beautiful art is not combined with an immediate interest, as it is in the case of beautiful nature. For the former is either such an imitation of the latter that it reaches the point of deception and then produces the same effect as natural beauty (for which it is taken), or it is an art obviously directed designedly to our satisfaction. In the latter case the satisfaction in the product would, it is true, be brought about immediately by taste, but it would be only a mediate interest in the cause lying at its root, viz. an art that can only interest by means of its purpose and never in itself. (144)

The beauty of nature alone deserves our interest, because only such beauty permits the attachment of an indirect and immediate moral appendage. If certain products of the beautiful arts happen to incite our interest, it is because they deceive us by taking on the appearance of nature. This, then, is the context within which Kant will briefly discuss the arts in the Third Critique. It is a context that shows that art is not the prime focus of Kant's aesthetics, and that its basic propositions are not derived from the study of the arts. Natural beauty is the paradigm for what Kant calls form, and the judgment of taste thereupon. Natural beauty is privileged as well when the question arises concerning beauty's relation to the morally good. This ascendance of nature over art in Kant's aesthetics is clear evidence of this aesthetics' proto-epistemological concerns. Kant's analysis of the arts in chapters 43 to 53 is an appendix of sorts to the beautiful of nature: all the more so, as its aim is to carve out within the realm of what Kant calls "only [*nur*] art," and of the beauties of which no immediate interest lets itself be attached, one, after all rather meager, domain of art—the art of genius—whose products look like products of nature without deception and that therefore can also legitimately demand interest.

NOTES

1. Immanuel Kant, *Critique of Judgment*, trans. J. H. Bernard (New York: Hafner Press), 151. All subsequent page references in the text refer to this work.

2. This motif of disinterestedness is not particular to Kant's aesthetics (as many of his commentators seem to believe). Narrowed down to designate the lack of concern in pure judgments of taste with the existence of the objects that are seen to be beautiful, the term not only becomes a concept in its own right, but its role in the Third Critique differs also from that which it plays long, before Kant, in the numerous other treatises on aesthetics throughout the eighteenth century. Yet even though disinterestedness acquires a novel meaning in Kant, this meaning is not without relations to the earlier uses of the term. Introduced into the language of German aesthetics by F. J. Riedel, who himself borrowed it from the British empiricist philosophers involved with aesthetics (Shaftesbury, Hutcheson, Addison, and Burke, for example), disinterestedness is a notion that originates in moral philosophy and theology in the seventeenth and eighteenth centuries, where it refers to a non-egoistic ethics or represents the principle of a non-instrumentalist theology, that is, a theology in which God is not a means for human needs. When one loves God disinterestedly, one loves Him, according to Shaftesbury, simply for His own sake, or because of the excellency of the object. For the history of the concept, and its antecedents in theology and moral philosophy in particular, see Werner Strube, "Interesselosigkeit. Zur Geschichte eines Grundbegriffs der Aesthetik," in *Archiv für Begriffsgeschichte* 22 (1979): 148–74. For the role of the term in British empiricist aesthetics, see Jerome Stolnitz, "On the Origins of 'Aesthetic Disinterestedness'," in *Journal of Aesthetics and Art Criticism* 20 (1960–1961): 131–43.

3. Louis Guillermit, *L'élucidation critique du jugement de goût selon Kant* (Paris: Editions du CNRS, 1986), 151.

4. See my "Leaps of Imagination" (in *The Path of Archaic Thinking: Unfolding the Work of John Sallis*, ed. K. Maly (Albany: State University of New York Press, 1995), 35–47), in which I show that the imagination in Kant is a "faculty" entirely determined by other faculties, hence without self-identity. Only by "depriving itself of its freedom [*der Beraubung der Einbildungskraft durch sich selbst*]," in sacrificing its sensible nature, and determining itself purposively "according to a different law from that of its empirical employment [by which it] acquires an extension and a might greater than it sacrifices" (109) does the imagination win a self of its own to begin with.

5. Considering the more empirical nature of the context in which Kant discusses certain affects such as enthusiasm and apathy, which have been privileged by a number of interpreters of Kant (Jean-François Lyotard or Paul de Man, for example), as entrance points into the question of the sublime, caution is warranted in not overdetermining the significance of these examples for the problematic of the sublime in general.

6. In the aesthetical reflective judgment upon the sublime, the relation between the powers in question is thus much more problematic than the relation between the imagination and the understanding in the beautiful. No simple symmetry obtains between both kinds of judgments. The nature of the relation between the faculties involved is quite different. Even though the understanding is active only as the power of cognition in general in judgments upon the beautiful, the imagination relates to it as to an actual power. In the sublime, the relation to reason is negative. Imagination does not "know" the rule to which it subjects itself. There is only the feeling that resistance to sensibility is subjectively purposive. Reason is only virtually present as it were.

7. As seen, the reason for the beautiful's potential with respect to representing the morally good hinges on the fate of sensibility in judgments concerning the mere form of an object. With the lack of interest in charm and the exclusive concern with the form of a thing, the judgment of taste about the beautiful reveals a subtle yet decisive "presence" of reason. The ideal of beauty invoked by Kant in chapter 17 anticipates the question of the beautiful's possible relation to the absolutely good. There is no turning point in Kant from a concern with form to so-called more serious questions. Rather, Kant's path is one of continuity.

CHAPTER 4

Gesture and Commentary

Jean-François Lyotard

The difficulty I have in talking about art is not feigned. This difficulty is a new one; at least it is a new one for me. This is not to say that it is recent. Rather, I would say that it has gotten worse over time, its nature has changed, and its effects have become so far-reaching as to lead me to believe that there is a deception involved each time I am called upon to discuss a work of art.

Over a span of several years it was not impossible for me to comment on a work of architecture, painting, or music. What authorized me to do so was a certain deference. The work, I told myself, is itself *already* a commentary. It is a commentary on a way of being toward chromatic or linear space, toward inhabitable extension, toward sonorous duration. And this is so much the case that the philosopher (or whoever passes for one)—that is, he who poses questions or to whom questions are posed regarding space, time, form, visible or audible color, the interior and the exterior, in short, so-called aesthetic questions—had to be so schooled in the commentary on whichever of these questions he thought were inscribed within the work at hand. For example, the philosopher had to be so schooled in the name of what was required for thinking about these questions, but also in the name of a certain debt. He was indebted to the work by the fact that, in its mere existence as a way of being toward space, time, form, and so on, it had preceded him in the elaboration of these questions, that it had been his mistress in these matters. He owed it thought, for he was in love with the work, his mistress; he was thus going to give it what he himself did not possess.

Reprinted with permission of the author and the publishers of *IYYUN, The Jerusalem Philosophical Quarterly*. The essay first appeared in *IYYUN* 42 (January 1993): 37–48. Trans. Stephen Adam Schwartz.

At that time, the work was not, or not only, a kind of prey upon which philosophical thought, or thought reputed to be philosophical, would have settled its grasp in order to incorporate it as a kind of factual example to be at once turned into a speculative example to integrate its still-unthought meaning into the philosopher's thinking discourse. What I wrote about art at that time was certainly not devoid of such contempt and violence. But is it not perhaps unnecessary for the philosopher to excuse himself and to seek to be pardoned for this intrusion, for this apprehension "against the grain" of the work within a problematic which is perhaps not the work's own? After all, the interested party itself, the interested party *par excellence*, the artist or so-called author of the work, has been and is *always*, in my experience, in favor of the violation of which I am speaking. The artist needs it and calls for it. With the passing of time, this appeal became more insistent. It became impossible for me to leave a studio without a request for a few pages, even a few lines, just because I had briefly thought out loud or had seemed to pay attention to allow myself to be disquieted by a work of art.

The reason for these recurrent requests was simple and is entirely to the credit of the artists: they have expected and will always expect the philosopher to render intelligible what they have made. Artists expect philosophers to transcribe their *gestus*. They expect them to transcribe into words their way of being toward space, color, tone, and so on, as it is delineated and rendered in the finished work, in the realized *res gesta*. And not into just any words, but into the strange words that philosophy uses when it distorts its learned vocabulary, its vocabulary of knowledge, in order to come into contact with what it does not know, with what it knows no better than does the artist or the art itself; when philosophy is committed to paying its debt to the *gesture* of color, volume, tone, and line, without the intention of peacefully *di-gesting* it within the organism of a system or, worse still, within a "worldview." At such times, the philosopher, like a desperate lover, attempts to give the work something he did not possess, namely, the words to carry on this gesture. And he attempts this even if it means changing the whole of what he thought he knew and was capable of signifying, just so as to be able to give the artist, whether dead or alive, the three words, or perhaps 300 pages, which would transcribe the absolute insignificance of the gesture that is the work of art.

In this way, the violation, the "going against the grain" of which I spoke, could only have been the rule, for no one could have explicitly stated what the work's inherent problematic was before any sort of thinking had taken the risk of explicating it, of unfolding it into phrases. This violation was the rule, but at the same time it was not a violation. It was rather a strong crossing or passage: a translocation, a transcription, a transposition, a transition, a translation, in any case an act of treason, but one that was also holy and wise.

The artist thus called for and continues to call for a philosopher, but one who has been divested and disarmed, resolved to neglect his vested interest, the knowledge that vests and protects him. The artist does not and cannot call for such words from the so-called theoretician out of anything other than the base motives tied to fashion and marketing interests, or out of a certain simplicity or lack of learning, which would lead him to confuse philosophers with "intellectuals" or with "researchers in the human sciences." That is, the artist cannot request such words from a type of thought which has been built and which has built up the organism by which it apprehends and assimilates "the given," and may I remind you that building was an art before it became either an industry or an intellectual industry. What art gives is not "the given." It gives to and gives rise to thought. But this is not a new idea.

The artist cannot even call upon an apparently more friendly type of thought, one that would digest what is to be thought in what the artist gives within, for example, a dialectics or a hermeneutics of *postponement*. That is, within a type of thought that knows that it does not know, that knows that its words are never the last words, that the commentary that it gives back to the art work and the artist is itself subject to the same conditions as the artistic gesture, that there will have to be still other words and other commentaries, and thus other gestures in order to perpetuate its own gesture in words. The artist would be wrong to place his trust in this type of thought, for it is immediately too general. It is a generalization of the gesture, of what is properly the artist's affair. It is a *robbery* but also an evasion (*dérobade*). It is a borrowed gesture that has been generalized into a doctrine. But it remains a doctrine. And in this way, such thought still digests the gesture that the work of art is, at the very same time that it seems to take pains to respect it.

What the artist sought from us philosophers was not this almost arrogant confidence in the infinite finitude of interpretation. Rather, it was this labor of bending ourselves—not only with our assumed philosophical knowledge but also without it—to the singularity of the canvas, drawing, or volume that has *in effect* been presented, exposed, or executed. When I say "in effect," I am making mention of what really matters: singularity. The artist asks of us philosophers that we think the perceptible singularity that is presented here and now: a work or works that are here, now, in the singularity of their occurrence. But we should bear in mind that this possessive of occurrence is only reconstituted by memory after the fact. It is reconstituted by both memory and the doctrine or system. When the work occurs, *advient, geschieht,* it *is* both the occurrence and the event. This is so for a very simple reason, which no mode of thought is capable of thinking, even that type of thought that is vowed to postponement, that thinking that seeks to show that the here and now have no assignable presence. This "reason," which is hardly reasonable, is that the work of art is, each time, an event in space-time-matter, a coming to space-time-matter, in and toward that with which the artist deals, in and toward which art makes its gesture, color, sound, form, and so on. For the sake of clarity, let us say that this alone—the fact that there is a gesture in space-time-matter, the fact that it *is* there and is a gesture—constitutes the impenetrability of the work for thought. It is precisely to the level of this enigma that the artist obligates the philosopher to place or displace his thought, and this is so whether the artist is aware of it or not. It is up to the philosopher, in the awareness of his debt, to know this for both himself and the artist.

This is the difficulty I alluded to at the beginning, a difficulty that is not recent. It is the result of the occurring, of the existing—and both of these words are inadequate—I would even want to say "of the presence," if this word did not bring with it all of the worst disputes among philosophers, finally of a sort of *actus* that is the gesture of a matter in, with, and toward space-time, of an *actus* that I would understand in the sense of the French expression *il s'agit*: the *actus is* a matter of space-time-matter. The philosopher's difficulty with the work of art is due to this *actus*, which is immediately also a *situs*. The gesture that is the art work is a *situs*, because in coming to space-time it immediately reorganizes it: it both is situated in and situates space-time. This gesture is an *actus*, because it is a movement and passage of colors, lines, volumes, or sounds. It is a *thrust* of matter (the Latin *agere* is to *ducere* as the English "to push," a *tergo*, is to the verbs "to pull," "to lead," *a fronte*).

The difficulty of having to philosophize about these gestures in which tones or volumes act and are acted upon, and in which space-time situates itself and is situated, is much greater than the one that opposes thought and what is called *experience*. For a philosopher, experience is so to speak predisposed toward comprehension. However one understands it, whether in the manner of Plato or empiricism, in the manner of Kant's first *Critique* or Hegel's *Phenomenology of Spirit,* experience is always the way in which the given is constructed so as to be grasped and incorporated within memory, to be digested by the mind. In other words, it is a way for the given to be laid out within a reasonable discourse. Mind or spirit is somewhat weakened in experience, for in it the mind encounters what it is not and what it does not know. But it is only somewhat weakened. In this experience, the mind puts itself to the test, but it also proves itself and approves of itself. Thought *acquires* experience; through experience, thought grows. Experience attests to just how lacking in reality the given is, just as the ruminations of ruminants attest to their skepticism with regard to the grass they eat.

But works of art do not allow themselves to be chewed or, at least, they do not allow themselves to be assimilated. When artists ask philosophers for a few pages about their work, their ingenuousness is not insincere, but it is nevertheless malicious, as always. They know full well that we will never accomplish the task, even by the most sophisticated gestures of which our discourse is capable.

I would like to say a few words about this gesticulation. If we philosophers are to divest ourselves of our knowledge in order to accede to the gesture that is the work and transcribe it within our own space-time-matter, we must obviously take care not to take this space, time, and matter itself for granted. Here I am referring to the space-time-matter of the philosophical discourse itself and not to the time, matter, or space that might offer themselves as *objects* for philosophical thought, objects to which philosophical thought might refer in order to elaborate their *theme,* setting them up within its *thesis* as the logical or grammatical subject of the various propositions, sentences, or judgments that philosophy attempts to articulate in reference to them. Our debt to art requires that we take care of that within and toward which our own phrases arise as we try to comment on or interpret works of art.

Consequently, we must rid our discourse of the referential, cognitive, or objectifying function that philosophy, like other intellectual disciplines, naively and unconsciously confers upon words and their arrangement, even if it does this in a different way than do other disciplines. We must go back and examine these words and their arrangement in order to recognize that the lexicons and syntaxes by which they have been imparted to us—and which make up the prevailing genre of philosophical discourse that the tradition calls "argumentation"—entail more than just arguments. They *at once* bring with them acts and sites in the space-time-matter of *language* itself. Thus we must recognize that the attention paid by philosophers to the referential function of discourse completely conceals from them those gestures that are involved in this discourse itself.

These gestures must both be directed at and take place within the space-time-matter that happens to be ours, namely, language, and they must do so as such and no longer as the unthought or the unconscious of our discourse. But as soon as they appear as such, the gesture that secretly supports argumentation loses its privilege as the philosophically correct way of organizing the space-time-matter of language, in much the same way that the exposure of the gestures underpinning the geometrical perspectivism of the Quattrocento not only divests this pictorial device of its princely privilege—that of the so-called legitimate perspective—but also liberates other possible gestures. It even makes possible and requires, in one and the same gesture, an entirely different approach to painting, one in which it will no longer be a matter of representing scenes (just as in the tradition of philosophical discourse, it was mainly a matter of debating about referents). Rather, it will be a question of receiving and welcoming spatial gestures, temporal gestures, linear gestures, and chromatic gestures. And so it is that the philosophers who are called upon by artists are put in the situation of welcoming and receiving discursive gestures effected *in* the time, space, and matter of language, and *toward* this time, this space, and this matter itself.

It is certainly not a question here of acquitting ourselves of our debt of transcription by miming the work of art that we are to transcribe. Moreover, such an imitation makes no sense. For a gesture in and toward the space-time-matter of the one has no *mimetikon* in and toward the space-time-matter of the other, notwithstanding the consoling dream expressed by the ancient formula *Ut pictura poesis*. Instead, we must receive and welcome rhythms, virtual sonorities, lines, angles, curves, and semantic colors, while also adroitly awakening the semantic layers that lie dormant within words and their sequences. The philosophers who are summoned in this way must thus begin to *write* and cease merely "to think." In other words, they must begin to think about thought itself as a work of art and no longer simply as an argument. This results in a profound change in the modes of their discourse, a discourse which, as a result, leaves the province of the philosophical community.

Such is the difficulty. It has always been with us. Though it had been suppressed at first, this difficulty became conspicuous when the rules governing painting, building, and composition went into decline and along with them the rules for commentary, which were known as *poetics* (you will forgive me for oversimplifying). In the eighteenth century, philosophy, under the name of aesthetics, was entreated to transcribe into its idiom the enigma of the work of art. And since the works in question are ones in which the adherence to rules is no longer the overriding consideration, this transcription essentially consists in recognizing that method (*modus logicus*) must give way to manner (*modus aestheticus*), even within the discourse of the commenting philosophers themselves. This is evident not only in the work of Kant or Diderot, but also in the later Boileau, the defender of Longinus.

In spite of everything that would be subsequently attempted by speculative thought—and this includes Walter Benjamin's book on the concept of art criticism in German romanticism—in an attempt to reestablish the reign of argument and the concept over works of art, the harm (or the good) has already been done. To the extent that philosophy is called upon to question itself about art, philosophy is challenged to accomplish its proper task, which is to understand objects of thought by defining them and debating their properties. Philosophy is no longer even asked to understand *itself* as an object of thought, as it always has whenever it attempts to understand other objects of thought. Whether knowingly or unknowingly, the artists who call for philosophical commentary on their works are also asking philosophy to *take itself* as an art. This is a familiar slippage, a turn that was most notably imposed on philosophy by Nietzsche and, in the French tradition, by Valéry, a devoted reader of Nietzsche. It is not insignificant that Valéry was also a disciple of Mallarmé, albeit a poor disciple at first glance. It is through Mallarmé's works and influence that precisely the same sort of *subreption,* as Kant would have called it, that affects philosophy, came to literature, the art of language. By this I mean the same move to abandon objectivities in favor of a labor on the gestural potential latent in the time, space, and matter of language.

So where does the difficulty of which I have been speaking lie? It seems to lie in the fact that, unlike those laborers of language, writers (or poets, if you will), we philosophers, who are called upon to comment on works of art, including literary texts, are still supposed to understand and explicate the gestures of others. And we have trouble seeing how our own gesticulation, within our own language, can serve to understand and explicate such works.

Speculative and romantic thought resorted to the principle that there was an organic continuity between plastic, sonorous, or theatrical gestures on the one hand, and the discourse bearing on these gestures on the other hand. This principle held that the commenting discourse had *emerged* from the artistic gestures themselves, developing in language what remained unspoken within them. This was also my initial assumption. Based as it is on a vitalist metaphor, a metaphysics of the "life of the mind," such recourse is no longer open to us. In the age of biochemistry, biophysics, genetics, and bioengineering, such a conception of life would be taken as little more than a fable.

What is more, we also cannot have recourse to a rationalism of models, even a flexible one: we cannot recover the power of explication held by theoretical discourse, which is today being developed by so-called modern logic, axiomatics, and epistemology in terms of a sophisticated technology of cognitive discourse, one that comes to be applied to domains of reference whose very data are already highly mediated.

The reason for this is clear. As Valéry has already shown, explications of the work of art that have been borrowed from psychology, psychoanalysis (or what passes for it), sociology, history, semiotics, and linguistics all commonly treat the work as a definable object. In the *Introduction à la poétique,* Valéry writes: "Everything that we can define is immediately detached from the productive spirit [this is how Valéry designates what I have here been calling "gesture"] and opposed to it. The mind at once turns it into the equivalent either of a matter [in the sense of an inert objectivity] on which it may operate or of an instrument with which it may operate."[1]

Given that classical poetics, on the one hand, and both knowledge gained through theoretical understanding and the speculations of reason, on the other hand, are no longer available to us when discussing works of art, how are we to answer the call to understand such works? To my mind, Kant remains the most advanced thinker with regard to this aporia. Through an approach that remained a quasi-method, *The Critique of Aesthetic Judgment* brought to light the extreme contortions that the categories of the understanding and the ideas of reason must undergo if reflection is to have access to what is at stake in works of art: the feelings of the beautiful and the sublime. It seems to me that Adorno's negative dialectic provided a minor correction rather than a refinement of these contortions of reason and the understanding. For his negativity is still too dialectical. Kant's subtractive aesthetics, with all of the transcendental philosophical power that it retained, left the field open for a greater cognizance of our difficulty than did the spasmodic and exasperated rough sketch in which Adorno's efforts resulted.

Evidently, this difficulty is not a recent development. If philosophy makes itself into literature, not in order to take up a position as literature's equal but as a way of hearing the silences of the work of art, then why do we continue to ask philosophy for clarifications that this mutation prevents it from providing? By considerably freeing what he called "reflection" from the categorical rules and ideas in order to draw near to what is most proper to art and aesthetic feelings, Kant was also announcing the dissolution of the argumentative power of philosophical discourse in these matters. The only guide left for reflection to follow was that which belonged purely and exclusively to it, namely, feeling. In other words, not thought insofar as it knows or wills but as it is affected—regardless of what it does—by its act and its site, as it feels itself to be happy or unhappy, or both at once (as in the case of the sublime). And this feeling or affect happens to thought immediately, that is, without having been relayed by the *consideration* of an end; by any practical, empirical, or pure interest; by any concept whatever. The *fact* of art was thus such that the critical concept of this great aesthetic doctrine could only derive the *power* to comprehend it by giving up its *own* power, the power of arguing.

The true stakes of art were thus fixed and established: to provide pleasure and/or pain to pure thought on the occasion of a given act in a given site. One question, though, remained pending: How is this feeling to be brought to light?

We can only take up the challenge of speaking about art under the regime or, if you prefer, in the tone of what I would call, by a sort of vague analogy with psychoanalytic practice, a *compte rendu d'affect*, a report or account of the affect provoked by the work. Now, one can only report on or account for an affect by transmitting it, and not by objectifying it, as Valéry has suggested. But such a transmission leaves no hold for any sort of regulation. For regulations can only bear on representations, as they used to be called, on visual, sonorous, or even verbal images, but in any case on representative elements that *stand for* and are equivalent to the affect. Now this relationship of *standing for*, which constitutes the substance of a sign, can in no way be generalized when what is to be signified is an affect. What I mean is that a given curve, chromatism, rhythm, tonality, or envelopment does not include its affect within it, nor does it include a group of affects that are definable in principle and in advance in the way that a word includes its meaning or meanings, or a concept the class of objects that belongs to it. Affect has no such credentialed representative in the world of what I have been calling gestures.

And this is why the work as gesture is still an event. The presence of this gesture immediately renders thought happy and/or unhappy, that is, before and without its having to think about, decipher, or decode the work. This does not mean that the work as gesture cannot be grasped within the network of a code, by the algebra of a symbol, or through critical analysis. But its encoding, encrypting, or its analytic will not have been what makes the work, here and now, an unpolished sentimental event that provokes or fails to provoke our love. I repeat: there is no method by which to account—since the question of how to speak about art comes to us in these terms—for this sort of stupor by which thought suspends all activity, takes a break or, in Kant's terminology, a *Verweilung*, in which it comes to a halt before the event of the work in order to linger near it. This is the same sort of stupor that Barthes attributes to lovers, who are only able to repeat untiringly the phrase "I love you." This sort of obtuseness does not bode well for those reports or accounts of affect that have become the task of the philosopher who discusses art. Deprived of the ability to argue, we here risk lapsing into aphasia.

It will be objected that the beautiful and the sublime are no longer at stake in contemporary art, and that the negative aesthetics I am relying on is inappropriate to such art. Well, I would like to argue for the opposing view. The effort or effect of what have been called *avant-gardes* can be summed up in the fact that they have slowly but surely eradicated everything that might be able to *stand for* a feeling, that is, whichever vocabularies and syntaxes—what are sometimes referred to as rhetorics—are suspected of ensuring determinate affective effects. From this point of view, Kandinsky's attempt to establish a lexicon of signs seems somewhat hopeless. Through a tremendous implosion of the relationship between sensibility and feeling, the work of the avant-gardes called into question all of the forms and deformities that had hitherto allowed coding and encrypting according to some alleged "rules" of taste—or, for that matter, rules of distaste—to the point where, with Marcel Duchamp, the question is no longer one of the beautiful and the sublime, but of art itself: What is *art*?

This question is usually understood as inquiring about the nature of the *object* that can be qualified as artistic, as though the question put an end to art as a conceptual or logical class by making it undefinable which objects belong to this class. But this question can rather be read as putting or seeking to put an end to every attempt to "read" the gestures made in and toward space-time-matter, to put to an end to every claim to qualify and signify such gestures to define, class, decrypt, and interpret them, in short, to put an end to every sort of conceptual operation on the work. Negative aesthetics, an aesthetics that is negative with regard to the powers of understanding and reason—an aesthetics that was begun with Kantian critique—takes a further step with Duchamp. For this conceptual artist, the force of the concept is weakened even further and is "undone" by paradox. The concept shows its force in its own weakness, in the deficiencies that the understanding discerns in paralogisms, antinomies, and aporias. Yet it was no more in Duchamp's power than it was in others' to put an end to our immediate susceptibility to the event of the gesture, what I would rather call "passibility." By introducing the sublime within the conceptual critique of so-called aesthetic sentimentality, Kant extended the inconceivable well beyond the principles of taste. How are we to name the immediate affect or sentiment provoked by the almost negligible, unperceived, and imperceptible gesture of Duchamp? Duchamp himself proposed the term *ironism* or humor. But these are terms that are still too closely related to the sublime, for in them what is at issue is still the *nothing*. The gesture of art has always been this nothing for the philosopher, because he or she cannot grasp it with the means provided by argumentation, while at the same time, this nothing, in and through the affect for which it is the occasion, insists and persists within philosophical thought itself. Such is the state of the difficulty I have in speaking about art today. As you can see, it is not the result of turns taken within the various arts in the last ten or twenty years under the name of "postmodernism." Am I perhaps too old to be affected by them? I am not a great believer in epochs and generations when it comes to aesthetic susceptibility or possibility, and I have fairly good reasons for such disbelief.

It seems to me that the philosopher must ask himself about the possibility of the gesture (the aptitude for being affected by it) as such. No matter how it operates, such a gesture always has *a place*, *an instant*, and *a matter*. It is always a site and an act in, with, and toward space-time-matter. To ask oneself about the possibility of the gesture means questioning the affective power hidden within the space-time-matter. We know how committed Duchamp was to parachronisms, paratopisms, and paralogisms. In contemporary technologies, we are confronted with something else that Duchamp anticipated in his artisanal way: parahyletisms, paradoxes of matter, a few examples of which were presented in the exhibition I entitled *Immaterials*. These paradoxes have always seemed to me essential to the sentimental effect of the artistic gesture. Indeed, they are in conformity with the paradoxes that are constitutive of any particular possibility, paradoxes that are themselves particular. Here I am speaking of the enigma that Freud called unconscious affect. This affect requires not memory but the working through of an anamnesis. It seems to me that the philosopher who is captivated with art today must set himself the task of practicing on a particular work an anamnesis of the space-time-matter that the work paradoxically makes into act, site, and gesture. But I cannot say what the idiom would be in which the philosopher—if indeed he even remains a philosopher—might bring to light such an anamnesis.

NOTES

1. Paul Valéry, *Introduction à la poétique* (Paris: Gallimard, 1938), 39.

PART II

Aesthetics and the Question of the Other

CHAPTER 5

Levinas and the Ethics of Imagining

Richard Kearney

La littérature est l'aventure unique d'une transcendance enjambant tous les horizons du monde. . . . La littérature rappelle l'essence humaine du nomadisme. Le nomadisme n'est-il pas la source d'un sens, apparaissant dans une lumière que ne renvoie aucun marbre, mais le visage de l'homme . . . l'authenticité de l'art doit annoncer un ordre de justice.

—Emmanuel Levinas, *Sur Maurice Blanchot*
(Paris: Fata Morgana, 1975)

I

Kierkegaard attributed the crisis of the "present age" to the fact that human subjects were lacking passionate commitment to thinking. Today, more than a century later, one is tempted to add that we are also lacking passionate commitment to imagining. We live in a "Civilization of Images," where human subjects are deemed less and less responsible for the working of their own imaginations. The citizens of contemporary society increasingly find themselves surrounded by simulated images produced, or reproduced, by mass-media technologies operating outside of their ken or control. Even artists, as Roland Barthes argues, are becoming "copyists" rather than "creators" of images!

In all of this, the dominant role of imaging becomes parody. The image ceases to refer to some original event—in the world or consciousness—and becomes instead a simulacrum: an image of an image of an image. In our *société*

Reprinted with permission of the author from *Poetics of Modernity* (Atlantic Highlands, N.J.: Humanities Press, 1995), 108–17.

de spectacle the imaginary circulates in an endless play of imitation, where each image becomes a replay of another that precedes it. The idea of an "authentic" or "unique" imagination becomes redundant.

I have analyzed this so-called postmodern dilemma of the image as parody/pastiche/simulation in some detail elsewhere.[1] Here I inquire whether the work of Emmanuel Levinas, one of the foremost ethical thinkers in continental philosophy, has anything to teach us about the ethical implications of this dilemma in contemporary poetics.

In his 1972 essay "Idéologie et idéalisme," Levinas offers an apocalyptic account of our society of simulation, where Sameness reigns supreme:

> The contemporary world—of science, technology, leisure—sees itself as trapped. . . . not because everything is now permitted, and thanks to technology possible, but because everything is the same. The unknown immediately becomes familiar, the new normal. Nothing is new under the sun. The crisis written of in *Ecclesiastes* is not one of sin but of boredom. Everything becomes immersed and immured in the Same. . . Everywhere the machinations of melodrama, rhetoric, and play accuse and denounce. Vanity of vanities: the echo of our own voices, taken as response to the few prayers which remain to us, everywhere fallen back onto our own feet as after the ecstasies of drugs. Except for the other whom, in all this boredom, we cannot let down.[2]

Levinas suggests that the best response to the collective solipsism of Western culture is the assumption of ethical responsibility for the Other. Responsibility breaks through the circular game of mirrors, which perpetrates the reign of sameness through blank parody and stakes a claim for Otherness. But how can such ethical responsibility resist the ideology of the simulacrum pervading our social imaginary? How, if at all, can we retrieve some ethical dimension of *poiesis* from the faceless Civilization of Images that informs our experience?

II

There are a number of tests where Levinas analyzed the aesthetic imagination, notably "La réalité et son ombre," *Sur Maurice Blanchot*, "La Transcendence des Mots" (on the writing of Michel Leiris), "Agnon/Poésie et resurrection," "Paul Célan/De l'être à l'autre," and "L'autre dans Proust."[3]

In "La réalité et son ombre," written largely in response to Heidegger's ontological poetics of dwelling, Levinas warns us against becoming engulfed in a "spellbinding world of images and shadows"—where enigma and equivocation rule and realities are evaded (*RO*, 117). He reminds us of the ethical motivation behind monotheism's proscription of idolatrous images of death (*RO*, 115). But he does not go so far as to suggest that the artistic imagination should be censored for ethical or religious reasons. He is calling for a mode of critical interpretation capable of retrieving art as "a relation with the other" (*RO*, 117). And he commends the practice of such reflective hermeneutics in avant-garde writing as a critical defense against "artistic idolatry." "By means of such intellectualism," he writes, "the artist refuses to be an artist only; not because he wishes to defend a thesis or a cause but because he needs to *interpret his own myths*" (*RO*, 117).[4]

Levinas repeatedly endorses such critical self-interpretation. In *Noms propres*, he praises Agnon for his invocation of a certain "Hebraic saying," which "unravels the ultimate solidity beneath the plasticity of forms that western ontology teaches" (*NP*, 18). He contrasts the captivating power of "imaginary presence" to Agnon's poetry of "resurrection," which goes beyond the idolatrous tendency of images and opens us to the "irrepresentable as an endless fission of all that has dared to tie itself into a substrate" (*NP*, 63). So also, in his texts on Célan and Proust, Levinas endeavors to develop a similar ethics of writing and reading, based on the simple observation that the writing of these two authors clears a path "toward the other" (*NP*, 63). This entails, in Célan's case, a body of poetry that opens up an alterity exceeding the imagination of the author himself. Célan, he claims, is a poet who "concedes to the other . . . the time of the other" (*NP*, 63).

But what, we may ask, is the motivation of Levinas' critique of poetic imagination? Some answer, I suggest, may be found in his contrast between the "face" and the "image" in *Totalité et infini*.[5] Here again we find Levinas deeply suspicious of the enchanting power of images once they cease to answer to the Other. The face is the way in which the Other, as nomad, surpasses every image I have of him or her. It is irreducible to a series of qualities that might be formed into some noematic representation, correlative to a noetic intention. Or, as Levinas puts it, "The face of the other destroys and surpasses at every moment the plastic image that it leaves behind" (*TI*, 51). The face transcends every intentional consciousness. It expresses rather than represents. So Levinas describes it as that which I receive from the Other rather than that which I project upon him. Face-to-face conversation becomes the ethical model of relation par excellence, for it is here that the Other comes to me in all of his or her irreducible exteriority, that is, in a manner that cannot be measured or represented in terms of my own interior phantasms.

Is Levinas not therefore privileging conversation over imagination as the proper mode of openness to the Other? Indeed, is he not condemning imagination out of hand as a subjective intentionality that reduces alterity to its own remembered or anticipated fantasies? Or, worse, as that perverse agency of one-way voyeurism, epitomized by the figure of Gyges, whose ring enabled him to see but never to be seen by others?

While this is partly the case, it is not the whole story. Levinas' suspicion of images is not directed against the poetic power of imagination per se but against the use of such power to incarcerate the self in a blind alley of self-reflecting mirrors. In other words, the exercise of a poetic imagination open to conversation with the Other (as Levinas claims is the case with Leiris, Célan, Jabès, and Blanchot, among others) is already one that allows the face to exceed the plastic form of the image representing it. Such poetic imagination responds to the surprises and demands of the Other. It never presumes to fashion an image adequate to the Other's irrecuperable transcendence. Consequently, an ethical imagination would permit "the eye to see through the mask, an eye which does not shine but speaks" (*TI*, 38). It would safeguard the saying of the face against the subterfuges of the said.

That is why, in Levinas' words, the face is that transcendence of the Other which "breaks through its own plastic image" (*TI*, 128). It is also why an ethical poetics responds to the face with the question "Who?" (disclosing the alterity of the other person) rather than the question "What?" (reducing alterity to an impersonal system of substances, structures, or signs). Moreover, poetic responsibility to the Other refuses the consumerist status of imaging as imitation without depth or reference. It challenges the claim by certain postmodern commentators, such as Baudrillard, that we are condemned to a culture of "simulation" without origin or end, sublimely "irreferent" to the other.[6] Faced with the postmodern crisis of endless self-mirroring, wherein the face of the Other is dissolved into a mask of fantasies, ethical language bears witness to the infinity of the Other. It is this infinity that testifies to "my responsibility, to an existence already obligated to the other, beyond the play of mirrors" (*TI*, 158). Over and against all of the fashionable talk about the "end of man," a poetics of responsibility remains committed to human conversation, to the possibility of imagination's recovering its hermeneutic power to speak one-for-the-other and to listen to the powerless cry of the stranger, the widow, and the orphan—a cry which, in demanding that I speak to the unseen other (*le tiers*), is already a demand for justice (*TI*, 215).

For Levinas, not surprisingly, the best poetry is unfinished poetry—like Célan's, whose exposure of nothingness within is in fact a recognition of Otherness without, a poetry that is always an "interrupted breath" (*une souffle coupée*, as in *Atemwende*) because haunted by the recognition that its own saying can never be said, completed, closed off. In this respect, Célan remains for Levinas the "nomadic" poet who gave voice to those who have no voice, who—like Beckett—was devoted to the failure of complete communication, to the impossibility of ending, to the refusal to bring saying to a full stop. Therefore, a poetics answerable to the Other resists the temptation to mask the face behind an anonymous game of vertiginous repetition (*TI*, 270). It insists that language always expresses more than any plastic representation can suggest. Ethics is there to remind poetics that the Other can never be captured in the lures of the imaginary. No matter how pervasive the persuasion that there is nothing beyond the image but other images, the ethical ear of hermeneutic imagination refuses to be taken in.

III

If a certain reading of Levinas' opposition of face to image in *Totalité et infini* leads us to believe that ethics is opposed to any poetic functioning of imagination, a reconsideration of this argument, in light of Levinas' texts on Célan, Proust, Blanchot, and others, redresses the balance. Here it becomes clear that it is not the speaking power of imagination that Levinas objects to, only its power to fetishize or idolize images in self-referential play. Bearing this distinction in mind, it seems that Levinas does suggest the possibility of an ethical reading of the contemporary crisis of poetics. I return, therefore, to my original question of how to form an alliance between an ethics of responsibility and a poetics of imagination.

Although Levinas never addresses this task directly, there are suggestive hints in certain texts. Before examining these, however, I would like to take an example not mentioned by Levinas himself but relevant to this problematic. I refer to the attempt by Claude Lanzmann, in *Shoah*, to portray the Holocaust in cinematic images. In this practical endeavor to combine an ethics of responsibility with a poetics of imagination, Lanzmann seeks to present the irrepresentable in and through the audiovisual medium of film. He is trying to recount what cannot be recounted, to demonstrate the impossibility of reproducing the event of the Holocaust in some kind of linear narrative while reminding us of the unforgettable—though usually forgotten—character of the event. Lanzmann refuses to portray Auschwitz in terms of spectacle or sensation. He shows no images of burnt bodies or SS commandants. He resists the temptation to imitate the inimitable in terms of dramatic reproduction or documentary newsreel. We do not see the victims—for that, Lanzmann believes, would reduce them to "objects" of genocide. What we do see are the faces of survivors, bearing witness to the impossibility of representing in images that which they witnessed firsthand. It is the use of cinema to express the unimaginableness of the Holocaust that succeeds in reminding us that we have forgotten how unimaginable it was, and that we must not be allowed to forget this forgetfulness.

Lanzmann's *via negativa* combines ethical and poetical moves. It uses images against themselves to suggest what they fail to capture (by their failure to do so). *Shoah* provokes what it cannot evoke. To Adorno's question, whether poetry can be written after Auschwitz, it answers that it cannot, but that we cannot stop trying. In that sense, we may describe it as a poetics committed to an ethics of responsibility. As a former disciple of Levinas, Jean-François Lyotard, observes:

> To represent "Auschwitz" in images, in words, is a way of forgetting it. I'm not just thinking here of B movies and soap opera series and pulp novels or testimonies. I'm also thinking of those representations which can and could best

make us not forget by virtue of their exactness or severity. Even such efforts represent what should remain unrepresentable in order not to be forgotten precisely as forgotten. Claude Lanzmann's film, *Shoah*, is perhaps a singular exception. Not only because he resists the use of representation in images and music, but also because he hardly offers a single testimony where the unrepresentable character of the extermination is not indicated, even momentarily, by an alteration of voice, a tightening of throat, a tear, a sob, the disparition of a witness out of frame, an upset in the tone of the narrative, some uncontrolled gesture. So that we know that the witnesses are surely lying, or "playing a role" or hiding something, however impassive they may appear.[7]

We are concerned here with self-negating imagination—one might even be tempted to add, self-deconstructing imagination. For at issue is a functioning of images that debunks its own claim to representational presence. We confront a series of cinematic signifiers that refuse to be tied to a "transcendental signified." Intentions without fulfillment, as phenomenology would put it, *visées à vide*. The poetic refusal of intuitive closure, completeness, certainty approximates to an ethical form of deconstruction—a proposition that becomes even more compelling in light of Levinas' account of deconstructive thinking in "Idéologie et idéalisme" as "signifiers playing in a game of signs without signifieds . . . a conceptual disillusionment with the possibility of positing sense, with Husserl's 'doxic thesis,' a denunciation of the rigor of logical forms as repressive, an obsession with the inexpressible, the ineffable, the un-said sought after the mis-said, in the lapsus." Are these not the very conditions of Lanzmann's *Shoah*? Or at least of Lyotard's reading of it? One is tempted to respond in the affirmative. But then we read Levinas' own concluding remark on such deconstructive discourse and take pause. "Such," writes Levinas, "is the painful rupture of modern discourse, exemplified by its most sincere representatives, but already trading on the false coin of primary truths and fashionable cant" (*II*, 31).

Although Levinas does not mention any poststructuralist thinkers by name, it is difficult not to associate such a description with philosophers like Lyotard, Foucault, and Barthes. But the important issue here is not who is who in Levinas' allusions but how Levinas himself is to retrieve an ethical poetics from a deconstructive discourse on imagination. How, in other words, is he going to distinguish between the "painful rupture of modern discourse" as ethical irrepresentability, on the one hand, and as mere fashionable cant, on the other hand? Some hint of a solution appears in a passage in *Totalité et infini*, which speaks of a primary mode of expression where the signifier as face transcends all signifying systems and allows the Other to express itself. Such language of proximity, which precedes linguistic signs, is actually an ethical language of the face as "original expression," as the "first word—you shall not kill" (*TI*, 157, 173). This is a language that explodes the "neutral mediations of the image" and imposes itself on us in a manner irreducible to the form of its manifestation (*TI*, 174).

But to admit as much is surely to admit that the face has nothing really to fear from mediating, or mediated, images as long as we who respond to such images respond to the underlying language of the face that speaks through them. The face is only threatened, is it not, by images that would have us believe that the language of poetics can definitively divorce itself from the language of ethics? If this is the case, Levinas' ultimate position would appear to be that poetic imagining is fine, as long as it remains answerable to an ethics of alterity. Answerablity would itself be seen as compatible with, and complementary to, a certain gesture of deconstruction. I refer here to the dismantling of modern claims (idealist or existentialist) that the transcendental ego or imagination remains the origin of all value. The deconstruction of such subjectivist claims might indeed serve an ethics of alterity.

Levinas appears to suggest as much in certain passages that acknowledge an ethical motivation behind anti-humanist critiques of the "self." The following admission from "Un Dieu Homme?" is a case in point: "The contemporary anti-humanism which denies the primacy of being enjoyed by the person taken as an end in itself has perhaps opened a space for the [ethical] notion of subjectivity as substitution . . . the infinite patience, passivity and passion of the self [soi] whereby being empties itself of its own being."[8] Viewed in this way, the debunking of the humanist subject, construed as self-identical Sameness [*idem*], can be seen as releasing a different kind of self, an ethical subject which, like Ricoeur's *ipse*, is open to alterity and transcendence. Such an ethical subject, Levinas insists, remains alert to the eschatological order of creation still to come, announced in Genesis 2:3, in which, Levinas insists, "everyone has a part to play."[9] The deconstruction of the humanist self in the name of eschatological poetics is only ethical, for Levinas, however, to the extent that it acknowledges that "responsibility as response is the primary saying; and that transcendence is communication which implies, beyond the simple exchange of signs, a 'gift', an 'open house'" (*II*, 33).

IV

This would certainly seem to be Levinas' thinking in his readings of Proust, Célan, Blanchot, and Agnon. It is time to take a closer look at some of these. In one essay in *Sur Maurice Blanchot*, "The Servant and Her Master" (published in 1966), Levinas praises Blanchot's writing for its "moral elevation, an aristocracy of thought." What he means is a cold neutrality in Blanchot's language that expresses the inexpressible—that experience of *désastre*, which he identifies with our contemporary culture of absence and death. "Objectivizing consciousness is replaced by a sense of being that is detached from cosmological existence, from any fixed reference to a star (dis-aster), a being that strains toward obliteration in an inaccessible nonlanguage."[10] What fascinates Levinas here is Blanchot's use of images as ciphers of infinity, gestures of interminable waiting that can never be fulfilled. Blanchot's words operate as intentional signifiers of a self that undoes its own self-centeredness, exceeds its own ontological ipseity, out of concern for something other, something beyond the said or the sayable, the imaged or the imaginable—what Levinas describes as a "first concern for justice" (*SM*, 150). Indeed, one is tempted to add that what distinguishes deconstructive writing as "moral elevation" from "fashionable cant" (*bavardage à la mode*) is just that: concern for justice.

Levinas makes a similar case for ethical poetics in his readings of Proust and Leiris. He interprets the Proustian author's endless quest for the lost self as an encounter with the "enigma of the other." The fact that Marcel never fulfils his desire for Albertine does not mean that he does not love her. On the contrary, "to the extent that Marcel struggles with her presence as absence in the narrative, this struggle is love, in that it is directed not by being-toward-death but by the death of the Other, not by Dasein, but by the responsibility for the Other's death which creates his infinitely answerable 'I'" (*SM*, 160). The Proustian drama of solitude and incommunicability is not about the retrieval of some ideal state of self-presence. It is about an ethical relation with the Other that remains forever Other. Levinas reads the Proustian imagination less as a quest for lost being than "as the relational space in which I am hostage to the other" (*SM*, 160).[11]

"Moral elevation" of a parallel kind is to be found in the writing of avant-garde author Michel Leiris. Here again the linguistic imagination is never allowed to slip away into empty imitations but is constantly recalled to critical vigilance. Images ceaselessly undermine their own mesmerizing power, generating a movement of nomadic transcendence toward the Other. They become genuine speech, which for Levinas means a "moment of critique" that shatters the *imaginaire* of self-sufficiency and opens us to a relation with someone.[12] As Levinas puts it, "This need to enter into a relation with someone, in spite of or over and above the peace and harmony derived from the successful creation of beauty, is what we call the necessity of critique" (*TW*, 147). At this point, Levinas contrasts writing that approximates to vision—where form is wedded to content in a way that appeases it—and writing that approximates to sound, where "the perceptible quality overflows so that form can no *longer* contain its content" (*TW*, 147). The necessity of critique is met by the latter kind, epitomized by Leiris' own texts. Here a rent is produced in our imaginary world; words are uttered that "surpass what is given." The ethical imagination of a writer like Leiris is acoustic rather than representational.

Leiris' *writing* is praised accordingly as a textuality of verbal sound that privileges "the living word, destined to be heard, in contrast to the word that is an image and already a picturesque sign" (*TW*, 147). Leiris invents a literature of bifurcations (*bifurs*) and erasures (*biffures*), writing that resists the idolatry of total meaning. Levinas explains: "Bifurcations—since sensations, words and memories continually turn a train of thought from the path it seemed to be taking toward some unexpected direction; erasures—since the univocal meaning of each element is continually altered" (*TW*, 145–46). Leiris reminds us that responsible art is in the first instance an act of speech, where we hear, and respond to, the words of the Other. But these words of transcendence can only assume a presence among us as a trace of the Other, precisely because they refuse to become flesh. Levinas spells out what he means by such an ethical *ascesis* of words:

> The use of the word wrenches experience out of its aesthetic self-sufficiency, the "here" where it has quietly been lying. Invoking experience turns it into a creature. It is in this sense that I have been able to say elsewhere that criticism, which is the word of a living being speaking to a living being, brings the image in which art revels back to the fully real being. The language of criticism takes us out of our dreams, in which artistic language plays an integral part. . . . Books call up books—but this proliferation of writings halts or culminates at the moment when the living word is installed. (*TW*, 148)

V

Leiris thus serves for Levinas—along with Proust, Blanchot, Agnon, and Célan—as a poet who responds to the fetishizing power of images by producing counter-images, word-images that disclose how being for the Other, in and through language, is the first event of existence. One is compelled to infer that it is just such a poetics of the "living word" that Levinas would recommend as an antidote to the proliferation of mirror images and mirror texts that characterizes contemporary culture. The best answer to the parodic imagination is an auditory imagination critical of its own images and attuned to what exceeds them.

But avant-garde literature is not the only poetical medium to testify to the ethical. The critique of our Civilization of Images does not—as thinkers, from Adorno and Marcuse to Steiner and Henri imply—require a retreat from the glare of popular culture to the inaccessible reaches of high art.[13] Levinas also acknowledges the possibility of media images bearing ethical testimony in his remarks on the TV news coverage of a dying Colombian girl buried up to her neck in mud after an avalanche in 1986.[14] Viewers can respond to such an image in a purely sensational or voyeuristic fashion. But they can equally respond to it as a naked face crying out in destitution. The choice of response is ours, but it is never ethically neutral. It is a response, one way or another, to the ethical cry of another. Even the decision to be sadistic in viewing such suffering—a decision to refuse to respond to the ethical cry— is itself a response to the Other, albeit negative. Before we are condemned to be free, we are condemned to be responsible.

Recognizing the ethical charge of media images is, I submit, a crucial step toward a hermeneutics of postmodern imagination. It is regrettable that Levinas himself never explicitly pursued this path, and that, furthermore, he adopts an elitist attitude to poetics in his almost exclusive attention to avant-garde writing. The closest he comes, perhaps, is when he acknowledges in "L'idée de la culture" (1983) that contemporary culture in the broad sense can serve the "irruption of the human in the barbarism of being." "Culture is not a surpassing or neutralization of transcendence," he goes on. "Rather it is an ethical responsibility and obligation toward the other, a relationship to transcendence as transcendence. One could call it love. Culture is obliged to the face of the human other, which is not a given of experience and does not come from this world."[15]

What Levinas manifestly fails to address, however, is the right of art as art to explore a realm of imagination that, in Ricoeur's phrase, "knows no censorship."[16] Even if one is prepared to admit that aesthetic images are derived from the primary expression of the face and remain, in the end of the day, answerable to the face, one still reserves the right of art to suspend judgment, however provisionally, while it explores and experiments in a free play of imagination. Levinas does not fully appreciate that if the ultimate origin and end of art is ethics, the rest belongs to poetics.

Without this alibi, however temporary, poetics would cease to play freely, would cease to imagine how the impossible might become possible, how things might be if all was permissible. Deprived of such leeway, we are ultimately left with Lenin's maxim that "Art is the hammer of the benevolent propagandist" or Sartre's "Words are loaded pistols."[17] Polemics notwithstanding, such slogans are the death of art.

Free play of imagining is indispensable not only for poetics but also, in a curious sense, for ethics itself. This Levinas failed to see. If ethics is left entirely to itself, or allowed to dictate to poetics at every turn, it risks degenerating into cheerless moralism. Ethics needs poetics to be reminded that its responsibility to the Other includes the possibility of play, liberty, and pleasure, just as poetics needs ethics to be reminded that play, liberty, and pleasure are never self-sufficient but originate in, and aim toward, an experience of the other-than-self. That is where ethics and poetics meet—in those words that the self receives from the Other and returns to the Other: the hermeneutic act of being-for-one-another.

NOTES

1. See my *Wake of Imagination* (London: Hutchinson, 1987; St. Paul: University of Minnesota Press, 1988) and *Poetics of Imagining* (London: Routledge, 1991). The practice of parody is sometimes termed *postmodern* insofar as it subverts the modern view of imagining as an original invention of a unique human subject. The term *postmodern* first gained common currency in architecture in the mid-1970s, when it designated a shift away from the late modernist international style of Corbusier and Mies Van der Rohe, with its emphasis on utopianism and novelty, toward a "radical eclecticism of pseudo-historical forms. Its main proponents were Charles Jencks, Robert Venturi, and Charles Moore. But the term was quickly taken up by the philosophers. Here it became synonymous with those structuralist and more particularly poststructuralist currents of thought which disputed the modern belief in the primacy of the humanist imagination as a creative source of meaning. The idealist and existentialist arguments for the centrality of the autonomous imagination have, since the 1960s, repeatedly run the gauntlet of critical deconstruction. Indeed, so vehement this dismantling process has been that one sometimes wonders if it is still possible to speak legitimately of a postmodern imagination at all. Several contemporary critics dismiss the very notion of the imaginary as an ideological ruse of Western bourgeois humanism, as little more than an illusion or effect of the impersonal play of language, a ludic mirage of signs.

2. Levinas, "Idéologie et idéalisme," in *De Dieu qui vent à l'idée* (Paris: Vain, 1982), 31; trans. in *The Levinas Reader*, ed. S. Hand (Oxford: Blackwell, 1989). Hereafter cited as *II*.

3. Levinas, "La réalité et son ombre," in *Les Temps Modernes* 38 (1948), translated as "Reality and Its Shadow" in *The Levinas Reader*, ed. Sean Hand; hereafter cited as *RO*; *Sur Maurice Blanchot* (Paris: Fata Morgana, 1975); "La Transcendence des Mots" (on the writing of Michel Leiris) in *Les Temps Modernes* 44 (1949); "Agnon/Poésie et resurrection," "Paul Célan/De l'être à l'autre," and "L'autre dans Proust," in *Noms Propres* (Paris: Fata Morgana, 1986). Hereafter cited as *NP*.

4. See M. P. Hederman's critique of Levinas' position on art and poetry, "De l'interdiction à l'écoute'," in *Heidegger et la question de Dieu*, eds. Kearney and O'Leary (Paris: Grasset, 1981), 285–96.

5. Levinas, *Totalité et infini* (The Hague: Nijhof, 1961; trans. Duquesne University Press, 1969). Hereafter cited as *TI*.

6. Baudrillard, *Simulations* (New York: Semiotext(e), 1983).

7. Lyotard, *Heidegger et "les juifs"* (Paris: Galilée, 1988), 51.

8. Levinas, "Un Dieu Homme?" in *Levinas: Exercises de la patience*, no. I (Paris: Obsidiane, 1980), 74.

9. Levinas, "Sur la mort de Ernst Bloch," in *De Dieu qui vent à l'idée*, 65n.

10. Emmanuel Levinas, "The Servant and Her Master," *The Levinas Reader*, ed. Séan Hand (Oxford: Blackwell, 1989), 150. All further references to this work will be marked in the text parenthetically as *SM*.

11. For a contrary reading of Proust on this issue, see Martha Nussbaum, *Love's Knowledge* (Oxford: Oxford University Press, 1990), 261–85.

12. Levinas, "The Transcendence of Words," *The Levinas Reader*, 144–49. All further references to this work will be marked in the text parenthetically as TW.

13. See in particular Herbert Marcuse, *The Aesthetic Dimension* (Boston: Beacon Press, 1988); George Steiner, *Real Presences* (London: Faber and Faber, 1989); Michel Henri, *La Barbarie* (Paris: Grasset, 1987).

14. Levinas, contribution to Cérisy Colloque on Levinas, August 1987.

15. Levinas, "L'idée de la culture" (1983), reprinted in *Entre nous* (Paris: Grasset, 1991), 207–08.

16. Ricoeur, *Time and Narrative*, vol. 3 (Chicago: University of Chicago Press, 1988).

17. Sartre, *Existentialism and Literature* (New York: Citadel Press, 1972).

CHAPTER 6

Disappearing Traces: Emmanuel Levinas, Ida Fink's Literary Testimony, and Holocaust Art

Dorota Glowacka

A face is a trace of itself, given over to my responsibility, but to which I am wanting and faulty. It is as though I were responsible for his mortality, and guilty for surviving.

—Emmanuel Levinas, *Otherwise Than Being or Beyond Essence*[1]

Figure 6.1 *Star of David and Number, Carved in Brick, Exterior of Block 9, Main Camp (Auschwitz).* From Joseph P. Czarnecki, *Last Traces: The Lost Art of Auschwitz* (New York: Atheneum, 1989), 159. Reproduced with permission of the author's estate.

Until recently, the so-called "theory" seemed ill equipped for the task of examining the Holocaust narrative, and "the resistance to theory," to recall de Man's phrase, has been prevalent among Holocaust scholars.[2] Yet the radical challenge of poststructuralism to the Western politics of representation and critical theory's "ethical turn" in the last decade, as reflected in influential writings by Jean-François Lyotard, Maurice Blanchot, Jacques Derrida, and Emmanuel Levinas, has allowed us to ask important questions about the relevance of traditional aesthetic standards to Holocaust narrative. With the current proliferation of works about the Holocaust, the stringent distinctions between ethically responsible representations and irreverent, "merely" aesthetic productions have become problematic. As a result, Holocaust literature has become a site par excellence where traditional notions of aesthetics as representation are being contested. In this context, Emmanuel Levinas' ethical philosophy in particular—his critique of the Western canons of the beautiful as injurious to the Other—makes it possible to engage in new ways of thinking about aesthetics, and consequently to conceive of a category of Holocaust art that respects and preserves the absolute alterity of the Event.

In one of the most haunting scenes of Claude Lanzmann's *Shoah*, Simon Srebrnik, the survivor of the Chełmno extermination camp, returns to the site of murder. We see him walking through a serene, rural landscape; suddenly, he points to a large field covered with grass and says, "*Ja, Das ist der Platz*" [Yes, this is the place]. Although this unremarkable scenery is now unscathed by the signs of violence to which it was witness, for Srebrnik, it bears the indelible image of the crime, the traces of which only his speech in front of Lanzmann's camera can etch in the viewer's imagination.[3] "The place" is an image of absence: it withholds the signs, draws them into itself, and even Srebrnik's testifying voice retreats from it. In an attempt to bring forth an image, the survivor walks away from the camera, retracing with his footsteps what must remain undisclosed to the viewer.

In Ida Fink's short story entitled "Traces" ["Ślady"], from the volume *A Scrap of Time*, the main character, the single survivor of a small-town ghetto, describes a photograph of the ghetto in its last stages: "There is a lot of white in it; that's snow. The picture was taken in February. The snow is high, piled up in deep drifts. In the foreground are traces of footprints; along the edges, two rows of wooden stalls. That is all. Yes. This is where they lived."[4] The speaker identifies the footprints as being most likely left by the members of the local Judenrat who were being marched to death, following the discovery of a group of children in the attic of the Judenrat building. The woman speaks reluctantly, but then she changes her mind and asks that what she is saying be written down. She wants a trace of those who perished to remain, and since she alone survived, only she can fulfil the task of bearing witness. Ida Fink herself fled from a small-town ghetto in Poland in 1942, survived the Holocaust on the Aryan side, and now lives in Israel. Thus the first person narrator of her stories, her *alter ego*, reenacts a paradoxical double role of one of the victims and the surviving witness to the events.[5]

In one of the interviews, Claude Lanzmann said about *Shoah* that he had to work with "the disappearance of the trace . . . with traces of traces of traces" (quoted in Robbins, 252). Similarly, the unnamed speaker in Fink's story is trying to capture in speech the materiality of the footprints left in the snow by the people who were just about to suffer a horrifying death. These footprints in turn lead her to recall that the group of children remained absolutely silent when the SS brought them out of the attic and shouted at them to identify their parents. Although the memory of the children's heroism has been eradicated—it is only their parents' footsteps that are visible in the photograph—the narrator's reminiscence will now provide testimony to the children's courage. It is in her speech, therefore, that the passage of the condemned ones into remembrance is effectuated. Since the attic above the Judenrat was liquidated and the hidden children murdered, the witness's language will now become a fragile shelter, protecting its inhabitants from oblivion.

A Doll of Auschwitz (see Figure 6.2), 1987, by Mordechai Ardon (Max Bronstein),[6] offers a visual commentary on the theme of disappearing traces. Ardon, a German Jew who fled to Palestine in 1933, painted the triptych in 1987, having been inspired by the poem *A Doll of Auschwitz*, which he heard recited in Paris. Like Fink's story "Traces," the painting evokes the collapse and disappearance of the child's world during the Holocaust. The icons of a doll's hands, stretching out among the abstractions of the dark colors in the second panel (entitled *The Road of Numbers*, in reference to cattle trains carrying their human cargo to the camps), and the tiny footprints in the third panel *The Shadows*—signify the Event as well as point to their own simulacral inadequacy to speak it.

The next image, *Disappearing Places (Tarnopol)* (see Figure 6.3),[7] 1988, by Robert Morris, is one of a series of lead reliefs in which the artist used Holocaust imagery in order to, in his own words, "counter the pernicious amnesia that is already at work, softening the contours of this mark on our time" (*DI*, 359). These plates refer to small camps in Poland that have never been documented in photographs and therefore are almost completely forgotten (the word *Tarnopol*, the name of one of the small camps, appears half-covered at the bottom of the panel). The imprint of a palm and the grooves in the lead bring to mind the grip lines clawed in the concrete walls of gas chambers by the victims in their last agonizing moments. *Disappearing Places* ponders this historical amnesia but also explores the way in which the Holocaust can break through obliterating plastic surfaces.

These images, effected in different artistic media, illustrate what I would like to call the art of disappearing traces. Starting from Levinas' discussion of the ethical function of language in relation to the Other, I will argue that the Jewish philosopher's critical interrogation of Western aesthetics is particularly relevant in discussions about representations of the Holocaust in literature and art. Levinas' own work is informed, in its entirety, by a protest against the atrocity of Auschwitz.[8] His ethics is a philosophy of peace and a cry against murder, which suspends ethics, on behalf of the Other to whom I am responsible; the Other, who resists appropriation in cognition and indeed is "the primordial expression of 'you shall not commit murder.'"[9] Levinas was one of the first philosophers to become disturbed by the phenomenon of National Socialism and to insist that the evil of Hitlerism has to be refuted philosophically.[10] His *magnum opus*, *Otherwise Than Being or Beyond Essence*, is dedicated to "the memory of those who were closest among the 6 million assassinated by National Socialists, and of millions on millions of all confessions and all nations, victims of the same hatred of the other man, the same anti-Semitism" (*OB*, Dedication). This paramount concern for the Other has led Levinas to search for radical ways of engaging with others, which would not reduce their alterity to the function of the same. The epistemological adventure of the Cartesian West is grounded in representation, which Levinas characterizes as "a determination of the Other by the same, without the same being determined by the Other" (*TI*, 168).

According to Levinas, philosophy is founded on the conquest of the Other, and works of art or, as he says disparagingly, "games of art" (347), epitomize this "exploitation and emprise" of alterity. In many of his works, Levinas has cautioned against the egotistic and totalizing dimension of aesthetics. Already in his early essays such as "Reality and Its Shadow" (1948), and especially in *Totality and Infinity*, he denounces aesthetics as complicit with totality and allergic to absolute alterity. Twenty years later, he reiterates this view in *Otherwise Than Being*: "Art is the pre-eminent exhibition in which the said is reduced to a pure theme, to absolute exposition, even to shamelessness, capable of holding all looks for which it is exclusively destined. The said is reduced to the Beautiful, which supports the Western ontology" (*OB*, 40). Ethics or justice, therefore, is the overcoming of aesthetics. Yet I would argue that Levinas' indictment of the Western politics of representation, his distrust of the image in which the Other is seized, actually opens up a possibility of thinking about aesthetics "otherwise." This alternative, nonviolent aesthetics is grounded in ethically informed artistic practice, "art for the other," in which the desire to produce a likeness of the Other already presupposes ethical responsibility.[11]

Levinas defines ethics as the calling into question of the same by the Other's absolute alterity. Within the ethical relation, the self is constituted in

Figure 6.2   Mordechai Ardon, *A Doll of Auschwitz*, 1989. Reproduced with permission of Butterworth Heinmann Publishers, a division of Reed Educationl and Professional Publishing Ltd.

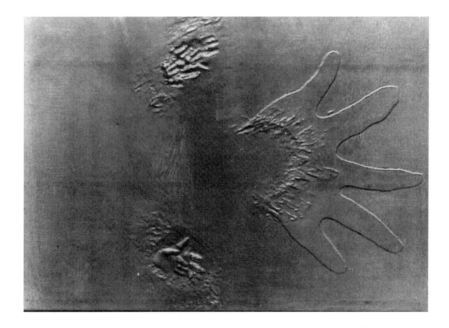

Figure 6.3   Robert Morris, *Disappearing Places (Tarnolpol)*, 1988. Reproduced with permission of Butterworth Heinmann Publishers, a division of Reed Educational and Professional Publishing Ltd.

its infinite obligation to another human being. In *Otherwise Than Being*, Levinas proposes an even more radical conception of the ethical subject, whereby I am responsible not only *to* but also *for* the Other. With respect to the Other, I am in the situation of a hostage, substituting for his or her pain and destitution but also assuming the burden of the Other's actions. My identity comes from the impossibility of escaping this responsibility: "The neighbour assigns me before I designate him" (*OB*, 87). Antecedent to its self-possession in enjoyment and in consciousness, the subject, the same for the other, is first and foremost a witness to the existence of the Other. Prior to disclosing myself to myself, my existence is a testimony to the life of the Other, who has traversed my horizon and disturbed my order of being.

The artists who incorporate Holocaust themes—writers, painters, film-makers—carry out a preponderant task of producing testimony to the unique individual suffering of the Other. In speech and image, they wish to bear witness to the victims' broken or extinguished lives in such a way that their traces will reverberate for both present and future generations of witnesses. In my reading of Ida Fink's stories, I will apply Levinas' conception of the ethical subject, emptied of its egoism by an absolute duty to aid the neighbor, to the writer or artist who has assumed the task of witnessing. It is the witness's speech that sustains the trace of the traumatic event. Such ethical speech carries a risk: in the process of bearing witness, even if it consists of passing on a story rather than providing firsthand testimony, the witness's own world has been irreparably fractured.

For Levinas, the ethical essence of language exceeds its communicative function. In its expressive function, over and above its manifestation as sign, language is a relation with an interlocutor, a response and nonappropriative reaching out to the Other, "before language scatters into words, into themes equal to words and dissimulating in the said the openness of the saying exposed like a bleeding wound" (*OB*, 151). Ethical "speech" is an interpellation, in which the Other is invoked but not grasped or comprehended. Since my absolute responsibility entails that I substitute for the Other, shelter the Other under my skin, the pronoun "I," as Levinas explains in his famous essay "Substitution" (*OB*, 99–129), first appears in the accusative rather than nominative form, indicating my guilt of usurping someone else's place "under the sun" (Pascal) and my readiness to respond to the call for help. Ethical speech, in which I have always already relinquished my possession of the realm I inhabit, means speaking the world to the Other—a gesture of absolute giving, for which I do not seek repayment or gratification. Since the Other invoked in ethical language retains his or her heterogeneity and singularity, in excess of the universalizing domain of concepts, ethical speech maintains the interlocutor to whom it is addressed. Yet the betrayal of alterity in thematization is inevitable, because the Other can only leave an imprint on the concrete surface of my language.

The opening to the suffering of the Other does not occur in disclosure and cannot be adequately described, and the Other arises behind the image in which he or she is presented. This nonphenomenal appresentation signals itself in my speech as a trace. In the trace, the undisclosable face of the Other accompanies its own manifestation in the sign and at the same time disengages itself from thematization. A trace of the Other signifies the presence of the Other who has never appeared within the coordinates of my world: "It disturbs immanence without settling into the horizons of the world."[12] A trace has interrupted the continuity of my representations and therefore cannot be mastered in consciousness. It is always slipping into the past more remote than any past recuperable in memory; it does not simply lead to the past, as memory would, but it signals a relation with the past that cannot be recovered in the present, outside every present and every presentation. The trace, which betokens the time of the Other, is "incommensurable with the present, always already in the past, over and beyond 'now,' which this exteriority disturbs and obsesses" (*OB*, 86). The trace signals the existence of the Other in a mode that is irreducible to manifestation and designates me in my irrecusable duty.

Ida Fink states her intentions in writing her literary testimony in the opening paragraph of the title story in the volume *A Scrap of Time*:

> I want to talk about a certain time not measured in months and years. For so long I have wanted to talk about this time, and not in the way I will talk about it now, not just about this one scrap of time. I wanted to, but I couldn't, I didn't know how. I was afraid, too, that this second time, which is measured in months and years, had buried the other time under a layer of years, that this second time had crushed the first one and destroyed it within me. But no. Today, digging around in the ruins of memory, I found it fresh and untouched by forgetfulness. (*ST,* 3)

Since, like the narrator in "Traces," she has become a precious repository of memory, sifting through the ruins of memory is her moral duty. This ethical dimension of storytelling is emphasized in all of her short narratives and plays. Many of the characters in the stories are eyewitnesses to murder, and they mention how excruciating it was for them to withstand the ghastly spectacle. For instance, in "Behind a Hedge," a housekeeper, Agafia, describes to her employer the trauma of secretly watching the execution of a group of Jews in the woods: "When they started shooting again, I jumped up and wanted to run into the woods, so I wouldn't have to see. But I didn't run. Something kept me there and said to me: 'Watch. Don't shut your eyes.' So I watched" (*ST*, 19). To those who do not want to listen to her gruesome report, Agafia retorts, "We have to know about it. And look at it. And remember" (*ST*, 17). Not averting one's gaze from the spectacle of murder is the witness's horrendous duty. A man in the story "The Pig" has been an inadvertent witness to four "actions," and although he yearns to see no more, he resumes the gruesome task again and again: "'I can't,' he said and slumped into a corner, but he stood up again and watched without blinking" (*ST*, 81). Indeed, the identities of Fink's narrators are constructed through their roles as witnesses, open to the flow of recollection and hospitable to the stories of others.

It is important to summon the circumstances of murder in a detailed image, to place each individual death in space and time in order to make it concrete and unique. In "A Scrap of Time," the narrator relates the death of her cousin David, who at the first shots "climbed a tree and wrapped his arms around the trunk like a child hugging his mother, and that was the way he died" (*ST*, 10). This caring description seems to release David's death from the bestiality of the circumstances in which it occurred and, perhaps even more importantly, it pries open the dimension of David's life in the small town prior to his murder. In "The Death of Tsaritsa," the narrator reminisces about a young girl, living on the Aryan side under an assumed name, who jumped out of the window after her identity was discovered. A certain B. "rescued Tsaritsa's death from anonymity" when he accidentally witnessed her suicide.[13] Although such remembrance compounds the horror, it is important for Fink that the details of the victims' deaths be preserved. Numerous descriptions of executions in the stories serve to accord the murdered people a measure of humanity, because they focus on the singularity of their suffering, against the anonymous statistics of mass extermination. Although none of the events can be undone or their horror sublimated into beautiful dying, by returning these deaths to language, where the victims' individual fates have left traces, the writer exposes and decries the acts of murder.

The decision to listen and respond to the Other's story, to assume its onus of pain and dread, is a difficult one. Several stories in both volumes tell about survivors' cautious attempts to share the story with a close friend or lover after the liberation, and their frustration when the interlocutors turn a deaf ear. In "Splinter," a young girl falls asleep when her boyfriend keeps telling her about his mother's murder. In "Night of Surrender," the survivor's boyfriend, an American soldier, advises her to continue her life under an assumed Aryan identity. Ironically, for what he believes to be in the survivor's best interest, he chooses to collaborate in the erasure of memory. He denies Klara *alias* Ann her desire to unburden herself of the past and of the fake identity she has constructed for herself. By remaining content with the girl's invented story of her Aryan life, he refuses to acknowledge the rent in the fabric of his world produced by her Jewish difference and inadvertently colludes with the murderer who forced her to conceal her Jewishness in the first place. It literally hurts the witness to receive the sharp splinter of memory in the openness to the Other. For the witness, the suffering of the Other is, in Levinas' evocative metaphor, "a thorn burning flesh" (*OB*, 50). Levinas emphasizes the bond between perceptions of the world through senses and the expressive function of language, which presupposes the attitude of listening. Sensibility itself is then first and foremost the vulnerability of the body, its sensitivity in the exposure to the Other.

In its expressive function, language is Saying, which coincides with the ethical essence of subjectivity animated by responsibility. It is always absorbed in the said, the plastic surface of language upon which it imprints itself as a trace, a surplus that signifies beyond being. Fink's storytellers are messengers who enable the recurrence of traces in language. Often the narrator in a story is a collector of pieces of conversation from which she will reconstruct what happened. In "A Spring Morning," she picks up a comment overheard by someone who watched a procession of people being marched to their deaths. As they were crossing a bridge, one of the condemned men suddenly said, "The water is the color of beer" (*ST*, 45). The witness saved the shred of a sentence, the sole testimony to an extinguished life, and by passing it on, released the trace into its unpredictable itinerary in language. In the story "Sabina," the narrator hears about the last moments of Sabina and her daughter, just before they were discovered in their hiding place under a pile of empty sacks in the corridor of the Judenrat. Such stories, she confesses, "float past the edges of our memory" (*T*, 101), and the storyteller has to make an effort to capture these fleeting bits of recollection, drag them from *their* hiding places and unlock the traces from the parentheses of history. In the already mentioned story "Traces," the events unfold from the blurred image in the photograph. Yet without the speaker's commentary, no one would even notice the footprints in the picture, or at best they would remain inconsequential. They are mute signs, whose meaning eludes the viewer. The narrator ponders, "The people are gone—their footprints remain. Very strange," and then she insists, "I wanted some trace of them to be left behind" (*ST*, 137). In several stories, the narrator describes the life of her own condemned community, as if posthumously bearing witness to herself. The narrative voice is painfully frayed between the instance of the storyteller and the subject of her narrative: unbearably close to the horror and infinitely removed from it at the same time: "Hidden in the dark interiors of our apartments, with our faces pressed against the window panes damp from rain and our rapid breath, we, reprieved until the next time, looked out at the condemned" (*ST*, 23). The collapsing of the instance of enunciation into the diagetic space of the story produces a sense of the imminent extinction of the witness, bidding us to listen to that fragile voice intently. Witnessing is no longer a recording from an objectifying vantage point but an incessant traversing of the distance toward the event.

Such movement of approach toward the invisible Other is for Levinas the essence of the ethical relation. It is this relation of responsibility that institutes language—language that, prior to its communicative function, presupposes an interlocutor and an eagerness to listen. The first-person narrator in Fink's stories is also an astute listener. Prior to reconstituting the others' lives in her language, she turns an ear toward the voice of the Other and listens with patience, allowing the stories to reach her from a distant shore. The act of listening eradicates the interval between the two times, of the past events and of the witness's later account, and collapses the aesthetic distance between the horror and its description.

The witness is burdened with an impossible task of searching for disappearing traces. A short, dramatic piece, also entitled "Traces" (from the volume *Traces*), describes a young woman's search for information about her sister. She conducts a series of interviews in the village where the sister was hiding during the war and examines what she believes was her hideout. She comes across a few clues, such as initials etched on a windowsill or scraps of a love letter, one of which indicates the hidden woman's own attempt to efface the signs of her existence: "have to wipe out every trace. I shall always" (*T*, 165). None of the pieces of information can be corroborated, and the woman's main source is a village idiot, which further undermines the validity of the clues. No one seems to be a trustworthy repository of memory, so the main character's quest for certainty is futile. Her stubborn desire to learn about her sister's fate, however, allows for the vanished life to etch itself in her speech. After the woman leaves, the villagers are recalling certain details, as if only now the girl about whom no one knew or wished to know during the Event suddenly became a presence among them. Other stories in both collections also portray survivors who are searching for their loved ones. It seems that the writer's task is analogous to these attempts, and it is invested with the same passion, devotion, love, despair, and often false hope.

Levinas emphasizes that a trace is not a cipher that the other leaves behind to be decoded. On the contrary, it reiterates in its own continuous effacement: "He who left a trace in wiping out his traces did not mean to say or do anything by the traces he left" (*TO*, 357). The erasure of traces is underscored in Fink's accounts: the witness's task is impossible from the start, not only because the murderer has destroyed the evidence of the crime, but also because during the Holocaust the only hope of survival for those in hiding was to obliterate the traces of their former lives. For instance, in the "Tenth Man," a handful of Jews who return to their native village after the liberation are unrecognizable to their former neighbors: the teacher's wife now has "a drawn face of a peasant woman" (*ST*, 103), and a dry goods merchant's features are hiding behind a perpetual smile. Ironically, only those who "lost their faces" have managed to survive. These masks also bring comfort to those who come into contact with survivors—they conceal the horror of what their owners went through, so that no questions need to be asked. Witnessing therefore becomes a quest for the face that the memory cannot conjure, as in the story "Henryk's Sister," in which a woman is searching for a glimpse of her murdered husband's features in the face of his twin sister. Levinas avers that, although in speaking I bear witness to the Other, the Other never speaks to me except as a mask. Yet in ethical speech, which designates me as a witness, I encounter the Other who is denuded of his or her image. Fink's stories are imbued with the same necessity of turning toward the Other in patience and humility, of enduring the pain afflicting me from behind the mask. Witnessing is a movement toward an encounter with the nudity of the face.

While emphasizing the need to recuperate the victim's voice from the silence of oblivion, the narrator is also weary of language, of its betrayal in the said. Her own sentences often falter as she realizes that words circumvent the events but never palpate the horror. In the process of testifying, words acquire an uncanny quality; the equivocations and tensions in the narrative and the instability of everyday expressions point to language itself as a suspect in the crime. As the chasm between words and what is happening in the story is widening, a sense of treachery of language creeps into the simplest phrases. Even the titles of many stories are misleading: "A Spring Morning," "Description of a Morning," and "An Afternoon on the Grass," as if the reader were to expect cameos of rural tranquility rather than reports of murder. Although language as the bearer of traces is accorded such value in Fink, it is always ethically equivocal. One can shield oneself with words against horrifying truths, as is the case in the story "Description of a Morning," in which the husband protects himself with the torrents of words against his wife's reticence and her memory of their daughter who died during the couple's escape from the ghetto. Speech can subdue the horror and thus facilitate physical survival, but at the same time it may drown the voices of others.

Fink's stories are fraught with the tension between speech and silence. The inflections of silence are many—the breathless silence of the hidden, the stillness of the earth just before the thundering arrival of the cattle train. Terror and imminent death are always announced by silence; for instance, the crowds waiting for deportation or marching to the places of execution are always mute, as if their speech had already been quelled.[14] One of the ponderous tasks the witness/narrator sets for herself is to bring out these individual, very different silences and let them "speak"; to use language in such a way that it does not engulf the disastrous spaces where words break off. It is in silences penetrating, interrupting, and questioning speech that the Other leaves a trace. For Levinas, even silence between two people is a relation of speech, while only murder is the absolute cessation of speech (*TI*, 232). Murder, therefore, is always directed at language, while justice, which is "a right to speak" (*TI*, 298), consists of making the expression of silence possible. It is in this sense that ethical responsibility amounts to "the impossibility of being silent, the scandal of sincerity" (*OB*, 143).[15] The Holocaust testimony's equivocation between speech and silence underscores what Levinas calls the expressive function of language, its very signifyingness, inconvertible into concepts or categories.

By insisting on the intranslatability of the events into known categories of thought, Fink asks that we respect the absolute impenetrability of these spaces and not reduce them to comprehensible images and familiar concepts. Irreconcilable with her own life in the present, impossible to domesticate in any rational framework, the "other" time seems to painfully furrow the surface of her memory. She discovers that the task of the storyteller as witness is to allow the time of the Other to creep into the interstices of the present and inflect by its difference the complacency of memory. During the events, the victims' experience was incommensurate with known conceptual frameworks, and Fink relates the disintegration of the fundamental categories of time and space in the lives of the condemned inhabitants of the ghetto—the "new zone" indescribable in everyday language. Their time was "not measured in months and years" (*ST*, 3) but in the escalating horror of the new words such as "round-up," "*Aktion*," "deportation."[16]

According to Levinas, chronological time is inseparable from consciousness and intentionality, and as such, it can be retained in memory (*OB*, 34). He repeats, after Husserl, that memory is the essence of selfhood, anchoring the I in the temporal continuum "after the event" (*TI*, 56), but he rejects Heidegger's ontology, structured upon the axes of Being and time, and he attempts to think of time in terms of ethics.[17] Heidegger claims Being-toward-death as the underlying ontological category and the ultimate horizon of the self's (*Dasein's*) projects, but to Levinas, Dasein's primordial anxiety is secondary to an ethical time of the postponement of death, in which I have time to be for the Other and thus can enact a meaningful life (*TI*, 237). The future does not arrive into my present as a swarm of possibilities, which I can apprehend and realize, but it comes to me across the absolute divide, from the invisible shore of the Other. Thus the common time of clocks presupposes a deontological relation with the Other, since a trace of the Other points to the past that no memory can follow—an immemorial, "utterly bygone past" (*TO*, 335). In the ethical relation, I am oriented toward the time of the Other, which I cannot

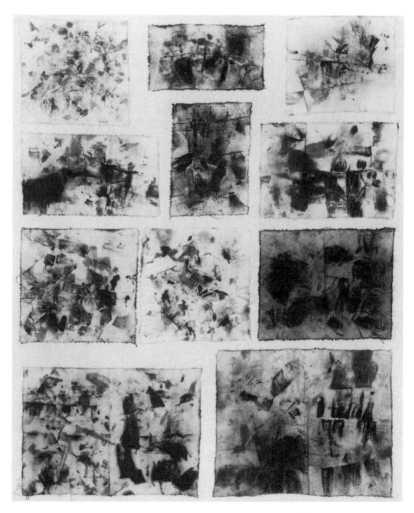

Figure 6.4 Herzl Kashetsky, *Dark Remnants*. Reproduced with permission of the artist.

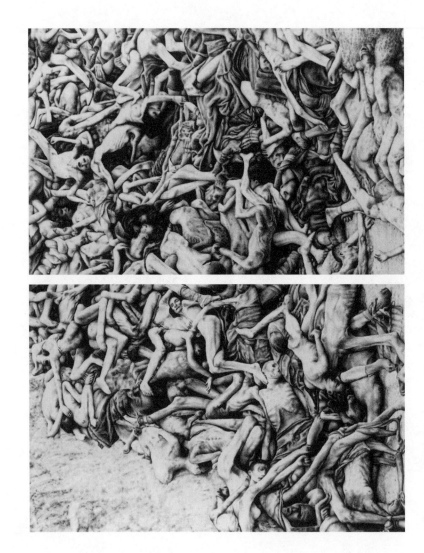

Figure 6.5 Herzl Kashetsky, *Mass Grave, Bergen Belsen* (diptych), 1995–1996. Reproduced with permission of the artist.

enter because it is unabsorbable into temporality. I would like to propose that Levinas' shattering of the temporal horizon circumscribed by the ego tensed on itself allows us to think of the self who, in her language, bears responsibility for the past in which she may not have been born and for the future in which she may no longer sojourn. To be for the Other means to be for what was before me and for what will come after me, and to which my language bears witness—the imperative particularly resonant in Holocaust literature. This entails that a work "spoken" in ethical language is undertaken as a passage to the time of the Other. In this movement, I am always already bereft of my work, since from the moment of its origin in me it is destined for the Other, for the time without me.

The past measured by chronology will eventually be assembled in the annals of history but, as Levinas insists, "When man truly approaches the other, he is uprooted from history" (*TI*, 52). Historiography abounds in examples of how the new generations appropriate for themselves the works of the dead, and the conquerors usurp the monopoly on historical truth. "The judgement of history," says Levinas, "is always pronounced *in absentia*" (*TI*, 242). It is only because ethics overflows recorded history, however, that beings "can speak rather than lend their lips to an anonymous utterance of history. . . . Peace is produced as this aptitude for speech" (*TI*, 23). Although it is incumbent on us that we continue to gather factual knowledge, recorded history will continue as a series of betrayals, while justice will write itself as traces, as equivocation and disturbance in the midst of evidence. It is imperative, then, to continue writing and rewriting history, so that the invisible can inscribe itself on its pages.

In "Nocturnal Variations on a Theme," Ida Fink speculates imaginatively on what it might have been like for the inmate to walk away from a concentration camp. Yet in each version of the event, through a series of detours, the prisoner returns to the camp, as if in a nightmare. The momentary exhilaration of freedom, the "almost winged step" (*T*, 109) toward a new life, invariably crumbles in front of the gate with the sign *Arbeit Macht Frei*. Even if the prisoner is now free to go wherever he wishes, he will remain forever imprisoned behind the barbed wire of memory. Even if the writer summons all of the powers of literature, she will still be unable to free him, and this failure marks the ultimate limit of artistic imagination. Yet it is imperative that a book in which I bear witness should be written, even if I am dispossessed of my work by the Other who has summoned me to pursue this task. Written in ethical language, my work is destined to "a history that I cannot foresee" (*TI*, 227), because it goes toward the Other in radical generosity, beyond aesthetic enjoyment and self-gratification. Justice requires representation in the said, in the book, in the image, despite the betrayal. The question asked by literature and art of the Holocaust is, invariably, how to reduce that betrayal. It is this "perpetual postponing of the hour of treason" that makes for the "infinitesimal difference between man and non-man" (*TI*, 35).

To conclude, I would like to briefly look at two Holocaust paintings by Jewish-Canadian artist Herzl Kashetsky. None of the painter's immediate relatives were directly affected by the atrocities of the Holocaust, yet for more than two decades, Kashetsky has been exploring the Holocaust themes in his art with deep spiritual commitment, and his Holocaust paintings have travelled as an exhibition entitled "A Prayer for the Dead." Kashetsky describes his work on the subject as "a trace of the event," giving "mute witness to horror," and commanding the viewer never to forget.[18] Most of Kashetsky's Holocaust art is in the convention of photorealism, so one is struck by the canvas entitled *Dark Remnants*, which, in its appearance of abstract expressionism, seems oddly out of place (see Figure 6.4). During his talk at the opening of the exhibition in Halifax, the artist explained that *Dark Remnants* presented scraps of cloth mounted on canvas, left over from the work entitled *Mass Grave, Bergen Belsen*, 1995–1996 (see Figure 6.5).[19] They were used to remove excess paint, and the artist simply could not bring himself to discard these material remains of his two-year labor on the horrifying diptych. These remnants became the relics recording the artist's approach toward the past in which the victims he was painting had suffered. Within the Levinasian framework of this discussion, Kashetsky, from the generation that has not been directly affected by the Holocaust, has become a witness, exposing himself without reserve to the Other, in vulnerability and pain. As Levinas contends in *Otherwise Than Being*, "the corporeality of the subject is the pain of the effort" (*OB*, 50).

Representation in the image, as understood by traditional aesthetics, allows for contemplative distance and mediation, which blunt the shock of the encounter with the Other. Bearing witness in the incessant search for the disappearing trace, however, occurs in proximity with the Other, where the impact of the Other on my life is crushing. The ethical witness does not bring the Other into a theme, an image, the light of the day. The I, as "here I am" for the Other, is a witness "whose truth is not the truth of representation" (*OB*, 146). The Levinasian art of disappearing traces radically calls into question traditional aesthetics: when Saying unsays the said, representation is undone by the trace which signifies as obsession, which inscribes itself in consciousness as interruption, frustration, and discomfort, and which registers itself in the vulnerability of my body, the beating of my heart, "even to the mucous membranes of my lungs" (*OB*, 107). It is this palpable breathlessness of Holocaust literature and art, the heavy stamp it leaves on those who choose to respond, that marks it as a unique challenge to what Levinas condemns as the hold of representation over ethics in the West.

NOTES

1. Emmanuel Levinas, *Otherwise Than Being or Beyond Essence*, trans. Alphonso Lingis (Pittsburgh: Duquesne University Press, 1998), 91. Hereafter cited in the text as *OB*.

2. See, for example, David H. Hirsch, *The Deconstruction of Literature: Criticism After Auschwitz* (Hanover: Brown University Press, 1991).

3. In "Writing of the Holocaust: Claud Lanzmann's Shoah," Jill Robbins discusses this episode at length in the context of Levinas' ethics. Robbins argues that Lanzmann's film is ethically significant, because it resists the reduction of the Holocaust to mere representation and thus implicates the viewer in the moral task of bearing witness. *Prooftexts* 7 (1987): 249–58.

4. Ida Fink, *A Scrap of Time* [Skrawek czasu], trans. Madeline Levine and Francine Prose (Evanston, Ill.: Northwestern University Press, 1987), 135. Hereafter cited in the text as *ST*.

5. Ida Fink was born in 1921 in Zbaraż, today's Ukraine. Before the war, she studied at the musical conservatory in her hometown. She fled the ghetto with her sister in 1942, equipped with fake birth certificates obtained by her father, and volunteered for work in Germany. She described her wartime ordeal of double identity, betrayals, and constant fear of being discovered in a semi-autobiographical novel *The Journey* [Podróż], trans. Joanna Weschler and Francine Prose (New York: Farrar Straus Giroux, 1992). Fink emigrated to Israel in 1957, and although she speaks Hebrew, all of her writings are in Polish. Despite international acclaim (*A Scrap of Time* received the Anne Frank Award in Holland), her works are relatively little known in Poland, and judging by the paucity and general tone of the reviews, their reception there has been lukewarm. Fink insists that all of her short stories are reconstructions of true events that she witnessed or heard about.

6. From Ziva Amishai-Maisels, *Depiction and Interpretation: The Influence of the Holocaust on Visual Arts* (Oxford: Pergamon Press, 1993), fig. 68. Hereafter cited in the text as *DI*.

7. *Depiction and Interpretation*, fig. 556.

8. For a discussion of Levinas' ethics in the context of Holocaust literature, see David G. Myers, "Responsible for Every Single Pain: Holocaust Literature and the Ethics of Interpretation," *Comparative Literature* 51 (Fall 1999). Myers turns to Levinas' notion of the absolute responsibility to and for the Other in order to argue that any response to Holocaust texts is always already ethical before it is interpretive. See also David Patterson's *Along the Edge of Annihilation: The Collapse and Recovery of Life in the Holocaust Diary* (Seattle: University of Washington Press, 1999) and the collection *Ethics after the Holocaust: Perspectives, Critiques, and Responses*, ed. John K. Roth (St. Paul, Minn.: Paragon House, 1999).

9. Emmanuel Levinas, *Totality and Infinity: An Essay on Exteriority*, trans. Alfonso Lingis (Pittsburgh: Duquesne University Press, 1986), 199. Hereafter cited in the text as *TI*.

10. In 1934, Levinas published "Reflections on the Philosophy of Hitlerism," which was one of the first attempts to understand the phenomenon of National Socialism. Even then, Levinas insisted that Hitlerism was not an anomaly but a menace deeply rooted in the mentality of the West. Therefore, it required philosophical inquiry and refutation.

11. In her essay "Aesthetic Totality and Ethical Infinity: Levinas on Art" [*L'Esprit créateur* 35: 3 (Fall 1995): 66–79], Jill Robbins argues that although Levinas denounces play, which is a central category of aesthetics, and excludes a possibility of ethical images, on the performative level of his own ethical discourse, his writings point to a way of conceptualizing the ethical and the aesthetic together, that is, of thinking the transcendence of the Other in a literary text. See also Jill Robbins, *Altered Readings: Levinas and Literature* (Chicago: University of Chicago Press, 1999). I also develop the idea of a Levinasian aesthetics, grounded in the responsibility to the Other, in my essay "Ethical Figures of Otherness: Jean-Luc Nancy's Sublime Offering and Levinas' Gift for the Other," in *Future Crossings*, ed. Krzysztof Ziarek (Evanston, Ill.: Northwestern University Press, 2000).

12. Emmanuel Levinas, "The Trace of the Other," *Deconstruction in Context*, ed. Mark C. Taylor (Chicago: University of Chicago Press, 1969), 352. Hereafter cited in the text as *TO*.

13. Ida Fink, *Traces*, trans. Philip Boehm and Francine Prose (New York: Henry Holt and Company, 1998), 63. Hereafter cited in the text as *T*.

14. For an extended discussion of the uses of silence in Fink's stories, see Marek Wilczyński, "Trusting the Words: Paradoxes of Ida Fink," *Modern Language Studies* 24: 4 (1994), 25–38.

15. The ambivalent dynamic between speech and silence has been a constant theme in Holocaust literature, art, and criticism. We recall that, immediately after the war, many writers turned to awed silence—the silence of biblical Aaron after the death of his sons, *va-yidom Aharon*—as the only appropriate response to the unspeakable horror. A group of German writers (such as Martin Walser and Peter Hamm) stopped writing altogether, and many others heeded George Steiner's famous remark that, "The world of Auschwitz lies outside speech as it lies outside reason" (George Steiner, "K." *Language and Silence* (New York: Atheneum, 1966), 123). They soon realized, however, that Europe was cloaking itself also in a silence of indifference, the silence that leads to forgetting and justifies ignorance. Elie Wiesel, who himself remained silent for ten years, began to ask for words that would testify to the crime. In 1990, he commented in an interview that now, when the floodgates of memory are finally open, "The problem is not to choose between speech and silence, but to try to make sure that speech does not become the enemy of silence. We must strive for the harmony of the two."

16. Polish Holocaust scholar Barbara Engelking examines the phenomenon of a different experience of time by the Holocaust victims in her study *Czas przestał dla mnie istnieć* [Time ceased to exist for me] (Warsaw: IfiS PAN, 1996).

17. Levinas pondered the relation between time and ethics already in 1947 in his essay "Le temps et l'autre," which subsequently became part of his book *Le temps et l'autre* (Paris: Fata Morgana, 1979), translated into English by Richard A. Cohen as *Time and the Other* (Pittsburgh: Duquesne University Press, 1987).

18. These comments are excerpted from a catalogue essay by Tom Smart, from the Beaverbrook Art Gallery in Fredricton, New Brunswick.

19. The artist did the oil painting, in two panels, through the period of 1995–1996. I would like to thank Herzl Kashetsky for his comments and clarifications and for permission to use the images of his work in this chapter.

CHAPTER 7

Poetry, Theology, and Ethics: A Study in Paul Célan

Martin Rumscheidt

"... der Tod ist ein Meister aus Deutschland"

"Passing through the thousand darknesses of deathbringing speech"

—Paul Célan

I

The above two statements by Jewish poet Paul Célan are brought together as an attempt to discern the call for a theology "after Auschwitz." I belong to a people who almost succeeded in their determination to "eradicate" in Europe those whom it designated as "the Others." My reflections on Célan's statements represent a theological attempt to bear respectful and nonviolent witness to the existence of those "Others." There is a dilemma in simultaneously claiming the Christian commandments, "Love God with all your heart, soul, and mind," and "Love your neighbor because she/he is like yourself." The disconcerting question that faces me is this: Can Christian theology so reconstruct itself after the Shoah, that in claiming the commandment "Love God with all your heart, soul, and mind," its construction of "Otherness" does not belie the second and equally important one: "Love your neighbor because she/he is like yourself?" In 1955, Theodor Adorno said that writing poems after Auschwitz is barbaric; is this also true for theology?

This chapter addresses the question by relating theology and literature and begins by elucidating what such a relation might be and what it looks like. It then examines Paul Célan's *Todesfuge*, from which the first statement is drawn. Finally, the poem is brought into conversation with "theology."

117

II

At this point, three observations are necessary. First, the conviction that Auschwitz signals the collapse of Western value systems and epistemic structures is foundational for this chapter. Second, the symbiotic relation of ethics and aesthetics is so devastatingly affected by the reality of the death camps that it may be irreparable. Third, since the Enlightenment, theology, in its form as an institutionalized and academic undertaking, has distanced itself—to its detriment—from the aesthetic, and in so doing has undermined the power of the ethical.

Institutionalized theology in the Christian West, particularly in modern times, has reduced literature, as well as visual art, to the level of a decorative servant. Under the rigorous control of theology, it was, at best, to provide a subsidiary or complementary interpretation to theology. As it had done for other domains of the life of the spirit, the Enlightenment loosened the bonds of theology's tutelage over literature. This resulted in the development of literature into something of quasi-religious significance. It is constructive to recall, for example, how the work of Johann Wolfgang von Goethe was interpreted by historian and theologian Adolf von Harnack (1851–1930), or the place the poet's famous *Faust* came to occupy in anthroposophy.[1]

And this is no mere mystification on the part of people for whom "established" religion no longer sufficed; literature took over, reflected on the substance of theology, and secularized it. One thinks of the poets Hölderlin (1770–1843) or Rilke (1875–1926) and how the former became the focus for Martin Heidegger's twentieth-century philosophy of Being. [It was Hölderlin who said "but what abides is founded by poets."] In my view, a false orientation in, if not the failure of, theology itself is the reason for literature becoming the "secular" bearer of religious substance. In the West, the religion that predominated for well over sixteen centuries was Christianity in its diverse denominations. Few of them can escape the indictment that they have failed the human being in the sense that they have held the human being in bondage. By this, I mean that religion was presented in a language of dominance most of the time. The most intense form of dominance is theology, a discourse among specialists often—and all too often—mysterious and esoteric, inaccessible to nearly the whole population. Much of regular preaching, too, was in the language of control: control both of the listening congregation and of the sacred. Even the reformative attempts to stop such domestication turned too easily into endeavors to coerce human beings into the petty orderliness of hierarchy, thereby enabling diverse secular and ecclesial orders of domination to maintain and strengthen themselves. The way the church presented religion, namely, by "predigesting" reality for people, has failed the human being, individually and collectively. What is named traditionally "The Word of God" is something "literary": it is a written and spoken communication. When transformed into a language of dominance, it becomes not what its substance is continuously asserted to be, namely, the liberation of people; instead, it cements their being in tutelage, blocking their coming of age. The Enlightenment's cry, "*sapere aude*," dare to use your reason, persuaded its followers to substitute "the Good, the Beautiful, and the True" for "religion," if they did not see art as religion itself. However this development is to be judged, the Enlightenment bequeathed its Western children the basic conviction that the aesthetic is a means of humanization.

In a radio broadcast, aired in the late 1960s, Nobel Laureate Heinrich Böll (1917–1985) said this:

> Literature and art respect . . . human beings in their lostness. That is why [literature and art] can never be optimistic, whereas religion must be, thus [making] art and literature inhumane. [We human beings] are qualified by mourning, by love, and by transitoriness. [Literature] proclaims this perduring transitoriness. Creating, . . . painting, . . . composing, . . . writing a poem or even prose . . . are themselves erotic processes that create relation; initially, an erotic relation between artist and artifact. . . . And the eros that comes into being here can, of course, also create a relation to human beings, possibly to God or the devil. . . . Now, it is my conviction that authors and artists, all creative people must enter into a relation of equality with the non-privileged, so that the art that is created does not become a domain for the educated elite, for that only turns art into a pseudo-religious esotericism.

The cult of the genius, the "great men" (Adolf von Harnack is an example of this "cult") who characterized the West's nineteenth century and its pseudo-religion, needed to be resisted with the ethical imperatives of *equality*. To resist in such a manner, Böll continues, is

> the task of the twentieth century artist to create it. No more elitist notion! . . . Religion, the churches and denominations are bankrupt because what they wanted was dominance. They existed by authoritarian means, falsely believing that religion was transferable and could be passed on like an inheritance. [As a result of the collapse of religion caused by this false belief, the aesthetic] is put into a position that it really cannot defend: it becomes religion, that is, the only expression of the Word, barely audible and barely understandable, in the midst of the corruption of God's Word by its representatives. . . . It might just be that it is precisely a decidedly non-Christian, that is, anti-Christian, even blasphemous literature that leads forward into humanization and creates the human being who can be addressed with the Word of the God of which it is said that it became itself human.[2]

Without expressly saying so, Böll describes the process that became so utterly unmasked in the Shoah: the inability of religion to provide through its institutionalized and "scientific" media an ethics of resistance, that is, an ethics *for* human beings. For those media were elitist, readily amenable to the elitism of the planners and practitioners of the *Endlösung*.[3] This elistism is what I called earlier the false orientation in and the failure of theology. And while Heinrich Böll directly names the elitism of religion "established" in the church institution, he also identifies it, albeit in its varying form, in the aesthetic domain. Here he provides an insightful answer to the question of why it was in the nation of Goethe, Bach, and Beethoven that the Holocaust came into being. This creation of German will, organization, and technology starkly manifests the climax of a century-and-a-half-long process, namely, the utter impotence of aesthetics and religion to concretize themselves in an ethic of resistance, perhaps even to imagine one at all!

One dimension of this impotence is what was earlier called the language of dominance: the language of purpose, control, and possession. In such language, relationships are seen not in terms of equality but of hierarchy. Hierarchy presupposes separation of those "above" from those "below," the "privileged" from the "nonprivileged." It is a language of dualisms. Its opposite would be an "anarchistic" one; it is close to what Böll refers to as non-Christian, anti-Christian, and blasphemous, the literature that may initiate humanization. It follows that stringent philosophical or scholastic conceptuality, as we know it in the Western tradition, is not expected to provide us with "anarchistic" language.

German feminist theologian and poet Dorothee Sölle argues that in shunning every attempt to impose "definitions," poetic language is able to render meaning audible and resonant precisely because of its narrative freedom and the plethora of linguistic means available to it. In particular, she names those used in mysticism: frequent repetition, comparison, exaggeration, hyperbole, antithesis, and paradox.[4] When theology and literature sever their relationship, both suffer. In that separation, theology seeks exile in "science," which, she argues, is finally something that is not of ultimate concern to human beings. What theology produced for the general population—rules and regulations, ecclesiastical ordinances, and catechetical pronouncements, declaring them to be for the good of the people—turned out to be detrimental to the existential nature of religion. The deep insights of theology—and indeed there are such— rarely found their way to the everyday world where human beings live much of their lives; rather, they were met with suspicion. This was less the result of the lack of interest in those insights than it was of the nature of theological language. Today, the language of dominance is being exposed as one that does not serve the emancipation and humanization of human beings, particularly the "non-elite." Thus the broadly "aesthetic," even in its weaknesses, is seen to be more credible and, for that reason, more decisive and significant.

I argue for a strong relation between theology and literature, for their mutual benefit. The separation of the domains of aesthetics, politics, and religion is the dogma of modernity, the modernity that Auschwitz exposed radically. Existing side by side in a spiritual "apartheid," a politics-free religion ends up venerating power and its idols, a religion-free politics decays into despising humanity itself, and an aesthetics-free politics and religion are mere utilitarian instruments of "principalities and powers" such as "globalization," as Victor Li describes it later in this book, or the "new European order," depicted in Alyss and Heim's work referred to above.

> Theology and literature is a *cantus firmus*, a lead-tune, in my life. . . . [My theological interest in literature] was aroused by the numerous traces of religious language in fiction writing that does not regard itself as religious at all; . . . In the course of a secularization process, the language of Christian faith has come to be at the disposition of indirect, metaphorical speech. It has taken on most diverse functions, anywhere between blasphemy and sacralization. It is the emancipatory use of religious language in fiction writing that justifies not only the theologian, but also the literary scholar to ask about the theological implications of such acceptance and appropriation. (*ALT*, 207)

She speaks of the damage that the lack of poetry has inflicted on the theology of the academy. For poetry can make, and has made, visible the seriousness and playfulness, that is, the beauty of theology.

> This kind of poetry is no luxury item; it is bread. It turns our planet, ever so beloved in spite of everything, more and more into home. . . . [P]oetry creates a boundary-dissolving freedom, . . . I really do not believe in the modern program of *poésie pure.* More precisely: wherever it happens successfully that the unmixed purity of the beautiful becomes sound and language, poetry is no longer "pure" and "for itself." Paul Célan's lyrical work serves as an example of how precisely, in most sparse, often hermetic language, the reality of the world of the extermination camp enters and the promises of tradition shine forth. When I learned Greek, the concept *kalonkagathon* became very dear to my heart. In my seventeen-year-old unintelligence, I wondered how the Greeks could take two words that for us have nothing to do with each other, and turn them into the one word: beauty-good. Where on earth would one find aesthetics and ethics in the same dish? . . . In order really to do theology we need a different language. Poetry and liberation is a topic central to my life.[5]

Today many of us experience our language as horribly corrupted, serving ever more to obfuscate and stupidify than to emancipate. For example, the term *collateral damage* is a manifestation of the triumph of the Nazis' language of instrumentality, of death. It is particularly the vocabulary of feelings that has sustained serious damage, I think especially the feelings of anger, revulsion, abhorrence, and shame. They are for me at the heart of every reflection by a German and Christian like me, who tries to think at all after Auschwitz. If

Karl Marx's observation is correct, that shame is a revolutionary feeling, then that word and others like those mentioned above need to be saved from the destruction of language. It is then that the destruction of human beings in language itself may be brought to an end, and we can begin anew to recognize ourselves in language, see again images of humanization, and become respectful of "the Other."

In one of her "eight theses on the criteria of theology's interest in literature," Dorothee Sölle states that theology needs to set itself apart critically only from that kind of art that denies what concerns human beings unconditonally and what, in so doing, denies the wholeness of the human being. For both theology and art, banality is a mortal danger. What is significant for theology in literature is what opens us, lifts us above the assurances of the known, confronts us with our own clichés, unmasks us, and transforms our relation to the world, to the Other, thereby transforming *us* (*ALT*, 211). In other words, the symbiosis of aesthetics and ethics and of poetry and theology needs to be rewoven if theology is to be reborn as a means of humanization, of finding and expressing the human being after Auschwitz—if this is even at all possible. For me, a child of Nazi Germany, if theology, my vocation, is to have any life whatsoever, the human being I need to find and hear above all is Jewish.

III

Paul Célan's *Todesfuge*[6] and its terse declaration that "Death is a master from Germany" situates me before the truth but in a place opposite to that from which Célan uttered those words. Célan experienced "the master from Germany" in the brutalization and degradation of his own family and people. As a German, not quite ten years old when Auschwitz was liberated by Soviet troops, I have "experienced" the master from my own home and native land and confront the *Meister* in what turns out to be a lifelong process wherein shame and humiliation have come to be decisive and possibly recreative feelings and motivations.

I do not here attempt a literary analysis of *Todesfuge*: John Felstiner has provided an excellent one in the chapter "A Fugue after Auschwitz (1944–1945)," to which I am gratefully indebted (*PC*, 22–41). However, I draw on his analysis to identify the literary, that is, the *aesthetic*, elements that summon theological reflection or imagination into an awareness of what Emmanuel Levinas calls "*la trace de l'autre*" which, understood in this context, is the trace and presence of the Jewish human being and a response that is respectful and nonviolent to the "Otherness" in which she or he is before me. In different words, I seek through *Todesfuge* to "do theology" in which, released by anger, revulsion, abhorrence, and shame, both personal and collective, an ethic may come into being that resists the "*Meister aus Deutschland*" in the service of life.

I seek to say something here that I believe is embodied in the beautiful word *tikkun olam* [mending the world].

Paul Célan (1920–1970) *wrote in German*! It was his mother's language. "And can you bear, Mother, as *oh, at home,* once on a time, the gentle, the German, the pain-laden rhyme?" (*PC*, 24). It is also mine: the language that articulated the death of his people in Europe, the language in which "the word was made flesh and, having become flesh, was eventually turned into heaps of cadavers."[7] Célan wrote in the language in which burned the fire that buried so many in "a grave in the air" (*PC*, 31). That language passed "through the thousand darknesses of deathbringing speech," which meant that his own writing also had to pass through those very darknesses (*PC*, xv). But "passing through," Célan's poetry also testifies to life: lost, taken away, clung to, longed for, and the like. "Like many people who lived through those years, he gave almost no factual testimony about them—which gives his poetry a testimonial charge" (*PC*, 22).

What first drew my attention to *Todesfuge* was not the statement "*der Tod ist ein Meister aus Deutschland.*" When in a public lecture the German essayist Walter Jens spoke of the poetry of Paul Célan, he cited another line from that poem: "*dann steigt ihr als Rauch in die Luft dann habt ihr ein Grab in den Wolken da liegt man nicht eng*" ("you'll rise then as smoke to the sky you'll have a grave then in the clouds there you won't lie too cramped") (*PC*, 31). According to Jens, for Célan, that line was not poetic license, not a metaphor. It struck me upon hearing this how radically the fact of Auschwitz must have affected the Jews' sense of identity, when the preceding generations that gave them their roots are buried in "a grave in the clouds." For example, in Célan's sentence, Jens shows how Auschwitz had radically touched the foundations of the Jewish culture. It was then that I first asked whether Adorno's dictum, cited above, did not also apply to the pursuit I was preparing myself for: theology.

Felstiner interprets Célan's work as an attempt to uphold humanness (*PC*, 15). It is the attempt on Célan's part to go on living himself and not to lose sight of what is good, true, and beautiful; or, in the words of Dorothee Sölle, cited earlier, not to lose sight of what may yet turn our world into "home," the exact opposite of "*l'univers concentrationnaire,*" the "concentrationary universe" of the Nazis (*PC*, 27).

> Out of those months that saw the war ending and its Jewish catastrophe revealed, Paul [Célan] wrote one lyric that drives far beyond private anguish, forming the benchmark for poetry "after Auschwitz": "Todesfuge". . . The *Guernica* of postwar European literature . . . The prolonged impact that "Todesfuge" has had stems partly from its array of historical and cultural signals—some overt and direct, some recondite or glancing. Practically every line embeds verbal material from the disrupted world to which this poem

bears witness. From music, literature, and religion and from the camps themselves we find discomforting traces of Genesis, Bach, Wagner, Heinrich Heine, the tango, and especially Faust's heroine Margareta, alongside the maiden Shulamith from the Song of Songs. To realize these traces in translating Célan's verse can identify the poem with its indictment of so-called Judeo-Christian culture. (*PC*, 26–27)

According to Felstiner, by the latter part of 1944, Célan was apprised of the fact that Jews were forced to play dance tunes or to sing nostalgic songs, while other Jews were forced to dig graves. When the poem first appeared in print, it was in a Romanian translation; the magazine *Contemporanul* published it in May 1947 under the title "Tango of Death." Felstiner explains, "For Célan to call the poem 'Death Tango' was to annul the dance that fascinated Europe during his childhood—the essence of life as urbane, graceful, nonchalant" (*PC*, 28). Camp inmates, whose highest duty, according to Jean Améry, was to die (*JSS*, 12), spoke of "Death Tango" when referring to the music that was played when other inmates were taken out to be shot (*PC*, 30). The switch to "Death Fugue" relates such music, whatever it was in each concrete case, to the music of quintessential German composer Johann Sebastian Bach, whose *Art of the Fugue* was heralded by Oswald Spengler as the pinnacle of music in the Western world, in his morphology of that world's culture *Der Untergang des Abendlandes* (1918; E.t. *The Decline of the West* 1926–1928.) Moreover, by changing the title to *Todesfuge*, Célan also annuls Nazi claims about the superiority of the Nordic race and its blue-eyed, blond-haired people. Instead, the title spells out that death, like Bach and his *Kunst der Fuge*, and like Beethoven and his *Grosse Fuge,* is a master from Germany. In the body of the poem, Célan speaks five times of "your golden hair Margareta," a totally unmistakable allusion to Goethe's *Faust*. Like death, Goethe *ist ein Meister aus Deutschland*: the eye of death, of the master from Germany; "it is blue." Death and music, death and the mathematical precision and beauty of the fugue, death and order, composition as act of aesthetic creation, and death as act of creating the super-mensch: Célan's title alone, relentlessly spelled out in the subsequent text, reveals that the music played for the inmates' death marches to the gas chambers is even more the funereal dirge of a culture in *Untergang* which, translated literally, is "going under," into its grave. Célan both undermines and simply annotates: the purely descriptive elements of this poem undermine whatever elevated sense there is about German culture ordering life. This is depicted equally in the gloomy phrase, repeated three times, "*da liegt man nicht eng*" ("there you won't lie too cramped") (*PC*, 31). The same precision that formed Bach's fugues as well as the automobiles of Mercedes-Benz or BMW calculated the "housing" of inmates in those relentless rows of bunks that one may still see today in Auschwitz-Birkenau: there even death happened according to strict rules of order. The "grave shovelled in the air," the "cemetery" of those gassed in the "showers" and reduced in the crematoria to smoke and ashes is, of course, such that no one lies too cramped. But the "order" of the "final resting place" itself collapses here into the disorder of the very "no place" of the air, annulling even the "order" of death.

Finally, what is the object of the first statement cited in this chapter's epigraph: *der Tod ist ein Meister aus Deutschland*? As Felstiner points out, "*Meister* can designate God, Christ, rabbi, teacher, champion, captain, owner, guildsman, master of arts, of theology, labor-camp overseer, musical maestro, 'master' race, not to mention Goethe's *Wilhelm Meister* and Wagner's *Meistersinger von Nürnberg*, which carries overtones of the 1935 Nuremberg racial laws and the post-war trials. Any other choice but 'master' would lose the loaded sense of *Meister*" (*PC*, 39). The sentence is repeated four times in the last thirteen lines—themselves a fugue-like structure. The whole poem is a fugue, and the basic melody line is "death is a master from Germany." The repetition of *der Tod ist ein Meister aus Deutschland* carries those who hear or read it into the thousand darknesses of deathbringing speech.

For me, personally, the darkness of this deathbringing speech looms largest in the final two lines: "*dein goldenes Haar Margarete dein aschenes Haar Sulamith.*" Felstiner leaves them untranslated. The golden hair of Margareta, the pure-blooded Aryan woman, is contrasted to the hair of Shulamith, "ashen," turned into ashes. "Instead of a promising Biblical parallelism, the figures of Margareta and Shulamith undercut each other—*dein goldenes Haar . . . dein aschenes Haar*. The German and Jewish ideals will not coexist. . . . Paul Célan's fugue runs out on [the Hebrew] name that resonates as strangely in German as it does in English, and which preempts them both. Darkened by ash, 'Shulamith' ends the poem holding onto what Nazism tried to erase: a rooted identity. Archaic, inalienable, she has the last word, not to mention the silence after" (*PC*, 40–41). Is Felstiner's conclusion true: that German and Jewish ideals will not coexist? Even though the Nazis did not utterly succeed in erasing the rooted identity of Jews, such an identity now does include that rootedness in the graves in the air. And is the silence after the last word the silence imposed by deathbringing speech?

IV

On that desperate morning of May 27, 1096, hundreds of Jews in the city of Mainz, having sought refuge in the Bishop's Court from the approaching hordes of the First Crusade, chose to end their lives *al kiddush hashem*, "for the sanctity of the divine name." Soon after, in deep despair, a survivor exclaimed, "My eyes dissolve in tears. Torah, now that your wise women and men are gone, who will lift you up?"[8] Eight and a half centuries later, that question was repeated:

"Torah, who is left to lift you up?" In the presence of that question, Christians need to keep silent, although it is a question that they dare not let disappear from their horizon. A question to which they *do* need to seek the answer sounds more like this: Can entering into the guilt and shame of Christianity's complicity in anti-Judaism and antisemitism and its deepest, most horrible abyss in Auschwitz lead Christians to a conversion that may create a new and respectful beholding of Jewish "Otherness" and, in metaphorical language, a new turning toward Jerusalem?

In my epistemological endeavor, I am guided by Dietrich Bonhoeffer's insistence that understanding cannot be separated from the existence in which it was arrived at. In addition, my theological hermeneutic was shaped by a small group of German theologians, of whom the poet Erich Fried, anti-fascist, Jew, and refugee from Nazism, once said that the fire that consumed the houses of God, albeit gone out long ago, still burns for them, even though they were not their houses of God.

Once the Christian concepts of repentance and conversion have been freed from the intentionality of sustaining the status quo of dominance, they may assist in the conversion of theology. In the face of the realism painted in Célan's *Todesfuge*, realism in and for theology can only mean turning back, changing ways and thinking on the basis of such turning and changing. In different words, to be converted, theology needs to incorporate anger, abhorrence, revulsion, and shame into its *method* and let them function destructively and constructively within itself. And that means that after it leaves the house of "scientific" and traditional institutionalized theology, its deepest insights may then also become accessible and helpful to the many who sought their new orientation in art rather than in religion.

> What are we to do . . . after Auschwitz? This continues to be the most haunting and, at the same time, the most impotent question. . . . Another question torments us as well: are we really at the place yet where we can discuss practical consequences? Is it not rather that Auschwitz is only just now beginning to enter our consciousness, that particularly we older ones are only just now ready to let the facts of Auschwitz enter our inner being, prepared only just now to look our guilt and complicity in the face? . . . But we do not want to relegate the question of what we are to do to the end of the line. We want to begin with it. But we ought to realize that whatever we might possibly do today, after Auschwitz, does not remotely come close to what Auschwitz means for us today. For Auschwitz stands before us as judgment on our Christianity, on the manner of how we were and are Christians; furthermore—seen with the eyes of the victims of Auschwitz—as a judgment of Christianity itself. Auschwitz stands before us as a call to conversion. Not only our behaviour is in need of change but our faith itself. In addition to ethical consequences, Auschwitz is to bring about faith consequences. Auschwitz constrains us to hear God's word

utterly differently from how we heard it before Auschwitz. . . . What is to be done after Auschwitz presupposes nothing other than our willingness to become aware of what has become in our remembrance of the victims who remained in Auschwitz, what has become of those who, incomprehensibly, escaped the Holocaust with their lives and, finally, what has become of us ourselves, what has happened within ourselves, the people who were and are closer to the perpetrators than to the victims. . . . And that brings us to what Christians can and must do first after Auschwitz. Christians must keep open the wounds. More precisely: they must not blind themselves to the fact that the wounds bleed as before. . . . How long Auschwitz is the present, we do not know. We know only that we must be present to it for as long as it is the present—not only in the memory alone but in its surviving victims and in the daughters and sons marked by their having to survive. Without this, we flee from the present. To keep ourselves equal to the present: that is the first thing we ought to do after Auschwitz.[9]

Todesfuge enables such "capacity for the present" insofar as, through its invocation of "the grave in the air," it firmly holds the hearer and reader before the severe challenge that not everything that happened decades ago is now in the past. Through its concluding juxtaposition of Margareta and Shulamith, of *goldenes* and *aschenes Haar*, "a cord that makes discord, a coda with no closure" (*PC*, 40), it blocks any attempt at cheap and false reconciliation and forgiveness; here, "making up" is unmasked as an ideological weapon of an unconverted and unrepentant status quo. In fact, Célan shows how in themselves these two important theological/religious concepts are a subterfuge when wielded by the dominant elite.

Our century's murders of Jews, what gave rise to and what followed from them, for which theology and church are accountable, are the signs of our times that make every theology utterly questionable in a manner hitherto unknown. . . . Slowly, very slowly there emerges the reflection of how deeply Christians are entangled in guilt as a result of the anti-Judaic elements of the New Testament's preaching of Christ, through the way that preaching was interpreted in the church's dogmas and theologies and how in the course of a millennium and a half the church made practical use of those elements in the Western world and, finally, through the church's failure to offer resistance against the crimes that rested on these elements and their interpretation. . . . As the Jews were abandoned, so was the action of divine election, the covenant and faithfulness of the God of Abraham, Isaac, and Jacob, the father of Jesus Christ; God was assaulted and denied in the center of his self-manifestation as the true and living God. But that means that Auschwitz has its own theological dimension. In its existence to date, theology is culpable and subjected to divine affliction. If we seek to remain theologians "before God," theologians before the living God, then we must not retreat before the doubtfulness of the theological enterprise posed by the historically given, concrete signs of our times. And that means: we have to fashion a particular consciousness from that doubtfulness.[10]

Such a consciousness begins when theology incriminates itself with Auschwitz, with what gave rise to and followed from it, and to take upon itself the weight of this incomprehensible and irreparable horror as an element constitutive of both its method and its substance.

Célan's *Todesfuge* rightly awaits the day when the Shoah becomes a component in and of Christian and theological identity. As I see it, a renewed endeavor of relating hermeneutically literature and theology, or in our specific discussion, Célan's *Todesfuge* and a Christian theology that shuns the contentment of the bystanders who saw the boycott of Jewish stores and workshops in April 1933, the passing of the Nuremberg Laws in 1935, and Kristallnacht in November 1938, and knew of the Shoah to which these events led with predictable logic, may perhaps allow theology to hope for something once again, if it may hope at all.

Heinrich Böll's assessment may be true that theology has failed the human being in the sense of holding in bondage and, consequently, dehumanizing the human being. If so, then theology stands indicted and convicted of having aided in eradicating the "traces of the Other," to use Emmanuel Levinas' phrase. The beauty of the others is destroyed by the totalitarian ethic of hierarchy, which ultimately cannot tolerate coexistence with others, whom it understands as alien, hostile, and less than human. But to reduce others to such contemptuous one-dimensionality and then to eliminate them is also to destroy one's own humanity. A theology instrumental in such development and reality may have no hope!

Doing theology "after Auschwitz" means finding a way to recover and restore our humanity, by rediscovering "the Others" as human, as beautiful. It may be that in repentance and conversion we can claim in "the Others" the neighbor, whom to love is to love one just like ourselves, whom to love is to love God, whom to love is to become and remain human.

My teacher, Karl Barth, taught us, his students, that we are human beings when we behold the other human beings and are ourselves, in turn, beheld by them, when we hear them and speak with them, when we stand with them and receive their standing with us. We are human beings when, not in coercion but in gladness, we are free to be and remain the companion of others.

NOTES

1. A highlight of Rudolf Steiner's anthroposophy was a full performance of Goethe's play *Faust* in Dornach, Switzerland.

2. Dorothee Sölle et al., eds., *Almanach für Literatur und Theologie* (Wuppertal: Peter Hammer Verlag, 1970), 97–98. Hereafter cited in the text as *ALT*.

3. See the meticulous development of this point in Götz Aly and Susanne Heim, *Vordenker der Vernichtung. Auschwitz und die Pläne für eine neue europäische Ordnung* (Hamburg: Hoffmann und Campe, 1991).

4. Dorothee Sölle, *Mystik und Widerstand. Du stilles Geschrei* (Hamburg: Hoffmann und Campe, 1997, 92). *The Silent Cry. Mysticism and Resistance*, trans. Barbara and Martin Rumscheidt (Minneapolis: Fortress Press, 2001), 64.

5. Dorothee Sölle, *Gegenwind. Erinnerungen* (Hamburg: Hoffmann und Campe, 1995), 285–86. *Against the Wind. Memoir of a Radical Christian*, trans. Barbara and Martin Rumscheidt (Minneapolis: Fortress Press, 1999), 151.

6. Paul Célan, *Gedichte in Auswahl* (Frankfurt am Main: S. Fischer Verlag, 1959), 8–9. An excellent translation is found in John Felstiner, *Paul Célan: Poet, Survivor, Jew.* (New Haven, Conn., and London: Yale University Press, 1995), 31-32. Hereafter cited in the text as *PC*. I agree with Felstiner's judgment that translating the poem's title into English, such as "Fugue of Death," "Death Fugue," or "Death's Fugue," loses the symmetry of the two words and how they make what belongs to death so visible. Cf. Felstiner, 32–33.

7. Jean Améry, *Jenseits von Schuld und Sühne. Bewältigungsversuche eines Überwältigten* (Stuttgart: Klett-Cotta, 1977), 12. *At the Mind's Limits. Contemplations by a Survivor on Auschwitz and Its Realities*, trans. Sidney and Stella Rosenfeld, (Bloomington: Indiana University Press, 1980), x. Hereafter cited in the text as *JSS*. Like Célan, Améry was a survivor and also chose to end his life. Cf. My "Dying is the Inmate's Highest Duty," in *Studies in Religion/Sciences Religieuses*, vol. 14, no. 4 (1985): 487–96.

8. Simon Hirschhorn, ed., *Tora, wer wird dich nun erheben? Religiöse Dichtungen der Juden aus dem mittelalterlichen Mainz* (Gerlangen: Verlag Lambert Schneider, 1995), 11.

9. Friedrich-Wilhelm Marquardt, "Christsein nach Auschwitz," in Friedrich-Wilhelm Marquardt and Albert Friedlander, eds., *Das Schweigen der Christen und die Menschlichkeit Gottes. Gläubige Existenz nach Auschwitz* (Munich: Chr. Kaiser Verlag, 1980), 9ff.

10. Friedrich-Wilhelm Marquardt, *Von Elend und Heimsuchung der Theologie. Prolegomena zur Dogmatik* (Munich: Chr. Kaiser Verlag, 1988), 74f.

CHAPTER 8

Between Ethics and Anguish: Feminist Ethics, Feminist Aesthetics, and Representations of Infanticide in "The Runaway Slave at Pilgrim's Point" and Beloved

Marjorie Stone

In the 1999 *PMLA* special issue on "Ethics and Literary Study," Lawrence Buell acknowledges, in a footnote, some "conspicuous omissions" in his introductory overview of "genealogical strands" within "ethically valenced inquiry." Collapsing two substantial omissions into one, he includes an undocumented reference to "the destabilization of gender categories by feminist and queer theory." Emphasizing the importance of Emmanuel Levinas to the ethical turn in literary studies, Buell subsequently alludes to Luce Irigaray's critique of Levinas' homogenizing concept of the "Other": that, as for woman as Other, Levinas "'does not note her existence.'"[1] But the existence of a well-established discourse of feminist ethics is not addressed by Buell, and there is little indication, either in his "Introduction" or in the *PMLA* collection as a whole, that feminism has significantly contributed to the resurgence of ethics within literary studies to which the special issue responds.[2] This chapter reflects theoretical contexts largely invisible in the *PMLA* issue on "Ethics and Literary Study." Drawing on the converging paradigms of feminist ethics and feminist aesthetics, I explore some of the questions generated by representations of infanticide in Elizabeth Barrett Browning's "The Runaway Slave at Pilgrim's Point" (1848) and Toni Morrison's *Beloved* (1987). I also argue that these two works share more features than one might expect, in portraying slave women who are "othered" not only by their gender and race but also by their acts.

There has been little work in either feminist ethics or feminist aesthetics directly relating to literary representations of slave infanticide. Addressing some of the reasons for this absence, I turn instead to the much greater body of feminist work that has accrued around the subject of abortion. I should make it plain at the start that I do not wish to confound abortion with infanticide. On the contrary, it is vitally important to maintain carefully reasoned distinctions at a time when, as Janet Hadley's 1996 global overview suggests, access to safe, therapeutic abortion remains unattained or under attack globally, and when new technologies are facilitating unprecedented forms of coercive reproductive control.[3] That said, I nevertheless suggest that theories of feminist ethics developed to address the complex moral questions of abortion also provide a helpful conceptual framework for approaching representations of slave infanticide. I furthermore question the relative neglect of the aesthetic in the developing work in feminist ethics and call for a more concerted analysis of the relations between feminist ethics and feminist aesthetics, between the "real" and the representational.

"IDEAL BEAUTY" AND THE "HOUSE OF ANGUISH": THRESHOLDS, QUESTIONS, AND CONTEXTS

I begin with a statue and a sonnet that have no direct relation to infanticide because, taken together, they illustrate the interlocking aesthetic and ethical regimes that writers have had to negotiate in representing the experience of slave women.

> They say ideal beauty cannot enter
> The house of anguish. On the threshold stands
> An alien Image with enshackled hands,
> Called the Greek Slave![4]

In "Hiram Powers' *Greek Slave*" (1850), a sonnet about thresholds of several kinds, Elizabeth Barrett Browning invokes the "alien Image" of a nude figure fashioned from chaste white marble that was widely exhibited by American sculptor Hiram Powers in the mid-nineteenth century (see Figure 8.1). "The ostensible subject is merely a Grecian maiden, made captive by the Turks and exposed at Constantinople, for sale," a pamphlet accompanying the exhibit stated, drawing attention to "the cross and locket visible amid the drapery" near the girl's chained hands, and presenting the Christian maiden as "a being superior to suffering": "a type of resignation, uncompromising virtue, or sublime patience."[5] Today Powers' *The Greek Slave* may seem to epitomize the triumph of safe Victorian sentiment, but in its own era, it encountered very different thresholds of acceptance.

Figure 8.1 Hiram Powers, *The Greek Slave*, 1846, marble. In the Collection of The Corcoran Gallery of Art, Washington, D.C. Gift of William Wilson Corcoran, 73.4. Reproduced by permission of The Corcoran Gallery of Art

Although Jennifer DeVere Brody claims that Powers' statue generated "unequivocal praise" and "overwhelming reverence," Jean Fagin Yellin and Joy S. Kasson have shown that it in fact provoked widespread controversy—in part because critics debated whether or not its pleasurable display of female flesh was "clothed" by its "virtuous sentiment," in part because it was appropriated by both the abolitionist and anti-abolitionist movements.[6] Frederick Douglass and Lucy Stone, for example, both used the statue as an emblem of the degradation that slavery imposed upon women. Meanwhile, anti-abolitionist newspapers mockingly observed that "no one had tried to liberate the *Greek Slave*," and one cynic noted, "[t]here were fair breasts that heaved with genuine sympathy" for the white Greek slave that "have never yet breathed a sigh for their sable sisters at the South!" Seizing upon such contradictions, John Tenniel published a parodic cartoon in *Punch* called *The Virginian Slave* when Powers' statue was exhibited during the 1851 Great Exhibition (see Figure 8.2). The cartoon was appropriated in turn by the black activist William Wells Brown, who staged a Crystal Palace demonstration in which he placed Tenniel's cartoon of a sardonically smiling black slave in front of Power's white marble and announced, "As an American fugitive slave, I place this 'Virginian Slave' by the side of the Greek slave as its most fitting companion."[7] As such incidents show, despite the transcendental aesthetic embodied in its "ideal beauty," Powers' *Greek Slave* became the focus of a storm of controversy in the politically charged world of art.

Entering this cultural debate, Barrett Browning's sonnet obliquely calls attention to what Powers' statue does *not* depict, given the norms policed by the faceless arbiters of art ("they") who have (or think they have) the power to "say" what "ideal beauty" can and cannot do. Powers hints at the probability of the Greek slave being raped by placing her chained hand over her pudenda, but he does not follow her into "the house of anguish." The "passionless perfection" of his "Image" is "Shadowed not darkened where the sill expands," the sonnet goes on to point out (in a significant choice of images). Nor does Powers portray a pubescent dark slave at the moment of sale, or such a woman being raped by a white man, even though, as someone who had lived in Cincinnati, he must have known that such acts were common events in his country. And certainly both prevailing "taste" and the limitations of his medium prevented him from portraying the experience, as opposed to the voyeuristic spectacle, of such a rape along with its aftermath in cases where it resulted in impregnation.

Powers' white, passive, mute Grecian maiden forms a strong contrast to the outspoken rebel slave Barrett Browning gives voice to—or appropriates the voice of—in "The Runaway Slave at Pilgrim's Point" (*CW*, 3: 268–75): a dramatic monologue completed in the months immediately following her marriage and flight to Italy with Robert Browning in September 1846. "I am black, I am black!" is the refrain of the nameless speaker in this monologue, whose skin is as "dark" as the "night" she has run through. Arriving as a fugitive on the

E PLVRIBVS VN

THE VIRGINIAN SLAVE.

INTENDED AS A COMPANION TO POWER'S "GREEK SLAVE."

Figure 8.2 *The Virginian Slave.* Illustration in *Punch, or the London Charivari* 20, (January–June 1851), p. 236. Wood engraving by John Tenniel. Courtesy of the Library of Congress.

shore at Pilgrim's Point, she invokes and curses the souls of the Pilgrim fathers and their "hunter sons," recalling how she was torn apart from her black lover; how she found his "blood's mark in the dust"; how she was tied up at "the flogging-place" and whipped as she "cursed" her oppressors "all round"; how she was raped, following her lover's death—as the plural form suggests, by more than one white man. "Wrong, followed by a deeper wrong!" she cries; "the white men brought the shame ere long/To strangle the sob of my agony." The bitter fruit of her rape is a white-faced child whom she stifles or strangles in turn, an act she recalls in tormented, protracted detail. The baby did not die quickly, as she first covered it up, then "twisted it round in [her] shawl": "he moaned and struggled"; "[h]e moaned and beat with his head and feet," striking his feet out against his mother's heart; "he moaned and trembled from foot to head, . . . till after a time, he lay instead/Too suddenly still and mute." If Powers' Greek slave is on the "threshold" of the "house of anguish," the runaway slave and her hapless child are fully inside it.

The attempt to portray the experience of a fugitive slave woman driven to commit infanticide in "The Runaway Slave at Pilgrim's Point" raises many questions, some of which arise with even greater intensity in reading Toni Morrison's *Beloved*. Most obviously, what right does Barrett Browning have to enter a slave woman's "house of anguish"? In doing so, does she simply perpetuate the construction of such a woman as a silenced Other? Or are there paradoxes in such appropriations that, as Elizabeth Spelman reminds us, justify the identification with another's suffering?[8] Putting aside such questions of identity politics for the moment, can any writer, even a descendant of black slaves herself like Morrison, enter a slave woman's "house of anguish" through the "palace of art"? Or can an art of "ideal beauty" at best produce artifacts or "Images" "alien" to extremities of human suffering? Conversely, are certain experiences alien to the pleasure we associate with art, creating a kind of impasse between aesthetics and ethics that itself has troubling ethical aspects? Or is it rather that we sometimes find too much pleasure in literary anguish and the pornography of representation that it may entail? Why, after all, "does the mind find pleasure in the representation of anguish?"—a question the young Elizabeth Barrett asked herself in a notebook she kept as a young woman, as she recorded her reading of some of the philosophers who helped found European aesthetics, including Hume, Hobbes, and Thomas Campbell.[9] (She may have had the pronouncements of these philosophers in mind in beginning "Hiram Powers' Greek Slave" with the unidentified deictic, "They say.")

To return to the more fundamental question at stake here, do certain experiences of human anguish become so intense that a threshold is crossed, when it is no longer a matter of pleasure or beauty or their absence because the very possibility of artistic expression and aesthetic response is annihilated? The substitution of *anguish* for *aesthetics* in my title is meant to shadow forth this possibility, as well as to pose the question of how such anguish affects the first (and some might say) the primary term in the coupling of ethics and aesthetics, a binary that may take the form of a dialectical opposition as well as a continuum or space of mediation. Does it become unethical even to attempt to represent what seems unspeakable? And does such unspeakable anguish also limit our ability to make ethical judgments in the realm of the "real" as opposed to the representational?

Such questions are far from new. In their most intractable form, they are often generated by the Holocaust which, in Elie Wiesel's words, is "not a subject like all the others. It imposes certain limits . . . in order not to betray the dead and humiliate the living."[10] In *Beloved*, these questions arise in the context of Morrison's decision to write about that other Holocaust of the "Sixty Million and more" whom the novel is dedicated to. "Some historians told me 200 million died," Morrison said. But it was not just the numbers, she testified: "The time—300 years—began to drown me. Three hundred years— think about that. Now, that's not a war, that's generation after generation." Paul Gilroy, who has eloquently argued for the importance of dialogue between "the histories of blacks and Jews," observes that black writers such as Morrison "have begun the vital work of enquiring into terrors that exhaust the resources of language, amidst the debris of a catastrophe which prohibits the existence of their art at the same time as demanding its continuance." Forcing herself to imagine, then to write about the "horror" of slavery and to do so in a way that was "not destructive," Morrison came up against the "unspeakable," yet persisted, thinking that, if her ancestors had "lived" the long historical trauma of slavery, it was not "beyond art" to tell it. Otherwise "[t]he slaveholders have won."[11] Morrison depicts differing dimensions of this historical trauma in *Beloved*, but in its most intense form, it is embodied in Sethe's reliving of the infanticide at the center of the novel's circling memories, and the ghost this act gives rise to: the ghost of the "already crawling" baby girl murdered by her own mother to save her from being taken back into slavery, the ghost who articulates the horrors of the Middle Passage and the "mumbling of the black and angry dead."[12] In Andrew Levy's words, "The story of Sethe's life and her infanticide is the story of *Beloved*," told "time and again" within the novel: "narrated by individual characters, retrieved from press clippings, passed on as abolitionist rhetoric, . . . told by Sethe herself. In any form, however, the story remains 'unspeakable': too painful, too perverse, to be told and understood."[13]

Sethe's act of infanticide has generated contradictory aesthetic and ethical reactions: some, like Levy, following Sethe's mother-in-law, Baby Suggs, in refusing either to "approve or condemn Sethe's rough choice" (*BL*, 180); some criticizing Morrison for representing a "crime" as if it is not really a crime at all in the context of the greater crime of slavery; some interpreting it as a heroic depiction of a "compassionate yet resolute self-emancipated mother's tough love" within a tradition of slave women's reproductive resistance.[14] Others have sought an artistic and ethical middle ground, emphasizing that Sethe is held to account by Morrison for her possessive motherly love.[15] James Berger situates *Beloved* in a political middle ground by interpreting its scene of "maternal violence"—of "unspeakable violence between blacks"—as Morrison's acknowledgment of the "alarming violence within African American communities" produced by systemic racial oppression; he then reads this acknowledgment of intra-familial violence within the context of "ongoing debates about American race relations" in the 1980s, shaped by the earlier controversy over Daniel Patrick Moynihan's report on *The Negro Family*.[16] In contrast, some conservative critics have distanced the entire novel from contemporary political debates and ethical questions rooted in historical realities. "*Beloved* was written in the palace of Art," Roger Sale declares; "Morrison's art makes us gasp" at the horror of slavery, but it also "insists that we not organize our feeling as if for protest or other action, but move back into the heavy verbal texture of the fiction." Harold Bloom similarly propounds, "I reread Morrison because her imagination, whatever her social purposes, transcends ideology and polemics, and enters again into a literary space occupied only by fantasy and romance of authentic aesthetic dignity."[17] Thus Sethe's "house of anguish" is transformed into a matter of textured words, a "literary space," an "authentic" chamber of "fantasy and romance" within the Palace of Art.

Although it has received less attention, Barrett Browning's "The Runaway Slave at Pilgrim's Point" has generated similarly contradictory responses. In the 1950s, Gardner Taplin condemned the poem as being "too blunt and shocking to have any enduring artistic worth"—presumably because of its graphic representation of infanticide, since the slave woman's rape is more elliptically portrayed. In contrast, Dorothy Mermin refers to the poem's presentation of an "idealized fantasy figure," even though she elsewhere describes the runaway slave "as a fully realized dramatic character." More severely, Sarah Brophy condemns Barrett Browning for the conservative, idealist poetics and the appropriation of voice that lead her to "inscrib[e] a melodramatic feminine voice within a patriarchal framework of reception." In the most theoretically sophisticated and historically sensitive interpretation to date, Susan Brown argues to the contrary that Barrett Browning's dramatic portrayal of a "socially contradicted" black female subject conducts a "sweeping critique" of "racism as a political and discursive system." Others see the poem's protagonist less as a conflicted subject than as a heroic spokeswoman. Helen Cooper, for example, argues that "[t]hough horrible," the "infanticide becomes, within the terms of the poem, tragically grand and inevitable, the logical conclusion of the slave's situation," while Ann Parry interprets the "dispos[ing]" of the child as the point of transformation when the slave assumes "mastery" over her own fate.[18] As Parry's term *disposing* suggests, in several of these readings the infanticide is treated in passing, and the ethical issues at stake, both in responding to the slave's actions and to Barrett Browning's portrayal of them, are not directly addressed.

These ethical issues, in their inescapable imbrications with aesthetic issues, are my principal concern in comparing Barrett Browning's representation of infanticide to Morrison's. But first, the yoking of authors and texts so differently situated calls for a word of explanation. One might legitimately expect these two texts to be a study in contrasts. Whereas Morrison is the descendant of American slaves, Barrett Browning was a privileged white Victorian poet supported in her artistic aspirations by legacies derived from Jamaican sugar plantations and colonial trade. While Morrison's engagement with the history of slavery grew out of her struggle to engage with the "horror" her people had pushed into forgetfulness in order to create a future, "The Runaway Slave" was Barrett Browning's first abolitionist work, an "occasional" poem composed in response to an invitation to contribute to the Boston anti-slavery annual *The Liberty Bell*. Morrison embeds her depiction of infanticide within a layered, experimental narrative incorporating the conventions of the slave narrative, the Gothic romance, and the historical novel, while Barrett Browning's dramatic monologue, which some dismiss as a melodrama, draws on the ballad tradition, Romantic monodrama, and early Victorian experiments with dramatic, first-person poems. More importantly, as I note below, while Morrison's focus on infanticide was suggested by the appalling lived experience of the actual slave Margaret Garner, Barrett Browning's was prompted by very different catalysts, some of them ethically suspect.

Nevertheless, across the divides created by racial heritage, historical context, and generic traditions, several features link Barrett Browning's representation of slave infanticide in "The Runaway Slave" to Morrison's in *Beloved*. These include the transgression of aesthetic thresholds through disturbingly graphic portrayals of a mother killing her child; the sympathetic inscription of maternal subjectivity in contexts where it is frequently erased or pathologized; a focus on the situational and psychological contradictions driving a slave mother to infanticide; and an emphasis on the ways in which the violence done by such a slave woman is inextricable from the violence done to her. In fact, neither work represents an act that can be categorized as "maternal violence" occurring "within" an African-American family, to use Berger's terms. The situational and motivational complexities represented in each work and the excess of anguish their protagonists experience pose a challenge to conventional systems of ethics, particularly those relying on a discourse of "rules" or "rights," or a separation of the private from the public sphere. As I argue in the context of *Beloved*, more adequate frameworks are found in theories of feminist ethics addressing the issue of abortion. Literary representations of slave infanticide point in turn, however, to the limitations of some influential feminist studies of abortion ethics—including their relative neglect of the Afro-American experience and their inattention to the realm of the aesthetic.

A WHITE WOMAN IN A BLACK WOMAN'S
"HOUSE OF ANGUISH": "THE RUNAWAY SLAVE"

"I will call them my people, which were not my people": Barrett Browning's poem seems to invite the criticism implied by Morrison's resonant biblical epigraph for *Beloved.* Is the poem an unpardonable act of literary appropriation, an extraordinary act of imaginative identification, or quite possibly both of these at once? Clearly, like "A Curse for a Nation," the anti-slavery poem Barrett Browning subsequently published in the 1856 issue of *The Liberty Bell,* "The Runaway Slave at Pilgrim's Point" indirectly reflected the guilt she experienced concerning her slave-holding ancestry. As she said to John Ruskin in 1854, "I come from a family of West Indian slaveholders, and if I believed in curses, I should be afraid."[19] Clearly, too, her composition of "The Runaway Slave" reflects the fact that she was a runaway herself when she completed it in December 1846, having recently escaped the house of the forbidding father and former slaveholder who utterly repudiated her after her secret marriage to Browning. Neither of the family legacies that Barrett Browning continued to receive came from her father, which gave her the freedom not only to marry Browning against his wishes but also to write poems that constituted an indirect curse on her own family.[20]

As well as using her enslaved speaker to exorcise her guilt about her ancestors and to express her anger against her father and the brothers who temporarily joined him in condemning her (projected as the Pilgrim fathers and their "hunter sons"), Barrett Browning may also have been projecting unconscious fears about her own bodily state at the time she was writing "The Runaway Slave." She sent the poem off to James Russell Lowell in America on December 23, 1846. Less than three months later, in mid-March 1847, she suffered a serious miscarriage "*of five month's date,*" terminating a pregnancy she had steadfastly denied the possibility of up until that time.[21] Considerable evidence, including the textual variants in the first rough manuscript of "The Runaway Slave," now at Wellesley College, suggests that the poem reflects repressed fears of a miscarriage or still birth, combined with terror of death in childbirth—not an unreasonable mix of fears for a recently married woman of forty with chronically frail health in the nineteenth century. In her recent biography of the Brownings, Julia Markus advances the different argument that Barrett Browning was afraid of bearing a child of mixed blood, because she secretly knew that she carried African blood in her veins. I have elsewhere argued that evidence for this claim is not convincing. Nevertheless, given the many relationships across the color line in colonial Jamaica, one cannot rule out repressed anxieties about "blood" in a descendant of Jamaican slaveholders who had married another such descendant (Robert Browning's father was the son of the Jamaican woman Margaret Tittle).[22]

If one combines this veritable witch's brew of repressed fears and anxieties with a Victorian cultural discourse projecting infanticide onto "savage mothers," to use Felicity Nussbaum's phrase, a damning portrait of an ethically compromised poet emerges. Early Victorian writers typically constructed infanticide as an evil committed by savage others in the remote reaches of the empire (particularly India), although in the 1840s, when Barrett Browning was writing, there was also growing concern about the evils of infanticide among working-class mothers in the heart of Britain. The same period saw the development of racial ideologies that cast Africans and Europeans as separate species. In the context of this imperial and class-inflected discourse of race and infanticide, Barrett Browning's focus on a night-black slave mother murdering a white-faced male child in an apparent act of revenge (instead of, as in *Beloved*, a slave mother murdering a black female child to save it from slavery) seems to speak to the deepest fears of a white colonial master class.[23]

It would be as much of a mistake, however, to see "The Runaway Slave" as a mere unconscious projection of imperial fears as it would be to reduce it to a text in which Barrett Browning compulsively inscribes her repressed anxieties concerning childbirth. The socialist reformer Romney in Barrett Browning's novel-epic *Aurora Leigh* declares that female artists can "generalise/On nothing—not even grief," and scornfully asks if any woman is capable of being deeply moved (as he is) by "the great sum/Of universal anguish?"[24] Romney is in good company. Susan Sherwin notes that "[m]ost of the influential theorists in the history of Western thought, including not only Kant and Aristotle, but also Thomas Acquinas, Jean-Jacques Rousseau, G.W.F. Hegel, Friedrich Nietzsche, and Jean-Paul Sartre, saw women as having a significantly different character from men, one they considered morally inferior because it was too focused on the particular and inattentive to the level of generality that moral thought was said to require."[25] In our own time, however, many would question Romney's gendered mix of aesthetic and ethical ideologies. Barrett Browning's poem has political, artistic, and philosophical contexts as well as biographical ones. Moreover, whatever the origins of her own particular neuroses may be, "The Runaway Slave at Pilgrim's Point" remains one of the most complex anti-slavery poems to appear in the nineteenth century. Just as some of the most powerful scenes and metaphors in Mary Shelley's *Frankenstein* mediate Shelley's traumatic experience of pregnancy and childbirth, yet nevertheless contribute to the resonance of her novel, so the psychic conflicts registered in Barrett Browning's poem helped generate an iconoclastic text that challenges the aesthetic and moral regimes making even Hiram Powers' idealized Greek slave a focus of debate. There is an ethics of reading as well as an ethics of writing and, as Derek Attridge points out, ethical reading entails engaging with a work as "Other," recognizing its "authoredness," and seeking to understand "its inventive reordering" of its cultural matrix.[26]

To appreciate the radical nature of "The Runaway Slave" within its mid-Victorian cultural contexts, we need to read the poem's dramatic depiction of the anonymous fugitive slave woman's experience against the erasure of maternal subjectivity increasingly evident in early Victorian treatments of infanticide. Whereas Dr. William Hunter's *On the Uncertainty of the Signs of Murder in the Case of Bastard Children* (1783) gives sympathetic attention to maternal circumstances and perspectives in infanticide cases, by the 1830s, a "medico-legal" discourse had been established that largely ignored the mother's experience and focused instead on a scientific examination of the dead child's body, laying the grounds for the medical fetalism shaping the treatment of abortion in our own time. William Cummin's *The Proofs of Infanticide Considered* (1836), in which he reprints Dr. Hunter's "influential and popular tract" but then disputes its anecdotal approach, reflects the development of this scientific discourse, evident as well in works on medical jurisprudence and obstetrical handbooks published in the 1830s.[27] A greater concern with the social and economic contexts leading women to commit infanticide is evident in William Burke Ryan's *Infanticide: Its Law, Prevalence, Prevention, and History* (1862). Nevertheless, Ryan also reflects an obsessive focus on the bodies of dead infants described in terms reminiscent of Victorian sensation novels: "In the quiet of the bedroom we raise the boxlid, and the skeletons are there. In the calm evening walk we see in the distance the suspicious-looking bundle, and the mangled infant is within. . . . [On the railroad] we find at our journey's end that the mouldering remains of a murdered innocent have been our travelling companion."[28]

The sensationalized reports of infanticide that began to appear in the 1850s and 1860s led to several literary works—most notably, George Eliot's *Adam Bede* (1859)—depicting the mothers of these "murdered innocents." Yet the subject remained hedged round with taboos. One critic responded to Eliot's representation of Hetty Sorel's infanticide by deploring the new "literature of pregnancy" and declaring, "This is intolerable. Let us copy the old masters of art, who, if they gave us a baby, gave it us all at once."[29] Moreover, even a writer with as highly a developed moral imagination as Eliot had limited sympathy for Hetty's anguish. In his passing reference to a newspaper account of a girl named Wragg in "The Function of Criticism at the Present Time" (1864), Matthew Arnold reveals how one prominent male arbiter of aesthetic standards responded to the subject of infanticide: "A shocking child murder has just been committed at Nottingham. A girl named Wragg left the workhouse there on Saturday morning with her young illegitimate child. The child was soon afterwards found dead on Mapperly Hills, having been strangled. Wragg is in custody." Arnold notes the dismal poverty of Mapperly Hills, the "bleak and inhuman" lopping off of Wragg's sex in the lopping off of her Christian name. But it seems that otherwise, Wragg is chiefly hauled in, like a pathetic rag doll stuffed with newspaper, to help Arnold make his polemical point that something is rotten in the heart of Philistine England. He condemns the ugliness of her name—Wragg, like "Higginbottom, Stiggins, Bugg," he observes is a typically "hideous" Anglo-Saxon name, the likes of which are not to be found in Classical Greece ("Ionia and Attica") where Arnold, like Hiram Powers, locates his realm of "ideal beauty." As a Hellenist preaching sweetness and light, however, Arnold is certainly not advocating that either art or criticism take the reader into Wragg's "house of anguish." On the contrary, the "function of criticism at the present time" is to embrace "the Indian virtue of detachment . . . abandoning the sphere of practical life," and to engage in the "*disinterested endeavor to learn and propagate the best that is known and thought in the world.*"[30]

Read against the backdrop of Victorian "medico-legal" constructions of infanticide and cultural assumptions about its decorous treatment in high art, "The Runaway Slave at Pilgrim's Point" is a startlingly unconventional poem. Drawing on Romantic ballads that sympathetically portray illegitimate mothers (like Wordsworth's "The Thorn") and fusing together abolitionist motifs common in the pages of the *Liberty Bell* (fugitive slaves, slave mothers, Pilgrim's Point as a symbol of liberty), Barrett Browning turned to new techniques of dramatic presentation she had learned in part from Browning to represent the consciousness of a speaker whose race and circumstances made her more alien than Wragg to many Victorian readers. The dramatic form, combined with the poem's twin focus on miscegenation and motherhood, generates some of its most subversive effects. In the condensations and ellipses of the slave's impacted recollections, there is no preparation for the child that simply appears upon her breast, like "[a]n amulet that hung too slack," following her bitter memory of the "deeper wrong" of her rape in stanza XV—a wrong that Barrett Browning made unconventionally explicit in adding this stanza at the fair copy stage. (Mostly, even in the outspoken *Liberty Bell,* writers simply referred euphemistically to the "pollution" of female slaves.) The "amulet" hung "too slack," the slave woman explains, because "hark! I will tell you low, low,/I am black, you see,—/And the babe who lay on my bosom so,/Was far too white, too white for me"—as white "as the ladies who scorned to pray" beside her in church, she adds in an aside, raising the possibility of hidden miscegenations. "My own, own child!" she continues; yet "I could not bear/To look in his face, it was so white." So she "covered" the child in her kerchief, and he moaned and struggled: "the white child wanted his liberty—/Ha, ha! he wanted the master-right." As Sally Shuttleworth has shown, "The image of the mother giving suck to her innocent babe was a potent one in Victorian ideology, but one that was riddled with class anxieties and demonic undertones," even when both the baby and the "bosom" represented were white. In Jill Matus' terms, the mid-Victorian construction of the maternal body was "unstable," as indeed our own still is, perhaps because, as Julia Kristeva's work suggests, the experience of abjection is indissolubly rooted in the experience of the mother's engulfing corporeal presence.[31]

What is remarkable about "The Runaway Slave at Pilgrim's Point" is that, despite the stilted diction ("hark!") and the stylized "attitudes" it inherits from Romantic monodramas, despite the primal desires and fears surrounding the maternal body activated by the poem, and despite the ideologically freighted spectacle of a black woman giving suck, then refusing suck to the "too white" baby she kills—the work's cumulative effect is to arouse pity and fear as well as admiration for the tragic dignity of the speaker in many readers. As one young African-American abolitionist, Charlotte Forten, observed in 1854, "[H]ow powerfully it is written! How earnestly and touchingly does the writer portray the bitter anguish of the poor fugitive as she thinks over all the wrongs and sufferings she has endured!" White Victorian readers, like Helen Whitman, a poet who later became Edgar Allen Poe's fiancée, responded similarly.[32] For the adolescent Forten, Barrett Browning is simply "the writer"; it is the poem that matters. But this, of course, was not the case for readers like Whitman. In 1850, Barrett Browning was named as a possible candidate for Poet Laureate. It is important to keep her authorial status in mind because, ironically, her reputation and race permitted her to take the licenses that she did. As Harriet Jacobs' adoption of a fictional mask suggests, an African-American woman who wrote frankly about rape and miscegenation would probably not have had her works published in the nineteenth century.

Forten chose to re-read "The Runaway Slave" to gather strength in the face of the suffering caused by the Fugitive Slave Act. As this choice implies, the nameless slave woman in the poem is not simply an object of pathos, nor is she simply a mother. She is also a fugitive (often a role reserved for male slaves), a religious questioner, and a political rebel who begins by cursing the land the pilgrim fathers blessed and ends by cursing their slave hunter sons, as she prophesies the civil strife yet to come out of slavery. Aptly, she defiantly compares herself to the "the black eagle at nest." Barrett Browning was strongly influenced by the female protagonists and ethical dilemmas depicted in Greek tragedy, as Morrison later was in *Beloved*. She had twice translated *Prometheus Bound*, and the runaway slave she depicts is cast as a black Prometheus—not, it should be noted, as a Medea figure. "It is *mothers* whom from the start dramatists portray as the mythological perpetrators of infanticide," Leslie Fiedler notes, even though "the practice of infanticide" was "usually at the father's behest" in many cultures.[33] But in "The Runaway Slave," as in "The Cry of the Children," where she takes her epigraph from the *Medea*, Barrett Browning presents the death of children in the context of the sins of the fathers.

At the same time, the text's graphic account of the innocent baby's struggle to breathe forces readers to engage with the ethical implications of the act the anonymous slave woman is driven to commit. The ethical questions are complex, because the act is not motivated simply by revenge. In fact, its etiology is far more ramified, reflecting the tortured complexity of the circumstances in which slavery has enmeshed the speaker. She acts not only out of the desire to deprive the white child of the "liberty" that is his "master-right," but also out of the traumatized fear of the "*master's* look" that used to fall on her soul "like his lash," which returns when she sees the "look" reproduced in the baby's face at her breast. As well, she is driven by the fear of being punished for bearing a child that is "too white" for her (this fear is brought out in the Wellesley manuscript, where there is more focus on the slave's conflict with judgmental white women). Paradoxically, too, she acts out of love. Read another way, the same lines that suggest her desire for revenge on the white child that "wanted the master-right" of liberty also convey her desire to prevent her child from being subjected to slavery and one day vainly struggling for liberty, "want[ing]"—or both lacking and desiring—the right reserved for masters. Love, in fact, is paramount in her recollection of the moment of murder: "And so, to save it from my curse,/I twisted it round in my shawl." However, she can only fully express her love when the white baby is buried in the "black earth—nothing white,—/A dark child in the dark!" Then she can sing to the child the song she learned in her maidenhood from the black lover murdered by her masters, the song repeating her forbidden lover's name.

These conflicted motives, a translation of the slave's entangled circumstances to her consciousness, are intensified by the state of spiritual despair precipitated by her reflection on her succession of ordeals. The return of repressed memories of murder, rape, pregnancy, and infanticide at the heart of the poem begins with the speaker's recollection of her vain attempt to justify the ways of a God who apparently casts away the black creatures He molded from clay, a God who sat "[c]oldly" behind the sun and did "not speak" when her black lover's blood was spilled in the dust. Stanzas IV to VIII of the poem constitute the beginnings of a black theodicy, reminiscent of the religious meditations that appear in the central chapter of the *Narrative of the Life of Frederick Douglass, an American Slave* (1845)—a possible influence on the poem, the Wellesley manuscript suggests. In the slave woman's case, however, the theodicy descends into a form of madness produced by the unendurable extremity of her anguish. As the speaker recalls, the "*master's* look" in her child's face "made me mad!", a madness she relives in her tortured recollections of God's "fine white angels" plucking her fruit "to make them wine" and "suck[ing] the soul" of her child as "the humming-bird sucks the soul of the flower." In a fair copy draft of the poem Barrett Browning had signaled the possibility of the slave's madness by using the title "Mad and Black at Pilgrim's Point." Wisely, however, she altered this. While the slave may remember a period of temporary madness, she is not mad as she speaks. As she says to the slave hunters who surround her at the poem's close, in a strategic variation of a line the poem has made a refrain, "I am not mad: I am black." In other words, her period of postpartum madness, like her religious questioning and her act of infanticide, is culturally configured by the institutionalized exploitation of slavery. She is not a "savage mother"; it is the culture of slavery, not nature, that is savage. The slave mother's act of infanticide in "The Runaway Slave at Pilgrim's Point" is as inextricably embedded in the violence generated by this savage culture as is Sethe's slaying of her child in *Beloved*.

INFANTICIDE IN BELOVED :
CONTEXTS IN FEMINIST ETHICS AND AESTHETICS

In Morrison's case, as opposed to Barrett Browning's, the epigraph of *Beloved* might well be altered to read, " I will call them my people, which were my people"—people not "[d]isremembered and unaccounted for" (*BL*, 274), but remembered and accounted for, despite the difficulties that representing the prolonged historical trauma of slavery entails. Even in the late twentieth century, Morrison's decision to focus her novel on infanticide poses particularly complex ethical and aesthetic challenges, given the uneasiness that historians have expressed in addressing this subject, as well as the controversy concerning the evidence for its use. Wilma King observes, "It is not easy to reconcile accounts of the unwavering love slave mothers had for their children with reports of infanticide," reflecting the ethical ambivalence the subject typically generates. Elizabeth Fox Genovese rightly points out that many deaths of slave infants may be explained by Sudden Infant Death Syndrome, "linked to their mother's labor in the fields," emphasizing as King does that historical hypotheses concerning infanticide as a form of reproductive resistance need to consider "the well documented attachment of slave mothers to their children." Nevertheless, James Berger's claim that "[h]istorians agree that slave infanticide was extremely rare" is open to question. King, for example, cites the case of a Virginian slave woman, convicted of "killing her mulatto child"—though she claimed that "'she would not have killed a child of her own color.'" Barbara Bush points out in her study of Caribbean slave women that "[i]nfanticide is the natural corollary of abortion, but historians, sociologists, and demographers rarely consider this subject because of strong taboos in Western culture."[34]

In *Beloved*, Morrison presents several instances of infanticide that entail slave women's acts of resistance against the sexual predations of white men, although none of these is depicted as violently as the infanticide in "The Runaway Slave at Pilgrim's Point." Sethe's mother-in-law, Baby Suggs, has a baby by a "straw boss" in exchange for keeping her third child, and when he betrays her and sells the child, she cannot love the fourth that she has by him. "'God take what He would,' she said" (*BL*, 23). Sethe learns that her own mother "threw away" the child resulting from the rapes the crew subjected her to on the Middle Passage, and that the "others from more whites she also threw away. Without names, she threw them." But Sethe she kept, and "gave the name of the black man" who fathered her (*BL*, 62). In this respect, Sethe's mother resembles the speaker in Barrett Browning's poem who can only love her white child when she buries it in the black earth, and sings to it the name of her black lover. Finally, there is Ella, who "had been beaten every way but down. She remembered the bottom teeth she had lost to the brake. . . . She had delivered but would not nurse, a hairy white thing" fathered by a man who had brutalized her. "It lived five days never making a sound" (*BL*, 58–59). These incidents in *Beloved* suggest that Morrison is acknowledging, with less ambivalence than some historians, the use of infanticide by slave women as a form of reproductive resistance. But the scene of apocalyptic violence at the center of her novel presents an act that is more ethically complex than these.

As the novelist has testified, *Beloved* grew out of her encounter with newspaper clippings concerning the story of Margaret Garner, who tried to kill her four children in Cincinnati, Ohio, in 1856, rather than see them taken back into slavery. "She succeeded in killing one; she tried to kill two others," Morrison said. "She hit them in the head with a shovel, and they were wounded but they didn't die. And there was a smaller one that she had at her breast. . . . She said, 'I will not let those children live how I have lived.'" Paul Gilroy points out that, although the newspaper accounts of Garner's story are contradictory, it exercised a "continuing symbolic power," particularly within women's anti-slavery discourse. Lucy Stone's response testifies to its haunting effect. The abolitionist and women's rights activist visited the fugitive in prison and tried to comfort her, but Margaret's "'only reply was a look of deep despair, of anguish such that no words can speak.'"[35] It is unlikely, however, that Morrison was influenced by such accounts. She observed, " I did not do much research on Margaret Garner . . . because I wanted to invent her life, which is a way of saying I wanted to be accessible to anything the characters had to say about it. Recording her life as lived would not interest me. . . . I got to a point where in asking myself who could judge Sethe adequately, since I couldn't, and nobody else that knew her could, really, I felt the only person who could judge her would be the daughter she had killed. And from there Beloved inserted herself into the text."[36] Morrison's comments reveal that her attempt to come to terms with the ethical dilemma posed by Margaret Garner's actions led to a shift from the register of historical "reality" to the register of fiction—from Margaret to Sethe. They also indicate, however, that once this shift to the aesthetic domain had taken place, the ethical question of how to judge a slave mother who kills her own child generated the novel's narrative form, as the ghost who shapes the plot "inserted herself into the text." In other words, the historical and the fictional, the ethical and the aesthetic, are dialectically folded into each other like the convolutions of a Möbius strip. Morrison did not simply move, as Sales and Bloom imply, into the protected space of the "palace of art," leaving history, politics, and actual ethical dilemmas behind.

Morrison seems to have found the Garner story resonant for some of the same reasons that George Eliot was drawn to the story of Antigone: because it epitomizes the tragic dilemma of an irresolvable conflict between an individual and her society. "[Q]uestions about community and individuality were certainly inherent in that incident as I imagined it," she stated. "When you are the community, when you are your children, when that is your individuality, there is no division . . . Margaret Garner didn't do what Medea did and kill her children because of some guy. It was for me this classic example of a person determined to be responsible."[37] In another comment, Morrison implies that Garner's story involved a characteristically female embodiment of tragic conflict. The significance of the Garner incident "didn't get clear for" her, she observes, until she connected it to another story she had read—a story about a Harlem girl shot by a jealous ex-boyfriend with a silencer on his gun at a party. The girl died rather than see him captured. Both stories, according to Morrison, epitomize, "at least on the surface," a "very noble" self-sacrificing love "peculiar to women [showing that] the best thing that is in us is also the thing that makes us sabotage ourselves . . . I had about fifteen or twenty questions that occurred to me with those two stories in terms of what it is that really compels a good woman to displace the self, her self."[38] As *Beloved* indicates, however, one story is more complex than the other, because in Sethe's act of displacing her self—the self that she eventually learns to recognize with Paul D's help as her "best thing" (*BL*, 273)—there is also the displacement of her daughter's self.

Morrison herself said of Sethe's act of infanticide that she "did what was right although she did not have the right to do it"—a statement rejected as "muddled" by some critics who cite it.[39] What is particularly interesting about the statement is that Morrison does not say of Sethe, "she did what she thought was right." If Morrison had said this, the first half of the statement, describing Sethe's "right," might have yielded before the second half, *the* right. But no such resolution occurs. And where both logic and conventional ethical assumptions might have expected an either/or, we encounter the logic of "both, and." And what? More: more that we have to take into account. No abstract system of rules and principles, of "right and wrong," or as we say in our racially coded language, "black and white," can accommodate the complexities of Sethe's act-in-context. The dilemma Morrison articulates is reflected in the narrative tensions of *Beloved* itself, where whatever judgment the ghost might make of her mother as her murdered daughter is complicated by the fact that she also speaks for the "Sixty Million and more" murdered and violated by slavery, including Sethe herself.

Although the ethical dilemma crystallized by Morrison's statement resists any resolution, the frameworks of feminist ethics developed in part to address the issue of abortion are useful in coming to terms with its intractable complexities. From the perspective of feminist ethics, in fact, her statement does not seem "muddled" at all. Instead, it presents a deliberate paradox that underlines the inadequacy of any discourse of "rights" to address the intolerably contradictory particulars of Sethe's situation and experience. As Sherwin observes, binding ethical laws such as those developed by Kant "pay scant attention to the specific details of individuals' moral experiences and relationships." An emphasis on accommodating the "specific details" of individual experience shapes the feminist studies of abortion that have emerged from a variety of disciplinary orientations, including philosophy, psychology, social science, political science, and law. Despite their disciplinary differences, these studies agree in rejecting traditional ethical systems relying on transcendental or universal moral laws, or an abstract discourse of "rights." In general, they argue instead not for an essentialized "feminine ethics" but for a theory of feminist ethics that approaches ethical questions within the contexts experienced by situated or embodied subjects, who live within networks of relations and responsibilities and particular historical and material circumstances.[40] In other words, as Barrett Browning implies through the metaphors of "Hiram Powers' *Greek Slave*," ethics, like anguish, lives in certain houses. It cannot be separated from the spirits, hearts, and bodies of the women, children, and men who struggle to make "rough choices" in their daily lives. Nor can ethical judgments be separated from the embodied experience and ideological frameworks of those who seek to assess these choices.

While the theoretical frameworks of feminist ethics are common in treatments of abortion, they are not often brought to bear in investigations of infanticide. Some of the reasons for this are immediately apparent, given the current cultural climate in which the fetalism of "pro-life" activists leads to mottoes on the Internet such as "Infanticide follows abortion as night follows day," along with implicit calls for the murder of "baby butchers." But the relative neglect of the ethics of infanticide by feminists is not merely strategic or determined by the philosophical and moral distinctions between abortion and infanticide. As Loretta Ross points out, feminist work on abortion has been dominated by a "white abortion rights movement" that has been slow to recognize the historical colonization of African-American women's wombs during slavery, their use of abortion and infanticide as resistance, and the continuation of state-sanctioned invasive practices in twentieth-century eugenic and fetal protection movements directed at African Americans and Hispanic Americans. While feminist writers on reproductive ethics and realities in the 1990s took steps to rectify this omission and also to give more attention to women's reproductive experience in Third World contexts, the paradigm Ross objects to has been difficult to alter. Judith Wilt's nuanced analysis of twentieth-century abortion narratives, for example, reflects its inflections, even though she includes a consideration of Afro-American women writers. Stating that "in the nineteenth-century novel of infanticide lie the seeds of the twentieth-century abortion narrative," Wilt traces a historical trajectory called into question by the revisionary swerve we encounter in *Beloved,* where Morrison returns to "seeds" of infanticide never fully accounted for in the nineteenth century.[41]

If feminist ethics has tended to pass over infanticide in focusing on abortion, it has given even less attention to literary representations of infanticide. Although philosophers such as Martha Nussbaum have argued, in relation to the law, for the value of the narrative instantiations that literature can provide, feminist ethics on the whole—particularly ethics centered on reproductive issues—has tended to privilege philosophical, historical, legal, or sociological approaches that seldom turn to the illuminations offered by artistic representations.[42] Literary critics such as Wilt, and Barbara Johnson, in her perceptive treatment of "Apostrophe, Animation, and Abortion," have been more inclined to try to map the complex interanimations of the real and the representational.[43] The neglect of the aesthetic in feminist ethics is ironic for at least two reasons. First, given the emphasis feminist ethics places on the circumstances and experiences of "embodied" subjects, literature and the arts provide an ideal medium for illustrating and understanding the situated complexities of moral choice. Second, as Peggy Zeglin Brand and Carolyn Korsmeyer in part point out, there are striking convergences between feminist ethics and feminist aesthetics that call for further investigation and application. In both bodies of theory, for example, the "disinterested, disembodied Cartesian knower" is replaced with a conception of the subject "as situated, as engaged and as part of a community"; in both, analysis is complicated by "issues of race, class, culture, and sexual identities"; in both, there is a rejection of abstract rules or principles and an emphasis on assessing art or moral actions within the "cultural frameworks" and "historical contingencies" that shape them; in both, there is skepticism of a totalizing construction of the feminine; and in both, not surprisingly, there is a strongly pragmatic emphasis. In feminist aesthetics, this is reflected in the affirmation of an activist art, or an art in "everyday use," to use the title of Alice Walker's influential story, as opposed to the traditional emphasis on formal properties and an art of transcendent, timeless value (Powers' "ideal beauty").[44]

An analysis of Sethe's act of infanticide in *Beloved* drawing on the frameworks of feminist ethics and aesthetics would argue that we cannot judge this act without entering and remembering Sethe's particular "house of anguish," while also acknowledging the implications of our own positionality.[45] It would not decontextualize Sethe's moral failings by criticizing her tendency to view her children as "property" and interpreting her as a character who is "acting freely" (in Sartre's existential sense) but overstepping "some boundaries" in slaying her own children.[46] In such an analysis, dependent on the assumption of a free Cartesian agent, the violations of slavery that permeate every aspect of Sethe's consciousness fall into the background. But for Sethe, slavery is not a background; it is the appalling foreground in which she is driven to do what she does. Nor would the theoretical assumptions of feminist ethics and aesthetics support isolating one experience from that foreground, as Ann-Janine Morey does in stating that, "Sethe is driven to infanticide by Schoolteacher's list of words dividing human from animal qualities"[47] They call instead for interpreting Sethe's act within the entire matrix created by its narrative context, in which Morrison gives continuous attention to Sethe's embodied experience of pregnancy and childbirth, interwoven with the subjugating violations of slavery.

While it is impossible to summarize the cumulative anguish that leads Sethe to begin butchering her own children, at the very least, as in the case of the fugitive slave woman in Barrett Browning's poem, we need to remember some of the more traumatic experiences that precede it: that Sethe has been separated from her husband and witnessed some (though not all) of the atrocities the men of Sweet Home are subjected to; that she has separated herself from her children, whom she has sent on over the river to Ohio to what she hopes may be freedom; that, pregnant and still carrying milk in her breasts for her two-year old girl, she is pinned down and in effect raped, in a grotesque scene in which her master's sons suck the milk from her breasts while "schoolteacher" stands by and discourses on her animal traits; that she is whipped until her back is laid open in wounds so severe that she is never able to feel the skin on her back again; that, against all odds, she succeeds in escaping and beginning the flight to join her children, with blood dripping from her back and milk from her breasts; that she almost dies and gives birth on the way, then is finally reunited with her children and her mother-in-law, Baby Suggs, in the free state of Ohio. Then the "four horsemen" of Sethe's apocalypse suddenly appear and come right into Baby Suggs' yard, because the Fugitive Slave Law gave them a legal right to do so. The event that occurs then cannot be categorized as an act of "maternal violence" "within" the African-American family, because there is no "within" for Sethe's family to escape to. Nor is it an act of existential freedom. When Sethe sees the horsemen, she "heard wings. Little hummingbirds stuck their needle beaks right through her headcloth into her hair and beat their wings. And if she thought anything, it was No. No. Nono. Nonono. Simple. She just flew. Collected every bit of life she had made, all the parts of her that were precious and fine and beautiful, and carried, pushed, dragged them through the veil, out, away, over there where no one could hurt them" (*BL*, 163). An older sense of the word "ecstasy," closer to its original Greek meaning of displacement or trance, refers to a state in which consciousness is eclipsed. What Sethe undergoes is an ecstasy of unendurable anguish.

We see Sethe's act first through the eyes of the slave catchers, and they see only "niggers" and blood pumping down a fugitive nigger woman's breast from the slit throat of her child, and nigger eyes, among which "the worst were those of the nigger [mother] who looked like she didn't have any. Since the whites in them had disappeared and since they were black as her skin, she

looked blind" (*BL*, 150). What the blind eyes of the slaveholder see is only ru-
ined property: "a dead nigger could not be skinned for profit, and was not
worth his own dead weight in coin" (*BL*, 148). As the successive versions of
this incident reveal, moving inward toward Sethe's story and the maternal subjectivity the slaveholders erase, this is a scene of madness, and the murder it
depicts is as much a matricide as an infanticide: a matricide intimated by
Sethe's eclipsed eyes. Sethe later recalls of this time and the following time of
Beloved's burial, "my mind was homeless then" (*BL*, 204). It is Baby Suggs
who calls the dead mother back to some kind of traumatized life, by trading
"the living for the dead." She hands Sethe's still-living infant to her for her to
nurse, and taking the body of her slain two-year old daughter, she places it in
the "keeping room" (*BL*, 152).

The word "keeping-room" is fitting, as the dead child's ghost keeps before
the reader the consciousness of the network of relationships and responsibilities that Sethe exists within, and the subjectivities of others who are irrevocably affected by the action that the unremitting violations of slavery lead her to
take: Beloved above all, but also her other children, and the members of her
community. Her community judges Sethe, and they are judged in turn by the
narrative, but throughout Morrison emphasizes the ways in which all of her
characters are shaped not only by their memories of slavery but also by the systemic racial violence that persists after slavery is abolished. Paul D may repudiate Sethe's actions as savage, saying, "Your love is too thick," and insisting
that, "There could have been a way. Some other way." But his judgment reflects
the "shame" bred by the degradations of slavery that he has internalized as
much as the shame he attributes to her (*BL*, 164–65). It is another woman with
her own dark memories who, with the help of Sethe's living daughter, Denver,
begins the movement toward Sethe's release from the ghost who embodies the
past. Ella is a "practical woman," who "junked" Sethe after a "crime" she regarded as "staggering." But she "didn't like the idea of past errors taking possession of the present" (*BL*, 256). Ironically, it is Ella's memory of her own
abandonment of the hairy white "pup" she could not bear to keep alive that is
the catalyst for a groundswell of newly positive feeling among the women of
the community toward Sethe (*BL*, 259). And it is this groundswell of feeling,
the voices of the women joining in the search for "the right combination" (*BL*,
261), that unites Sethe again with her people and permits the exorcism of
Beloved. Thus Morrison links one act of infanticide to another, situating both
within the "holocaust" that slavery constituted for her people, but also within
the communal feeling that permitted those who endured slavery to sometimes
survive it. Not always, and not everyone. That is why the last words are given to
the ghost of the slain girl: "In the place where long grass opens, the girl who
waited to be loved and cry shame erupts into her separate parts," her story dissolving now, "not a story to pass on" (*BL*, 274).

Both *Beloved* itself and Morrison's statements about the novel indicate that, like Ella, she is a "practical woman," and that she is concerned with developing a pragmatic aesthetic in order to articulate an ethics of survival: an aesthetic and an ethics complex enough to encompass the appalling contradictions that slavery imposed on people's lives. She is not creating an object of "ideal beauty," although the incantatory lyricism and haunting images of her cadenced narrative are integral to its power. In suggesting that feminist ethics, as it has been developed to address abortion, and feminist aesthetics, with its emphasis on an art that can be "of use," are helpful in approaching Morrison's representation of slave infanticide in *Beloved*, I have necessarily passed over many complicated questions. Others will no doubt arise from my comparison of Morrison's novel with Barrett Browning's more problematic representation of a slave woman's "house of anguish." But as Charlotte Forten's response suggests, despite the appropriations it entailed, "The Runaway Slave at Pilgrim's Point" was of some use to those fighting against slavery in the nineteenth century. As for *Beloved*, it remains of immeasurable use in illuminating both slavery's effects on those who lived under its law and the continuing trauma that its legacy creates for those whose ancestors survived it.

NOTES

1. Lawrence Buell, "In Pursuit of Ethics," *PMLA* 114 (1999): 11, 16–17. The other omitted "strands" are "Bakhtinian dialogism," "Habermasian discourse ethics," and "ecocriticism."

2. The ratio of female to male contributors is 1 to 6, and the single essay by a female contributor—Mary Beth Tierney-Tello's "Testimony, Ethics, and the Aesthetic in Dialmela Eltit," 78–6—is more concerned with ethics in postcolonial contexts than with the feminist contexts its subject matter might also invite.

3. Janet Hadley, *Abortion: Between Freedom and Necessity* (Philadelphia: Temple University Press, 1996).

4. *The Complete Works of Elizabeth Barrett Browning*, ed. Charlotte Porter and Helen A. Clarke, 6 vols. (New York: Thomas Y. Crowell & Co., 1900: New York: AMS rpt., 1973), 3: 275. Hereafter cited in the text as *CW.*

5. [Miner Kellog], *Powers' Statue of the Greek Slave* (New York: R. Craighead, 1847), 4.

6. Jennifer DeVere Brody, *Impossible Purities: Blackness, Femininity, and Victorian Culture* (Durham and London: Duke University Press, 1998), 67, 69; Jean Fagin Yellin, *Women and Sisters: The Anti-Slavery Feminists in America* (New Haven, Conn., and London: Yale University Press, 1989), 99–124; Joy S. Kasson, "Narratives of the Female Body: *The Greek Slave*," *The Culture of Sentiment: Race, Gender and Sentimentality in Nineteenth-Century America*, ed. Shirley Samuels (New York and Oxford: Oxford University Press, 1992), 173–90. Commentators stressed that the statue's nudity was in effect sanctioned by its moral purpose, while some protested, "Take off that chain—present no fiction of its being a helpless slave, and what remains but a licentious

exhibition?" (Yellin, 109; see also Kasson, 179, 181, for descriptions of the slave "clothed all over with sentiment" or "clothed with chastity.") Brody—mistakenly in my view— interprets Barrett Browning's sonnet as an expression of unquestioning reverence for Powers' statue and the reified Victorian connections between "whiteness, beauty, and purity" it embodies (68); Yellin more accurately describes it as "the most important critique of the passivity" of Powers' figure to appear (123–24).

7. See Yellin, *Women and Sisters*, 109–12, 122. Ellen and William Craft also participated in this demonstration, Ellen dressed in drag to call attention to the circumstances of their sensational escape from Georgia, effected through her "passing" as a white master attended by the slave who was in fact her husband.

8. Elizabeth Spelman, *Fruits of Sorrow: Framing Our Attention to Suffering* (Boston: Beacon Press, 1997), 113–32. I am indebted to Sue Campbell for calling my attention to the usefulness of Spelman's analysis.

9. Unpublished notebook containing Elizabeth Barrett's comments on her reading from 1824 to 1826, p. 95. I am grateful to the English Poetry Collection, Wellesley College Library, for permission to examine and cite this notebook.

10. Cited in Susan Bowers, "*Beloved* and the New Apocalypse," *Toni Morrison's Fiction: Contemporary Criticism*, ed. David L. Middleton (New York and London: Garland Press, 1997), 212.

11. Danille Taylor-Guthrie, ed., *Conversations with Toni Morrison* (Jackson: Mississippi University Press, 1994), 256–57; 247–48, 244–45; Paul Gilroy, *The Black Atlantic: Modernity and Double Consciousness* (Cambridge, Mass.: Harvard University Press, 1993), 213, 218. Morrison elsewhere observes, "If Hitler had won the war and established his thousand-year Reich, at some point he would have stopped killing people . . . because he would have needed some to do the labor for nothing. And the first 200 years of that Reich would have been exactly what that period was in this country for Black people . . . Not for five years, not for ten years, but for 200 years or more" (*Conversations*, 235).

12. Toni Morrison, *Beloved* (New York: Penguin, Plume Group, 1988), 198. Hereafter cited in the text as *BL*.

13. Andrew Levy, "Telling *Beloved*," *Texas Studies in Language and Literature* 33 (1991): 114.

14. Levy, "Telling *Beloved*," 117; Martha Bayles, "Special Effects, Special Pleading," *New Criterion* (January 1988): 36; Bernard W. Bell, "*Beloved*: A Womanist Neoslave Narrative: or, Multivocal Remembrances of Things Past," *African American Review* 26 (1992): 9.

15. Wilfred D. Samuels and Clenora Hudson-Weems, *Toni Morrison* (Boston: G. K. Hall, Twayne Publishers, 1990), 106.

16. James Berger, "Ghosts of Liberalism: Morrison's *Beloved* and the Moynihan Report," *PMLA* 111 (1996), 410–11.

17. Roger Sale, "Toni Morrison's *Beloved*" and Harold Bloom, "Introduction," *Modern Critical Views: Toni Morrison*, ed. Harold Bloom (New York and Philadelphia: Chelsea House Publishers, 1990), 165–66, 2. Such aestheticizing co-optations seem particularly disturbing in light of *Beloved's* relevance to the continuing racial violence the legacy of slavery breeds: for example, the racially motivated murder of James Byrd Jr. in

Jasper, Texas, in June 1998, an African-American disabled man who was beaten and then dragged by a chain from a truck until his head and right shoulder were torn from his body ("Jury Selection Begins in Texas Racial Killing," *The Toronto Star,* January 25, 1999, A10).

18. Gardner Taplin, *The Life of Elizabeth Barrett Browning* (New Haven, Conn.: Yale University Press, 1957), 194; Dorothy Mermin, *Elizabeth Barrett Browning: The Origins of a New Poetry* (Chicago and London: Chicago University Press, 1989), 161, 187; Sarah Brophy, "Elizabeth Barrett Browning's "The Runaway Slave at Pilgrim's Point" and the Politics of Interpretation," *Victorian Poetry* 36 (1998): 277; Susan Brown, "'Black and White Slaves': Discourses of Race and Victorian Feminism," in *Gender and Colonialism,* ed. Timothy P. Foley et al (Galway: Galway University press, 1995), 129; Helen Cooper, *Elizabeth Barrett Browning: Woman and Artist* (Chapel Hill: University of North Carolina Press, 1988), 119; Ann Parry, "Sexual Exploitation and Freedom: Religion, Race, and Gender in Elizabeth Barrett Browning's *The Runaway Slave at Pilgrim's Point,*" *Studies in Browning and His Circle* 16 (1988): 124–25.

19. *The Letters of Elizabeth Barrett Browning,* ed. Frederic Kenyon, 2 vols. (New York: Macmillan, 1897), 2: 220.

20. Her indirection itself may be ethically suspect, since in both of her *Liberty Bell* poems she chooses to write a harsh critique of American slavery, making no mention of the Jamaican slavery that had enriched her. However, this focus was also called for by the context. Moreover, cursing in Barrett Browning's poetry takes complex and rhetorically sophisticated forms, resulting in powerful political interventions in the anti-slavery debate. See my article, "Cursing As One of the Fine Arts: Elizabeth Barrett Browning's Political Poetry," *Dalhousie Review* 66 (1986): 155-73.

21. *The Brownings' Correspondence,* ed. Philip Kelley and Scott Lewis, vol. 14 (Winfield, Kans.: Wedgstone Press, 1998), 86, 155.

22. Julia Markus, *Dared and Done: The Marriage of Elizabeth Barrett and Robert Browning* (New York: Alfred A. Knopf, 1995), 106. I question Markus' claim in "Elizabeth Barrett Browning," *The New Dictionary of National Biography* (forthcoming). On Browning's Jamaican ancestors, see Jeannette Marks, *The Family of the Barrett: A Colonial Romance* (New York: Macmillan, 1938), 102–33.

23. See Felicity Nussbaum, "'Savage Mothers': Narratives of Maternity in the Mid-Eighteenth Century," *Cultural Critique* 20 (1991–92): 123–51. Colin Ramsey notes the demonizing of Amerindian mothers in "Cannibalism and Infant Killing: A System of 'Demonizing' Motifs in Indian Captivity Narratives, " *Clio* 24 (1994): 55–68. As an example of the steady stream of studies decrying infanticide in India during the nineteenth century, see J. Peggs, *India's Cries to British Humanity, Relative to the Suttee, Infanticide, British Connexion with Idolatry, Ghant Murders and Slavery in India; to which is added Humane Hints for the melioration of the State of Society in British India,* 2d ed. ([London]: Seely & Sons, 1830). On British working-class infanticide, see William Ryan and Jill Matus, cited below. The connections between Victorian racial ideologies and "The Runaway Slave" were addressed by Cora Kaplan in a paper, "Giant Propensities: Gender and the Rise of Racial Thinking in Victorian Britain, 1838–1865," delivered at the Birkbeck College Women's Poetry Conference, July 1995.

24. Elizabeth Barrett Browning, *Aurora Leigh,* ed. Margaret Reynolds (Athens: Ohio University Press, 1992), Book II, ll. 183–84, 206–09.

25. Susan Sherwin, *No Longer Patient: Feminist Ethics and Health Care* (Philadelphia, Temple University Press, 1992), 43.

26. Derek Attridge, "Innovation, Literature, Ethics: Relating to the Other," *PMLA* 114 (1999): 26–27.

27. William Cummin, *The Proofs of Infanticide Considered, including Dr. Hunter's Tract on Child Murder, With Illustrated Notes, and a Summary of the Present State of Medico-Legal Knowledge on that Subject* (London: Longman, Rees, Orme, Brown, Green, and Longman, 1836). For additional evidence of the developing forensic discourse of foetalism and the erasure of maternal subjectivity, see Thomas Stewart Traill, *Outlines of a Course of Lectures on Medical Jurisprudence* (Edinburgh: Adam and Charles Black, 1836) and Charles Severn, Surgeon, *First Lines of the Practice of Midwifery: To Which Are Added Remarks on the Forensic Evidence Requisite in Cases of Foeticide and Infanticide* (London: S. Highley, 1831).

28. W. B. Ryan, *Infanticide: Its Law, Prevalence, Prevention, and History* (London: J. Churchill, 1862), 45.

29. Cited in Jill Matus, *Unstable Bodies: Victorian Representations of Sexuality and Maternity* (Manchester and New York: Manchester University Press, 1995), 1. Matus discusses *Adam Bede* in the context of medical debates about wet-nursing and treatises on infanticide (see pp. 157–67).

30. Matthew Arnold's italics. *Lectures and Essays in Criticism,* ed. R. H. Super, with the assistance of Sister Thomas Marion Hocter (Ann Arbor: University of Michigan Press, 1962), 273, 270, 283.

31. Jill Matus, op. cit.; Sally Shuttleworth, "Demonic Mothers: Ideologies of Bourgeois Motherhood in the Mid-Victorian Era," *Rewriting the Victorians: Theory, History, and the Politics of Gender* (New York and London: Routledge, 1993), 38. For Julia Kristeva's theory of abjection, see, in particular, her *Black Sun: Depression and Melancholia,* trans. Leon S. Roudice (New York: Columbia University Press, 1989).

32. See Charlotte Forten, *The Journal of Charlotte Forten,* ed. Ray Allen Billington (1953; rpt. New York: Norton, 1981), 44–45, and Anne Lohrli's reprinting of Whitman's poems praising "The Runaway Slave," among other poems ("Sonnets to Mrs. Browning," *Studies in Browning and His Circle* 6 [1978]: 71–73).

33. Leslie Fiedler, "On Infanticide," *Journal of Popular Culture* 14 (1981): 677.

34. Wilma King, "'Suffer with Them Till Death': Slave Women and Their Children in Nineteenth-Century America," *More Than Chattel: Black Women and Slavery in the Americas,* ed. David Barry Gaspar and Darlene Clark Hine (Bloomington and Indianapolis: Indiana University Press, 1996), 160; Elizabeth Fox Genovese, "Strategies and Forms of Resistance: Focus on Slave Women in the United States," *In Resistance: Studies in African, Caribbean and Afro-American History,* ed. Gary Y. Okihiro (Amherst: University of Massachusetts Press, 1986), 158; Berger, 417; Barbara Bush, "Hard Labor: Women, Childbirth, and Resistance in British Caribbean Slave Societies," *More Than Chattel,* 207–08. Bush argues that, "If infanticide existed in the Old South where better material conditions prevailed, even stronger arguments apply for its practice in the Caribbean. In 'letting' their children die, women slaves would release them from a dismal future." Moreover, West African religious beliefs provided an ethical rational,

because a newborn infant "is not regarded as part of this world until eight or nine days have passed, during which period it may be ritually neglected."

35. Taylor-Guthrie, ed., *Conversations with Toni Morrison*, 207; Gilroy, *The Black Atlantic*, 65–67. Morrison gives 1851 as the date of the Garner incident, but the newspaper accounts Gilroy analyzes indicate it was 1856.

36. Taylor-Guthrie, ed. *Conversations with Toni Morrison*, 238.

37. Cited in Gilroy, *The Black Atlantic*, 219.

38. Taylor-Guthrie, ed., *Conversations with Toni Morrison*, 207–08.

39. Samuels and Hudson-Weems, *Toni Morrison*, 111. See also Taylor-Guthrie, ed., *Conversations*, 272.

40. Sherwin, *No Longer Patient: Feminist Ethics and Health Care*, 38. As Sherwin points out, Kant does not accord any prominence to the context of individual women's experiences, since he assumed that only men can fully "qualify as moral agents," and that women—like children and idiots—are either incapable of or unwilling to "ignore personal sentiments in their moral decision-making." Janet Hadley similarly emphasizes the limitations of a discourse of "rights" in addressing the ethical complexities of abortion in *Abortion: Between Freedom and Necessity*, 77–93. For other important studies of abortion ethics, see Carol Gilligan's *In a Different Voice: Psychological Theory and Women's Development* (Cambridge, Mass.: Harvard University Press, 1982), Rosalind Petchesky's *Abortion and Women's Choice: The State, Sexuality, and Reproductive Freedom* (1984; rev. ed. Boston: Northeastern University Press, 1990); Catriona Mackenzie's "Abortion and Embodiment," *Troubled Bodies: Critical Perspectives on Postmodernism, Medical Ethics and the Body*, ed. Paul A. Komesaroff (Durham and London: Duke University Press, 1995). 38–61; and *Reproduction, Ethics and the Law: Feminist Perspectives*, ed. Joan C. Callahan (Bloomington and Indianapolis: Indiana University Press 1995).

41. Loretta J. Ross, "African-American Women and Abortion: 1800–1970," *Theorizing Black Feminisms: The Visionary Pragmatism of Black Women*," ed. Stanlie M. James and Abena P. A. Busia (London and New York: Routledge, 1993), 142–44; Judith Wilt, *Abortion and Women's Choice: The Armageddon of the Maternal Instinct* (Chicago and London: University of Chicago Press, 1990), 23. The revised second edition of Petchesky's *Abortion and Women's Choice* reflects her attempt to address her earlier neglect of Afro-American perspectives, although Gayatri Chakravorty Spivak remains critical of Petchesky's First World focus and assumptions (see "Diasporas Old and New: Women in the Transnational World," *Textual Practice*, 10 [1996]: 265). Studies like Hadley's that do extend the North American white middle-class focus on abortion "choice" to include various aspects of reproductive control in a global context emphasize the forced infanticide of female children in countries such as China and India, given the contemporary urgency of this subject, not infanticide under conditions of slavery. For a survey of changing paradigms in an American political context, see Marcy J. Wilder, "The Rule of Law, The Rise of Violence, and the Role of Morality: Reframing America's Abortion Debate," *Abortion Wars: A Half Century of Struggle 1950–2000*, ed. Rickie Sollinger (Berkeley: University of California Press, 1998), 73–94.

42. Martha Nussbaum, *Love's Knowledge: Essays on Philosophy and Literature* (New York: Oxford University Press, 1990) and *Poetic Justice: The Literary Imagination and Public Life* (Boston: Beacon, 1995). Gilligan's *In a Different Voice* is an important

exception to the neglect of the literary; this may in part explain why her work has been so widely used by literary critics. Spelman's *Fruits of Sorrow*, although it is not concerned with abortion ethics, is another important exception, particularly relevant here because of the attention it gives to suffering caused by slavery.

43. Johnson's article (*Diacritics* 16 [1986]: 29–39) demonstrates how the ethical dilemma of abortion produces transformations in aesthetic form by complicating the structures of address in poems about abortion, such as Gwendolyn Brook's "The Mother." Although I do not have space to address them here, similar complications in the structures of address characterize "The Runaway Slave at Pilgrim's Point" and *Beloved.*

44. *Feminism and Tradition in Aesthetics,* ed. Peggy Zeglin Brand and Carolyn Korsmeyer (University Park: Pennsylvania State University Press, 1995), 13–18. In "Why Feminism Doesn't Need an Aesthetic (And Why It Can't Ignore Aesthetics" (in Brand and Korsmeyer), Rita Felski argues that we need to go "beyond feminist aesthetics" because of the tendency, even within a self-critical feminist theory, for female experience or artistic practice to be invoked as a "unproblematically universal category" that ignores the "discursive, institutional and material conditions" within which philosophers, artists and their audiences are embedded (434). Such a distinction is analogous to Sherwin's distinction between "feminine ethics" and "feminist aesthetics" (45–48).

45. Such an acknowledgment need not prohibit the shared regulative standards of "interactive universality," according to Seyla Benhabib in *Situating the Self: Gender, Community and Postmodernism in Contemporary Ethics* (New York: Routledge, 1992). In her terms, "'universality'" should be a regulative ideal "that does not deny our embodied and embedded identity," not the "ideal consensus of fictitiously defined selves" (153).

46. See Samuels and Hudson-Weems, *Toni Morrision*, 106, 111.

47. Ann-Janine Morey, "Margaret Atwood and Toni Morrison: Reflections on Postmodernism and the Study of Religion and Literature," *Toni Morrison's Fiction,* op. cit., p. 254. Morey compares *Surfacing* to *Beloved,* but she does not focus on the ethical aspects of abortion in Atwood's novel and infanticide in Morrison's.

PART III

AESTHETICS AND POLITICS

CHAPTER 9

Feminine Writing, Metaphor, and Myth

Drucilla Cornell

THE SIGNIFICANCE OF MYTH, AND THE FEMININE
AS AN IMAGINATIVE UNIVERSAL

The inability to simply escape our genderized context explains why the role of myth in feminist theory is essential to the reclaiming, and retelling, of "herstory" through the mimetic writing that specifies the feminine. I am again emphasizing the word "myth" deliberately, to emphasize the hold that myths of Woman and the feminine have over both individuals and cultures. They are remarkably unchanging. Hans Blumenberg has defined myth as follows:

> Myths are stories that are distinguished by a high degree of constancy in their narrative core and by an equally pronounced capacity for marginal variation. These two characteristics make myths transmissible by tradition: their constancy produces the attraction of recognizing them in artistic or ritual representation as well (as in recital), and their variability produces the attraction of trying out new and personal means of presenting them. It is the relationship of "theme and variations," whose attractiveness for both composers and listeners is familiar from music. So myths are not like "holy texts," which cannot be altered by one iota.[1]

Myth is one important way in which the feminine achieves what Blumenberg calls "significance." Significance is the deeper meaning we associate with myth's

Reprinted from Drucilla Cornell, *Beyond Accomodation: Ethical Feminism, Deconstruction, and the Law*, new ed. (New York: Rowman and Littlefield Publishers, 1999), 172–96, with permission of the author and the publisher.

capacity to provide our life-world with symbols, images, and metaphors that not only give us a shared environment but an environment that matters to us and inspires us. It is the constancy of myth that allows us to continue to recognize ourselves in the great myth-figures of the feminine, and to engage with them as touchstones for a feminine identification, if not identity. Hélène Cixous, for example, has powerfully evoked mythical figures in order to give significance to the deliverance of the feminine writer, seeking to find her way beyond a system of gender representation that she finds crippling. And, indeed, Irigaray has appealed to Ariadne to give mythic expression to *derelection*. The appeal to the mythic heightens the intensity associated with our own struggles to survive within patriarchal society and to find our ways out, our *sorties*. It is precisely the shared sense that our struggle "really matters" that is heightened through the engagement with mythical feminine figures.

The reinterpretation and recreation of mythical figures can also help us give body to the dream of an elsewhere beyond patriarchy and the tragedy imposed by a gender hierarchy that blocks the alliance between the sexes of which Irigaray writes. In her "Sorties," Cixous engages with mythical figures to indicate the "way out" from the Lacanian tragic-comedy in which—as it is beautifully evoked in Duras' allegory of thwarted desire, *Blue Eyes, Black Hair*[2]—the two sexes are fated to miss one another. For Cixous, there has to be an elsewhere in which love can be lived, in which lovers can meet in an alliance.

> There has to be somewhere else, I tell myself. And everyone knows that to go somewhere else there are routes, signs, "maps"—for an exploration, a trip. That's what books are. Everyone knows that a place exists which is not economically or politically indebted to all the vileness and compromise. That is not obliged to reproduce the system. That is writing. If there is a somewhere else that can escape the infernal repetition, it lies in that direction, where *it* writes itself, where *it* dreams, where *it* invents new worlds.[3]

But this reinvention can only begin where we "are" and where we "have been."

> If woman has always functioned "within' man's discourse, a signifier referring always to the opposing signifier that annihilates its particular energy, puts down or stifles its very different sounds, now it is time for her to displace this "within," explode it, overturn it, grab it, make it hers, take it in, take it into her women's mouth, bite its tongue with her women's teeth, make up her own tongue to get inside of it. And you will see how easily she will well up, from this "within" where she was hidden and dormant, to the lips where her foams will overflow. (*S*, 95–96)

For Cixous, we can read and reread certain important myths, particularly as they have been retold, as routes "out." For example, in her reading of Penthesileia, she finds signs that indicate the possibility of the elsewhere, a woman's community not dominated by men. In Penthesileia, Cixous reveals what first appears as "feminine" desire unleashed. The Law of the Father does not seem to constrain the woman warrior. She lives as if she were free. She acts as she pleases, indulges her own desire, fights back in the glory of her own strength.

> But the essence of Penthesileia is pure desire, frenzied desire, immediately outside all law. She is absolutely unbridled: unbounded flight, panicked by any shadow of a boundary-stone. And this pure desire, which has no other law than the need to reach its object, is absolutely, with no uncertainty, the one she wants; she saw it—like lightening she recognized it. A bolt of lightening itself. (*S*, 117)

Yet the "law" catches up to her precisely because the code of reversal demands that "[f]or a free woman, there can be no relationship with men other than war" (*S*, 116). The law of reversal only puts women where men have been, in the role of domination. But the sado-masochist machine continues to run. There is no place for love in the Amazons' code, only the war against domination. MacKinnon's ideal of a "sex for itself" turns against its own aspirations to be free of domination and ends in Penthesileia's death, the death that is "the vengeance of castration." Under Cixous' interpretation of the myth, Penthesileia had to die.

> And Kliest-also-dies, from being Penthesileia, from not being able to be Penthesileia without dying, as Penthesileia had to die from being too close to the shadow of the law, from having been afraid of the old ghosts, from having seen life itself get by within reach, within sight, from having brushed against it, from having felt the caress of its flaming hair, from not being able to hold onto it.
>
> How love a woman without encountering death? A woman who is neither doll nor corpse nor dumb nor weak. But beautiful, lofty, powerful, brilliant?
>
> Without history's making one feel its law of hatred?
>
> So the betrothed fall back into dust. Vengeance of castration, always at work, and which the wounded poet can surmount only in fiction. (*S*, 122)

The mistake of dreaming of a sex-for-itself in which the women are united against men is given mythical significance and played out in the lives of feminists who can only survive as the "warriors" responsible for keeping the boundaries intact so that men will not violate the border. The Law of the Father is reinstated at the same time that it is supposedly dominated. More precisely, to dominate the Law is to reinstate it. What is erected, according to Cixous' interpretation, is a barrier against the love that demands the new choreography of sexual difference, the multiplication of voices of lived sexuality.

Why obstacles to love? Accidents maybe. But anyway, in history, the first ob-
stacle, always already there, is in the existence, the production and reproduction
of images, types, coded and suitable ways of behaving, and in society's identification with a scene in which roles are fixed so that lovers are always initially
trapped by the puppets with which they are assumed to merge. (*S*, 113)

But sometimes, by playing, yet knowing we are playing, with the "role of
the ideal woman," we unchain ourselves. This possibility is the hope of Irigaray's *mimesis*. Cleopatra, for Cixous, is the mythical figure for such a woman.
Through her retelling of the story of Antony and Cleopatra, the couple in
which history becomes myth, she gives body to the dream of love that evokes
the elsewhere, indeed, demands it, as she gives another figure of Woman, the
woman who restyles herself playing with the role of being the phallus. Cleopatra, as read by Cixous, is the figure of feminine difference, a complete stranger
to "their" conventions that continuously restore the law of castration. She is the
threshold that Antony must cross to find love. Nor for Cixous—herself Alger-
ian—is it a coincidence that Cleopatra is from the "Third World." She is the
figure of the "other" woman who refuses to adjust to a culture that would deny
her the life she seeks.

But in the Orient, the Impossible is born; she who is incomprehensible, who
exceeds the imagination, who rewards the most powerful of men, she who has
all, and who is more than all, no existence can contain her, no man has been
able to equal her in radiance, in the length of ardor, in passion, yet the greatest
ones have adored her, have approached her, she has not fled, it is herself in flesh
and in reality who welcomes him, it is herself without making use of the glamour of absence who shows herself, unveiled, given to touch, to taste, but no
man has ever equaled her. Except, at the end of her life, Antony. (*S*, 126)

But she is also, for Cixous, the woman who knows that in order to survive,
she must play her role as the signifier of their desire.

She is woman made Art: each moment of her story with Antony is created, at
the same time ardently lived and immediately multiplied by incessant tensions, trans-formations, recreations that open and echo the thousands of
scenes in which love can infinitely inscribe its need of no limit. All her art in
the famous staging of her appearance to Antony's eyes. Entrance that has not
ceased repeating itself over the centuries. (*S*, 126)

But as she plays her role, she transforms it by affirming for herself the
abundance and beauty of her flesh. She is not the distant object, the signifier of
absence, she is "there," enacting in herself the art that makes love possible. The
lovers, in Cixous' interpretation of the myth, meet and mingle their bodies.

Abundance of fantasies and metaphors that inscribe the dialectic of this desire in figures of nourishment—heavenly foods, meats, wines. Everything exchanged between the two boundless lovers is received as the child receives mother's milk: on Antony's word, Cleopatra's ear breakfasts, and that is the right way. We are far from object "a," from the fatality of its absence, from its evasions that only sustain desire by default. (*S*, 127)

At the end of her quest, Cleopatra "finds" a lover who does not demand that she be less, or so the story goes, as Cixous dreams it. As Cixous writes, she consciously takes on the self-dramatization of expressing her own longing through myth. She knows that this is not the "real" story. Of course, she knows the danger of self-dramatization is the reinstatement of romanticism that glories in the self. Yet what *matters* is to "preserve" her dream of a love beyond the machinery of sado-masochism. Cixous will not settle for the ideology of lesser expectations that would say such a love is "unrealistic." Of course, it is "unrealistic" in the world as it is. Nor is she afraid to write erotic love in all of its chaos, as opposed to Kristeva's more cautious affirmation of caring love, or *agape*, as our hope. "Romantic" language is one rhetoric among others that Cixous plays with to evoke her Other-Love. Undoubtedly Cixous' seemingly "romantic" language can almost be embarassing to the Anglo-American feminist, more cautious before the apparent pitfalls for women of such language and such longing. Is it not this dream of Other-Love that always got us into trouble? But from whose theory, whose vantage point is "it" trouble? Not Cixous', as she celebrates that trouble, a celebration that itself is transformation through mimetic enactment of the feminine.

At the beginnings of *Other-Love* there are differences. The new love dares the other, wants it, seems in flight, be-leaves, does some stealing between knowing and making up. She, the one coming from forever, doesn't stand still, she goes all over, she exchanges, she is desire-that-gives. Not shut up inside the paradox of the gift-that-takes or in the illusion of onely uniting. She enters, she betweens—she mes and thees between the other me where one is always infinitely more than one and more than me, without fearing ever to reach a limit: sensualist in our be-coming. We'll never be done with it! She runs through defensive loves, motherings and devourings. (*S*, 99–100; emphasis in original)

Runs through, but does not merely repeat. "Elsewhere she gives," and what is given in Cixous' interpretation is precisely the elsewhere, ungovernable by the machine of sado-masochism.

They have—from the moment Antony saw Cleopatra coming to him—abandoned the minuscule old world, the planet—the shell with its thrones and rattles, its intrigues, its wars, its rivalries, its tournaments of the phallus, so grotesquely represented by the game of penis-check played by the imperialist superpowers of the triumvirate, with the mean solemnity that makes history. And with a leap, it is toward the new land they go to look for an entirely different life. (*S*, 128)

Cleopatra, in Cixous' rendering of the myth, refigures Woman as she who plays with the effects of her castration so as not to accept it. Cleopatra is already the Queen. Even Dido, for Cixous, is not a Woman within whom she can self-dramatize her own experience and find significance. But Cleopatra, as figured by Cixous, is:

profusion, energy, exuberance. That is what she is. To be sure, she has at her disposition material reserves from whose magnificence her generosity can draw. Absolute Queen of several countries, she can give more than anyone. But also, all the splendor of the life that Antony and Cleopatra make together is commensurate with the fabulous grandeur of their investments, material, fleshly, symbolic, spiritual: not only do they have everything, strength, power—almost absolute—but it is nothing. They do not take all this for something, they reduce it, with a kiss, to the nothing that it has never ceased to be, save in the eyes of beings who know nothing of love, that is to say, everybody. At no moment do all these glories, all these treasures, for which men make peoples kill each other, make them bat an eye. (*S*, 127)

Cixous' tone undoubtedly has a Nietzschean exuberance to it. With him, she celebrates through her retelling of myth the Woman of style. But the difference is that she tells the myth by emphasizing the side of the feminine from within and as the threshold that gives as "elsewhere." "And far from kingdoms, from caesars, from brawls, from the cravings of penis and sword, from the unnameable 'goods' of this world, far from show and self-love, in harmony with each other, in accord, they live still" (*S*, 130). Cixous refuses the Lacanian lesson that love must be "banging your head against the wall."[4] Says who?

In Cixous, we remember the dream of living beyond castration by giving the dream expression and dramatic significance through the retelling of the myth. This memory is recollective imagination. We recollect the mythic figures of the past, but as we do so, we reimagine them. It is the potential variability of myth that allows us to work within myth, and the significance it offers, to reimagine our world and by so doing, to begin to dream of a new one. In myth we do find Woman, with a capital letter. These myths, as Lacan indicates, may be rooted in male fantasy, but they cannot, as he would sometimes suggest, be reduced to it. The "reality" presented in myth cannot be separated from the performative capacity of language. This is why we can work within to create an artificial mythology. As a result, even in myth, "reality" is always shifting as the metaphors in which it is presented yield a different and novel interpretation of the myth's meaning. I want to suggest that the feminist reconstruction of myth, such as we find in Christa Wolf's *Cassandra* and in Carol Gilligan's recent lectures on love, involves recovering the feminine as an imaginative universal, which in turn feeds the power of the feminine imagination and helps avoid the depletion of the feminine imaginary in the name of the masculine symbolic.[5] This use of the feminine as an imaginative universal does not, and should not, pretend to simply tell the "truth" of Woman as she was, or is. This is why our mythology is self-consciously an artificial mythology; Woman is "discovered" as an ethical standard. As she is "discovered," her meaning is also created. In spite of Cixous' wariness of her defeat, better to love like Dido than found the Roman Empire. In like manner, we have no doubt after reading Wolf's *Cassandra* that Achilles had his priorities all wrong, and that Cassandra should have been listened to, because she saw the connection between destruction and masculine subjectivity. In this sense, the reconstruction of myth can bring the *differend* out of the shadows.[6] Moreover, the reconstruction of myth also involves making explicit the utopian aspiration that the reinterpretation expresses. As Wolf explains: "The Troy I have in mind is not a description of bygone days but a model for a kind of utopia" (*C*, 224). That utopian Troy is Cassandra's Troy, not Achilles'! But we also are given a different definition through the reinterpretation of the myth of feminine power.

The feminist visionary who sees the world *differently* and tells us of her world may be ignored, but her vision cannot be taken away from her, as MacKinnon would argue, because the only viewpoint available is male. Wolf's allegory of the feminine indicates that Woman is the *seer* precisely to the degree that she skirts castration by the symbolic order. Cassandra saw "the truth" of Troy. In the feminist retelling of the myth, she was not mad, only true to her "reality." Feminine power as defined in the myth is the gift and the burden of "seeing." Of course, we can enter, and indeed to some degree we are forced to enter, the realm of the symbolic as we write, and by so doing we undermine our power of seeing differently. The price we pay for seeing differently is great. We know what Wolf's Cassandra suffers.

But, of course, there is also an implicit retelling of Oedipus in Wolf's *Cassandra*. The ascension into the symbolic for the masculine subject is the acceptance of castration. Blindness is what follows, the price to be paid. The illusion that having the penis is having the phallus protects against "seeing." The price that has been paid is that *man* cannot see his own castration. But Cassandra *sees* that he does not have what he thinks he has. If there is a central mistake in Andrea Dworkin's *Intercourse*,[7] it is to accept the masculine illusion that having the penis is having the phallus. In the end, it is just a penis.

When we, as women, speak of Wolf's *Cassandra*, of her experience as reinterpreted, of her Troy as retold, we do not return to essentialism; we dream from the standpoint of the mythical figures who could redeem the feminine as the threshold to a life beyond castration. We are imagining, not describing.

THE CRITIQUE OF STRATEGIC ESSENTIALISM

But this process of reinterpretation and reimagination should not be thought of as strategic essentialism. Gayatri Spivak has argued that, in spite of the postmodern deconstruction of gender identity, and more specifically of Woman, we need to speak and write of Woman, or in Spivak's case, the shared conditions of women, in order to promote the politics of feminism.[8] This writing and speaking of Woman she refers to as strategic essentialism; strategic, because it is consciously directed toward a political goal, and essentialism, because it reinstates some version of the essence of Woman and the feminine, even if only temporarily and for a political purpose. To quote Spivak:

> To begin with, I think the way in which the awareness of strategy works here is through a persistent critique. The critical moment does not come only at a certain stage when one sees one's effort, in terms of an essence that has been used for political mobilization, succeeding, when one sees that one has successfully brought a political movement to a conclusion, as in the case of revolutions or national liberation movements. . . . . It seems to me that the awareness of strategy—the strategic use of an essence as a mobilizing slogan or masterword like *woman* or *worker* or the name of any notion that you would like—it seems to me that this critique has to be persistent all along the way, even when it seems that to remind oneself of it is counterproductive. Unfortunately, that crisis must be with us, otherwise the strategy freezes into something like what you call an essentialist position. (*IW*, 126–27)

For Spivak, then, the very word strategy implies a critique of postures toward essentialism, which attempts to give us more than strategy. As she explains, a strategy is not necessarily a position, which can too easily be frozen into a supposed explanation. As she also explains, "[a] strategy suits a situation; a strategy is not a theory" (*IW*, 27).

Therefore, embracing essentialism strategically need not lead necessarily to the normative injunction of a movement—in this case, identification as a woman, a worker, and so on—masquerading as a statement about ontology. Spivak emphasizes the appeal to essentialism as strategy and, therefore, as an explicitly political posture. If there were a "timeless" essence, it could not be strategically affirmed or rejected. It would remain. In a sense, the word strategy contradicts essentialism, if understood as "something" always "there," even if distorted in form.

For Spivak, the more profound point is that we cannot help but risk essence. For example, for the anti-essentialist, anti-essentialism becomes the essence of feminism. According to Spivak, deconstruction does not dismantle "essentialism" altogether as much as it shows us "the unavoidable usefulness of something that is very dangerous" (*IW*, 129). But she not only embraces "strategic" essentialism, she also distinguishes essentialism from an appeal to "context" and thus from attempts to write of the specificity of any particular group, including women. The debate over essentialism has become obstructionist for Spivak, precisely because the anti-essentialists tend to identify all attempts to specify female national or class difference as essentialist. Her objection to the form in which this debate has recently taken place is political, and explicitly so.

In a similar manner, in the sense of being inspired by a political positioning, Diana Fuss has argued that Irigaray's "essentialism" should be understood politically.[9] Her "essentialism" is necessary, in other words, within the gender hierarchy of Western philosophy that has reduced Woman to lack, the ground of man's essence.

> Irigaray's reading of Aristotle's understanding of essence reminds one of Lacan's distinction between *being* and *having* the phallus: woman does not *possess* the phallus, she *is* the phallus. Similarly, we can say that, in Aristotelian logic, a woman does not *have* an essence, she *is* essence. Therefore to give "woman" an essence is to undo Western phallomorphism and to offer women entry into subjecthood. Moreover, because in this Western ontology existence is predicated on essence, it has been possible for someone like Lacan to conclude, *remaining fully within traditional metaphysics,* that without essence, "woman does not exist." Does this not cast rather a different light on Irigaray's theorization of woman's essence? A woman who lays claim to an essence of her own undoes the conventional binarisms of essence/accident, form/matter, and actuality/potentiality. In this specific historical context, to essentialize "woman" can be a politically strategic gesture of displacement.[10]

My disagreement with Spivak and Fuss is twofold. First, as I have argued, the writing of the feminine need not be essentialist or naturalist, as these two terms are technically understood. Deconstruction shows us the limit of essentialism as one specific discourse in which the being of the thing is unveiled in its universal properties or grasped in its general form. But deconstruction shows the limit of essentialism as it is thought to encompass all attempts to write specifically of any group or context. Thus there is a difference between an appeal to essence and the illumination of feminine specificity as an explicit ethical and political position. Spivak, in other words, is right to claim that not every appeal to "context" involves essence. Her mistake is that we should even adopt the word "essence" when we are indicating specificity. It is precisely the confusion of essentialism with any writing of the specificity of feminine difference that leads to the belief that we risk either "essentialism" or indifference to the suffering of women. The solution is precisely the one of deconstruction: to show the limit of essentialism through—at least in the case of Husserl—its self-contradictory positioning within language.

As Fuss herself reminds us, Irigaray directly states that what she seeks "is not to create a theory of woman, but to secure a place for the feminine within sexual difference."[11] Thus the thinking of feminine difference, as we have seen with Derrida, cannot be separated from the problem of thinking difference more generally. The difficulty, of course, is that to conceptualize difference is once again to reinstate the identity through its very determination as a concept. As a result, Derrida engages multiple rhetorical strategies—supplement, difference, and so on—to indicate the difference that cannot be conceptualized. In like manner, Irigaray does not want to conceptualize Woman, nor determine her essence, even as the basis for her subjecthood, precisely because this determination through the concept would inevitably reinstate the specific, phallogocentric structure of identification in which subjecthood had been defined. To define through the concept, and more specifically the concept of essence in which the thing is understood with its own negativity—as we learn from Hegel[12]—is still to define difference within a pregiven totality of ideality, even in the unique Hegelian sense of essence. The Derridean demonstration is that this reinstatement of difference within ideality is inadequate to difference.

Within Irigaray, the demonstration is also of the specific inadequacy of the relational ideality that has confined woman in her role as complement. Therefore, Irigaray does not write of woman as if she is to be reconceptualized as an essence or a subject; rather, she writes from the side of the feminine, a positioning that has been imposed by the gender hierarchy. However, this being said, we cannot simply place ourselves outside of the ideality in which the masculine and the feminine have been defined.[13] We cannot just drop out of gender or sex roles and pick them up again when we feel like it. Disruption takes place from "within." The writing of the feminine does not, then, displace through the reconceptualization of Woman's essence but through *mimesis* as *de-sistance*. The feminine, through *mimesis*, is no longer repudiated as an imposition but affirmed as a positioning. Such an affirmation is clearly both ethical and political.

This leads me to my second objection to Spivak and Fuss. In one sense, to write from the side of the feminine could be considered strategic, adopted for the purpose of achieving a political goal. But such writing is not simply strategic, in the sense that it is a *conscious* manipulation. We cannot escape the hold of the feminine on the unconscious, which is precisely why we work within myth to reinterpret and transform rather than merely reject. Theoretically, identity may be deconstructed as pure form or structure, as the *de-sistance* of *mimesis;* but gender identity is, practically, very much in place and enforced by the law. *Mimesis* is our only other option if we are not to repudiate the feminine. More importantly, the affirmation of the feminine, and indeed, of the irreducibility of the feminine, is not simply strategic, goal oriented, but also utopian, in that it tries to keep alive an "elsewhere" beyond our current conception of the political as an instrumental struggle for power. As we have seen in

Cixous, the feminine encompasses the possibility of Other-Love. The maternal, as one figure, embodies the utopian possibility of a different nonviolent relation to Otherness. In Irigaray, the feminine as threshold is the limit to what is, while *as fantasy*, it is the overflow that cannot be contained. The recasting of immanence and transcendence is metaphorized by Irigaray's writing from the position of the feminine, and more directly from within the female "sex."

> We need both space and time. And perhaps we are living in an age when *time must redeploy space*. Could this be the dawning of a new world? Immanence and transcendence are being recast, notably by that *threshold* which has never been examined in itself unto *mucosity*. Beyond the classic opposites of love and hate, liquid and ice lies this perpetually *half-open* threshold, consisting of *lips* that are strangers to dichotomy. Pressed against one another, but without any possibility of suture, at least of a real kind, they do not absorb the world either into themselves or through themselves, provided they are not abused and reduced to a mere consummating or consuming structure. Instead their shape welcomes without assimilating or reducing or devouring. A sort of door unto voluptuousness, then? Not that, either: their useful function is to designate a *place*: the very place of uselessness, at least on a habitual plane. Strictly speaking, they serve neither conception nor *jouissance*. Is this, then, the mystery of female identity, of its self-contemplation, of that strange word of silence: Both the threshold and reception of exchange, the sealed-up secret of wisdom, belief and faith in every truth?[14]

IRIGARAY'S ETHICAL EVOCATION OF THE BODY OF WOMAN

Is Irigaray, in her evocation of the language of the feminine body, writing literally of the characteristics of that body? Is this a description of what a woman's body *is*, and therefore an identarian logic: so the body is, so Woman is? Is she mapping the feminine on to femaleness, and therefore reverting to the essentialism of universal properties? Irigaray herself has explicitly distinguished between the anatomical and the morphological in her writing of the body, a distinction that many Anglo-American feminist theorists have found unconvincing. Beyond this distinction, however, should be the realization that Irigaray's evocation of the threshold in which difference could be lived differently is not a *description* at all. It is an attempt to give body to the threshold of the phallocentric order as feminine difference, to be sure. But such writing is explicitly *ethical* in that it tries to offer us an engagement with the Other that confounds the mirror symmetry that annihilates the difference in identity. The feminine body is no longer sentenced to confinement within their vision of "it" as lack. In other words, her writing does not give us a description of the woman's body as the essence of femaleness. Instead, she denies the truth of their description. Anatomy is *not* destiny, as essence or as imposed by the law of gender identity. The *feminine body* "figures" as an ethical relation that includes carnality and, indeed, is embodied as the woman sex that is not one. "The lips that touch" figure a connection to one's self that does not involve the illusory projection of the subject as one consolidated entity. When we try to envision a "new world," a destiny that is not the fate imposed upon us by the phallogo-centric machine, we rely on literary techniques, here not the literality of the body, but the feminine body returned as the symbolization of the nonviolatable relationship to difference, embodied in the sex that is not one.

> (Superimposed, moreover, these lips adopt a cross-like shape that is the pro-totype of the crossroads, thus representing both *inter* and *enter,* for the lips of the mouth and the lips of the female sex do not point in the same direction. To a certain extent they are not arranged as one might expect: those "down below" are vertical.)
>
> Approached in this light, where the edges of the body join in an embrace that transcends all limits and which nevertheless does not risk falling into the abyss thanks to the fertility of this porous space, in the most extreme mo-ments of sensation, which still lie in the future, each self-discovery takes place in that area which cannot be spoken of, but that forms the fluid basis of life and language. (*SD*, 128; emphasis in original)

For this love of the Other, that celebrates the love of oneself as Other, Iri-garay evokes God—"or a love so scrupulous that it is divine" (*SD*, 128), but God is embodied through the redeployment of space. The challenge to the tra-ditional categories of immanence and transcendence—necessary to the rede-ployment of space to save the utopian possibility of Other-Lover—is done more specifically through the evocation of the "difference" of the female body. Certainly, this is an explicit challenge to the phallogocentric metaphors through which we can only conceive of difference through identification of the object as "for" the subject, Irigaray's "mirror symmetry." Fuss, for example, has argued that Irigaray's "two lips" is a metonymic figure deliberately opposed to the reigning metaphor of the phallus, and with the phallus, to the reign of metaphor itself. Fuss' reliance on the "two lips" as a metonymic figure, as against a metaphorical figure, is too neat, since the refiguration is inescapably metaphorical. When Irigaray evokes the threshold as feminine difference, and the proximity to difference in oneself as feminine and as figured by the two lips in contact, she relies on the power of metaphoric transference (i.e., the thresh-old "as"). But Fuss is certainly correct in her interpretation of Irigaray's writing of the body as literary refiguration, not just description. My addition here is that this refiguration through the feminine body is necessary for a carnal ethics.

The sexualization of the ethical relation is deliberate and is a denial of the rejection of the flesh often associated with the very idea of a moral subject. We saw earlier that the writing of the maternal body "presented" a "subject of heterogeneity" in which the One is tied to the Other and, therefore, is not truly One. This writing is also explicitly ethical in that the "maternal body" presents us with an image of love through non-identity. But Irigary's suspicion of the identification of the feminine as the maternal function has turned her away from this image of the One with the Other. Instead, we are presented with the carnality of the feminine "sex" as the embodiment of a proximity that is not appropriation, nor even an encompassing of the Other by the self. There is a broader theoretical point to be made here: the evocation of the ethical relation, as Other-Love beyond the current identity structures established by phallogocentrism cannot rely on an appeal to what "is" either as mere description, or as a reality given to us in "the conversation of mankind." Difference is also differentiation in time, what is different from what is. The future is not conceived as an evolution of the present, which would be the perpetuation of the same, and in this case, the same old story of gender hierarchy. Feminine writing, in this sense, turns us toward the future.

The politics of difference demands that we think the new, the different. But, of course, whenever we think the new, we can only conceive of it within the pregiven ideality. The pregiven ideality, which undoubtedly establishes the intelligible, also serves as an undertow to repetition. The role of the aesthetic in the dreaming of the new, the different, beyond the current machine of sadomasochism, lies precisely in its power to evoke, and indeed to challenge, the very conventions of intelligibility that make us "see" the world from the viewpoint of the masculine. The explicit "use" of feminine language is one tool in undermining current conceptualizations in which the world, ethics, and politics are perceived. It would be a mistake, then, to think that writing of the feminine is apolitical, or even that it replaces the political with the aesthetic. Rather, the politics of difference and the difference of the feminine demand the evocation of utopian possibility and, therefore, inevitably have an aesthetic dimension. Without the aesthetic evocation of utopian possibility of feminine difference, we are left with the politics of revenge to which MacKinnon calls us. Feminism becomes another power seeking ideology, a reversal that inevitably reinstates the old economy. As Irigaray reminds us, on the contrary, "the transition to a new age coincides with a change in the economy of desire, necessitating a different relationship between man and god(s), man and man, man and the world, man and woman" (*SD*, 120). Put very simply, the politics of feminism needs its poetry for the redefinition of the goal of feminist politics and, indeed, of the very content of politics itself. Politics is now not only the struggle for survival within patriarchy, as important as that struggle obviously is, but also the struggle through the dream for a new world, a different future.

We can now "see" how Catharine MacKinnon has obscured the real power of the celebration of the utopian potential of feminine difference. As we have seen in her debate with Gilligan,[15] MacKinnon challenged her opponent for affirming the conditions of women's oppression. MacKinnon was not concerned to challenge Gilligan's empirical findings over the question of whether this "ethic of care" was actually correlated with women. She argued that to the degree that women demonstrated different characteristics, it was because they had been subordinated. As a result, these characteristics should be rejected as suspect. On the perspective I have offered here, it is not important whether women have *actually* achieved a different way of loving that is superior and therefore to be valued. Gilligan's and Wolf's narrations are a part of our artificial mythology. As we tell the story, we are in part creating the reality in which this is the case. What matters is that the retelling of the feminine as an imaginative universal gives body to the "elsewhere," which makes this one appear "fallen" and gives us the hope and the dream that we may one day be beyond it. But it also allows us to affirm the feminine.

DOUBLE WRITING AND LITERARY LANGUAGE

The need to pay attention to the specificity of literary language and to avoid a literal interpretation of feminine writing and mythology also has been evidenced in another debate within feminist circles. Some literary critics have challenged the recent writings of Afro-American women for mistaken idealizations of that experience that reinstates the philosophy of full presence. The attempt is to give specificity and, indeed, mythological significance to the unique experience of Afro-American women. For example, Hortense Spillers challenged author Toni Morrison for privileging speech—or, more specifically, a primordial, musical language–over writing, as she writes of the "lost origin" of the Afro-American mother-tongue.[16] "Nan," the woman who "mothered" Sethe and others, still spoke that language. She, in Sethe's memory, still lived with the mother-tongue.

> Nan was the one she knew best, who was around all day, who nursed babies, cooked, had one good arm and half of another. And who used different words. Words Sethe understood then but could neither recall nor repeat now. She believed that must be why she remembered so little before Sweet Home except singing and dancing and how crowded it was. What Nan told her she had forgotten, along with the language she told it in. The same language her ma'am spoke, and which would never come back. But the message—that was and had been there all along.[17]

I use this quote deliberately. There are certainly other places in the novel where Morrison seems to appeal to a lost language that is different, and fundamentally so, from the white man's. There are many different levels on which the passage I have chosen can be interpreted. The first is that Sethe, the runaway slave forced ultimately to kill her own children in order to save them from slavery, is mourning her own lost possibility of a return to the mythical, "true" mother who knew the secret and could unlock the message. "Nan," on this reading, is the allegorical figure of the loss of the mother and with her, her magic to give counter-structures of identification, and with them a different language. "Holding the damp white sheets against her chest, she was picking meaning out of a code she no longer understood" (*BL*, 62). On this reading, Morrison's allegory of the lost mother who could provide the basis of identification, and thus of meaning, should not be identified with a statement about what Afro-American language is. Her language is the imaginary through which Sethe dreams of a different life whose possibility as a real alternative has now been forgotten. Sethe herself is the figure of the mother who had to kill her children to prevent their enslavement. Thus the tale of loss doubles in on itself. Sethe is left with the white man's language, which blocks her from recovering "the message."

Here we have a brilliant narration through the character of the Afro-American woman, Sethe, of how the loss of the "true" mother leaves only the white man's realm of the symbolic, in which the Afro-American woman cannot "find" herself. She can only remember herself through a future that is not yet. In Morrison's evocation of the lost or spectral mother, and with her a different language—what Kristeva has referred to as the semiotic—we also have the expression of one of the most profound tragedies imposed by racism and imperialism, the suppression of the Other's language and culture. Certainly, no one has written more sensitively than Derrida about the suppression of the Other's language and culture associated with imperialism and its racist justifications. The attempt to recover a language other than theirs, always an act of creation although frequently sought through the memory, motivated by loss, is part of the resistance of the imperialists' attempt to be the sole defining power of who the oppressed people are. To stress the difference of Afro-American speech can only be done through contrast with "theirs." This is a similar point to the one that Kristeva makes, that the semiotic is ultimately still dependent on the symbolic, since it relies on its point of contact where break and resistance are defined.[18]

Thus when the "lost" language is given specification as different from theirs, it can only seem to take on characteristics reminiscent of the privilege of full presence, voice over writing, musical repetition over the distance of articulated language, and so on. When we speak *of* the semiotic, we are not writing from within "poetic" language. When the women in *Beloved* hollered, "[t]hey stopped praying and took a step back to the beginning. In the beginning there were no words. In the beginning was the sound, and they all knew what that sound sounded like" (*BL*, 259). The "lost" language escapes capture by the white man's imposed conventions. "They sang it out and beat it up, garbling the words so they could not be understood; tricking the words so their syllables yielded up other meanings" (BL, 108).

But it would be a mistake, since this is a novel, to quickly identify the fictional specification of the lost language—itself, as I have suggested, connected to the allegory of the spectral mother—as replicating the error of the "philosophy of presence." The technical interpretive danger is that such an interpretation potentially fails to take into account the distinctiveness of literary language. Such a language has the power to formulate itself as act. The performative aspect of this language creates its own reality. In the great "novel" *Finnegans Wake*, the reality of "fici-fact" that is written is constantly being undermined, put back into motion, by the very language in which it "is."[19] The language of the night blows apart the seemingly static articulations and conventions of day-to-day life. But such "night" language is not the only way to write, which is consistent with "the double gesture." One must be careful of bringing the charge of reinstating "the philosophy of full presence" against a novelist who, as such, is engaging in the distinctive genre of literary discourse, but particularly in this case, where Morrison's "references" to the characteristic lost language should themselves be interpreted within the allegory of the unrepresentable "past" of the spectral mother. *Beloved* is best read as an allegory of the loss of identity of Afro-American women imposed by slave society. The dead baby, taken away from mother by a society that could give her no possibility of life, other than one of enslavement, returns as the ghost that keeps the past in the so-called identity of the escaped slave. But as such, the ghost allegorizes the disruption of that present identity. As an apparition, there can be no coming to a permanent identity that is fully present. *Beloved* is the allegory of this absence in the present. There can be no adequate account of her loss in their language, other than as allegory.

> Everybody knew what she was called, but nobody anywhere knew her name. Disremembered and unaccounted for, she cannot be lost because no one is looking for her, and even if they were, how can they call her if they don't know her name? Although she has claim, she is not claimed. In the place where long grass opens, the girl who waited to be loved and cry shame erupts into her separate parts, to make it easy for the chewing laughter to swallow her all away.
> It was not a story to pass on. (BL, 274)

To pass on the story would require its translation into a language inadequate to its expression. The Law of the Father cannot identify the Afro-American woman, nor can she identify herself within the law.

In her powerful article "Sapphire Bound!" Regina Austin has also shown us that "the law" cannot conceive of the Afro-American woman other than as a combination of "black" and "female" and therefore cannot think of her at all.[20] In an analysis of several legal cases, she demonstrates how problems of jurisdiction in employment discrimination and constitutional law cannot be adequately resolved, because judges have been incapable of thinking of exactly what "quantities" of "blackness" and "femaleness" actually make up a "black woman" for purposes of the law. Is she one-third "woman," two-thirds "black"? Or is she instead half and half? Or two-thirds "woman," one third "black"? Is she, at least in some ways, more "black" than "woman," or more "woman" than "black"? Such questions *matter.* But courts go around and around again. In "Sapphire," Austin shows that the very conception of the person used to analyze what it is to be "black" and "woman"—cutting her into properties and defining "blackness" and "femaleness" as separate—fails, and inevitably so, to "represent" her. An Afro-American woman is not divisible into her "blackness" and "femaleness." It is not that she is both "black" and "female." She is an Afro-American female, whose purported property of "blackness" can in no way be separated from who she is as a woman. Woman is lived differently when one is an Afro-American female. Austin brilliantly shows that the concept of "woman" itself is thought to be primordially white, with "blackness" thrown in later. When the courts, in other words, speak of "woman" as something separable from Afro-American descent, they are postulating a kind of femaleness, as a property or substance, that all women share. Femaleness is a universal that can "be" shared. Then we add race or nationality. But as Austin demonstrates, it is precisely femaleness that is lived differently when the woman is Afro-American. The specificity that must be sought is that unique to the Afro-American woman.

Austin herself adopts an innovative style—certainly innovative for a law review article—to give body to what cannot be conceived under the analytic structure of the person. The figure of Sapphire exposes the impossibility of finding her "reality" under their system of representation. As they struggle to know her, to capture her in their categories, she remains beyond, figuring herself in a way that cannot be grasped by them, and yet she is figured as Sapphire. Austin's discourse thus avoids the danger of "indifference" in which nothing is said or written about the specificity unique to Afro-American women, at the same time that she exposes the fallacy of the assumption that all women share femaleness as a property, in the same way.

To summarize, the "double gesture," as I have interpreted it, does not by definition have to belie any attempt to give body to the specificity, or more generally to the specificity of the feminine, as it is lived by women of color. If it did, it would be a necessary risk to "indifference."[21] Reliance on allegory can never be fully separated from the metaphorical attempt to give body to the figures of Woman who are evoked. Sapphire speaks for herself.

THE CRITIQUE OF MYTH

The Appeal to Identity

The danger of reinstating the myth of full presence is only one objection to the affirmation of the need to interpret, rather than reject, the myths of the feminine. And indeed there are at least two different conceptions of what this objection involves, both with an explicitly ethical dimension. The two different conceptions should be kept separate, for one involves an appeal to individual identity, and the other, at least on one level, to individual and social difference.

The first was made by Simone de Beauvoir in *The Second Sex.*[22] The myths of the feminine according to de Beauvoir reflect the refusal of the male to understand that woman is not his Other but a being like him, given to transcendence. More specifically, myth reflects the social containment of women in a gender identity, which marks them as the Other. The identification of Woman as Other is what the myths justify. Yet it is precisely this structure of justification that prevents Woman from living out her singularity. Each woman becomes Woman. But Woman is nothing other than the projection of "their" fantasy of Otherness that sustains "their" identity, "their" primacy. Once the role of myth in the perpetuation of the fantasy made reality of Woman as Other is exposed, it leads to de Beauvoir's conclusion that feminism must dethrone, rather than affirm, even if through reinterpretation, myths of the feminine. The myths, in other words, can only reinforce the conceptualization of Woman as Other, which in turn justifies femininity as the fate that undermines every woman's destiny as an individual human being.

> The women of today are in a fair way to dethrone the myth of femininity; they are beginning to affirm their independence in concrete ways; but they do not easily succeed in living completely the life of a human being. Reared by women within a feminine world, their normal destiny is marriage, which still means practically subordination to man; for masculine prestige is far from extinction, resting still upon solid economic and social foundations. (*SS*, xxxv)

Obviously de Beauvoir recognizes that the actual subordination of women finds its basis in economic and social forms of oppression. But for de Beauvoir it is not a coincidence that the justificatory apparatus of patriarchal society demands the creation of myths of Woman. Men are the subjects; as subjects they are the myth makers. Therefore, there is a significant difference between the mythologization of Woman and the celebration of masculinity through heroes, even if done in myth. It is enough for a man to be a man. As man, according to de Beauvoir, he is singular, himself. It is his uniqueness as an actual subject that is celebrated.

> A myth always implies a subject who projects his hopes and his fears toward a sky of transcendence. Women do not set themselves up as Subject and hence have erected no virile myth in which their projects are reflected; they have no religion or poetry of their own: they still dream through the dreams of men. Gods made by males are the gods they worship. Men have shaped for their own exaltation great virile figures: Hercules, Prometheus, Parsifal; woman has only a secondary part to play in the destiny of these heroes. No doubt there are conventional figures of man caught in his relations to women: the father, the seducer, the husband, the jealous lover, the good son, the way-ward son; but they have all been established by men, and they lack the dig-nity of myth, being hardly more than clichés. Whereas woman is defined exclusively in her relation to man. The asymmetry of the categories—male and female—is made manifest in the unilateral form of sexual myths. We sometimes say "the sex" to designate woman; she is the flesh, its delights and dangers. The truth that for woman man is sex and carnality has never been proclaimed, because there is no one to proclaim it. Representation of the world, like the world itself, is the work of men; they describe it from their own point of view, which they confuse with absolute truth. (*SS*, 161)

In her description of the asymmetry between men and women embodied in the mythological status that Woman as Other takes on in patriarchal society, de Beauvoir comes very close to MacKinnon. As they represent the world, so it is. Myth, with its deep hold on the unconscious, simply masks that reality, that they are representing us as Other. As in Lacan, in de Beauvoir we cannot find ourselves in the feminine embodied in myth. We cannot identify with their fantasy of us. To dethrone myth is to expose the fallacy—which preserves the illusion that their point of view is rightfully identified as absolute truth—that their point of view deserves the status of myth. The only "truth" that is em-bodied in myth is precisely their fantasy projection of Woman as Other, which belies our singularity. Translated into de Beauvoir's existentialist idiom, we re-main in our transcendence from the immanence that the species seemingly im-poses upon us because of our femininity, even if it is undoubtedly the case, as de Beauvoir sees it, that femininity is the imposition of the species on us.

But in her next paragraph she concedes:

> It is always difficult to describe a myth; it cannot be grasped or encompassed; it haunts the human consciousness without ever appearing before it in fixed form. The myth is so various, so contradictory, that at first its unity is not dis-cerned: Delilah and Judith, Aspasia and Lucretia, Pandora and Athena—woman is at once Eve and the Virgin Mary. She is an idol, a servant, the

source of life, a power of darkness; she is the elemental silence of truth, she is artifice, gossip, and falsehood; she is healing presence and sorceress; she is man's prey, his downfall, she is everything that he is not and that he longs for, his negation, and his *raison d'être*. (*SS*, 161-62)

At the heart of de Beauvoir's analysis of myth is her desire to return Woman to humanity. Men and women are to affirm "their brotherhood" as fellow human creatures, irreducible to their supposed divergent essences as males and females. As with MacKinnon, what sexual difference might mean in the future, freed from patriarchal ordering, is unimaginable now. The goal of feminist politics is to be like them, no longer burdened by the demands of the species and the constraints of a structure of gender identity in which "the male seems infinitely favored" (*SS*, 36).

The free woman is just being born; when she has won possession of herself perhaps Rimbaud's prophecy will be fulfilled: "There shall be poets! When woman's unmeasured bondage shall be broken, when she shall live for and through herself, man—hitherto detestable—having let her go, she, too, will be poet! Woman will find the unknown! Will her ideational worlds be different from ours? She will come upon strange, unfathomable, repellent, delightful things: we shall take them we shall comprehend them." It is not sure that her "Ideational worlds" will be different from those of men, since it will be through attaining the same situation as theirs that she will find emancipation; to say in what degree she will remain different, in what degree these differences will retain their importance—this would be to hazard bold predictions indeed. What is certain is that hitherto woman's possibilities have been suppressed and lost to humanity, and that it is high time she be permitted to take her chances in her own interest and in the interest of all. (*SS*, 795; quoting a letter from Rimbaud to Pierre Demeny, May 15, 1871)

The dethroning of the myths of femininity is a necessary, even if not a sufficient, step in dismantling patriarchy. In de Beauvoir, it is evident that women, once freed from complicity in their perpetuation of their oppression and from economic subordination, will find their opportunity to achieve "full membership in the human race" (*SS*, xxxiv). De Beauvoir must assume that women are like men; it is only their "false" projections of us that disguise this reality.

Now, what peculiarly signalizes the situation of woman is that she—a free and autonomous being like all human creatures—nevertheless finds herself living in a world where men compel her to assume the status of the Other. They propose to stabilize her as object and to doom her to immanence since her transcendence is to be overshadowed and forever transcended by another ego (*conscience*) which is essential and sovereign. The drama of woman lies in this conflict between the fundamental aspirations of every subject (ego)—who always regards the self as the essential—and the compulsions of a situation in which she is the inessential. (*SS*, xxxiii–xxxiv)

Thus the first objection to the reinterpretation of the myths of the feminine postulates a universal human subject with certain characteristics, even if those characteristics are defined as the inevitability of transcendence and individual liberty. In that sense, the objection appeals to identity. To make the feminine different is only to deny her the subjectivity she can still live up to. I use the words "live up to" deliberately. There is perhaps no greater example of the writer who constantly call us "to be" like them than de Beauvoir. It is we who have to try harder. It is no coincidence that the relief that comes with the affirmation of feminine difference does so, at least in part, because we can at last stop trying so hard to be *like* them. As Irigaray reminds us, it is time for women to stop trying so hard. De Beauvoir's existentialist subject is masculine. Our femininity is our deficiency, an unfortunate imposition. I cannot describe in detail the way in which *The Second Sex* tragically reflects the repudiation of the feminine at the same time it holds out the hope for emancipation. I only want to emphasize here that de Beauvoir's call to dethrone mythology is based on an underlying truth that, in spite of the imposition of femininity, we are still subjects *like them*. We must at last give up the "bad faith" that protects our difference, but only at the expense of denying our freedom. Part of giving up the "bad faith" involves dethroning the myths of the feminine, and with it the recognition of our shared status as "subjects."

THE APPEAL TO NATIONAL, RACIAL, AND CLASS DIFFERENCE

If de Beauvoir's suspicion of the myths of the feminine rests on a postulated projection of a "universal" subject—at least in the sense that all subjects are marked by transcendence—the second criticism of the reinterpretation of the myths of the feminine turns rather on the danger inherent in myth to deny difference, to speak of Woman when there are only women. Myth, in other words, can never be "fair" to the extremely variegated nature of the lives of actual women. The word "fair" is not a coincidence, because the critique of any attempt to speak or write of women is ethical as well as methodological. Methodologically, the charge is that gender never exhibits itself in pure form, so that we can know the essence of Woman herself but only as the feminine as expressed in the lives of actual women who, if they are women, are also women of a particular national, ethnic, cultural, and class background. To speak or write of Woman thus obscures these differences. Here we have the ethical critique. To write of Woman homogenizes, masking the differences. In its worst case, it simply validates the experience of white, middle-class women as being

that of Woman. If done in the name of creating solidarity through gender co-
herence, such theorizing, including through the reinterpretation of myth,
would seem to risk racism, national chauvinism, and class privilege.

But let us reexamine the charge of homogenization by looking again at the
retelling of the Medea myth in Toni Morrison's *Beloved*. In *Beloved*, the mother
decides to kill her children to protect them from slavery. There are, of course,
many interpretations of Medea, but there is certainly one interpretation that
emphasizes the mother's protectiveness of her children. It is not her revenge on
the Man, but her desire to protect her children from the vengeance of the Father that leads her to kill her children. This protectiveness can be interpreted as
the most horrifying example of the overprotectiveness associated with the cas-
trating mother, who denies, in the most graphic sense, the autonomous lives of
her children.

In *Beloved*, however, the one life that the mother cannot give them, or
at least guarantee them, is an autonomous life in even the most minimal
sense. She cannot protect them from slavery. And so she protects them from
the white patriarchal order in the only way she can. She takes their lives before they are turned over to him. The Man will not get these children. In
Beloved, the myth is retold, and as it is retold, the "meaning," the deep significance of killing one's children, is problematized, by the slave "reality" in
which the mother is allowed to bear the children but not to "raise" them. As
we have seen, *Beloved* challenges on a very profound level the idealization of
mothering as the basis for a unique feminine "reality." In the context of slavery, mothering (in the sense of bearing and raising children) tragically takes
on its own meaning through the stark denial of maternal control, or even of
intervention into her children's lives. What does it mean to kill one's children
when, by definition, they are denied full lives as human beings by the Laws
of the Father? Could we possibly understand this act, except within its own
context, the context of slavery? The answer, I think, is no. But at the same
time, the reliance on one of our most profound myths, the "killing" mother,
dramatically exposes the tragedy of slavery, and more generally, the "impotence" of the mother to "raise," resurrect, her children, even if she could free
herself. Her freedom cannot be guaranteed by a law and a social order from
which she is excluded. She can leave no trace of herself behind. She erases
her progeny.

> Down by the stream in back of 124 her footprints come and go, come and
> go. They are so familiar. Should a child, an adult place his feet in them, they
> will fit. Take them out and they disappear again as though nobody ever
> walked there.
> By and by all trace is gone, and what is forgotten is not only the foot-
> prints but the water too and what is down there. The rest is weather. Not the

breath of the disremembered and unaccounted for, but wind in the eaves, or spring ice thawing too quickly. Just weather. Certainly no clamor for a kiss. (*BL*, 275)

Far from homogenizing the situation of Woman, the allegory of *Beloved* relies on myth to dramatize the very difference of the Afro-American mother's situation. In this sense, the "universals" expressed in myth are not and cannot be just the mere repetition of the same. Indeed, the "universal," the symbol of the "killing mother," cannot be known, except as it is told in context. The "universal" in myth, in other words, is much closer to what Michael Walzer has called the "reiterative universalism."[23] The "universal" is only as it is told, in its difference.

The tragedy in *Beloved*, in other words, is symbolized as the tragedy of Medea. It is told through myth that brings forth the full weight of the oppression of the Afro-American woman in slavery. But as the tragedy of the Afro-American mother, the meaning of this tragedy shifts. Sixty million and more. The story is that *significant*. In itself, it is myth.

In this sense, to affirm that in a bipolarized society of gender identity Woman signifies, particularly through myths, does not mean that the feminine can be reduced to a set of shared characteristics or properties. I return to Austin's allegory of Sapphire, of the Afro-American woman who cannot be represented in the conception of the person as a collection of properties, including "black" and "woman." Sapphire is feminine, but as Woman she "is" differently. She "is" an Afro-American woman.

To say that we can simply escape myth, particularly myths of the feminine, is to once again reinstate the "neutral" conception of the person. As in de Beauvoir, myth can only be dethroned if we can finally raise the veil and "see" that women are *fully human*. But what does it mean for de Beauvoir "to see" that women are potentially fully human? It means, ultimately, that we "see" that they can be like men. The "myths" only disguise that "reality." Supposedly overcoming the gender divide only reinstates it. If de Beauvoir is right, we can only escape "myth" completely once we have been freed from patriarchy. Walter Benjamin once said that as long "as there is one beggar, there will be myth." Transposed into the gender hierarchy, I would argue that as long as there is the gender hierarchy, there will be myth. We cannot simply erase myth. Nor can we dethrone myth altogether without a "neutral" concept of the person. Our only option is to work within myth to reinterpret it.

Of course, to recognize that we are operating within myth and not an "essential" female nature is already in one sense to dethrone "myth," for it denies the myth's claim to an atemporal universality. So it was, so it will be. As the myth is retold—think again of Wolf's *Cassandra* or Morrison's *Beloved*—"the so it was," as determinative of "the future," is itself called into question. Indeed, the "so it was" is "seen" differently once it is "seen" from the "feminine" perspective. There is always, of course, the danger that myth reifies through its very power to give significance. My only reminder is that this danger cannot be solved through the denial of myth's hold on us in a genderized society. The way beyond is to retrace the circle that seemingly encircles us. The retelling of myth begins—and perhaps we will always "be" so beginning—to specify the feminine, so that "herstory" can be told, in all of its suffering and pain, as well as in all of its glory. "Riverrun, past Eve and Adam's."[24]

NOTES

1. Hans Blumenberg, *Work on Myth*, trans. Robert M. Wallace (Cambridge: MIT Press, 1985), 34. Originally published as *Arbeit am Mythos* (Frankfurt am Main, FRG: Suhrkamp Verlag, 1979).

2. Marguerite Duras, *Blue Eyes, Black Hair*, trans. Barbara Bray (New York: Pantheon Books, 1987). Originally published as *Les yeux bleus cheveaux noirs* (Paris: Les Éditions de Minuit, 1986).

3. Hélène Cixous, "Sorties: Out and Out: Attacks/Ways Out/Forays," *The Newly Born Woman*, Hélène Cixous and Catherine Clément, eds., trans. Betsy Wing (Minneapolis: University of Minnesota Press, 1986), 72. Originally published as *La jeune née* (Paris: Union Générale d'Éditions, 1975) (emphasis in original). Hereafter cited in the text as *S*.

4. Jacques Lacan, *Feminine Sexuality: Jacques Lacan and the école freudienne,*. ed. Juliet Mitchell and Jacqueline Rose, trans. Jacqueline Rose (New York: W.W. Norton and Company, 1995), 170.

5. Christa Wolf, *Cassandra: A Novel and Four Essays*, trans. Jan Van Heurck (New York: Farrar, Straus, and Giroux, 1984). Hereafter cited in the text as *C*.

6. Jean-François Lyotard, *The Differend: Phrases in Dispute*, trans. George Van Den Abbeele (Minneapolis: University of Minnesota Press, 1988), 150–51. Originally published as *Le Differend* (Paris: Les Éditions de Minuit, 1983).

7. Andrea Dworkin, *Intercourse* (New York: Free Press, 1987).

8. Gayatri Spivak, "In a Word," *differences,* vol. 1, no. 2 (1989): 124. Hereafter cited in the text as *IW*.

9. Diana J. Fuss, "Essentially Speaking: Luce Irigaray's Language of Essence," *Hypatia*, vol. 3, no. 3 (1989).

10. Fuss, "Essentially Speaking," 76 (emphasis in original, citation omitted).

11. Irigaray, *This Sex Which Is Not One,* trans. Catherine Porter (Ithaca, N.Y.: Cornell University Press, 1985), 159. Originally published as *Ce sexe qui n'est pas un* (Paris: Les Éditions des Minuit, 1977).

12. See generally, Georg W. F. Hegel, *Hegel's Science of Logic*, trans. A.V. Miller (Atlantic Highlands, N.J.: Humanities Press International, 1969).

13. Such is the status of women that the appeal to feminism is critical. As MacKinnon notes:

> Women's situation offers no outside to stand on or gaze at, no inside to escape to, too much urgency to wait, no place else to go, and nothing to use but the twisted tools that

have been shoved down our throats. There is no Archimedean point—or, men are their own Archimedean point, which makes it not very Archimedean. If Feminism is revolutionary, this is why.

See Catharine A. MacKinnon, *Toward a Feminist Theory of the State* (Cambridge: Harvard University Press, 1989), 117.

14. Irigaray, "Sexual Difference," in *French Feminist Thought: A Reader*, ed. Toril Moi (New York: Basil Blackwell, 1987), 128 (emphasis in original). Hereafter cited in the text as *SD*.

15. See, for example, Isabel Marcus et al., "The 1984 James McCormick Mitchell Lecture: Feminist Discourse, Moral Values, and the Law—A Conversation," *Buffalo Law Review*, vol. 34, no. 1 (1985): 73–75.

16. See Hortense Spillers, *Conjuring: Black Women, Fiction, and Literary Tradition*, ed. Marjorie Pryse and Hortense Spillers (Bloomington: Indiana University Press, 1985).

17. Toni Morrison, *Beloved* (New York: Penguin Books, 1987). Hereafter cited in the text as *BL*.

18. See, generally, Kristeva, *The Kristeva Reader*, Part I, "Lingustics, Semiotics, Textuality," ed. Toril Moi (New York: Columbia University Press, 1986), 23–136.

19. James Joyce, *Finnegans Wake* (New York: Penguin Books, 1939).

20. Regina Austin, "Sapphire Bound!" *Wisconsin Law Review*, 3 (1989).

21. Naomi Schor, "This Essentialism Which Is Not One: Coming to Grips with Irigaray," in *differences*, vol. 1, no. 2 (1989).

22. Simone de Beauvoir, *The Second Sex*, trans. H. M. Parshley (New York: Random House, 1974). Originally published as *Le deuxieme sexe* (Paris: Alfred A. Knopf, Inc., 1952). Hereafter cited in the text as *SS*.

23. Michael Walzer, "Two Kinds of Universalism" (1989), p. 9 of unpublished manuscript on file with the author.

24. Joyce, *Finnegans Wake*.

CHAPTER 10

Aesthetics and Politics

Terry Eagleton

The phrase "political aesthetics" would seem as much an oxymoron, as blatantly self-contradictory as military intelligence, or Mormon intellectual. How can aesthetics be political, when it was actually constituted as the very opposite of all that? And that this is the case is surely obvious from all of the dust and heat that has been raised recently over this rather modest, unassuming, academicist little enterprise known as literary theory. Why do people get so steamed up about a project that, face it, is of interest to only a few hundred thousand politically not very important people, eminently dispensable that we regrettably are for all our Lacanian-imaginary illusions that the world would crumble to nothing if we were not around to have it center on us? Why has there been so much blood on the senior common room floors over this matter, some of it looking alarmingly like mine? Why does this strange, hybrid nonsubject called literary theory even from time to time hit the pages of the posher newspapers, so that oil executives are treated to a brief, bewildering exposition of Saussure and Derrida over their fried eggs? It cannot, surely, have anything to do with literature, or reception theory, or any of those other arcane pursuits. Face it, nobody cares a great deal, in the great scheme of things, and certainly not in the White House, about whether your approach to the minor poetry of Sir Walter Raleigh is hermeneutical or poststructuralist, Marxist or postcolonial. (Speaking of the latter, some people seem to labor under the consoling illusion that the relations between the North and the South of the globe are importantly to do with something called "culture." They may have to do with trade or drugs or oil or armaments or air bases, but questions of value, meaning, language, identity, and hybridity come a dismally long way down on the list. One can sympathize with literary people liking to feel themselves globally relevant, but there is a thin line between relevance and megalomania.)

187

Nobody gets especially steamed up about the politicization of sociology or economics or the discourse of human rights. One expects these sorts of things to be political. But every society also carves out a sort of quasi-sacred realm for itself, over and above these pragmatic affairs, in which it seems possible for one blessed moment to be free of all that turgidly prosaic stuff and brood instead on the very meaning of the human. The names of this space are historically various: you might call it myth, or religion, or a certain brand of idealist philosophy, or culture, or aesthetics, or the Humanities, or—metonymically—Literature. These latter candidates for the job are of course of very recent historical provenance. The whole task was performed far better by religion, which hooks up the very sensuous texture of my experience to the most fundamental possible questions about what it means to be alive, and why there is anything at all rather than just nothing; and if the idea of culture has one supremely important source in the nineteenth century, one could do much worse than name it as the final failure of religion as an ideological force. (Though when I am speaking in the United States, I must always recall what a very *godly* society it still is—how U.S. politicians can still make solemn appeals to the Almighty, which make us jaded Europeans wince with embarrassment and shuffle our feet.) Anyway, whatever the transient names of this space, its ideological function was, and remains, entirely necessary: to furnish us with that protected enclave, that range of accessible imagery and archetypes, which we could point to when somebody asked us—not the least at times of political crisis and upheaval—what really, in the end, do you live by? A society that *needs* to drag out its fundamental values and expose them to the light of day is already, you might say, in a certain crisis, since these values work far better by being tacitly assumed, by intertwining themselves so subtly with the roots of our identity that even to scrutinize them would be like trying to leap on our own shadows or haul ourselves up by our bootstraps. But this privileged or protected space remains essential, even in the jaundicedly rationalist, technologizing, remorselessly secular and disenchanted world of advanced capitalism (I do not say "late," since we have no idea how late it is), and it is always handy to have these values available in readily packaged and, as it were, portable form. And the name of *this* phenomenon is Literature—though it could always have been something else, and indeed used to be before the quite recent invention of something called the Humanities.

One can begin to understand then about all that dust and heat and blood. Because if the whole *point* of this area is to be constituted as the very antithesis of the material or historical, and if the materialists and historicists then begin to get their grubby paws even on *that*, then there is really nowhere else for liberals or conservatives to retreat to, in a world drained of significance where the aesthetic provides one of the last, lonely, fragile outposts of value *as such*. And of course I thoroughly understand the panic and anxiety to which this gives rise—some of my best friends are liberals and conservatives, and of course no document has more unstinting praise for the capitalist middle class than the *Communist Manifesto*. These liberal and conservative critics understand, absolutely rightly, that the construction of this demarcated area was historically speaking a most generous-spirited, even utopian gesture: an attempt, forlorn but nonetheless noble, to *redeem* those human values and energies for which a brutally utilitarian capitalism has absolutely no time at all, by syphoning them off somewhere else, where they could be nurtured and tended, vigorously flourish, but—here was the price—flourish in splendid isolation from the other social practices of which they were supposed to provide a living critique. The moment when art becomes critical in its very form and being is also the moment when it is struck politically impotent, a contradiction inscribed in the very body of the modernist work of art. But this very impotence could always be turned into triumph, victory snatched from the very jaws of defeat, virtue plucked out of dire necessity. Because if the aesthetic work was now apparently entirely pointless, without function or rationale, curved back upon itself in glorious, anguished autonomy, conjuring its own substance miraculously out of its unfathomable depths with its back turned aloofly to the workaday world, then it was here, in its very inner structure, that it could be read as most profoundly political and utopian. For what it then figured was a frail image of how men and women themselves might be, in a socialist society that had finally given the slip to exchange value, the sway of utility, the sovereignty of instrumental reason. Now works of art looked like nothing quite so much as us, or at least us as we might be under transformed political conditions, and looked like this precisely because the political was the last thing they had any truck with. They looked this way because of something that could be shown but not said. Where art was, there humanity shall be.

So it is that the political ethics of Karl Marx are of a full-bloodedly aestheticist kind. What pains Marx so deeply is the thought that human powers and capacities, as he calls them, should ever be importantly subdued to an instrumentalist logic—that they should need any rationale, metaphysical or utilitarian, other than their own self-delighting development, in which, like the newly defined work of art, they furnish their own immanent grounds and ends. The only good reason for being a Marxist is that you can stop being one as soon as possible and just lie around all day in various interesting states of *jouissance*—what Marx rather more prosaically referred to as the abolition of toil. To him, there is absolutely no *reason* we should live like works of art, any more than there is any metaphysical foundation to a song or a smile; it just belongs to what he would call our species being. Marxism is ultimately all about the aestheticization of human existence, the release of sensuous particularity from the metaphysical prison-house of exchange value and bourgeois abstraction. But of course for Marx this is very far from some sort of callow, laid-back, hedonist, postmodern celebration of pleasure or plurality or the body (that latest fetish of cultural theory), since as a thoroughly traditionalist, indeed Aristotelian moral- ist, he understands that such a condition could be made available to all men and women only by the most rigorously instrumental forms of thought and action, and by the willing sacrifice of such self-realization on the part of some for the sake of others. Marx has his Kantian side, too, quite properly, and by no means regards the dutiful, deontological, necessary repression of pleasure as a mere hangover from the grand narratives of the boring old men.

Even so, his political ethics are much closer to Oscar Wilde's than they are to John Stuart Mill's. It is just that he understood that in order to gener- ate that surplus or sheer gratuitous abundance, which is the very mark of our species' being, we first need a material surplus as well, which the bourgeoisie have been kind and altruistic enough to hand down to us, along with a pre- cious tradition of liberal humanism. Any socialism that lacked these material and spiritual conditions—that tried, for example, to build itself from the ground up in conditions of extreme scarcity, without usable capitalist and lib- eral heritage—would inevitably find itself having to generate wealth by the coercive power of an authoritarian state and so, tragically and criminally, would destroy the very political structures of socialism in the attempt to con- struct its material base. This is the phenomenon we know as Stalinism, which only Marxists have really been able to explain. And of course all of this is of great relevance in the world of revolution and incipient insurrection that we witness around us today: the overthrow of apartheid, of the neo-Stalinist regimes of the East, the mass popular rebellions of South Korea, the persis- tent struggles against colonialism, the militancy of the French working class, and the like. Perhaps none of this has yet reached the pessimistic postmodern ears of those in the Ivy League universities who have been too busy reading Baudrillard to bother reading the newspapers.

In none of this, of course, is culture in the least central. The first move of a materialist cultural theorist must be suitably self-humbling: to recognize how relatively unimportant we are. But not to be central is not necessarily to be nothing. What characterizes the three forms of political struggle that have dominated the global agenda over the past few decades—revolutionary nation- alism, feminism, and ethnic conflict—is exactly, and most unusually, that "cul- ture," in the anthropological rather than the aesthetic sense of the word, has become the very medium in which political contentions are being fought out. Indeed, this is one vital reason for the crisis of the notion of culture in our day—that it has imperceptibly shifted from being part of the solution to being part of the problem. What began as an essentially transcendent reality, a kind of higher or deeper ground on which mere sublunary quarrels could be imagi- narily resolved, has become the very language in which those quarrels articulate themselves. But we must not exaggerate here even so in that fashionable reductionism known today as culturalism. The conflict between Catholics and Protestants in Northern Ireland has something to do with culture, but not fundamentally. Culturally speaking, Northern Catholics and Protestants understand each other only too well. And even if culture has for the moment become part of the material problem rather than the idealist solution, we should surely nonetheless continue to hope for the political and material conditions in which we will be able for the most part to live by culture alone, which is to say, anthropologically speaking, to be free. (For Marx, only gratuitous production, free of the goad of necessity, can finally be the index of our liberty.) Then indeed we shall be free of all of this tiresome, utterly essential concern with class and gender and ethnicity and neocolonialism and talk about something more interesting for a change, such as the curious way in which Prince Charles's ears protrude from his head, or why it is that British Rail public announcements are garbled just at the most vital points.

The conflict between socialists and postmodernists can thus be seen as one between two different senses of the aestheticization of politics. If socialism is—I hesitate even to pronounce this demonized term—teleological, it is among other reasons because it believes that the material conditions for what I might call an anthropological aestheticization of politics have yet to be constructed, and that one thing that forestalls that project is the aestheticization of politics in another way: in the specularization of the political, for example, or in that aestheticization of the economic that we call commodity fetishism. Or—in the theoretical sphere—in that monstrous form of dogmatism known as intuitionism, in which I make incontrovertible appeals to something called my immediate political experience in much the same way that old-style aesthetics makes an appeal to taste. Or, indeed, that neopragmatist assault on the cognitive for which truth is whatever is agreeable or convenient to the mind, or to our given discourses, which is yet another form of aestheticization. However philosophically plausible some of these cases may be, none of them has the faintest chance of succeeding in a social order which, while dismantling the metaphysical or foundational in its most routine *material* behavior, nevertheless still cannot get on *ideologically* without it. Which is why all of those U.S. politicians still talk of the Almighty's special regard for the nation at the very moment they have their fingers in the till.

Advanced capitalist orders cannot afford to take the Nietzschean way out of the structural contradiction in which they have landed themselves—I mean the irresolvable contradiction between the fact that they stand in need ideologically of a metaphysical foundation which their own rationalizing, secularizing activity continually undermines. Nietzsche had a sort of solution to this—not in so many words, to be sure—which ran as follows: If the spiritual superstructure keeps entering into embarrassing contradiction with your material basis, then just throw away the superstructure. Forget about high-sounding metaphysical rationales. Nobody believes the stuff any more: God is dead, the superstructure has crumbled to dust, and the *hypocrisy* by which you still strive to square this impossible circle is itself ideologically disabling. So take instead the aestheticizing way out: renounce absolutes, and just allow your values to be generated up, transiently, perspectively, by that infinite textual spawning of conflictive energies which is the very stuff of the cosmos, and to which we give the name of will-to-power. Now in one sense this is a highly alluring escape hatch for a middle class in a metaphysical mess. For of course the sorts of values you conjure directly out of your practical life activity are always going to be considerably more plausible, ideologically speaking, than those you parachute in from some metaphysical outer space, where the hiatus between what you do and what you say you do—the performative contradiction between them—will itself necessitate reaching for yet another kind of discourse to square this incongruous gap. No ideological value that is not in some sense, however obliquely, anchored in men's and women's lived experience stands any chance at all of surviving for very long, as socialism must be among other things an unabashed appeal to people's self-interest. Nietzsche's (implicit) recommendation is aestheticizing because it asks us, audaciously, to found our being merely in ourselves. The *Übermensch* is he who had become autotelic, self-legislating, self-grounding, just like the aesthetic artifact. But if you *do* conjure up your values directly from what you do, the danger is that you will end up, in this sort of society at least, with all the worst kinds of values: aggression, domination, competition, and so on. If Nietzsche's recommended escape route is finally too hair-raising for the bourgeoisie to tread, it is because it overlooks the fact that values must not just be *expressive* of what we do but must also help *legitimate* it. Value must here have an *active* role, as of signifier to signified, in relation to our social behavior, not just the passive reflection of that behavior of an ironic sign. It must rationalize, totalize, displace, dissemble, sublimate, naturalize and the like; but this then opens up a necessary hiatus between what we do and what we say we do, into which the thin end of critique can always be inserted.

Various forms of neo-Nietzschean pragmatism then are fair enough for academic type, but hardly adequate if you are trying to run a country rather than just a philosophy department. For people have an annoying habit of inquiring after the foundations of their world and grow restless with aestheticizing answers such as "it just stands on itself." Theorists are really those adults who have never properly grown up, who continue, like a child not yet "naturalized," to find our most commonplace activities puzzling and estranging and persist in raising the most embarrassingly large questions about them. Theory is difficult not just because it uses phrases such as "hermeneutical phenomenology," but because of its sheer childlike naivety: "Where does capitalism come from, mummy?"; it pipes up and generally receives for its pains a late Wittgenstein sort of reply: "This is just what we do, dear."

Theory is thus among other things a kind of Brechtian alienation effect and only tends to happen when for some reason or another our habitual practices begin to break down, to come apart at the seams, to hit some logjam beyond which they are incapable of proceeding. When theory breaks out on a virulent, positively epidemic scale, as it has over the last few decades in the West, you can be sure that something has gone awry. The conservative's mistake is to think that what has gone awry is the emergence of theory itself rather that the situation of which this appearance is symptomatic. Theory in this sense is just a social practice being thrust into a new kind of self-consciousness, and there is thus always something unpleasantly navel staring or narcissistic about it, as anyone who has the misfortune to encounter some leading literary theorists will no doubt be aware. Theory comes about, historically speaking, when it is both possible and necessary for it to do so—either when we need to find a new set of rationales for what we have been doing anyway, or when we need to change the agenda. A long time ago, people used to just drop things occasionally, without giving it much thought. Then along came physicists to instruct them in the gravitational laws by which objects fell to earth, philosophers to query whether there really were any discrete objects to be dropped in the first place, sociologists to speculate that all this dropping was the result of intensifying urban pressures, psychologists to admonish us that it was really all symbolic of trying to drop our parents, poets who wrote of dropping as symbolic of death, and critics who saw it as a sign of the poet's castration complex. Now, suddenly, dropping could never be the same again: we could never get back to the happy garden where we just zapped round all day dropping things in fine careless rapture without a worry in the world. Theory had now set in; we still dropped things, of course, but now tentatively, self-consciously, with an exquisite sense of the arbitrary, unfounded nature of the action.

Consider all of this an an allegory of modernism. Modernism is the moment when words come to be about words, paint about paint, stone about stone—when, under the pressures of a commodifying society in which the very experience that art might take as its subject-matter is felt to be degraded, sinisterly complicit with power—the work of art begins to bend back upon itself and take its own form as theme. The structure of this gesture then resembles the structure of theory, as the work of art must now, to be authentic, fold within itself some sort of awareness of the shameful fact that in a nonfoundational universe, it might just have well never have been. And of course around the time that the artwork is growing in this way "theoretical," theory for its part is waxing more aesthetic, in that distinguished lineage of antiphilosophers, from Kierkegaard, Marx, and Nietzsche to Heidegger, Adorno, Wittgenstein, and Derrida, who are opposed to philosophy in a philosophically fascinating way—for whom, since what has now become problematic is not just this or that philosophical topic but the whole nature and status of the discourse itself, a new style of writing might provide a formal resolution to certain substantive difficulties. Seen as a proleptic gesture, prefiguring some future condition in which we all—and not just philosophers—might think otherwise, this is a rich, fertile strategy; seen—as it must also be, I think—as a rather desperate *displacement* of, or compensation for, a political aesthetics that is yet to arrive in practice, it runs the risk of idolatry, believing as idolaters do that you can have the future in your pocket, even now. Indispensable though it is, it thus stands under the judgment of the Judaeo-Christian prohibition on graven images (since the only image of God is humanity), or under the judgment of E. M. Forster's *Passage to India*: not here, not now, not yet.

CHAPTER 11

An Ethics of the Name: Rethinking Globalization

Victor Li

Even if any terminology is *a reflection* of reality, by its very nature as a terminology it must be a *selection* of reality, and to this extent it must function also as a *deflection* of reality.
—Kenneth Burke, "Terministic Screens," *Language as Symbolic Action.*

The essentially performative character of naming is the precondition for all hegemony and politics.
—Ernesto Laclau, "Preface" to Slavoj Žižek's *The Sublime Object of Ideology*

Much breathless talk about globalization we hear all around us is what the late Clare Boothe Luce used to call globaloney.
—Richard J. Barnet and John Cavanagh,
*Global Dreams: Imperial Corporations
and the New World Order*

The term *globalization* invokes an overwhelming sense of magnitude. Magnitude can, in turn, summon up what Jacques Derrida, following Kant, calls the colossal sublime.[1] Immeasurable and equal only to itself, the colossal sublime breaks with all previous examples and measures just as the concept of globalization claims to be unequalled in its magnitude and power to shape a world

A longer version of this work, entitled "What's in a Name?: Questioning Globalization," appeared in *Cultural Critique* 45 (spring 2000). Published here with permission of the University of Minnesota Press.

like no other we have known. In this sense, globalization is our contemporary or postmodern sublime. At the same time, capitalism, acknowledged generally as the central driving force of globalization, resembles the artistic avant-garde in its use of the aesthetic of the sublime to break with preestablished rules and conventions, as Jean-François Lyotard has noted: "There is a kind of collusion between capital and the avant-garde. The force of scepticism and even of destruction that capitalism brought into play . . . in some way encourages among artists a mistrust of established rules and a willingness to experiment with means of expression, with styles, with ever-new materials. There is something of the sublime in capitalist economy."[2]

Such a view of the connection between political economy and aesthetic culture is usually ignored in those accounts of globalization that stick solely to the mantra of global economic competition and free-market fundamentals. In these standard accounts, globalization forecloses all forms of inquiry except that of a hard-headed economic and instrumental rationality. It is against such a foreclosure that my chapter is directed. I will argue that the term or name "globalization" has itself a kind of aesthetic or shaping quality that in avant-garde or sublime fashion seeks to be self-determining and equal only to itself. I will contend, however, that the sublime aesthetic of globalization has to face up to something like an ethical demand that, in Simon Critchley's words, "seeks the location of a point of alterity . . . that cannot be reduced to the Same."[3] In other words, the concept of globalization that performatively seeks to become global or universal has to be questioned by an alterity or otherness that resists globalization's putative universality. In fact, to return to our analogy between globalization and the sublime, Lyotard warns us that the aesthetic of the sublime, if it is to remain true to itself, must question its own accomplishment, lest it fall victim to a hegemonic desire for closure that would in fact destroy the sublime itself. By stating that "the sublime feeling is the name of privation" (SA,107), Lyotard acknowledges that it is through incompletion and alterity that the aesthetic remains open. Capitalist globalization may therefore appear to resemble the aesthetic of the sublime, but it is ultimately a false sublime because it cannot, in the final analysis, question its own raison d'être or entertain the thought of a difference that opposes it. It cannot envisage its own antinomy.

Incompletion and alterity are important features in the first part of my chapter, which explores what I call an ethics of the name. Drawing on the work of Jacques Derrida, Kenneth Burke, Pierre Bourdieu, and Slavoj Žižek, I will argue that we need an ethics that will reveal the performative, conditional, and incomplete nature of the name, and that such an ethics can be linked to practical and political issues in the world. To this end, in the rest of my chapter I show how an ethics of the name can be applied to the term globalization and to the theories that discuss its primacy. I will also examine the inconsistencies and contradictions in the use of this term and suggest that we should "forget glob-alization" in order to reorient our way of looking at the world.

I

In the famous balcony scene of William Shakespeare's *Romeo and Juliet*, Juliet unburdens her heart and laments her separation from Romeo, a separation caused, as she sees it, by their feuding family names. It is to the problem of the name that her utterance is directed.

> 'Tis but thy name that is my enemy.
> Thou art thyself, though not a Montague.
> What's Montague? It is nor hand, nor foot,
> Nor arm, nor face, nor any other part
> Belonging to a man. Oh, be some other name!
> What's in a name? That which we call a rose
> By any other name would smell as sweet.
> So Romeo would, were he not Romeo called,
> Retain that dear perfection which he owes
> Without that title.
>
> (*Romeo and Juliet*, II, ii, 39–47)[4]

Juliet is of course painfully conscious of the power of names. But it is precisely because she is aware of their power that she also questions their claim to refer-ential identity. "What's in a name?" she asks pointedly, as she proceeds to un-couple name from referent, Romeo Montague from the man with that given name. The name, Juliet argues, is not what it claims to be; the name's title is neither necessary nor absolutely tied to the entity so named. For Juliet, the be-lief that names are tied to reality must be dispelled; after all, "any other name" would do for both the rose and Romeo.

What can be called Juliet's "deconstruction" of the identity logic of the name has attracted the attention of Jacques Derrida, who has described Juliet's balcony speech as "the most implacable analysis of the name."[5] Commenting on Juliet's uncoupling of name from referent, Derrida says: "The name would only be a 'title,' and the title is not the thing which it names, any more than a title of nobility participates in the very thing, the family, the work, to which it is said to belong" (*AC*, 428). Both Juliet and Derrida understand the inade-quacy of names and titles; but, equally, they also understand the powerful human need to name and then to identify the name with the thing named. It is their recognition of the symbolic power of the name as title and distinction that compels them to analyze the name's inadequacy, its lack that incessantly calls for supplementation, for something other than itself. As Juliet puts it: "Oh, be some other name!" It is the otherness of the name, the otherness the name both resists and retains, that leads Derrida to remark in another essay that "when a name comes, it immediately says more than the name: the other of the name and quite simply the other whose irruption the name announces."[6]

As it turns out, what Derrida describes as "the other of the name" that "says more than the name" haunts his own first name, Jacques. In an interview with Derrida, François Ewald suddenly posed this surprising question: "Your name is Jackie. Did you yourself change your first name?" Resisting the somewhat frivolous and journalistic curiosity of the question, Derrida responded in a thoughtful way:

> You are asking me in fact a very serious question. Yes, I changed my first name when I began to publish, at the moment I entered what is, in sum, the space of literary or philosophical legitimation, whose "good manners" I was practising in my own way. In finding that Jackie was not possible as the first name of an author, by choosing what was in some way, to be sure, a semi-pseudonym but also very French, Christian, simple, I must have erased more things than I could say in a few words (one would have to analyze the conditions in which a certain community—the Jewish community in Algeria— in the '30s sometimes chose American names, occasionally those of film stars or heroes, William, Jackie, and so forth). But I never would have changed my last name, Derrida, which I have always found to be quite beautiful, don't you think? It has a good resonance in me—but precisely like the resonance of another.[7]

Though somewhat defensive about his family name, Derrida admits to the duplicity of his first name. His response uncovers the double logic of the name as performative construction and accompanying disruption. First, we learn about the propriety of names, the ways in which names are made to fit certain social, cultural, or institutional codes and requirements. Thus while Jacques is more fitting or appropriate for a philosopher than Jackie, Jackie is quite appropriate for a star such as Jackie Gleason or Jacky Chan. Similarly, we find it appropriate to have a Johnny Halliday but not a Johnny Sartre, a Micky Rooney but not a Micky Foucault. But we also learn from Derrida's answer that the name that is appropriate, acceptable, or sanctioned also summons up another name whose irruption can never be wholly foreseen or prevented, another name that bears the mark of difference—in Derrida's case, a difference marked as colonial and at least twice removed from metropolitan Parisian "norms." What we learn from the interview is that every name has its other, every Jacques its Jackie, every proper designation its different and thus disruptive double. The name "says more than the name"; the name is always more than itself. Desiring to be firmly referential, its identity forever fixed, the name discovers that it is duplicitous and excessive, that it always carries at least another name.

We can give Derrida's somewhat abstract examination of the name's un-containable otherness a more methodical, sociopolitical orientation by relating it to Kenneth Burke's theory of "terministic screens" and Pierre Bourdieu's analysis of the act of naming as the exertion of power. Any name or term, according to Burke, functions as a screen directing our attention into some channels while simultaneously deflecting it from others. In Burke's words:

> We must use terministic screens, since we can't say anything without the use of terms; whatever terms we use, they necessarily constitute a corresponding kind of screen; and any such screen necessarily directs the attention to one field rather than another. Within that field there can be different screens, each with its way of directing the attention and shaping the range of observations implicit in the given terminology.[8]

The Freudian concept of repression provides an example of how a term or name can focus our attention on a particular view of things while screening out other views. Freudian terminology, argues Burke, "is highly serviceable in calling attention to ideas that are not given full conscious recognition because they are *repressed*" (*TS*, 51). But in doing so, it ignores those ideas that are unclear, not because they are repressed but because we have not yet become familiar with them and cannot therefore understand them adequately. "Would not a terminology that features the unconscious *repression* of ideas," Burke asks, "automatically deflect our attention from symbols that are not *repressed* but merely remote?" (*TS*, 51). It appears from Burke's analysis that the Freudian term *repression* opens up certain lines of inquiry by paradoxically *repressing* other epistemological possibilities. That which enables a term or name to function properly is thus precisely also that which prevents it from perceiving other meanings. For the name to be, its other must be screened out.

Kenneth Burke's discussion of the antinomy of the name is given a sociopolitical inflection in Pierre Bourdieu's analysis of how the social operations of naming structure our understanding of the world. For Bourdieu, language in general and names in particular play an important part in the classificatory struggles of social life, struggles for the power to construct and control social meanings. As he puts it: "The categories of perception, the systems of classification, that is, essentially, the words, the names which construct social reality as much as they express it, are the crucial stakes of political struggle."[9] The power of names is thus, for Bourdieu, linked directly to the power of social agency: "There is no social agent who does not aspire, as far as his circumstances permit, to have the power to name and to create the world through naming" (*SS*, 105). What to Burke is the power of the name to both focus and deflect attention becomes for Bourdieu naming as the exercise of power. To Burke's more formalist account of the power of names, Bourdieu adds the dimension of so-cial agency. For Bourdieu, the power of names to constitute or elicit meanings is not merely a formal or semantic property of language but part of a political or an ideological constitution of social power and domination. However, be-cause Bourdieu is more interested in nominations as domination, he does not seem to notice as much those moments when, like an emperor losing his clothes, the name sheds its power. As Richard Jenkins notes in his critique of Bourdieu, "Words have power in Bourdieu's world, but that power seems only to flow in one direction."[10] Focusing on the power of naming, Bourdieu pays less attention to the accompanying forces of counter-nomination. More than Burke, Bourdieu understands the political and material power of the name, but he is also less sensitive than Derrida to the name's antinomy, the otherness the name can never rid itself of.

Keeping in mind Burke's description of "terministic screens" and Bour-dieu's analysis of naming as the exercise of power, we can return to Juliet's and Derrida's argument that the name is other to itself and reconceptualize it in the following manner: the name is an expression of power that shapes and directs our perceptions and understandings, thus constituting the reality we know. But the name's performativity, its power to classify and construct our reality, is also its limitation, since its act of screening out or excluding other realities returns to challenge its putative singularity.

Such a challenge constitutes what can be called an ethics of the name. It is an ethics that compels us to treat every name as capable of both invention and suppression; an ethics that urges us to see names as creating certain ef-fects, allowing the production of certain forms of knowledge while, at the same time, preventing other aspirations, denying other kinds of knowledge. An ethical reading of the name would thus seek to trace the other histories, meanings, and uses of a name or term in a manner not unlike that suggested by Raymond Williams's *Keywords*, a work that seeks to go beyond the dictio-nary's range of "proper meaning" to uncover "a history and complexity of meanings" and, by doing so, to bring us to "the sharpest realization of the dif-ficulties of any kind of definition."[11] It should be clear that an ethics of the name does not preclude a practical politics that may require us to choose one name over another. But an ethics of the name also reminds us that any politics of the name must acknowledge that no name can ever be definitive without risking reification and injustice.

It can in fact be argued that an ethics of the name allows for the possi-bility of politics. The questioning of the singularity of the name enables us to rethink and displace its discursive grip, thus opening the way for other names, other political possibilities. Moreover, an approach, such as Bourdieu's, alert to the name's performative or constitutive nature, allows us to see that nam-ing is not an ontological act of reference but a thoroughly political intervention. To understand how this comes about, we must briefly consider how names refer to objects.

Drawing on the work of philosopher Saul Kripke, Slavoj Žižek argues that there are roughly two ways of approaching the problem of naming—the descriptivist and anti-descriptivist approaches. Descriptivists believe that a name is meaningfully linked to an object; that is, a name contains a cluster of descriptive features and refers to an object or objects in the real world that possess those descriptive features. Anti-descriptivists, on the other hand, hold the view that the name refers to the object through a "primal baptism," and that the name continues to be associated with the object, even with the disappearance of the descriptive features possessed by the object at the time of its baptism. Žižek favors the anti-descriptivist view, but he also seeks to explain why the name remains a "rigid designator," still associated with the object, even after the disappearance of the descriptive features that initially linked object to name. Žižek's explanation is that the link remains because the name not only designates but also retroactively constitutes its own reference, the object itself. As he puts it: "What is overlooked, at least in the standard version of anti-descriptivism, is that this guaranteeing the identity of an object in all counterfactual situations, that is, through a change in all its descriptive features, is the *retroactive effect of naming itself*: it is the name itself, the signifier, which supports the identity of the object."[12] Žižek's point that the name not only designates but also constitutes its reference is absolutely crucial for any political analysis, as Ernesto Laclau is quick to discern. In Laclau's words:

> [I]f the unity of the object is the retroactive effect of naming itself, then naming is not just the pure nominalistic game of attributing an empty name to a preconstituted subject. It is the discursive construction of the object itself. The consequences of this argument for a theory of hegemony or politics are easy to see. If the descriptivist approach were correct, then the meaning of the name and the descriptive features of the objects would be given beforehand, thus discounting the possibility of any discursive hegemonic variation that could open the space for a political construction of social identities. But if the process of naming of objects amounts to the very act of their constitution, then their descriptive features will be fundamentally unstable and open to all kinds of hegemonic rearticulations. The essentially performative character of naming is the precondition for all hegemony and politics.[13]

An ethics of the name will insist on the performative character of naming and work to show that the name's seemingly definitive grasp of the reality it names is in fact only a "self-referential, tautological, performative operation" (*SO*, 99) and, as such, will be vulnerable to the challenge of other names, other performative variations and interventions.

It is with such an ethics in mind that I want to examine a name, a word that has entered our lexicon and our consciousness with great force. The word is, of course, "globalization," a word that has ambitions to become a master word that will name the overwhelming processes shaping our contemporary world. The very term *globalization* presents itself as a universal, and an all-inclusive theoretical concept that is sufficient unto itself. As I will argue, not only are there theoretical inconsistencies in the totalizing or universalizing claims of globalization, but there is also the danger that "globalization," as a master term or meta-narrative, may swallow up and encompass even those discourses or narratives opposing it. Such a danger has been noticed, for example, by political economist J. K. Gibson-Graham, who confesses that in her earlier work she had ignored the performative character of conceptual categories and as a result discovered that her critical portrayal of a powerful global capitalism merely confirmed and further entrenched its monolithic, all-encompassing power. In her words:

> When theorists depict patriarchy, or racism, or compulsory heterosexuality, or capitalist hegemony they are not only delineating a formation they hope to see destabilized or replaced. They are also generating a representation of the social world endowing it with performative force. To the extent that this representation becomes influential it may contribute to the hegemony of a "hegemonic formation."[14]

Similarly, in our critical depiction of globalization, we may in fact end up confirming its globality, its universality, and, as a consequence, we may end up accepting its inescapability. To talk about globalization may be to entrench it further, to "acknowledge that we live within something large that shows us to be small . . . [and] in the face of which all our transformative acts are ultimately inconsequential" (*EC*, 253). No wonder, then, that an astute critic of globalization like Ian Robert Douglas has provocatively counseled us to "forget globalization."[15] For, indeed, we have to forget globalization in its constative form as a statement describing the reality of our contemporary world in order to remember its performative status as a discourse that actively constitutes and shapes the very reality it names. We must understand that globalization does not name a reality that has already taken place; globalization is a tautological, performative discourse actively seeking to convince us that globalization is our inescapable contemporary reality. Consequently, its performative, rhetorical force can be challenged, contradicted, and rearticulated differently. The name "globalization," which pretends to totality or universality, can thus be shown to be partial in all senses of the word—a name that is both incomplete and ideologically selective. An ethical approach to the name "globalization" will challenge its claim to hegemony, singularity, and globality and seek to reveal its unavoidable duplicity, the otherness that disrupts it.

II

According to Richard Barnet and John Cavanagh,

> "Globalization" is the most fashionable word of the 1990s, so portentous and wonderfully patient as to puzzle Alice in Wonderland and thrill the Red Queen because it means precisely whatever the user says it means. Just as poets and songwriters celebrated the rise of modern nationalism, so in our day corporate managers, environmental prophets, business philosophers, rock stars, and writers of advertising copy offer themselves as poet laureates of the global village.[16]

Like all buzzwords, the popularity of globalization depends on its flexible application. But, as Barnet's and Cavanagh's list of globalization's celebrants illustrates, the term often calls up the affirmative, "we are the world" version of global unity, economic plenty, and joyful cultural exchange. Ella Shohat and Robert Stam have called such a view the "euphoric version" of globalization and have described how it evokes

> the mobilization of capital, the internationalization of trade and tariffs, a salutary "competitiveness" on the part of labour, and the transformation of the world into a seamlessly wired global village. The term evokes a cybernetic dance of cultures, "one planet under a groove," the transcendence of rigid ideological and political divisions, and the worldwide availability of cultural products and information, whether it be CNN, world beat music, American serials, or Brazilian telenovelas.[17]

What stands out in such evocations of globalization is its economic and cultural promise. Euphoric or pop globalization not only describes but also actively pursues the free-market dream of a borderless world that is also a global emporium filled with all manner of cultural and consumer goods. Moreover, it is multicultural and syncretic in its orientation, as evidenced in Planet Reebok commercials, Planet Hollywood franchises, Virgin Records' Real World label and, in one of my favorite examples, Dan Piraro's "Bizarro" cartoon, which depicts a waiter in hybrid costume in a restaurant called "The Melting Pot" describing to a pair of customers "tonight's specials," which include "Mesquite Barbecued Sushi" and "Szechuan Enchiladas Alfredo."

But the euphoric version of globalization, available only to some and highly profitable to a few, acts as a terministic screen that keeps out of view the darker exploitive side of globalization. A critical examination of the negative character of globalization can be found in the Marxist world systems theory of Immanuel Wallerstein and, in its more contemporary form, Fredric Jameson's and David Harvey's analysis of the postmodern condition as the product of late global capitalism. These theorists see globalization as the historical progress of capitalism, with contemporary globalization as a manifestation of late capitalism's power to penetrate and capture all cultures and all levels of everyday life. Simplifying greatly, one can say that in their view the global village is nothing but an immense capitalist colony. Such a view, however, not only confirms globalization as the overwhelming progress of capital but also results in the paradoxical reduction of critique to paralysis. Global capitalism becomes the postmodern sublime to which a Marxist critic such as Fredric Jameson can only respond with a mixture of fear and awe. The unity, totality and singularity of global capitalism lend it a dominance before which critique pales. As J. K. Gibson-Graham argues, in the representations of global capitalism developed by Marxist theorists such as David Harvey, Fredric Jameson, and Immanuel Wallerstein, capitalist globalization becomes "an object of transformation that cannot be transformed" (*EC*, 253).[18]

Roland Robertson, a leading theorist of globalization, similarly critiques Marxist theory for tying globalization too closely to the capitalist economy. Robertson argues that despite Wallerstein's increasing interest in cultural factors and Jameson's sophisticated understanding of postmodern culture, both theorists still

> sustain the view that in a globalized world the major point of reference is *still* the economic "infrastructure" rather than globality itself, which . . . transcends, though it certainly includes, the global economy. On top of that, in a situation of increasing consciousness of the world as a whole one would expect civilizational conceptions of the entire world which *pre*date the "emergence" of the "infrastructure" to be activated. In other words, even though national, regional and other "cultural patterns" have undoubtedly been formed partly as responses to the growth of the capitalist world-system, the contemporary concern with the world as a whole—with *globality*—recrystallizes, in varying degrees, the historic philosophies and theologies of ancient civilizations concerning the structure and cosmic significance of the world.[19]

Robertson's attempt to theorize globalization as a historical, civilizational process of increasing global consciousness rather than as a manifestation of capital's expansionary logic may appear to be tainted by idealism to some. Yet it has the advantage of refusing to conceive of globalization as a process that follows a single, determined trajectory, namely, that of the spread of Western capitalism. As Robertson puts it: "[C]oncentration almost exclusively on the global economy exacerbates the tendency to think that we can only conceive of global culture along the axis of Western hegemony and non-Western cultural resistance" (*G*, 113). But in attempting to avoid the reductiveness of global economism, Robertson, in my opinion, tends to install another metanarrative which, for all its complexity, nevertheless subsumes all discourses or forms of action under the rubric of "globality," which is defined as "extensive awareness of the world as a whole" (*G*, 78). Thus even inward-looking religious funda-mentalisms and indigenization movements which, on the surface, may appear to resist global culture are seen by Robertson as products of globality, since it is only in reference to an awareness of the world that these assertions of identity and difference make sense. While we can agree with Robertson's point that particularization and relativization depend on consciousness of universaliza-tion, we may want to argue that Robertson's central concept of globality or awareness of the world as a whole is unevenly distributed and thus not equally present worldwide. In other words, while it is true that deglobalizing discourses depend on access to the notion of globality, that access to global consciousness may be uneven and unequal, given the scarcity of material and cultural re-sources in some communities. This uneven and unequal access may in turn pre-vent in part or in whole the formation of global consciousness and the accompanying means of resistance to global discourses. Thus though aware of heterogeneity and contestation, Robertson's theory of globalization remains, in the last instance, both totalizing and tautological, in that it allows for nothing that is not part of a consciousness of the whole. What is lost in such an ulti-mately totalizing view of globality are the dimensions of relationality and con-text, especially asymmetrical relations or unequal contexts of power and wealth. Marilyn Strathern's criticism of self-totalizing globalization theories is well taken: "Appeals to globalism conceal the relational dimensions of social life on two accounts—first, when the concept of culture is globalized on the presump-tion that cultures manifest a universal form of self-consciousness about iden-tity; second, when global culture appears to constitute its own context."[20]

If Robertson's globalization theory, with its "Euclidean orderliness,"[21] de-flects attention from the uneven and fragmentary acquisition of global con-sciousness, then Arjun Appadurai's approach stresses precisely the disjunct and fissiparous nature of contemporary globalization. Emphasizing irregularity, disjunction, complex overlappings, instability, and flux, Appadurai argues that globalization processes can no longer be understood in terms of world systems theory with its model of a developed capitalist core spreading to the undevel-oped periphery or any other theory that produces a unified conceptual scheme for global complexity (even one as flexible as Robertson's).

Noting that new technologies of travel and communication have speeded up global interactivity, Appadurai points out that any attempt to analyze what he calls the "new global cultural economy" must "look at the relationship between five dimensions of global cultural flow which can be termed: (a) ethnoscapes; (b) mediascapes; (c) technoscapes; (d) finanscapes; and (e) ideo-scapes."[22] Appadurai stresses that all five of the categories overlap each other in complex, disjunct, irregular, and unpredictable flows of people, media images, technologies, money, and ideas and ideologies. Moreover, he argues that analytical terms "with the common suffix-scape also indicate that these are not objectively given relations which look the same from every angle of vision, but rather that they are deeply perspectival constructs, inflected by the historical, linguistic, and political situatedness of different sorts of actors" (DD, 275). Since these actors can range from nation-states to diasporic communities to transnational companies (or TNCs) and right down to a local, individual actor, it appears that there will not only be a multitude of perspectival "scapes" but also an infinite variety of global views. Appadurai's approach to the new global cultural economy seems to result in a kind of *chacun son monde*, every person to his or her world. Appadurai is of course aware that such a form of analysis risks becoming radically indeterminate and unworkable; but he insists that we must avoid "the kind of illusion of order that we . . . impose on a world that is so transparently volatile" (DD, 292). Though "the great traditional questions of causality, contingency, and prediction in the human sciences" are still relevant, Appadurai argues that

> in a world of disjunctive global flows, it is perhaps important to start asking them in a way that relies on images of flow and uncertainty, hence "chaos," rather than on older images of order, stability, and systematicity. . . . This does not mean that the causal-historical relationship between these various flows is random or meaninglessly contingent, but that our current theories of cultural "chaos" are insufficiently developed to be even parsimonious models, at this point, much less to be predictive theories. (DD, 292)

Though we may wish to support Appadurai's attempt to deconstruct theories of global order and systematicity, his admission that no other theory has developed sufficiently to make sense of global complexity leaves us with neither critical purchase or political leverage. As Frederick Buell points out, "[Appadurai's decentering analysis] describes a world that no longer has a center to resist in the old way, one in which power is fragmented and diffused according to a wholly different geometry. . . . In a world so fragmented into disparate imagined communities, the old rationales for collective action disappear, and new, heterogeneous oppositional alliances are deprived of the cultural and political boundary lines upon which they depend" (NC, 322–23).

Though Appadurai rightly points to the inadequacy of current theories gathered under the name of globalization, his own approach results in an unmanageable perspectivism. If innovations in technologies of communication and transportation no longer allow power to be unproblematically centered in the new global space, power is nonetheless not so completely decentered that one cannot discern the shape of what Doreen Massey has called the "power-geometry" of the world. According to Massey, global flows are less irregular and unpredictable and more channelled than Appadurai makes them out to be:

[D]ifferent groups and different individuals are placed in very distinct ways in relation to these flows and interconnections. . . . Different social groups have distinct relationships to this anyway differentiated mobility; some people are more in charge of it than others; some initiate flows and movement, others don't; some are more on the receiving end of it than others; some are effectively imprisoned by it.[23]

A character named Alix Bowen in Margaret Drabble's novel *The Radiant Way* says something similar:

They are still talking about travel and mobility. The eighties will be the global decade, everyone says, . . . but if this is so, why don't Brian and I ever go anywhere? I spend all my time driving from Wandsworth to Wanley, or sitting on the bus between Wandsworth and Whitehall. That's mobile, but it's not global, is it?[24]

The important point to glean from Massey's and Drabble's observations is that the disjunctions and unevenness of global flows, as noted by Appadurai, are not wholly indeterminable or unpredictable, and that we can discern the asymmetrical shape of the world's "power-geometry." Globalization *is*—it exists for those who are in its pathways and may stand to gain or lose by it; globalization *is not*—it does not count for those who have fallen out of its circuit and to whom little or nothing flows.

In what follows, I want to examine how the term *globalization* both *is* and *is not*; how its use summons other meanings that question it; how, in short, the name "globalization" may be seen as a misnomer. My discussion will stress the unevenness of global flows and the unequal acquisition of global consciousness but, unlike Appadurai's decentering approach, which too quickly dissipates any meaningful analysis of power, I want to insist that the unevenness of globalization be tied to the question of global resources and power and their unequal distribution. As one critic of globalization puts it: "The global village, after all, is the fantasy of the colonizer, not the colonized."[25]

To see globalization in terms of the inequities of power is to understand, first, that globalization which seeks to be all-encompassing is, in fact, geographically, economically, and culturally partial and sectoral. Globalization does not extend its reach globally; it is not truly global. Second, since globalization is not global, it can be seen as local. The processes and discourses of globalization tend to originate from and remain concentrated in a number of metropolitan locales. Globalization can thus be regarded as parochial, even ethnocentric, despite its claim to be universal. Let us look in more detail at these two instances where the name of globalization is called into question.

III

How can we even begin to talk about economic or cultural globalization when a report released in 1995 by the United Nations Conference on Trade and Development (UNCTAD) disclosed that the world's Least Developed Countries (LDCs) are worse off today than they were a decade ago? Out of the 185 countries in the world, UNCTAD classifies 48 as LDCs, 33 of which are in Africa. The LDCs have a combined population of 560 million, or roughly one-tenth of the world's population—a significant number by any reckoning. The populations of the LDCs are clearly not part of the new global economy or culture. With an average per capita income of U.S. $30 in 1993 (compared to U.S. $906 for developing countries and U.S. $21,598 for developed economies), the LDCs contribute next to nothing in terms of global trade, global production, or global consumption. The UNCTAD report shows that the LDCs' share in world exports and imports in the early 1990s was 0.4 percent and 0.7 percent, respectively. Foreign direct investments in 1993 amounted to merely 0.4 percent for LDCs, compared to 39 percent for developing countries.[26] Not only are LDCs completely marginal to globalization, they cannot even be seen through the lenses of dependency theory as victims of capitalist neoimperialism, since capital can see nothing to exploit in them. Thus economists and political scientists have started to call the LDCs "basket cases" and have downgraded them from "Third World" to "Terminal World" status.[27]

The LDCs' exit from globalization's map is well illustrated in an advertisement by Royal Trust, the investment arm of the Royal Bank of Canada. Entitled "The World According to Stock Market Capitalization," the advertisement displays a map of the world in which the sizes of nations are not geographically represented but scaled according to the amount of their stock market capitalization. As a result, we are presented with a rather surprising map in which whole continents and countries have shrunk or disappeared, while others loom disproportionately large. The United States, the European countries, and Japan occupy large areas on the map, while Russia and most of the East European countries are missing. The continents of South America and Africa have largely disappeared and are dwarfed in size by geographically small but financially wealthy islands such as Hong Kong, Taiwan, and Singapore. The text of the advertisement, clearly relegating a large portion of the globe and its population to nonexistence or invisibility, proclaims of its revisionist cartography: "This is the real world. The world that makes money go round" (see Figure 11.1).

Globalization is, therefore, not truly global. Despite the increased use of the term *globalization* in corporate boardrooms, financial institutions, management schools, and media circles, globalization remains confined to several clearly defined areas of the world. In portentous language that resembles the Royal Trust's selective globalization, the Japanese business guru, Kenichi

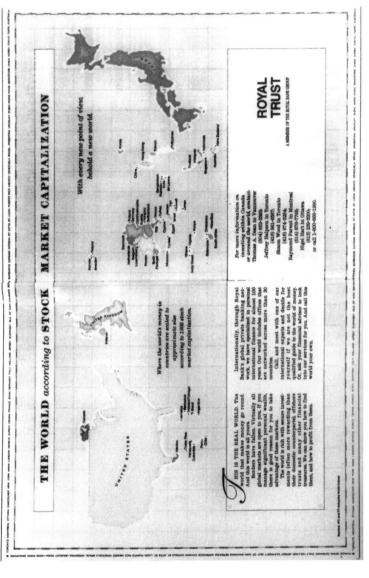

Figure 11.1 "The World According to Stock Market Capitalization," an advertisement by Royal Trust. Originally in *The Globe & Mail*, September 1991. Reproduced by permission of Royal Bank of Canada.

Ohmae, declares: "An isle is emerging that is bigger than a continent—the Interlinked Economy (ILE) of the Triad (United States, Europe, and Japan), joined by aggressive economies such as Taiwan, Hong Kong, and Singapore."[28] Clearly, however, despite the pun, an ILE does not a globe make. But, then, as Benjamin Barber points out: "[I]n speaking of global companies and global markets, the globe encompasses only designated players in the game. The geography of the whole planet is not at issue" (*JMW*, 54). Even ardent advocates of globalization are aware of the geographically and economically limited nature of the term. Thus Pedro Belli, a senior economist at the World Bank, in an article in *Harvard Business Review*, states bluntly:

> Globalization—the defining term for the economy of the 1990s—is today a misnomer. True, the economies of industrialized nations have become increasingly intertwined through "global trade" and "global products." But globalization has largely left out two huge regions of the globe, encompassing more than 60 countries that account for roughly 20% of the world's population and a major share of its natural resources: Africa and Latin America.[29]

How can these countries enter globalization's map? Belli's answer is of course the classic free-market solution to all ills: that protectionism and statism must be dropped, and economic liberalization and privatization must be embraced. Belli's view—what he calls the true "globalization of globalization" (*GR*, 55)— offers not just a description of the current economic scene but also a prescription and a warning: Globalize or perish—embrace the market, or you will literally vanish from the world's map. Globalization is thus not just about expansion, integration, and inclusion; it is also about exclusion, especially if you do not do what the market regards as the right thing. As Hans Magnus Enzensberger has cynically remarked: "In New York as well as in Zaire, in the industrial cities as well as in the poorest countries, more and more people are being permanently excluded from the economic system, because it no longer pays to exploit them . . . there is only one thing worse than being exploited by the multinationals, and that is not being exploited by them."[30]

Despite the dream of global corporations to have everyone on the globe dressed in Levis and Nikes, fed on Big Macs and Coke, and wired for infotainment by Sony and IBM, the reality is in fact less global and more restrictive. Richard Barnet and John Cavanagh report that "marketing departments of global corporations focus on the two dozen wealthiest countries of North America, Europe, and East Asia" (*GD*, 178). Marketing departments know that in most of the poorer countries the majority of people just do not have enough income to purchase the global goods they are pushing. In Barnet's and Cavanagh's pithy formulation: "Most will not have spare change even for Pringle's or Cheez Whiz" (*GD*, 170). Moreover, corporations channel the flow of goods in such a way that products match the particular segment of the market that can afford them. By this measure, the most global of products is cigarettes, since they can be "sold on the street by the 'stick' (in the jargon of the trade) to millions too poor to buy a pack" (*GD*, 182). Household appliances and consumer electronics, on the other hand, are less global because they can be afforded only by the top tenth of the population in developing countries. In the Philippines, for example, "Sony and Matsushita can expect to reach no more than the 3.5 percent of the population that earn $5,000 a year or more" (*GD*, 182). The global flow of consumer goods is thus more like a trickle in some parts of the world.

A similar exaggeration of global culture is evident in media reports, popular journalism, and academic studies. There is a growing list of books and articles that debates whether the world is becoming a culturally homogeneous "McWorld" through Western cultural imperialism, or whether we are seeing the emergence of a complex, syncretic, or hybridized global space in which Western culture is but one of the players, though admittedly a dominant one.[31] Both sides of the debate, however, are quite convinced that some kind of global culture is being produced, disagreeing only over its composition and shape. Thus a popular travel book such as Pico Iyer's *Video Night in Kathmandu*, whose very title suggests the bizarre intermingling of Western high-tech and ancient monastic culture and Hollywood entertainment and Eastern spirituality, can be read either as an account of the global spread of Western goods and culture, or as a description, in Frederick Buell's words, "of a new, syncretic, hybridised, media-based global culture" (*NC*, 5). But read either way, the globalization of culture recounted in Iyer's book is very much a subjective, one-sided affair. It is the first-person "I" who notes, while in Bali, the names of stores such as the "Hey Shop, the Hello shop, Easy Rider Travel Service, T.G.I. Friday restaurant." It is the "I" who lists the availability of "New Wave Japanese T-shirts and pretty sundresses in *Miami Vice* turquoise and pink." It is the "I," addressing a sophisticated global readership, who remarks: "After dinner, I had made my way to a nearby cafe for a cappuccino. Next to the cash register were enough stacks of old copies of *Cosmo*, *Newsweek*, and the *London Sunday Times* to fill six doctor's waiting rooms."[32] It is the erudite cosmopolitan "I" who entitles the chapter on Bali, "Prospero's Isle." There is a point of view clearly at work here, driven by a metropolitan agenda that sees cultural globalization everywhere: "No man, they say, is an island; in the age of international travel, not even an island can remain an island for long" (*VN*, 21). What is missing, however, in Iyer's book is an account of what the natives think about all this global culture talk. To be sure, we do get the odd native's view, such as that of Maung Maung, the Burmese trishaw driver. But these native informants are usually involved in the tourist business, have thereby been "globalized" to some extent, and can thus be made to fit the narrative of cultural globalization. But what about the others who do not work in the tourist trade, and whose everyday routines and concerns may touch tangentially, if at all, the world of *Cosmo* and cappuccino, *Dallas* and Def Leppard. Is there not a certain arrogance involved in the claim to see the world in a grainy Rambo poster encountered in some tropical village? Is there any basis to the argument that jet travel and the information highway are turning the world into a global village when there are still many parts of the world without highways, where travel to the neighboring village may take the better part of a day's hike? The processes of globalization so enthusiastically recorded by privileged travelers and cultural studies theorists may not figure at all in the consciousness of a native farmer, whose acre of maize may be to him more important than the knowledge that we can watch *Baywatch* in Benares.

Even in those places where so-called global products and culture have established their presence strongly, globalization, in either its homogenizing or hybridizing form, need not necessarily occur. Another recent traveler to Bali, Stephen Greenblatt, has jotted down his impressions of a festival in Amlapura in which a Charles Bronson movie *Death Wish II*, a local Indonesian movie about rich yuppies in Jakarta, and a traditional *wayang kulit* (a shadow puppet play) were simultaneously on show:

> The Balinese were moving gaily and apparently at random from one of these shows to another, crowding in to witness a few illuminating minutes of American screen violence, moving outside to listen to the chanting of the *dalang* [storyteller and puppeteer] and watch the shadow puppets flickering across the screen, . . . crossing the square to see the gilded youth in Jakarta race around in red sports cars. In the context of this festive perambulation, the villagers whom on my first night I had seen huddled together before the television set seemed part of a larger Balinese fascination with images on screens. Though the *wayang* scaffold was propped against the movie house, it seemed far more plausible symbolically at least to imagine the movie house propped against the ancient puppet theater, with its intimations of the unreality of the world.[33]

Greenblatt, puzzled by the Balinese audience's untroubled equanimity and unquestioning acceptance of what to him were bizarre and heterogeneous cultural juxtapositions, reaches for a culturalist explanation; he attributes their serenity to an ancient Balinese fascination with the unreality of images, with the world as shadow theatre. While this may be a plausible explanation, one can equally argue that no recourse to a Balinese metaphysics of the image is needed to explain Greenblatt's puzzlement. Greenblatt is puzzled because what he sees in Amlapura does not fit the current globalization paradigms of cultural homogenization, cultural resistance, or cultural hybridization. He is puzzled because the metropolitan categories he is in possession of do not appear to be relevant to the

Balinese. He thus proposes an indigenous cultural answer to his puzzle. But no answer may be needed, because there need not be a puzzle to begin with. The puzzle may be a puzzle, only because the observed facts do not fit a preconceived thesis—the thesis of cultural globalization. The Balinese may or may not be under the grip of a metaphysics of the image, but their lack of puzzlement, their serenity before the intrusions of alien cultural forms, may have a simpler explanation: they are not puzzled because they are not beholden to and thus are not troubled by the particular set of problems that engages Greenblatt. Global products may well enter Balinese society with ease, because to the Balinese, their global status may not be a matter of great theoretical or academic concern.

IV

My discussion of Iyer's travelogue and Greenblatt's Balinese anecdote shows not only the partiality of cultural globalization but also the metropolitan perspective behind globalization discourses. That is, globalization discourses originate from and circulate in certain specifiable locales and can thus be seen as parochial, despite their claims to be global. Marilyn Strathern points out that "theories or models, and especially models that purport to speak of universal conditions, are produced out of specific circumstances. How the universal is apprehended may even be taken as a veritable index of the parochial" (*SC*, 4). Similarly, Meaghan Morris warns that "loose talk about globalization can be intensely parochial. . . . [D]iscourses that deploy, as universals, certain power—saturated and generative oppositions like 'modernity' and 'tradition' are actually *limited*—or 'place-based,' even parochial—in their descriptive, let alone their predictive value; they help to produce, from a particular position, the phenomena they claim to describe."[34]

We can see the justice of Strathern's and Morris' argument when we take stock of the sites of production, circulation, and reception of globalization theories and discourses. A basic list of these sites would include the North American, European, and Japanese governments and government agencies, major universities from the same regions, policy pronouncements by TNCs, journals on the right such as *Fortune*, *Forbes*, *The Economist*, and *Harvard Business Review*, journals on the left, such as *Public Culture*, *Social Text*, *boundary 2*, *Alternatives*, and *Theory, Culture and Society* (and their respective readerships), and publishers such as Routledge, Sage, HarperCollins, leading university presses, and so on. Most of the sites mentioned are located in America or Europe. Quite clearly, then, the debates on globalization are what Anthony King calls "self-representations of the dominant particular" and illustrate Morris' point about how they help produce, from a particular position, the very issues and problems they claim to debate. In short, it is the particular that produces the global, though the former is claimed to be subsumed by the latter.

An illuminating example of the localism or parochialism of global discourse is provided by John Tomlinson in his description of academic publishing in the West. After meeting various criteria, of which market demand is paramount, an academic book will be published and will then circulate in those affluent nations that can afford it. "This circulation," Tomlinson argues,

> will generally be taken to represent the material existence of the "global debate" on any particular issue. Yet it is clear that this circulation of texts is determined, at one level, by the interests of the (relatively) affluent academic institutions of the capitalist West which provide the market for the (often multinational) academic publishing houses. It is by no means clear that this situation can be seen as a "global argument" in the fullest sense of the term.[35]

Moreover, Tomlinson notes, there is the question of translation. Most academic books are never going to be translated into languages such as Guarani or Quechua, because there is never going to be a viable market for such translations. Consequently, says Tomlinson, there will be "the effective exclusion of certain cultures . . . from the 'global conversation' of intellectuals and scholars [and this] indicates how loosely we speak in speaking of a global community of scholars" (*CI*, 14). The discourse of globalization, seen from such an angle, can therefore only ever be *potentially* global, though its particular and parochial Euro-American provenance is never in doubt.

Both in a cultural and an economic sense, globalization, as discourse and as practice, appears to be centered not only in the Triad Zone that Ohmae has delineated but, to be even more precise, in a network of urban formations, a kind of "high-tech Hanseatic league,"[36] anchored by the "global" cities of London, New York, and Tokyo. These three cities, according to urban geographer Saskia Sassen, contain "the largest concentrations of leading producer services firms, the top twenty-four securities houses in the world, sixty-three of the top one hundred banks in the world, 84% of global capitalization, and the largest concentrations of a variety of commodity and currency markets."[37] We see in such statistics confirmation of the view that globalization is not only nationally or regionally based but even more narrowly located in certain urban centers.

We can further claim that globalization's parochialism is not only space bound but also class based. Thus depending on access to material resources and educational or cultural capital, some residents of New York will be more globally conscious and participate in globalization processes more actively than others. In fact, some of them will feel that they share the same global discourse with others a continent away, and not with those across town. Manhattan yuppies may have more in common, in terms of lifestyle and taste, with their counterparts in Bombay or Bangkok than with poorer residents in Brooklyn or those even a block away. The discourse of globalization is therefore also a discourse of class. Globalization is a concept that matters most to a small but powerful and influential fraction of the world's population, a transnational professional class made up of "commercial pilots, computer programmers, film directors, international bankers, media specialists, oil riggers, entertainment celebrities, ecology experts, movie producers, demographers, accountants, professors, lawyers, athletes" (*JMW*, 16–17). Though transnational or global in their orientation, this professional class can be regarded as parochial insofar as their idea of the global is made possible and thus also shaped and limited by their links to capital, information, and technology. In other words, it is the class-specific nature of their professions—the fact that they speak the same global jargon, have access to and consume the same global products, interact on the same electronic networks, share the same mobile, border-crossing lifestyles, and owe their jobs and careers to transnational cultural and economic institutions or corporations—that limits their view of globalization and makes it class bound and parochial. Their consciousness of globalization reflects their own class interests and sets them apart from the vast majority of people, the "great unwired," as journalists have taken to calling them, whose circumstances no doubt shape a different view of the world, one perhaps not unlike that of Margaret Drabble's character, whose mobility is limited to bus rides between Wandsworth and Whitehall.

V

If I have called globalization's name into question, it is because I think we should effect a hermeneutic shift that will lead us away from both the model of market integration, multicultural consumption, and sentimental "one-worldism" offered by euphoric globalization and the lugubrious alternative of a globe completely saturated and dominated by capital presented by world systems theorists. It is in this context that we should endorse the slogan: Forget globalization. If globalization is far from being truly global, as we have seen, then perhaps the term *globalization*, riddled by contradictions and inconsistencies that render its use problematic, ought to be discarded. Like Juliet, we may wish to say of globalization, "Oh, be some other name!" Should we decide to "forget globalization" and come up with another name, we may wish provisionally to settle on that of "The New International," a name that acts, according to Jacques Derrida, as a remembrance of our world's "violence, inequality, exclusion, famine and economic oppression"; a name that calls for a new justice.[38] For globalization need not be about the advancement of some at the expense of others. It can be renominated and rearticulated as the search for global justice and equality. Thus while acknowledging the marginalization of large parts of the world by the global economy, Mexican social critic Carlos Vilas nonetheless finds it possible to affirm that globalization processes also imply "that broad sectors of the world's population are today conscious of the injustice in which the majority of their peers live, creating the initial condition for a true universalization of the idea of justice and the undertaking of action conducive to making it a progressive reality."[39]

As we enter the new millennium, it is anyone's guess as to whether such a global consciousness of injustice will help us achieve "The New International" that Derrida calls for. What is clear, however, is that globalization, as I have described it in its euphoric or triumphalistic mode, cannot claim to be the single, totalizing master-word or metanarrative that explains what is or ought to be happening in our world. It is a selective, performative discourse that finds what it seeks and believes what it creates. In that sense, globalization's hegemony is built on self-referential and tautological grounds and is thus open to dispute and rearticulation; it is not a singular, unchangeable name.

NOTES

1. Jacques Derrida, *The Truth in Painting*, trans. G. Bennington and I. McLeod (Chicago: University of Chicago Press, 1987), 135.

2. Jean-François Lyotard, "The Sublime and the Avant-Garde," *The Inhuman: Reflections on Time*, trans. G. Bennington and R. Bowlby (Stanford: Stanford University Press, 1991), 89–107. Hereafter cited in the text as *SA*.

3. Simon Critchley, *The Ethics of Deconstruction: Derrida and Levinas* (Oxford: Blackwell, 1992), 5.

4. William Shakespeare, *Romeo and Juliet*, in *Shakespeare: The Complete Works*, ed. G. B. Harrison (New York: Harcourt, Brace, and World, 1968), II, ii, 39–47.

5. Jacques Derrida, "Aphorism Countertime," *Acts of Literature*, ed. D. Attridge, trans. N. Royle (New York: Routledge,1992), 427. Hereafter cited as *AC*.

6. Jacques Derrida, "Khora," *On the Name*, ed. T. Dutoit, trans. I. MacLeod (Stanford: Stanford University Press, 1995), 89.

7. Jacques Derrida, "A 'Madness' Must Watch over Thinking," *Points. . . .:Interviews, 1974–1994*, ed. Elizabeth Weber, trans. Peggy Kamuf et al. (Stanford: Stanford University Press, 1995), 343–44.

8. Kenneth Burke, "Terministic Screens," *Language as Symbolic Action* (Berkeley: University of California Press, 1996), 50. Hereafter cited as *TS*.

9. Pierre Bourdieu, "Social Space and Symbolic Power," *In Other Words: Essays Towards a Reflexive Sociology*, trans. Matthew Adamson (Cambridge: Polity Press, 1990), 123–39. Hereafter cited as *SS*.

10. Richard Jenkins, *Pierre Bourdieu* (London: Routledge, 1992), 157.

11. Raymond Williams, *Keywords: A Vocabulary of Culture and Society* (London: Fontana, 1976), 15.

12. Slavoj Žižek, *The Sublime Object of Ideology* (London: Verso, 1989), 94–95. Hereafter cited as *SO*.

13. Ernesto Laclau, "Preface," *The Sublime Object of Ideology*, by Slavoj Žižek (London: Verso, 1989), xiv.

14. J. K. Gibson-Graham, *The End of Capitalism (as we knew it): A Feminist Critique of Political Economy* (Cambridge, Mass.: Blackwell, 1996), x. Hereafter cited as *EC*.

15. Ian Robert Douglas. "The Myth of Globalization: A Poststructural Reading of Speed and Reflexivity in the Governance of Late Modernity." Paper presented at the 37th International Studies Association Convention, San Diego, April 16–20, 1996, 25.

16. Richard J. Barnet and John Cavanagh, *Global Dreams: Imperial Corporations and the New World Order* (New York: Touchstone, 1994), 13–14. Hereafter cited as *GD*.

17. Ella Shohat and Robert Stam, "From the Imperial Family to the Transnational Imaginary: Media Spectatorship in the Age of Globalization," *Global/Local: Cultural Production and the Transnational Imaginary*, eds. Rob Wilson and Wimal Dissanayake (Durham, N.C.: Duke University Press, 1996), 146.

18. For Marxist accounts of capitalist globalization, see Immanuel Wallerstein, "Culture As the Ideological Battleground of the Modern World System," *Theory, Culture, and Society* 7: 2/3 (1990): 31–57; Fredric Jameson, *Postmodernism or, the Cultural Logic of Late Capitalism* (Durham, N.C.: Duke University Press, 1991), and David Harvey, *The Condition of Postmodernity: An Enquiry into the Origins of Cultural Change* (Oxford: Blackwell, 1990).

19. Roland Robertson, *Globalization: Social Theory and Global Culture* (London: Sage, 1992), 77. Hereafter cited as *G*.

20. Marilyn Strathern, "Foreword," *Shifting Contexts: Transformations in Anthropological Knowledge*, ed. Marilyn Strathern (London: Routledge, 1995), 157. Hereafter cited as *SC*.

21. Frederick Buell, *National Culture and the New Global System* (Baltimore: Johns Hopkins University Press, 1994), 305. Hereafter cited as *NC*.

22. Arjun Appadurai, "Disjuncture and Difference in the Global Cultural Economy," *The Phantom Public Sphere,* ed. Bruce Robbins (Minneapolis: University of Minnesota Press, 1993), 269–95, 275. Hereafter cited as *DD*.

23. Doreen Massey, "A Global Sense of Place," *Marxism Today* (June 1991): 26–27.

24. Margaret Drabble, *The Radiant Way* (Harmondsworth: Penguin, 1988), 164.

25. Cited in D. A. Leslie, "Global Scan: The Globalization of Advertising Agencies, Concepts, and Campaigns," *Economic Geography* 71 (1995): 411.

26. Summary of UNCTAD figures in Irene Ngoo, "World's Poorest Nations 'Worse Off Today Than a Decade Ago'," *The Straits Times* (Singapore) September 29, 1995, p. 9.

27. Benjamin R. Barber, *Jihad vs. McWorld* (New York: Times Books, 1995), 34. Hereafter cited as *JMW*.

28. Kenichi Ohmae, *The Borderless World: Power and Strategy in the Global Marketplace* (London: Harper Collins, 1994), x–xi.

29. Pedro Belli, "Globalizing the Rest of the World," *Harvard Business Review* (July–August 1991): 50. Hereafter cited as *GR*.

30. Enzensberger, cited in Bruce Robbins, "Some Versions of US Internationalism," *Social Text* 14: 4 (1995): 14.

31. See, for example, *National Culture and the New Global System*; *Global/Local*; and *Jihad vs. McWorld*.

32. Pico Iyer, *Video Night in Kathmandu* (London: Black Swan, 1989), 21. Hereafter cited as *VN*.

33. Stephen Greenblatt, *Marvellous Possessions: The Wonder of the New World* (Chicago: University of Chicago Press, 1991), 5.

34. Meaghan Morris, "Future Fear," *Mapping the Futures: Local Cultures, Global Change*, ed. Jon Bird et al. (London: Routledge, 1993), 30, 36.

35. John Tomlinson, *Cultural Imperialism: A Critical Introduction* (Baltimore: Johns Hopkins University Press, 1991), 14. Hereafter cited as *CI*.

36. Arif Dirlik, "The Global in the Local," *Global/Local: Cultural Production and the Transnational Imaginary*, ed. Rob Wilson and Wimal Dissanayake (Durham, N.C.: Duke University Press, 1996), 29.

37. Scott Lash and John Urry, *Economies of Signs and Space* (London: Sage, 1994), 290–91.

38. Jacques Derrida, *Specters of Marx: The State of the Debt, the Work of Mourning, and the New International*, trans. Peggy Kamuf (New York: Routledge, 1994), 84–85.

39. Carlos Vilas, "Latin America and the New World Order," *Social Justice*: 23 1/2 (1996): 300.

CHAPTER 12

The Social Figure of Art: Heidegger and Adorno on the Paradoxical Autonomy of Artworks

Krzysztof Ziarek

If at present nothing is self-evident about art, as Adorno remarks in the first sentence of *Aesthetic Theory*,[1] then art has perhaps become a preeminent locus of questioning, a site where not only the reason for the existence of art is repeatedly called into question but also the modern organization of social life and the technological determination of being are brought into view. As art continues to doubt, at least since Hegel, its own existence, this uncertainty is directly linked to the unsettled, and multiply unsettling, question of the social role of art. No one would disagree that art is dependent on the social organization of labor and that it inscribes the relations of production that obtain at the time of its origin. Where the issue becomes contentious is with respect to whether the figuration of forces in the work of art—which I will explain later, by way of Heidegger's thought, as a poietic figure—is, in fact, a *refiguration*, which transforms the social/technological forces, that is, whether the work that art performs amounts to a different disposition of forces than the one that, socially and historically, gives origin to the work. I would argue, in agreement with Adorno and Heidegger, that aesthetic, historicist, or cultural explanations of how art works socially, of what it accomplishes in relation to the world from which it originates, fail to address this crucial transformation or redisposition of forces—the redisposition which, in my mind, constitutes the very work art performs. Underneath aesthetic concepts, cultural inscriptions, and material entanglements, this work is what might decide whether art, the modern proliferation of artworks notwithstanding, retains relevance and force. To examine this work is to attempt to think art beyond the scope of aesthetics, to begin to address art, as I suggested elsewhere, "after aesthetics."[2] But it also means keeping alive the uncertainty as to whether modern art is capable of such work, and as to whether its recipients can respond to it or become affected by it.

This "refigurative" work marks the ambiguous, though critical, element of art's autonomy. I want to underscore in this context a certain streak in Marxist thought, crucial especially to Gramsci's reflections on culture[3] and Adorno's *Aesthetic Theory*, which insists on such a paradoxical autonomy of art: even though art is a social fact, its work is "more" than what its sociohistorical context and its origin as a cultural artifact could account for. This position keeps us on guard against two distinct forms of approaching art that evacuate the paradox of this autonomy: formalist aesthetics and materialist critiques of art. Formalist readings of modernism annul the paradox of art by insisting on a quasi-organic unity of the artwork, whose aesthetic integrity would remain separate, "uncontaminated" by a social-historical context. Cultural-materialist analysis, on the other hand, downplays this paradox by equating art to its social provenance. Materialist aesthetics explains art's role and even its critical effects as co-extensive with art's status as a cultural product, the position that forecloses the possibility of a more radical critical edge in art, the edge kept alive by Adorno's thought under the idea of the paradoxical autonomy of art. My suggestion is that the social role of art should be explained apart from the constrictive and misunderstood opposition between formalist and materialist aesthetics which, increasingly, has come to determine, and polarize, contemporary debates within literary studies. If art retains social importance, its significance is not adequately explainable in terms of cultural production, social effects, or aesthetic ideology. Rather, it resides in what I call merging and renegotiating Adorno's and Heidegger's concerns and concepts, the social figure of art. My intention is not to compare Adorno and Heidegger,[4] or to limit their encounter to Adorno's mostly acrimonious and often misleading remarks about Heidegger's thought but instead to bring out unacknowledged proximities between them and radicalize them in ways that would allow us to rethink art beyond the scope of either Heidegger's or Adorno's positions.

My approach focuses on how the work of art produces, or *figures*, a constellation of forces alternative to *both* the sociocultural formations from which it arises and the forms of critique extant in them. Like Adorno, I argue for the recognition of a "different" status of art in relation to forces—life, material, social—a peculiar status that does not make art separate from society but allows it, even though it remains embedded in and shaped by society, to redispose its forces into alternative and transgressive configurations that operate outside of the dialectic of critique. As my title indicates, I call these alternative dispositions *figures* (as distinct from the idea of form)—working configurations whose meaning is intrinsically social. The revision I propose responds to an increasing marginalization of aesthetic and poetic considerations in contemporary cultural discourses, which define art as, essentially, an effect of *other* forces—social, economic, or political—rather than as a discrete force, which is capable not only of describing or reflecting but also of critically refiguring the forces operating within the social domain. This culturalist revision of aesthetics is certainly a justified reaction to formalism but, in its attempt to theorize art from within the nexus of cultural and institutional forces, it explains art's force as borrowed from society, as an extension of its historical-material conditions. Against formalist aesthetics, I argue, therefore, that art is not an *object* to be perceived or judged aesthetically and, in distinction from materialist aesthetics, I propose that art's signification is not limited to being an effect of the play of various social forces. Rather, art has its own specific force, with a "poietic" dynamic, which must be considered in relation to the "external" social and political forces but cannot be satisfactorily explained in their terms. What I call art's social figure reaches beyond the terms of both *social* and *formalist* aesthetics.

The notion of the figure that I plan to develop here is borrowed from Heidegger's "The Origin of the Work of Art," but it is used here to mediate between Heidegger's *Gestalt* and Adorno's concept of form, in a gesture that keeps in play both elements of the social figure. The use of the term *figure* rather than *form* is meant to forestall an all too easy misunderstanding, which reduces the "formal" tensions in the work of art to "empty" or "self-interested" formalism. Juxtaposing Adorno and Heidegger in this way allows us also to keep in play the social relevance of the figure, which often evaporates from readings of Heidegger.

Probably the most important contribution of Adorno's *Aesthetic Theory* lies in its insistence on the fact that art's role as a social critique is not carried out by means of content or themes but is figured into form: "Real denunciation is probably only a capacity of form, which is overlooked by social aesthetic that believes in themes" (*AT*, 230). Adorno insists on the radical social significance of the formal figuration in modern art, defending it against the naive misconception of the social aesthetic, which equates social critique to thematic, content-based commentary or political commitment and reduces formal aspects of art to empty formalism or disengaged, autotelic play. Likewise, art's role as a *fait social* cannot be adequately addressed by socially oriented criticism, which implicitly values positivist discourse over the "artistic" language of art. Cultural criticism operates on the assumption—a false one in Adorno's view—of the translatability of art's workings into the propositional discourse of knowledge, equating art's social significance to its historical, institutional, and cultural effects: "Once art has been recognized as a social fact, the sociological definition of its context considers itself superior to it and disposes over it. Often the assumption is that the objectivity of value-free positivistic knowledge is superior to supposedly subjective aesthetic standpoints. Such endeavors themselves call for social criticism. They tacitly seek the primacy of administration, of the administered world, even over what refuses to be grasped by total socialization or at any rate struggles against it" (*AT*, 250). What complicates cultural readings is that art is both less *and* more than social praxis: it is less because it does not conform or register properly as praxis in accordance with the pragmatic notion of action and the ends-means rationality. Art's nonconformity, though, enacts a critique of the narrow idea of practice: "Art, however, is more than praxis because by its aversion to praxis it simultaneously denounces the narrow untruth of the practical world" (*AT*, 241).

Still, Adorno's notion of form as the locus of social critique has to be complicated. Although certainly far from conventional, Adorno's understanding of form operates within the framework of the aesthetic conceptualization of art, on the intersection between spirit and senses, at the point where spirit both produces the image of forces in the artwork and explodes its own configuration within this image. Heidegger's rather different take on art becomes important in this context, because his notion of *Gestalt*, or figure, is a vehicle for an explicit critique of aesthetic approaches to art, especially the category of form pivotal to them. In the first part of "The Origin of the Work of Art," Heidegger critiques the idea of form/matter as inadequate, even misleading, for thinking about art, because the notion of formed matter is the basis for defining equipment and thus belongs to the ends-means rationality. The fact that "[t]he metaphysics of the modern period rests on the form-matter structure" gives rise to "a mode of thought by which we think not only about thing, equipment, and work but about all beings in general."[5]

Determining the constitution of beings in modernity, the matter-form doublet becomes the anchoring structure of aesthetics, which also predetermines the boundaries of aesthetic inquiry. Heidegger's diagnosis of the metaphysical *provenance* and *limitations* of aesthetic categories makes it possible to critique in one swoop both formalist aesthetics and the thematic readings of art, which fall short of bringing into the open the work that takes place in art. Since Adorno's *Aesthetic Theory* explicitly sets up art against the ends-means rationality, which rules the over-administered world of modernity, it is imperative to nuance Adorno's notion of form, in fact, to "deform" it, so that it does not remain as heavily implicated in the metaphysics of the spirit which it, in other ways, tries to critique. Heidegger's alternative to the idea of form—*Gestalt* or figure—is neither image nor representation. It is certainly not contentless, even though its operation cannot be explained in terms of meaning, theme, or interpretation. Heidegger situates the notion of the figure beyond the opposition of form and content, reinscribing in the *Gestalt* a dynamic tension—a rift (*Riss*), as he calls it—between world and earth. While world refers to the open relational context that the work inaugurates and in which it exists, earth indicates a withdrawing, a certain impenetrability or Otherness, which "rifts" the world, disturbs its openness and contests its intelligibility. Thus the figure plays its rifts beyond the opposition of form and content, beyond the formal features of the work of art and its thematic concerns, as it constitutes the very outline or the blueprint—a kind of a writing or a breaking through—of the active conflict between world and earth: it is a figure of the alethic play of concealment and unconcealment. Fundamentally historical in its nature, the artwork projects into its figure the relations that structure the very world into which the work arises. As Christopher Fynsk suggests, art continues to perform the very occurrence of relations through which it figures its event: "The work fashions and bears *in itself* the event out of which it comes to stand."[6]

What I would like to take over from Heidegger's discussion is the way in which it pushes beyond the aesthetic categorization of form and matter, destructures it and reinscribes its tension across the layered working of art. The figure is, therefore, never "spiritual"; it is not spirit sublating the material, giving form to or unifying the sensible aspects of the work. Rather, the figure remarks the Otherness of materiality in which art works in the impenetrability associated with the earth. In a similar vein, the figure cannot be confused with the sensible form or outline of the work, because the idea of sensible form is undone and reinscribed across the rift between world and earth: on the one hand, form shapes the material, brings out, as Heidegger remarks, its quality as material (in opposition to equipment, in which the material disappears into the usefulness of the object) and, on the other hand, world unfolds into a "form," its context always opening up into a historical shape. There is ultimately a correlation between the thingly character of the work in Heidegger and the resistance to the spirit that Adorno detects in the material of art. The ungraspable or unconceptualizable materiality in which art cuts its figure echoes in the element of concealment that destructures truth and in the withdrawal that marks the limits of any "world."

Artwork understood as a figure is not an object but a *work*: in the active sense of an occurrence, an event, or an act. The accent in the word "work" falls not on the fact that it has been created but rather on how and what it *works*, on what kind of work art performs. The active sense of working, of art working on its audience but also soliciting the audience to work with and through it, deemphasizes the static concepts of form and content and draws attention to the temporality operating in art. As Adorno puts it: "The artwork is at once process and instant" (*AT*, 100).[7] Working with Benjamin's dialectical image, Adorno describes art as a becoming, or *ein Werdendes* (*AT*, 132), as a process or an activity, which, sedimenting history, explodes, as an instant, the continuity of its own inner time. Defining art as an act, as the tension between process and instant, which characterizes the inner time of art, Adorno comes close to explaining art in terms of the temporality of the event. The advantage of the notion of the event is that it further radicalizes temporality, placing historicity that marks, and mars, each moment of presence, beyond the opposition of process and instant.

The event occurs as an instant, but as a moment (an *Augenblick*) in which the eyes become closed—a rupture and a necessary blindness that indicates how historicity refracts the grasp of time as a linear progression. The notion of *das Ereignis*, or "propriative event," was introduced by Heidegger and has been reappropriated in different ways by various poststructuralist thinkers such as Foucault, Deleuze, Derrida, and Lyotard. What counts in those various elaborations of the event is its specific temporality, its "eventness," as Jacques Derrida calls it in *The Spectres of Marx*.[8] This eventness marks the historicity of experience, which *Being and Time*, still within the optics of Dasein, refers to as the being-constitution or composition of the occurring of Dasein (*Geschichtlichkeit meint die Seinsverfassung des "Geschehens" des Daseins als solchen*).[9] As the event-constitution of occurring, historicity marks a remainder over the linear temporality, a kind of a residual happening, giving presence but itself withdrawn from it and, thus, always already without place or presence in the present, the past, or the future. Historicity is what, composing or writing at any moment the relations between the three dimensions of time, does not belong to those dimensions: it does not constitute a past origin, a present instant, or a future presence. Without a dimension of its own, it marks the futurity of the present, that is, it unfolds the present as coming from what has been and dislocated toward what is to come. The work of art secretes this historicity, not as a hidden dimension or meaning to be discovered by interpretation but as the work that art performs in its figure. The figure can be described then by reference to the event and, more specifically, to the historial residues that art "figures" to unsettle presence, articulated forms, and closures of representation. It is a work that guards experience against both the schematization into the teleology of process and an arrest within the punctuality of an instant. We could say that art not only represents history and sediments it into itself but, staging the very happening of history, its event, puts into question the very principle of representation. Artworks default from history and historicism in order to keep in view the historicity of being.

How are we then to understand the relation to art *as work*? I will remain here concerned only with that specific mode of relation in which art is encountered as a work, in which, according to the definition I have been developing, art comes to be constituted as a figure that reworks the forces that bring it into existence and make up its social and historical context. I would suggest that such a relation could be described as a thinking or a knowing, but a knowing that needs to be carefully delimited and defined in terms of a certain alternative (to) praxis. Such a thinking or knowing is never simply "contained" in art but unfolds as an interaction with art, as a mode of relating in which art is allowed to happen as a work. In his reflections on the avant-garde, Lyotard explores this kind of relation in terms of "letting-go of all grasping intelligence and of its power, disarming it."[10] This releasement from mastering intellect performed by the work of art is explicitly modeled on Heidegger's notion of *Ereignis* and frames the event in terms of freeing from relations of power: "An event, an occurrence—what Martin Heidegger called *ein Ereignis*—is infinitely simple, but this simplicity can only be approached through a state of privation. That which we call thought must be disarmed" (*LR*, 197). Signification and representation are called into question, because the infinite simplicity of the event precedes and escapes the grasping power of thought; in fact, it makes thought, in all of its various modalities, possible. "The event happens as a question mark 'before' happening as a question" (*LR*, 197). The event both releases thought and, as a question mark before the question can even be formulated, it also releases, in the same gesture, happening from the cognitive and practical grasp of the intellect. For Lyotard, such a moment of a double release, which protects happening from representations and explanations that thought ascribes to it, constitutes the rigor of avant-garde art: "guarding the occurrence 'before' any defence, any illustration, and any commentary, guarding before being on one's guard, before 'looking' (*regarder*) under the aegis of *now*, this is the rigour of the avant-garde" (*LR*, 199). As the most rigorous realization of such an unbinding in writing, Lyotard singles out Gertrude Stein. One look at Stein's texts suffices to realize that they indeed release language from the power of grammar as well as social and literary conventions, and they do so to an extent that renders them difficult to read and impossible to interpret. I mean "impossible" here literally: Stein's writings are deliberately set up against interpretation, they disallow it, or, to put it differently, they release literature from the grasping power of interpretation.

Stein's works, though, are never just presentations of the unpresentable which, for Lyotard, reincarnate the modern sublime or, on the other hand, the "negative" imprints of the social world that Adorno finds in Beckett. As *How to Write* suggests, Stein is after a new vocabulary of thinking or, as she puts it in "Poetry and Grammar," after a new way of knowing things intensely, that is, of writing them in the intensity of their happening. Temporality and event underpin Stein's idiosyncratic writing, a writing that does not "use" language but instead invents or refigures it as it goes along. It functions as a writing not *in* language but *of* language. In this respect, it seems to resemble *Finnegans Wake*, but nonetheless it remains crucially different. While Joyce produces an interlingual, "international," so to speak, tissue of words, which keeps recreating itself on the morphological and semantic level, Stein remains within English, and her new "vocabulary" of thinking operates on the syntactical level. It dislodges syntax and revels in the indeterminate parts of speech and "grammatical incorrectness" in order to write a language underneath the rules and conventions of English. Stein's vocabulary of thinking is not that of single words or terms, but it produces infrasyntactic amalgamations which, instead of defining or meaning something, perform it as an event:

Out of kindness comes redness and out of rudeness comes rapid same question, out of an eye comes research, out of selection comes painful cattle. So then the order is that a white way of being round is something suggesting a pin and is it disappointing, it is not, it is so rudimentary to be analyzed and see a fine substance strangely, it is so earnest to have a green point not to red but to point again.[11]

This fragment comes from a section of *Tender Buttons*, entitled "A Box," which, rather than defining what a box is or naming its essence, performs first the containment suggestive of a box, then the expectation and surprise of opening, and, finally, the continuous pointing or differentiation that situates and makes up a box's being. The connections or pointings that this "parody" of description and definition develops are primarily not logical or semantic; more often, as is the case with all of *Tender Buttons*, these relations become constituted through syntactic, grammatical, and phonic connections. For example, "redness" comes out of "kindness" through parallel derivation of nouns, "redness," "rudeness," and "rapid" become associated through sound and letter variation, and so on. This does not mean that Stein eliminates logical or representational connections that structure and support the everyday world; she downplays, even minimizes, their importance and generates new practices of pointing that transform the everyday objects, foods, and spaces. The new hinges on which Stein's writing works are no longer those of the order of representation or signification, with the "invisible" syntactic meshing supporting them, but the lexical, syntactic, and phonic joints themselves.

What is interesting about Stein is how she explicitly makes a move away from words, terms, or concepts and performs a breakaway from a dictionary-limited and essence-oriented sense of language, which Heidegger, in his own way, repeatedly critiqued. Stein writes in infrasyntactic phrases that stage rather than name or define and that transcribe the temporality of the event. Her writings allow us to distance the work performed by art from the idea of negative presentation, to which Lyotard's and Adorno's different accounts remain riveted. Texts such as *Tender Buttons* or *Stanzas in Meditation* obviously play with and refuse the principles of representation, syntactical ordering, or semantic consistency, but they certainly do not exhaust themselves in this negativity. On the contrary, theirs is primarily a force of positivity (and even joy), a force that unfolds or performs without submitting to the power and strictures of articulation or presentation. Not an anxiety of "Is it happening?" that Lyotard ascribes to them[12] but a force of "it is happening," a giving of what comes to be, which is closer to the subjectless but positive force of the Heideggerian event and its destructured unfolding of *es gibt*: it gives/there is.

The first feature of the thinking "figured" in art—a "letting-go of grasping intelligence"—can be described as positive, in terms of a residual release of forces. This entails a second important and more difficult characteristic: the "positive" releasement is never passive, because it constitutes a mode of knowing and, as such, initiates a possibility of a new idea of praxis which, as Adorno argues, denounces the restricted, "untrue" instrumental sense of praxis. In conformity with his overall conception of the modern artwork in *Aesthetic Theory*, Adorno understands this possibility in a negative sense, as a denunciation of praxis as it exists, limited and caught up in the impossibility of another praxis. A more "positive" approach to such a praxis, though one with its own problems,[13] is proposed by Heidegger in "The Origin of the Work of Art." Heidegger suggests that, in its reception, or preservation, as he calls it, the work opens up a certain mode of knowing.[14] This knowing (*Wissen*) that *works* in art is not a matter of cognition (*Kennen*) or representation (*Vorstellen*); it is not a theoretical or propositional knowledge, just as it is not aesthetic "knowledge," perception, or judgment. "Yet knowing does not consist in mere information and notions about something. He who truly knows beings knows what he wills to do in the midst of them" (*BW*, 192). At the time of "The Origin of the Work of Art" (1935–1936), Heidegger thinks within the influence of the Nietzschean rhetoric of the will and, what is more disturbing, remains close to the sense of acting he endorsed during the period of his engagement in National Socialist politics. It is important to note, though, that the will Heidegger has in mind is not the will to power but a kind of a knowing how to will, and a knowing how to act.[15]

As is well known, shortly after "The Origin of the Work of Art," Heidegger begins an extensive reading of Nietzsche and a decisive critique of the concept of will, in particular, of Nietzsche's will to power as the culmination of metaphysics. He abandons terms such as *willing, resoluteness*, and *truth*, and new terms such as *event, letting-be*, and *releasement* gain prominence. This is not the place to consider the ramifications and the specifics of this significant change,[16] but I would like to bring its general tenor to bear upon my re-reading of the relation between art and praxis in "The Origin of the Work of Art." In this text, *Wissen*, or knowing, is tied to acting but not as a matter of a clear-cut decision. On a closer look, it is a knowing that takes the form of preserving the strife figured in the work of art, of the space of deciding, in which one confronts the temporality and undecidability of the identities—material and "spiritual"—at play in art. Heidegger never says what or how one knows or wills "in the midst of beings," but he makes clear that this knowing has to do with historicity. The work of art opens up history, which means that in art one comes face to face with the *essenceless* occurring of what is, with the fact that being does not give stable identity, truth, or knowledge but keeps displacing them, always singularly. Historicity marks the withdrawal from presence and manifests the undecidability opened up by this retraction as what is *decisive* about being— a decisiveness of depresencing, which art keeps staging in its figure. This decisive undecidability that marks the being-constitution of occurring is what must confront and critique Heidegger's own work of the early 1930s.

The fact that historicity is what is decisive about Being and what remarks its undecidability is to be taken here as "positive": it problematizes the notions of identity, truth, meaning, representation, and so on, without disqualifying them. It exposes their fiction, their disregard of historicity, their logic of identification that maintains the power of a presence that can never materialize. It is this kind of a difficult work of thinking, figured in art, that I would like to reread within "The Origin of the Work of Art," focusing especially on the idea that this kind of work is not just critical or negative but, as Heidegger indicates, constitutes a transformative displacement. Describing the figure as a multiple thrusting (*Stossen*), a patchwork of forces of sorts, Heidegger writes, "But this multiple thrusting is nothing violent, for the more purely the work is itself transported into the openness of beings—an openness opened by itself—the more simply does it transport us out of the realm of the ordinary. To follow (*folgen*) this displacement means to transform our accustomed ties to world and earth and henceforth to restrain all usual doing and prizing, knowing and looking" (*BW*, 191/*Holzwege*, 52–53, modified). The relation to art is not defined as an aesthetic judgment or interpretation but in terms of following the displacement the work opens up. This shift or displacement cannot be explained as a different, new, or unfamiliar "content," which art (re)presents. Instead, it is an act of transformation, a *Verwandlung*, which alters the entire complex of relations to and within the world. It transfigures the usual forms of perception (*Blicken*), knowing (*Kennen*), valuing (*Schätzen*), and doing (*Tun*). Nothing short of a complex change of the entire being-in-the-world—in its sensible, cognitive, evaluative, and practical aspects—occurs in the work. What undergoes transformation, however, is neither the "content" of the world nor the "form" of its reality, its *Weltanschauung*, but the composition and modality of relations that constitute a world—the very disposing or giving upon which both the content or the matter of the world and the historical forms it takes depend.

When art's figure works, it opens up a world. This world does not constitute an imitation of the existing reality or an imaginary realm that provides an avenue of escape from what exists as the real. World is not meant here as a spatio-temporal container for a totality of beings or, in the sense of a worldview, a form of representation. Rather, world is an occurrence that breaks open radically historical modes of relating covered over by the structurations of being that organize everyday commerce and make these other modes that "world" in art nonexistent or unreal. If we call this approach to art and worlding Heideggerian, then perhaps the most Heideggerian work of modern art in this respect is Stein's *Tender Buttons*. But to the extent that *Tender Buttons* performs the displacement of the everyday world, at least on the level of language and rhetoric, more radically than Heidegger would have ever imagined, or maybe even wanted, Stein's text is also non- or more than Heideggerian. That such a radical displacement is in the works is signaled already by the final two sentences of the first entry of *Tender Buttons*, entitled "A Carafe, That is a Blind Glass": "All this and not ordinary, not unordered in not resembling. The difference is spreading" (*TB*, 9). Indeed, *Tender Buttons* is all spreading difference which, without becoming extraordinary, remains "not ordinary" and "not unordered in not resembling" everyday being. *Tender Buttons* lures us, a little like Cubist paintings, with the promise of the ordinary and familiar world of everyday objects, events, meals, and domestic spaces, all the more sharply to transform this everyday world. It makes a gentle mockery of our, and language's, compulsion to defining and describing: if we listed the section titles in *Tender Buttons*, they would make up a sort of mock encyclopedic table of contents of domesticity. Underneath headings such as "Apples," "Lunch," "Cups," "Rhubarb," "A Table," "A Shawl," and so on, we encounter, though, an undoing of definitions, a simultaneous unmasking of the power and the shortcomings of representation. Producing definitions and images, representation covers the "presenting" or the occurring and evacuates the historicity of what it presents. Perhaps the most obvious weakness of definitions that *Tender Buttons* lays open is the tendency to isolate things and obscure their "existential" entanglements which, in Stein's eyes, constitute the very intensity of their actual being. To counter this proclivity of thought and language, Stein rejects conventional grammar, refuses to use the name of the things she describes, and writes things through a tangle of indeterminate and temporalized relations, which situate them in their everyday occurrence: "I had to feel anything and everything that for me was existing so intensely that I could put it down in writing as a thing in itself without at all necessarily using its name."[17] The thing in itself is not an isolated entity, defined in the particularity of its essence, but a kind of ecstasis of relations, which keeps represencing the thing within the changing bearings of its worldly occurrence. To unmask the temporal strictures of representation, Stein's sentences develop, as if on the spur of the moment and its irreducibility to expression, their own individual structures, without adhering to syntactical patterns and grammatical or semantic routines. Stein's importance lies indeed in foregrounding historicity through a radical remaking of language, through producing "unthought" modalities of bearing among things, that let them "be" instead of naming or representing them. Stein teases out of language the possibility of a different being in the everyday world, one that is, she writes, more intensely, or we could say, after Heidegger, *seiender* more "in being."

I would like to flesh out this notion of being "more in being" in the context of Heidegger's re-reading of *poiēsis*. In "The Question Concerning Technology," Heidegger defines *poiēsis* very broadly as the force of bringing forth and unfolding.[18] *Poiēsis*, then, is never simply a making but has to be thought of in terms of Being and its force of giving, which, in the case of art, becomes channeled through the artist. I would argue that the conflict between *poiēsis* and *technē* at issue in art concerns not technology or poetry per se but the question of how the force of giving (i.e., *Ereignis* or event) becomes disposed: what constellation it forms, whether or what power formation it produces, whether the disposition in question lets forces unfold in their historicity. That this is indeed the case is signaled in Heidegger's discussion of the ambiguity at the core of *technē* and technology. The Greek *technē* is the name not only for a skill or a craft but also for "the arts of the mind and the fine arts. *Technē* belongs to bringing-forth, to *poiēsis*; it is something poetic" (*BW*, 294). Ancient *technē* is a modality of revealing or unfolding. Modern technology, too, Heidegger argues, is a revealing (*BW*, 296), but one that is only ambiguously related to the ancient multiple sense of *technē*. As a revealing, modern technology is a modality of challenging and forcing out (*Herausfordern*) the energies of nature. It unlocks these energies in a way that compels and orders them, it discloses everything into resources, a standing-reserve (*Bestand*): measurable, ready to hand, controllable. The chief characteristics of such a revealing are regulation, ordering, calculation, in a word, *Gestell*, or enframing. Enframing has achieved such a prominence and pervasive presence in modernity that it covers over the poietic sense of *technē*, it renders *poiēsis* forceless, unreal as a force. "Above all, enframing conceals that revealing which, in the sense of *poiēsis*, lets what presences come forth into appearance" (*BW*, 309). As the firmly entrenched standard of revealing, modern technology renders any other forms of revealing "unreal" and thus, Heidegger argues, "also conceals revealing itself and with it that wherein unconcealment, i.e., truth, comes to pass" (*BW*, 309).

But this is where art comes into play, so to speak. Art is *technē*, and as such, it might be thoroughly technological itself, in the modern sense of technology. But it might also remain *technē* in a poietic, and not exclusively technological, way. If that is the case, then art could figure the very ambiguity of *technē*, which still could mark, perhaps even refigure, modern technology. If technological revealing of what is as resource is, at its core, a certain deworlding of experience, then art does nothing more than break this world open again. Against the technological organization of forces, it liberates the worlding of experience.

It seems, though, that for modern art to be at all able to sustain the ambiguity of *technē*, it has to radically deaestheticize itself, for instance, in the manner of dadaism or Duchamp's ready-mades. An important feature of Duchamp's ready-mades is their ephemeral character which, in an almost emblematic manner, counters the idea of art as an object. By making ready-mades transitory, keeping them in existence only as photographs or replicas, Duchamp ironizes the ideas of originality and authenticity and shifts the emphasis, in agreement with much of dadaist art, on art's character as event. While it is generally accepted that the ready-mades such as "The Fountain" are explicitly directed against the very idea of art, I see their primary target in aesthetics, or in the aesthetic idea of art, and thus also in technology. Duchamp's ready-mades break with the idea of artistic material and employ mass-produced objects: urinal, bottlerack, bicycle wheel, snow shovel, as the technological, already fabricated, "material" in which art works. One could say that the ready-mades are, to use Heidegger's vocabulary, equipment deliberately rendered out-of-work, displaced from its context of usefulness and reliability and transferred into the alternative and "impractical" sphere of art. The ready-mades pivot on the idea of instrumentality—as the structuring principle of modern everydayness—only to subvert it and show that art begins perhaps where technology, which I understand here in Heidegger's sense of a modality of revealing, is put out of work. "The Fountain" is a mass-produced urinal, turned upside down, explicitly disconnected from its intended function, and ironically called "The Fountain." It could easily be seen as a joke that defies not only aesthetic traditions but even the modernist challenges to such conventions that are not willing to give up on some notion of aesthetics. The idea of beauty, perhaps the central tenet of aesthetics, is ridiculed in the act of making an artwork out of a technological contraption for disposing human waste. But "The Fountain" is also playing with technological assumptions through a double reversal: the literal reversal of the physical shape of the urinal, which stands, so to speak, on its head, is replayed in the title, which reverses the urinal's function and changes it into a source or a fountain, presumably of art. The figure in "The Fountain" is obviously not the form of the manufactured object turned upside down but rather the interplay of the technological and poetic forces, which this ready-made keeps transfiguring and mobilizing into an anti-aesthetic gesture. The importance of "The Fountain" and other ready-mades lies in their explicit linking of the possibility of modern art to a certain subversion of technology. This subversion is encoded into what might be called a defunctionalizing, which exposes functionalistic organization of being in modernity. Mocking aesthetics, Duchamp may be suggesting that art, when conceived of in terms of aesthetics, becomes immediately trapped within its aesthetic, cultural, and ideological functions to the detriment of the work that it might perform, a work that remains "invisible" and "unreal" within the technological parameters of modern existence.

There are two important implications of this approach to Duchamp. First, the ready-mades suggest that to think art aesthetically is to already remove art from its poetic "realm" and to transpose it into aesthetics—it amounts, therefore, to de-arting.[19] Such a shift effectively evacuates or covers over art's force, as it renders art into an object no longer capable of work. To think art aesthetically is to reduce it, to mute its poietic force and circumscribe it within the notion of a cultural phenomenon. Clearly, one of the things that "The Fountain" illustrates is a difference between the techno-functional idea of work and the notion of the artwork, which it portrays no longer in aesthetic terms. Second, to think art culturally or sociologically, as a sector of culture or as an effect or a product of ideology, may not, contrary to appearance, really change the situation all that much. It is true that, in such approaches, art is taken out of the isolated sphere of aesthetics and inscribed into a larger picture of cultural and historical forces. Still, what takes place in the work of art continues to be explained in aesthetic terms, except that those terms become revised and refracted through the notions of cultural and discursive formations. What is not questioned, however, is the limitation that the notion of culture and the idea of art as a cultural product impose upon art. Unthought remains also the link that Heidegger detects between the technological revealing of being and the understanding of art as a sector of cultural activity. There seems nothing more evident in the ready-mades than the intimate, maybe even "essential," link between modern art and technology, a link that cannot be satisfactorily explained by reference to the increasing influence of technology and technological inventions on how art gets made but has to be discussed in terms of different modes of revealing constitutive of being in modernity. My remarks here should not be misunderstood as somehow downplaying the significance of historicist work but rather as suggesting that cultural contextualization, as important as it is to understanding art, usually cannot take into consideration the moment of "the more," the poietic event, which makes art what it is and which, as Adorno suggests, inscribing the historical-social forces into it, breaks out of their spell and, I would add, attempts to redispose them.

Such a redisposition or transformation, if it comes to pass at all, remains, characteristically for radical twentieth-century art, abstract. Notwithstanding their differences, Stein's texts and Duchamp's works are related by their poignantly abstract treatment of social, linguistic, and aesthetic forces. The structure of *Tender Buttons*, at least on the surface, resembles an abstract, dictionary-like mapping of everydayness and domesticity, which arranges and schematizes the singular incidents and objects of everyday life into ready-made and superficially transparent definitions. Relying on the generality of meaning and the structuring properties of language, such definitions reflect the invisible syntax of the modern world, whose workings become visible indirectly through the ease with which experience can become abstracted into conceptual entries. Duchamp's ready-mades, using manufactured objects to problematize the artistic idea of original and natural creation, make also a more general and more important comment on the prefabricated character of modern experience, whose events come to resemble the repetitive routine of an assembly line. Like bicycle wheels or snow shovels, moments of being forfeit their event character and become stamped with categorial determinations, which renders them usable and exchangeable with an almost mechanical facility. The manufactured objects become signs of a more pervasive and "invisible" tendency in being itself, which orders and abstracts the singularity of experience into a readily available stock of limpid, self-evident definitions and schematizations.

Adorno explains this tendency toward the abstract in modern art by reference to the increasing abstractness of the social relations in the administered world of modernity: "New art is as abstract as social relations have in truth become. . . . At ground zero, however, where Beckett's plays unfold like forces in infinitesimal physics, a second world of images springs forth, both sad and rich, the concentrate of historical experiences that otherwise, in their immediacy, fail to articulate the essential: the evisceration of subject and reality" (*AT*, 31). Beyond thematic or formal treatment of "real life issues," even beyond art's inscription within its historical-cultural scene, artworks such as Beckett's unfold a layer of relations between forces that organize the purported immediacy of empirical life. It is because this "second world of images" springs from the precariously nonpresent, though never absent, historicity of being, that they strike us with such a quality of abstractness and irreality. In Adorno's estimation, these images stay confined to "the negative imprint of the administered world." Stein's *Tender Buttons*, however, clearly unfolds each redefined object or event into a transformed or an alternative play of forces. These are the infinitesimal forces of being, of "intense existence," which Stein's writing unfolds into figures that not only refuse language's syntactic administration of meaning but also try to break free from what might be called the technological "physics" of the modern world—the unfolding of its forces into definable, calculable, and administrable "images." Stein's parodies of definitions deliberately refuse to become images; they destructure representation, to figure being, as it were, against its own impetus of unfolding into administrable rationality. It is perhaps through this tension between "figures" and "images" that Stein's text attempts to break open the abstractness of relations in the social world and almost literally release the infinitesimal forces of singularity. It is in such figures that art may retain what, for lack of better terms, might be called a "radical" or "postaesthetic" social relevance.

It is against the backdrop of the critique of aesthetics outlined here that I would like to rethink this postaesthetic significance of art in terms of a release or a redisposition of forces. Linking what I have termed the social figure of art to the idea of a disposition of forces will allow me to show that at stake in art's figure is the question of freedom and the modern forms of its foreclosure. This link will require a long and careful explanation, an analysis that would have to be conducted between Nietzsche, Heidegger, Foucault, and Adorno. Let me briefly suggest its outline here. Elsewhere, I began to redescribe the relationship between force and art through an analysis of Heidegger's reading of force-enhancement (*Kraftsteigerung*) in Nietzsche in the context of Foucault's reflections on power.[20] Such an approach makes it possible to define the figure in art as a kind of *forcework*, which might be thought of in terms of producing an alternative disposition of forces, a different, poietic modality of being-in-the-world. I would suggest that, opening up the historicity of experience, the figure loosens and disrupts the social objectivization of forces into forms of power. Art's force-work consists in transforming the very dynamic of force and relations among forces and therefore in changing the valency of relations: from power relations to letting-go of grasping intelligence and possibly also of the forms of power. It is a social force-work in the sense that it undoes the disciplining of forces and the disposition of force into constellations of domination. I indicate in my reading of Foucault and Heidegger that forces at work in the figure—which are *not* all the forces or constellations of forces operating in art—are forces related in ways that do not produce power. And they do not do that in a very specific sense: the enhancement of force that Heidegger interprets out of Nietzsche is such a disposition of forces that allows what is Other to be more in being (*seiender*);[21] in other words, it enhances not itself but its relation to what is Other. "Enhancing" the alterity of what remains Other, this change in relationality has a distinctive ethical dimension. In fact, it resituates ethics with a view to the modality of relation to the Other and reveals the juncture between ethics and aesthetics.

This enhancement, as opposed to a measurable or calculable "technological" increase in forces, is a form of relation between forces that might avoid issuing into power. In this sense, it resists or declines power but not as a counter-power or in opposition to power; instead, it indicates a "powerless" enhancement of force. This happening, as a disposition of forces, refuses the dominant disposition of the modern world: calculability and exchange. If technology reveals in the manner of deworlding, then perhaps we could think about the force-work of art in terms of a reworlding—of opening up spaces of relations and references that remain foreclosed and "unreal," within being as technology. Technology deworlds being by constraining and organizing it into resource. Art's force-work undoes or counters "domination" on this specific level of deworlding, because it attempts to refigure the very way that forces work: forces in art might be poietic, which means that they unfold terms of multiply enhanced references and relations that fall outside of the formalizable and measurable forces, that is, forces that are intrinsically technological. In my account, art's figure does not produce new forces, revolutionary, or counter-forces to the powers at play in society. It may only change the valency of relations between forces and perhaps inflect the dynamic of their formation from technological to poietic. This inflection, though, has unmistakable political and ethical implications.

NOTES

1. "It is self-evident that nothing concerning art is self-evident anymore, not its inner life, not its relation to the world, not even its right to exist"; Theodor W. Adorno, *Aesthetic Theory*, trans. and ed. Robert Hullot-Kentor (Minneapolis: University of Min-

nesota Press, 1997), 1. Hereafter cited as *AT.* The German edition, *Äesthetische Theorie* (Frankfurt am Main: Suhrkemp, 1993), hereafter cited as *ATG.*

2. Krzysztof Ziarek, "After Aesthetics: Heidegger and Benjamin on Art and Experience," *Philosophy Today* 41: 1 (1997): 199–208.

3. "Two writers may represent (express) the same socio-historical moment, but one might be an artist and the other just an unctuous individual. If the treatment of the question amounts to nothing more than a description of what the writers represent or express socially—that is, a more or less reliable summary of the characteristics of a specific socio-historical moment—it means that the question of art has not even been broached. . . . This is not criticism and history of art, nor can it be presented as such." (Antonio Gramsci, Notebook 23, section 3). Quoted after Joseph Buttigieg, "Antonio Gramsci" entry in *Encyclopedia of Aesthetics*, vol. 2, ed. Michael Kelly (Oxford: Oxford University Press, 1998), 333.

4. Hermann Möerchen's *Adorno und Heidegger* discusses what he calls an "exemplary" failure of communication between the Heidegger and the Adorno schools of thinking and attempts to stage a very interesting dialogue between the two thinkers. In the process, Möerchen lists and remarks on Adorno's quotations from Heidegger and comments extensively on Heidegger's explicit and implicit presence in Adorno's work. Perhaps the most valuable part of the book is the section detailing the often unacknowledged converges between Heidegger and Adorno, especially in relation to technology, power, and language. *Adorno und Heidegger: Untersuchung einer philosophischen Kommunikationsverweigerung* (Stuttgart: Klett-Cotta, 1981).

5. Martin Heidegger, "The Origin of the Work of Art," *Basic Writings*, ed. D. Krell (New York: Harper & Row, 1977), 159–60. Hereafter cited as *BW.* For the entire discussion of the form-matter structure in relation to the thing-being of artworks, see pages 157–60.

6. Christopher Fynsk, *Heidegger, Thought and Historicity* (Ithaca, N.Y.: Cornell University Press, 1986), 146.

7. "Das Kunstwerk ist Prozess und Augenblick in eins" (*ATG*, 154).

8. Derrida's phrase is "l'événementialité de l'événement"; Jacques Derrida, *Spectres de Marx: L'État de la dette, le travail du deuil et la nouvelle Internationale* (Paris: Galilée, 1993), 56.

9. "Historicity means the constitution of being of the 'occurrence' of Da-sein as such"; Heidegger, *Being and Time*, trans. Joan Stambaugh (Albany: State University of New York Press, 1996), 17. See *Sein und Zeit* (Tübingen: Niemeyer, 1986), 20.

10. *The Lyotard Reader*, ed. Andrew Benjamin (Oxford: Basil Blackwell, 1989), 199. Hereafter cited as *LR.*

11. Gertrude Stein, *Tender Buttons* (Los Angeles: Sun and Moon, 1991), 11. Hereafter cited as *TB.*

12. "In Stein's text, a phrase is one time, an event, it happens. The anxiety that this will not start up again, that Being will come to a halt, distends the paragraphs"; Jean-François Lyotard, *The Differend: Phrases in Dispute*, trans. Georges Van Den Abbeele (Minneapolis: University of Minnesota Press, 1988), 68.

13. I do not mean here only the closeness of "The Origin of the Work of Art" to the period of the rectorate or Heidegger's continuing proximity to the language of National Socialism. Obviously, Heidegger's work after 1934, his investment in both early Greek thought and Hölderlin's writings, is never reducible to the Romanticism that "both in its caricatural forms (for mass consumption) or its more elaborate (but still degraded) ones, [structures] the official—though not always very homogeneous—ideology of the Reich." In Lacoue-Labarthe, *Heidegger, Art and Politics: The Fiction of the Political*, trans. C. Turner (Oxford: Blackwell, 1990), 57. Hereafter cited as *HAP*. Although in his readings of Hölderlin, Heidegger begins to critique National Socialist "thought," he does not make, as Lacoue-Labarthe points out, a clean break from it (*HAP*, 135–36). But Heidegger's reflections on art are limited and problematic on another count: his readings remain largely limited to a number of German poets and rarely, with the exception of Klee or Char, engage with radical modernist aesthetics. In this respect, part of my project is to mediate Heidegger's interesting insights through Adorno's explicit elaboration of the significance of modernist revolution in art and eventually reach even beyond the scope of Adorno's reflection in order to explore avant-garde art, which Adorno largely dismisses.

14. What Heidegger means by preserving (*Bewahren*) is not perpetuating or safeguarding the unchangeable "truth" of a work of art but instead a kind of "keeping true" to the work character of art, to its working as a displacement and transformation of the usual ties to the historical world around us (*BW*, 181).

15. Undoubtedly, there are echoes here of the need for a decision, so crucial to Heidegger's rectoral address of 1933, and a suspicion of what Lacoue-Labarthe calls "national-aestheticism" may be justified. Focusing on Heidegger's readings of Hölderlin and "The Origin of the Work of Art," Lacoue-Labarthe characterizes Heidegger's thought at that time as "national-aestheticism" which both contests the official Nazi ideology and yet remains in a dangerous proximity to the language of National Socialism: "In all of this discussion of art, there is fierce competition with the *Weltanschauung* (Hitler's favorite concept) of the party and of its master thinkers and Heidegger, however immeasurably different his language and his thought, is always in a dangerous— and clearly perceived—proximity to the language and 'thought' of National Socialism" (*HAP*, 57). Even so the figure, as Heidegger elaborates it, breaks out of these aestheticizing entanglements; not free from them, it already performs their critique.

16. An illuminating and a complex reading of some of those changes in relation to the question of politics is presented by Miguel de Beistegui in his book *Heidegger and the Political: Dystopias* (New York: Routledge, 1998).

17. Gertrude Stein, "Poetry and Grammar," *Lectures in America* (New York: Random House, 1935), 242.

18. "Not only handicraft manufacture, not only artistic and poetical bringing into appearance and concrete imagery, is a bringing-forth, *poiēsis*. *Physis*, also, the arising of something out of itself, is a bringing-forth, *poiēsis*" (*BW*, 293).

19. I am modifying here Adorno's notion of *Entkunstung* from *AT* (16). Adorno's *Entkunstung* refers to the pressure that modern culture exerts on art to relinquish "aesthetic pretense" and merge with consumerist society. In other words, *Entkunstung* signifies the disappearance of art's difference. The de-arting I suggest in

reference to Duchamp works differently: it is a critique and rejection of aesthetics, a parody of art that appears to reduce the artwork to the culture at large only to lay bare another nonaesthetic layer of art, which calls into question both aesthetics and culture. De-arting indicates, then, a reformulation of art's difference or Otherness beyond the scope of aesthetics.

20. I am referring here to my essay "Powers to Be: Art and Technology in Heidegger and Foucault," *Research in Phenomenology* vol. xxviii (1998): 162–94.

21. "[S]uch enhancement of force must be understood as the capacity to extend beyond oneself (*über-sich-hinaus-Vermögen*), as a relation to beings in which beings themselves are experienced as being more fully in being (*seiender*), richer, more perspicuous, more essential. Enhancement does not mean that an increase, an increment of force, "objectively" comes about. Enhancement is to be understood in terms of mood (*die Steigerung is stimmunghaft zu verstehen*)." Martin Heidegger, *Nietzsche*, vol. 1, *The Will to Power As Art*, trans. David Farrell Krell (San Francisco: Harper & Row, 1979), 100. In the German original, these remarks can be found in the first volume of *Nietzsche* (Pfullingen: Neske, 1961), 120.

CHAPTER 13

Politics, Aesthetics, and Ethics in Joseph Brodsky's Poem On the Death of Zhukov

David MacFadyen

I had to eat a lot of crap together with this [poem]. . . . For long-time émi-
grés . . . Zhukov is associated with the most horrible things; those people escaped from him. That's why there's no sympathy for Zhukov.

—Joseph Brodsky, *Brodskii o Tsvetaevoi*

The Russian poet and Nobel Laureate Joseph Brodsky was born in St. Petersburg (then Leningrad) on May 24, 1940. He remained a resident of the
Soviet Union until the summer of 1972, when he was exiled by the authori-
ties. Such an extreme expression of disapproval ended an increasingly antag-
onistic relationship between the poet and his city. Tried and convicted in
1964 on the farcical charge of "parasitism," Brodsky spent one and a half
years in internal exile. Once back in Leningrad, the growing (and officially
embarrassing) discrepancy between the poet's literary and social status led to
extradition proceedings.

His subsequent success in America as a bilingual poet, professor, and recipient of the Nobel Prize (1987) led to increased attention to Brodsky's
post–Soviet life and work. The transformation of a Russian poet into an international one has proved to be the most attractive aspect of his literary evolution. Little, however, has been written about Brodsky's relation to Russian
poetry, to what he read in Leningrad, and how it fashioned his further development. How and why did the Soviet teenager and bibliophile Joseph Brodsky
become a poet of sufficient—and sufficiently irksome—repute that the most
powerful nation in the world wished to expel him forever?

239

A clear answer emerges from the proud ethical stance he always adopted in the face of Soviet imperialism and its noisy grandiloquence. The most famous of all of Brodsky's pronouncements upon ethics and its importance for contemporary poetics is heard in his Nobel speech, in the axiomatic declaration that "aesthetics is the mother of ethics." Ethics, he maintains, is a linguistically managed notion, which leads the poet and state into direct conflict over the rights to the same medium:

> The philosophy of the state, its ethics—not to mention its aesthetics—are always "yesterday"; language, literature are always "today," and often—particularly in the case where a political system is orthodox—they may even constitute "tomorrow." One of literature's merits is precisely that it helps a person to make the time of his existence more specific, to distinguish himself from the crowd of his predecessors as well as his like numbers, to avoid tautology—that is, the fate otherwise known by the honorific term "victim of history." What makes art in general and literature in particular remarkable, what distinguishes them from life, is precisely that they abhor repetition.[1]

How does a poet make use of his youthful reading, so that he and his own language do not, like the state, perpetuate "yesterday" (i.e., simply repeat themselves and thus fail ethically to realize the world-building potential that is inherent in any text)? One of the most radical responses to this question comes in a poem that allows Brodsky to cast a glance back at three such "yesterday's": the Russian language of his Soviet childhood, the workings of Soviet oration per se, and the eighteenth-century tradition that informed such imperial discourse. The poet's retrospective investigation of his aesthetic medium and its recent ethical misuse is most odd, for the following reason.

In scanning Brodsky's aesthetic constancy, an attentive reader will note something of a blip on the screen in 1974. In that year the poet, who owes much to the casual wit of those such as Auden and Frost, suddenly swaps his ballpoint pen for a quill and composes an epicedium on the passing of Marshal Zhukov. Why on earth is a young poet of Jewish extraction lauding an inspired military tactician of WW II, a four-time Hero of the Soviet Union? Why is a poet, twice exiled by that regime, mourning the demise of its fantastically successful defendant? The very basis for such questions is that Brodsky's reputation in the West, especially since his investiture as American Poet Laureate in 1991, helps foster two fundamental paradigms: homesick Jewish dissident or—once in New York—whiz-kid manipulator of the Western literary canon. What has yet to be considered is Brodsky's very odd (and very clever) relationship to his aesthetic and ethical *antithesis*, the Soviet rhetoric that both inspired and was inspired *by* those such as Marshal Zhukov. A definition of this relationship will explain first of all *why* Brodsky wrote his monody.

The 1960s, the last full decade that Brodsky spent in the Soviet Union, is sometimes assessed as a time of new ideas, tolerance, and polyphony. In the recent words of two émigré Russian sociologists, however, only "slogans changed, not methods." The *illusion* of change and ideological challenge was embodied by the speech of Khrushchev himself: "In essence, his main tenet was flexibility and plurality, *but* within the prescribed framework of a formal worldview."[2]

Let us assume—as did Brodsky—that within this narrow worldview, the creation of any contrary, innovative work of linguistic art is fashioned upon a divine prototype. The utterance of a new word, a novel definition of reality, in fact, *creates* a new reality: an object is perceived, named, and evaluated anew. It becomes something *else*. If there are no novel words, then novelty evanesces, and without the cosmogonical potential of new speech, immobility and stasis render the world lifeless. The rigid "framework" of a Soviet worldview turns into concrete and starts inching its way across the fields of Central Germany.

Trouble is, though, that the prescribed rhetoric that corresponds to this dull, *ex*clusive architecture does not, in its turn, actually correspond to objective reality at all. As Soviet propagandistic language grows increasingly fantastic in its refusal to deal with a markedly less rosy reality, a parallel, extensive semiotic system is engendered. An awful discrepancy emerges between words and what they designate: the monologic intoning of state-sponsored speech constitutes a whole system of signifiers. Russian scholar Mikhail Epshtein has neatly likened this state of affairs to Potemkin villages, to the wooden facades placed along roads traveled by Catherine the Great in the eighteenth century to give the *appearance* of an ameliorated present.[3]

This linguistic facade, however, does not cancel the abundance of ignored, undesignated, and unevaluated objects behind itself. The world is empty of words and sounds. It needs to be filled with such objects or spoken anew. This need, it would appear, was in part why Ernest Hemingway enjoyed such great success in the Soviet Union at this time, especially his novel *For Whom the Bell Tolls*. During 1995, I conducted a series of interviews with Brodsky's contemporaries, both in St. Petersburg and Moscow. When I raised the issue of youthful literary inclinations, not only of Brodsky but of each interviewee, Hemingway's name was by far the most frequently mentioned. Hemingway's general significance is formulated in an overview of the Soviet Sixties by P. Vail' and A. Genis: "The main American in Soviet life was Ernest Hemingway. In his books, Soviet readers found ideals, the formulated worldview of an entire generation. . . . Hemingway did not exist for reading. More important were the perceptions of life, set out by the writer. Such forms could be imitated. One needed only add one's context" (*MSC*, 64–65). The consequences of this oft-imitated, simple, and bold style can be seen if one takes a broader view of the decade and considers forms of popular entertainment over and above literature. Cinema audiences of the 1960s, for example, "especially young ones . . . were entranced by acting styles, adventure, and music.

Moscow youths emulated the gestures and memorized lines of American macho actors such as James Cagney and Johnny Weismuller."[4]

For Whom the Bell Tolls concerns itself with similar, bold attempts to define an *incontrovertibly* "good" reality in wartime (i.e., when ethics are weakly defined). The need for a new, reliable, and therefore good word becomes an existential responsibility. To just accept the status quo and shut up is a great deal easier : "It was easier to live under a regime than to fight it. . . . But this irregular fighting was a thing of great responsibility . . . I think that we are born into a time of great difficulty."[5] During such times of semantic instability, utterances become morally significant events, for to name an object is to both change and fix—at least for awhile—the nature of a thing. As Hemingway's hero notes of an acquaintance: "He had said [this] and it was true."[6] Speaking and making become synonymous commitments.

While the battle for significances is going on, Hemingway's world remains full of unclaimed objects: "His world is abundant with things, behind which there stand no ideas. . . . This is a deliberate simplification, a severing from polysemy: There is what there is, and nothing more" (*MSC*, 66). Polysemy, perhaps, is unnervingly close to semantic emptiness, to the "non-sense" of war. The answer to this emptiness, odd though it may sound, is for "ignored" poets such as Brodsky to fill it up with an assured, unambiguous *monologue*, known in Russian as *pafos*. "Pathos" is understood here in the Bakhtinian sense as a proud, often versified monologue that impedes the intrusion of other voices or accents. The testing of such a monologue, of a (seemingly) irrefutable worldview is how Bakhtin defines the emergence of so-called "superfluous men" in Russian literature, such as the hero of Dostoyevsky's *Notes from the Underground*. Vail' and Genis note a similar phenomenon in Soviet society: the self-assured rhetoric of Hemingway bumps up both against the need to marry word to deed (the American existential dilemma) and the inability to do anything (the Soviet political morass). "The example of Hemingway created a strong, beautiful, upright man who did not know what to do. Once again there appeared in Russia 'superfluous men'" (*MSC*, 72–73).

Russian *pafos* differs from its English counterpart in that it means enthusiasm, passion, and a general leaning toward bombast. Pathetic discourse in Russian is often associated with the odic leanings of the eighteenth century, with the time of Potemkin villages and the poem on which Brodsky models his dirge for Marshal Zhukov.

Brodsky chooses Gavrila Derzhavin's forgotten poem "The Bullfinch" (*Snigir'*) as his model for a new, pathetic word to challenge the vacuous Soviet rhetoric. The poem laments the passing of Generalissimo Aleksandr Suvorov five months after the end of the eighteenth century. Suvorov was one of the greatest field commanders in the history of Russian warfare, and the drama of his death is captured in Derzhavin's poem. I offer the following translation:

Wherefore your music's martial demeanor,
Finch dear, that fife-like hastens to play?
Who will direct us 'gainst the Hyena?
Who is our chief? Our hero today?
Whither the strong, bold speed of Suvorov?
Buried, the northern thunders repose.

Who 'pon his nag will gallop now, ardent,
Prior to battle (nibbling a rusk)
Where, in all climes, his sword he will harden,
Sleep upon straw, keep vigil 'til dusk,
Such that scant Slavs would vanquish in chorus
Ramparts, doors bolted, enemy droves?

Whose austere nerve is constantly zealous;
Prays to the Lord, to end fate's ascent,
Ridicules envy, falls upon malice?
Scepters he shuns and freely depends,
Suffers for virtues known amongst equals:
Who lives for Czars, when strength is all gone?

Gone from this world are men of such luster:
Cease with your song of war, little bird!
Joyless today are tunes of such bluster:
Distant, dull wailing of lyres can be heard.
Heart of the lion, wings of the eagle:
Gone from amongst us—why battle on?

May 1800[7]

The first strophe consists of a chain of substantives, arranged in ascending order of grandeur: leader—folk hero—Suvorov himself. The final step of this ascent moves even beyond tangible reality, up to thunderclouds. The transformation of the Generalissimo into an elemental noise is immediately followed by the interruption of that thunder, because the physical being, upon whom the production of that noise is dependent, has fallen down and fallen silent. The strophe therefore scribes an arc of ascending grandeur, or *pafos*, which is bound to its origin or source in the human body. The ascent and stalling of this body, as it were, take place simultaneously in two realms: in both war and the "martial music" (*branna muzyka*) inspired by that war. Derzhavin is equating two processes: warring and the struggle to interpret or designate the world. If Suvorov has died and will no longer wage battle, then—as the poem puts it—"why battle on?" Suvorov was a stable support of the state, and pathetic discourse has vanished. Derzhavin, in discussing problems akin to Hemingway's, is asking the following question: If the reason for pathos has vanished, then what are we to *do or make*, if we have no idea what to *say*? The first and last questions of the poem turn out to be identical. Now let us consider Brodsky's response to the same question in *On the Death of Zhukov*, couched in the same, stately (even ponderous) meter:

> Columns of grandsons, stiff at attention;
> gun carriage, coffin, riderless horse.
> Wind brings no sound of their glorious Russian
> trumpets, their weeping trumpets of war.
> Splendid regalia deck out the corpse:
> thundering Zhukov rolls towards death's mansion.
>
> As a commander, making walls crumble,
> he held a sword less sharp than his foe's.
> Brilliant maneuvers across Volga flatlands
> set him with Hannibal. And his last days
> found him, like Pompey, fallen and humbled—
> like Belisarius banned and disgraced.
>
> How much dark blood, soldier's blood did he spill then
> on alien fields? Did he weep for his men?
> As he lay dying, did he recall them—
> swathed in civilian white sheets at the end?
> He gives no answer. What will he tell them,
> meeting in hell? "We were fighting to win."
>
> Zhukov's right arm, which once was enlisted
> in a just cause, will battle no more.
> Sleep! Russian history holds, as is fitting,
> space for the exploits of those who, though bold,
> marching triumphant through foreign cities,
> trembled in terror when they came home.
>
> Marshal! These words will be swallowed by Lethe,
> utterly lost, like your rough soldier's boots.
> Still, take this tribute, though it is little,
> to one who somehow—here I speak truth
> plain and aloud—has saved our embattled
> homeland. Drum, beat! And shriek out, bullfinch fife!

1974[8]

What is the significance of Brodsky's text, and why did he decide to use Derzhavin's *Bullfinch*? The twentieth-century situation is different in that whereas Suvorov died a faithful servant of both Czar and God, Zhukov was not so easily subsumed into the epic hierarchies upon which state-sponsored *pafos* is composed. Due to the great popularity he enjoyed after his martial triumphs over the Third Reich, Zhukov appeared to both Stalin and Khrushchev to have an unnervingly cultic personality. Whereas the pathos of Suvorov's achievements serves to keep him subservient to earthly and heavenly thrones, Zhukov—by *embodying* that pathos, by living it out—used it as a tool of *self-definition* and raised himself to eye level with the state. In terms of language, his death marks the silent end to that ascent and the end of a noisy competition between two worldviews. No longer will the Marshal subvert the stability of the Soviet monolog. In an age where polysemy was rarely suffered, Zhukov is silenced, objectified by the state and turned into an object. He is dumb and therefore becomes the object, rather than the walking, talking, lyrical subject of Soviet pathetic discourse.

In the summer of 1997, a short book was published in Russia that discusses the relationship between Brodsky and poetess Marina Tsvetaeva. The book commences with an interview Brodsky gave to émigré critic Solomon Volkov. Volkov laments the absence of good political poetry in Russia over the last few decades, especially when one considers the high quality of Tsvetaeva's work in a similar vein after the revolution. When talk turns to Brodsky's few overtly political texts, *On the Death of Zhukov* is immediately mentioned. Volkov explains in part his interest in the poem, because although much younger than Zhukov, he saw the marshal in retirement. The soldier's behavior during that encounter is a fine example of how state prestige can be turned to private ends, but *not* for the sake of fame. Although (driven) far from the structures of military power, Zhukov uses precisely their modes of expression to display his proud independence.

> *Volkov*: Once—it was probably at the end of the 1960s—in a concert hall near Riga . . . I noticed a man sitting near me. On his jacket were four gold stars, in other words he was a four-time Hero of the Soviet Union! The lights went out quickly and I wasn't able to make out his face. And, looking at the gray buzz-cut and fleshy nape of the stranger's neck, I was left guessing right up to the interval. Who could this possibly be, with what looked like an unheard-of number of "Heroes" on his chest. When in the interval Marshal Zhukov—it was him, of course—stood up, the entire hall was already scrutinizing him greedily. And I remember what surprised me: why did Zhukov, who had won such fame and respect in life, need to pin his medals on a civilian jacket and then attend a concert?
>
> *Brodsky*: Seems completely natural to me. It's a different mentality, after all, a military one. The issue here isn't a hunger for fame. Anyway, hadn't they chased him absolutely everywhere by that time? [Volkov agrees] And in general, as we know, Heroes of the Soviet Union get beer without queuing.[9]

I have been lucky enough to gain access to Brodsky's archives in St. Petersburg, and to my amazement I found many other versified attempts among his unpublished materials to redefine the intent of Soviet *pafos*. Brodsky, it appears from these comments to Volkov, wrote this one published stylization out of *sympathy* for Zhukov and is therefore not writing with true Soviet *pafos* but composing in a manner not unlike Zhukov, who stole, as it were, from hegemonic rhetoric in order to further his own subjective intent.

The first strophe of *The Bullfinch* manifests that intent. It finishes with a silent, supine corpse. The first stanza of Brodsky's poem finishes in a similar fashion (i.e., with the Marshal's surname and another corpse). This objectification of the deceased justifies Brodsky's references to three ancient warriors: Hannibal, Pompey, and Belisarius. Hannibal struggled all his life against the *Roman* empire, a conflict that resulted ultimately in his suicide. Pompey was one of the late Roman Republic's greatest supporters, though he too clashed with moribund, imperial immobility in the form of Caesar. Fleeing from Caesar, Pompey fell into the hands of some traitors and was reduced to the same inactive state as Suvorov and Zhukov. As for Belisarius, a Byzantine general, he suffered—again like Zhukov—the suspicion of his native peoples after some dazzling military victories, and he was accused of both political infidelity and subversion.

In unifying these three objects of deafening, state-sponsored monologs, I should note that Brodsky uses the adverb *glukho* to define in particular the last few days of Hannibal's life. This word in Russian has several meanings: deafness (i.e., the absence of sound), distance or isolation, and deathliness. All three soldiers, on the edge of either literal or metaphorical empires, jar—sooner or later—with the intolerance of imperial monologs. All three men are deprived of their clamorous, stormy existence by a ruling, dogmatic power that prefers silence to dissent. Zhukov, as one of these heroes, is turned into a lifeless body, the significance of which is determined and then used by the state.

The theme of objectified soldiers is inherent in the paronomasia of Brodsky's fourth stanza: "Zhukov's right arm which once was enlisted/in a just cause will battle no more." The pun here on what is right or just shows what connects these two poems over the span of two centuries. Before God—or the state, if we are speaking about the military figurehead of a godless system that aspires to similar omnipotence and omniscience—a speaking individual belittles himself in order to magnify the importance of that which he serves. The logical limit of this process is the transformation of a previously animate individual into an inanimate one (i.e., one devoid of free will or speech), who accepts everything unquestioningly and refuses nothing.

In Zhukov's objectified state, he contains "some-thing" right or just in himself. The pun upon a right idea and a right hand expresses the *potential* of any speaker to objectify himself *correctly*—before the divine, world-creating potential of a word. Zhukov used *pafos* to shape his world, and now, sadly, it has shaped him. The physically *right* deeds of Zhukov enter, therefore, into history books.

The rise and fall of Hannibal, Pompey, and Belisarius come to us now only in established formats—these soldiers become objects of an abbreviated, diminished
"de-scription" of the world. As such, the deeds of Zhukov are reduced to one
page. Brodsky, with his own pathetic word, his own "little" tribute, tries to turn
everything back to front or upside down. The poet sympathizes with the Marshal
and surrounds him—*re-elevates* him—with the very pathos that he once served.

The entire tricky problem of using politically loaded aesthetics to do
something *else* is touched upon in the aforementioned interview with Solomon
Volkov. The critic sees *On the Death of Zhukov* in the light of what it is imitat-
ing. Brodsky claims to have little sympathy for Zhukov, but his poem and
words below suggest otherwise.

> *Volkov*: It's what is called a "state" poem. Or, if you like, an "imperial" one.
>
> *Brodsky*: You know, in this case, I actually like the definition of it as a "state"
> poem. Generally it seems to me that, in its time, this poem should have been
> printed in *Pravda*.
>
> *Volkov*: But your poem really shows no sympathy for Zhukov. On the emo-
> tional level it's extremely restrained.
>
> *Brodsky*: Absolutely right. But for a reader who's insufficiently intelligent or
> completely unintelligent, those kind of things aren't especially interesting. He
> reacts to a red flag. Zhukov—and that's all there is to it. I've also heard all kinds
> of things out of Russia. All the way to the absolutely ridiculous: they said that
> with this poem I'm plonking myself at the authorities' feet. But, you know,
> many of us owe Zhukov our lives. It wouldn't hurt to remember that Zhukov,
> and no one else, saved Khrushchev from Beria . . . Zhukov was the last of the
> Russian Mohicans. The last "Red Indian Chief," as they say. (*BT*, 45–46)

Zhukov, the last Chief, is dead. The brave officer, the embodiment of Soviet rhetoric, has left. An immediate consequence of the marshal's demise is silence: "Wind brings no sound of their glorious Russian/trumpets." A new
noise is required—"Drum, beat! And shriek out, bullfinch fife!" This reference
and request to the finch leads us *back* to the *start* of Derzhavin's poem. Zhukov
is dead, and Brodsky has wound up, so to speak, his clockwork songbird.
Derzhavin, hearing the song that interrupts the silence, asks, "Wherefore your
music's martial demeanor/Finch dear, that fife-like hastens to play?" The poem
by Derzhavin begins all over again!

Derzhavin says: be quiet, because pathos has gone quiet. Brodsky answers:
speak up and fill the emptiness *caused* by a quieted pathos . . . in fact, create a
formally similar, but qualitatively different rhetoric! The vital dialogue between
these two funeral laments, 174 years apart, shows clearly the reason Brodsky resorted to an alien discourse. A sacrilegious use of the Word is altered in favor
of a "creative" one: Brodsky is acquiescing *not* to Soviet aesthetics but to the

formally similar mode of expression that Soviet *pafos* usurped. The whole process is neatly formulated in an essay of ten years hence, one that shows how the fantastic hyperbole of Soviet pathos can be used by "outsiders" to subversive ends, how the tendency of impersonal *pafos* to think in generalizations and to objectify can be transformed into a subjective triumph. This fantastic reversal, paradoxically, is done through an *apparent* aesthetic or ethical surrender to the source of negation—which in this case is Soviet bombast: "Evil can be made absurd through excess . . . through dwarfing its demands with the volume of your compliance, which devalues the harm. This sort of thing puts a victim into a very active position, into the position of a mental aggressor."[10]

NOTES

1. Joseph Brodsky, "Nobel Lecture," *Brodsky's Poetics and Aesthetics*, ed. L. Loseff and V. Polukhina (Houndmills: Macmillan, 1990).

2. P.Vail' and A. Genis, *Mir sovetskogo cheloveka* (Moscow: Novoe literaturnoe obozrenie, 1996), 223. Hereafter cited in the text as *MSC*.

3. M. Epshtein, *Vera i obraz: Religioznoe bessoznatel'noe v russkoi kul'ture 20-go veka* (Tenafly: E'rmitazh, 1994), 111.

4. R. Stites, *Russian Popular Culture* (Cambridge: Cambridge University Press, 1992), 125.

5. Ernest Hemingway, *For Whom the Bell Tolls* (New York: Charles Scribner's Sons, 1968), 367.

6. Hemingway, *For Whom the Bell Tolls*, 406.

7. G. Derzhavin, "Snigir'," *Stikhtvoreniia* (Moscow-Leningrad: Sovetskii pisatel', 1963), 292–93.

8. Joseph Brodsky, "On the Death of Zhukov," trans. George L. Kline, *A Part of Speech* (New York: FSG, 1980), 78.

9. Joseph Brodsky, *Brodskii o Tsvetaevoi* (Moscow: Nezavisimaia gazeta, 1997), 47. Hereafter cited in the text as *BT*.

10. Joseph Brodsky, *Less Than One*, trans. George L. Kline (New York: FSG), 389.

PART IV

Toward an Ethical Art Practice?

CHAPTER 14

Beauty and the Beast

Alex Colville

I suggest that when we think of "beauty" we think of something pleasurable—and possibly bad, self-indulgent; when we think of "beast" we think of an animal—large, strong, capable of, and inclined to, violence. We are not sure that "beauty," though attractive, is necessarily good, and we are not sure that the "beast," though powerful, can be beautiful, or that it may be good—power always having the capacity to be good or bad. I think we know that the two have an important, even an inseparable, relationship, but a complex and difficult one. A dictionary definition of "beauty" includes the phrase "especially, a woman widely regarded as beautiful." Beauty tends to be thought of as female, power as male.

Aesthetics is more abstract than beauty, but I am of course suggesting that we think of it in a similar way. I think of the writings of Walter Pater, which I read as a fine arts student: his idea of "burning with a pure, gem-like flame." Perhaps serious people should not be concerned with aesthetics; possibly it is a concern of late, end-of-cycle, cultural periods—the late nineteenth century or the end of the second millennium. Maybe it is a field for lightweights.

Ethics is more abstract than beast, but it does have a heavyweight connotation. Blackstone says, "Jurisprudence is the principle and most perfect branch of ethics." I think of the image of Justice: a blindfolded woman holding a scale (measuring is serious) in one hand and a sword (serious and lethal) in the other. It is interesting that this figure is a woman. Is the implication that Justice, and so perhaps Ethics, is also beautiful? The iconography of this figure should be looked into, possibly originating in Roman times.

The idea of measuring, as in the scale of Justice, is of course quantitative, intellectual, and Apollonian (as distinct from Dionysian) and expresses a concept of the world, of the human condition as being real (George Steiner's book is called *Real Presences*), comprehensible (as distinct from absurd), and capable

Figure 14.1   Alex Colville, *Child and Dog*, 1952. Reproduced by permission of the artist.

to some degree of being controlled. Much has been said of the relation of form to content in the arts; McLuhan's dictum, "The medium is the message," thought to be so electrifying in the 1960s, states what anyone working in the arts cannot help knowing, that the content is inextricably woven into the form of the work. I suggest that the presence of formal mathematical elements in a work of art, whether in an Egyptian relief, a medieval chant, a Russian film of the 1920s, or a novel by Milan Kundera, is an indication that the artist is always in one sense an artisan, a fabricator, a former of content. Can we speculate that the content is always truth? It may be that truth, ethos, has to be released, revealed, by form. In "When the Cathedrals Were White," the architect Le Corbusier describes how a master mason of the thirteenth century, using only a square, a compass, and a plumb bob, would pass on geometric formulae to his apprentices only after the exchange of secret signs, which indicated that the apprentices were members of an elect.

I have thought for a long time that aesthetics and ethics cannot be separated, and of course I am not alone in this conviction—I think of Keats' affecting lines on beauty and truth. Heidegger says, "Beauty is one way in which truth occurs as unconcealedness"; it seems to me that he means that truth is essentially abstract. There is a practical sense of "telling the truth" about a sequence of events that has taken place, as in a court of law, but Heidegger is talking about a revelatory truth that is conceived, dug up as a treasure, perhaps laboriously fabricated, and so revealed—that is, unconcealed. Hemingway, an important sensibility in this century, spoke of "moments of truth"; I think we have experienced these illuminations, but it is the job of the artist to make them manifest, so that the moment exists as a protracted sequence in time, and the fragment becomes an extended spatial arrangement.

It has been said that the mark of a first-class mind is the ability to hold two equal and opposite ideas in a kind of equilibrium. Jane Jacobs, perhaps the most distinguished living thinker on urban life and urban planning, has written *Systems of Survival*, which proposes a duality that I think may be germane to the one we are discussing. Her book is projected as a long discussion of our society by a disparate group of serious people. To grossly simplify her thesis, she conceives of a good society as consisting essentially of two types, each of which fundamentally differs from the other. She calls these two types "guardians" and "traders." Guardians respect discipline, order, and confidentiality; traders are open, exchange information freely, move casually through different strata of society, and so on. Society benefits from their dual presences, but interestingly, society benefits most when each stays within its appropriate realm of activity. Almost exactly a year ago I was discussing this book with the late Jerry Godsoe, a brilliant and sagacious lawyer—he was advising me on a tax matter, but our conversation strayed into philosophy. He said to me, "So—are you a guardian or a trader?" I will not supply the answer to this question, but it may be worth thinking about.

A meditation on aesthetics and ethics can be one on culture and politics. Earlier in this century, the "advanced" arts were usually associated with "advanced" politics; the arts in Russia before 1930, the admirable communist mural paintings in Mexico, a school such as the Bauhaus in Germany, in which all the visual arts were conceived of as being a part of building, imbued with liberal political aspirations. This phase was, of course, followed by the official and banal art of Stalinist Russia, Nazi Germany, and Fascist Italy and Spain, and still later, Communist China. In general, the arts now seem apolitical or anarchic, but current issues such as the support of cultural organizations by tobacco companies, censoring pornographic material, and government-sponsored gambling indicate that politics cannot stay out of culture.

Two years ago, I was walking through the new wing of the National Gallery in London when I came upon a series of paintings I had not known before—the artist unknown to me. This was a work from the Middle Ages, when the connection between the good and the beautiful was so evident. The subject was the life of St. Francis of Assisi, told in a series of panels depicting episodes of his life. One of the last was called "The Wolf of Gubbio." This is an actual village— I looked it up. The town of Gubbio had been harassed by a grey wolf; when St. Francis came to the town, he was told of this problem. He had a solution: he told them to simply feed the wolf. In the painting, he and the wolf of Gubbio are shaking hands, or shaking hand and paw.

CHAPTER 15

The Banal Profound and the Profoundly Banal: Andy Warhol

Elizabeth Edwards

Andy made nothing happen.

> —Fran Lee Woods, from the film *Superstar:*
> *The Life and Times of Andy Warhol*

There is nothing to say about Warhol, and Warhol has said just this.

> —Jean Baudrillard, *The Perfect Crime*

Does the work of art really have any autonomy at all? Is it not rather the case that every single gesture of so-called art in the direction of autonomy from the social good has called forth the most massive recuperation projects, fueled by an anxiety that continues to proclaim that the real problem is the reverse, to find a way in which art can and will speak ethically? A clear imperative is at work here, one that works doubly, it seems, to both cede and at the same time protest the "autonomy" of the work of art. Autonomy is claimed as established at the same moment as theories of the aesthetic arise, in the eighteenth century—to the extent that theorists can in practice conflate the two terms, so that "aesthetic" *means* the autonomy of the work of art. Art, in the disassociated sensibility of modernity (and now postmodernity)[1] goes its own way; we wish it would not; if only it can be shown that art is involved in the good, that there is an ethical ground that can rehabilitate this errant art! The problem can probably only continue to be recycled, and not solved, as it is recycled throughout the modern era, and pop art is only one of the art movements of the twentieth century that resists the assimilation to ethics. Given the recent "turn to ethics" in contemporary theory, I question whether "the autonomy of art" was ever really possible, and if it is possible, what might be gained from such an autonomy. Here I look at the work of Andy Warhol, as particularly complicating any question of ethics and aesthetics, for the enigma of Warhol's product is the uneasy sense that it may affirm what it apparently also criticizes, those banal objects of mass consumer culture that surround us, dull our senses, moronize us. Moreover, his approach to his subjects works largely by dismantling the "high art" categories of classical aesthetics, simply by the intrusion of those soporific banal objects. In short, shall we be free from ethicizing and aesthetics, only to be in thrall to the mass anaesthetic of our times?

It is to stage a confrontation with certain current ethicizing theories of art—theories that I have sometimes found persuasive and that are central to the concerns of this book—that I have fixed on the figure of Warhol, who seems to have all his life aspired to banality in thought, word, and deed. In his writing and pronouncements, vacuous; in paintings and writings preoccupied with surface; in his choice of subjects interested in the everyday, the commonly seen, the mass-produced; and in his methods given to a repetition, which in itself stales and bewilders the eye, with a kind of pleasantly numbing effect. Moreover, he is given to rendering what is not banal *as* banal, of depoliticizing his subjects—witness the charming *Mao* series (1972–1973) or the *Vote McGovern* (1972) poster of Nixon. My engagement here with theorists of art and ethics is first with the configuration of the ethical as critique, a position most succinctly and cogently expressed in the work of Benjamin Buchloh in his essays on Warhol, and secondly with the alluring ethics of the sublime, as developed by J.-F. Lyotard. Underlying my account is what I can only describe as an allegiance to the Warhol effect, to a certain amoral pleasure, or pleasure in amorality, which strikes me as lighthearted. Much of his work seems derived from the spheres in which lightness prevails, the ephemeral rather than the permanent, the joke, the lighthearted, the spoof, the pleasantly vacuous. For pop is, as its name suggests, a "light" or possibly "lite" incarnation of art. I am then on the terrain most interesting to Milan Kundera, interesting because it raises the question of whether such light phenomena evade or escape from the ethical demand; at least they certainly show the ethical demand as rather dismal and, in its taste for the profound—indeed its insistence on profundity in its objects—raising the suspicion of a kind of aggressive, gloating pleasure in its own agonisms. The confrontation with Warhol is not used to confound the general theory with the anomalous particular, or theory with practice, but in the hope of revealing the stakes in certain theories, and of opposing the lightness of being I find in Warhol to the weight, the *gravitas*, of the ethical claim.

Warhol is remarkable for his lifelong refusal of what Levinas calls "the summons to responsibility."[2] His "signature" was literally a rubber stamp; or works were signed by his mother; and Gerald Malanga painted "so many" of them. The refusal to respond is a feature of his interviews—he is not answerable for his art, though he wrote entire books on the subject. His own stance is a kind of affectless ambivalence: "A person can cry or laugh. Always when you're crying you could be laughing, you have the choice. . . . You decide what you want to do and how you want to spend your time. Remember, though, that I think I'm missing some chemicals, so it is easier for me than for a person who has a lot of responsibility chemicals."[3] In *POPism*, Warhol (or possibly Pat Hackett, the ghostwriter) recounts his lack of affect on hearing of the Kennedy assassination: "I was alone painting in my studio. I don't think I missed a stroke. . . . It didn't bother me that he was dead. What bothered me was the way the television and radio were programming everyone to feel bad."[4] This is, at the well-established level of the artist as work-of-art found in Warhol, the corollary of the famous "emptiness" of his paintings.

Warhol's success as a cult figure is largely because of his fortitude in resisting the perpetual temptations or incitements to explain himself, critique himself. He is a kind of hero of the banal; he never lapses. And his success as a cult figure is indubitably one of his "works of art," in that the presence of the real person behind the art is part of what is being exploded. He seems to have tried not to be a person at all; to Baudrillard, his success lies in being a machine.[5] An amusing and edifying exchange among the participants at a DIA Art Foundation Symposium, whose members included Benjamin Buchloh, Rainer Crone, and Nan Rosenthal, inter alia, best shows the frustrations of attempting to co-opt Warhol for an ethical art and as an ethical person, to secure him as the intentional agent behind his own art. The debate concerns such political idiocies as putting Imelda Marcos on the cover of *Interview* magazine, as contrasted to, for example, the "biographical detail" that Andy "went every Easter and Christmas to give soup to people in the South Bronx"(*WAW*).[6] The desperation of basing the ethical claim for the artist on his giving alms to the poor is risible—certainly to Buchloh. Even more fascinating is Nan Rosenthal's intervention on Warhol's supposed affirmative stance: "Do you imagine that Warhol was positive about or admired all the traffic going through the Factory in the sixties? Second question, do you think he really enjoyed going to all those dinner parties every single night?" Here we rise to the truly *hilarious*, in the spectacle of Andy's iron duty to the shallow, the trivial, to vapid herd socialization.

In the attempt to establish an ethical artist-agent beyond charitable donations, we find a particularly nauseating example in the words of Simon Watney:

> We may revisit the question of how a "life" relates to a body of "work." Warhol lived through, and mapped out, relations of power rooted in every kind of institutionalized fantasy. His work and life are intimately tied up with the great themes of violence, desire, and death. Above all, he established a poetics of the provisional, an ultimately tragic recognition that there are no nec-

essary connections between the different areas of ourselves as individuals or as members of social groups. (*WE*, 121–22)

The tired rhetoric of heroics here seems totally out of synch with the *shallowness* of the Warhol effect, its own banality, its refusal of profundity and depth. If he is intimately tied to these great themes, then he has totally failed to do them justice. His work is a failure of adequacy to their being—an interesting failure. This may even be the point of his work.

In choosing the term *banality*, I choose a phenomenon central to the subject matter of pop art and to its relation to the mass-produced products of a consumer society that presents a scandal for aesthetics and, in its Warhol manifestation in any case, for ethics. I associate banality most evidently with the mechanically reproduced, with the advertising image that infiltrates every home and every psyche via the mass media, with the collective trashy fantasies about products and celebrities, with all of those phenomena held to dull the senses and intellects of modern people, by dint of their sheer ubiquity, endless repetitions, and sourcelessness—in short, with Warhol's subjects. Although the source of words related to the modality of banality, such as cliché and stereotype, comes from the domain of mechanical reproduction, as might be expected (both come from the stereotyping process of replication, the *cliché* being the plate used in the process), banality does not. It is a much older word, from the medieval French for "of or belonging to compulsory feudal service," part of the legal sphere of custom, and rights established by custom, which, through an intermediate sense of "common to all," arrives in current usage as what is trite, trivial, stale.[7] Thus the banal can be seen profitably as the compulsory-customary, for it is the element of compulsion that disgusts us about the banal, the sheer inescapability of the images and products in which our lives are steeped—the Pepsi generation and the Kodak moment as compulsory cultural knowledge. Further, the term has affinities with *habitus* in some of the senses advanced by Bourdieu, as those conditions of modern life that are unavailable to consciousness because of their sheer ubiquity. I am taking as my definition an offhand remark of Roland Barthes', in which he refers to "this difficulty in existing which we call banality"[8]; this difficulty in existing has a peculiar and distinctive character, and a distinctively modern character. What are these things that are ontologically stalled, that have a kind of ontological paleness, a ghostliness? It is that which is not seen though in full view, or perhaps more precisely, that which does not have to be looked at, though in full view, that which may be overlooked on the grounds that custom has staled it, that it has already been seen. Thus Warhol's subject is not quite that of Duchamp's ready-mades, but of the ready-seen, *the not very there* of ubiquitous mechanical reproduction. He does not paint Marilyn Monroe, but projects on a screen the simulacrum Marilyn; the so-called return to representation does not represent a person, but a screen phantom, and does it by producing yet another screen phantom, a replication of an image already stale. One of the peculiarities is that such staleness *really* makes it impossible to take in the truly banal; in other words, this is not simply an evasion on the part of consciousness, not a failure of attention (this is not your fault), but a constitutive part of banality. The failure in the banal is not that of badness. I therefore take this term and bypass the interesting light of the notion of "camp," to which Warhol's work does not seem to me to conform particularly well (neither the "it's so bad it's good logic," nor the complete, over-the-top seriousness of certain art forms is his domain). But it is also to be noted that the charge of banality is an aesthetic judgment— the force of the charge appears when it is leveled against art, when what is supposed to produce the fresh or refreshed, the unique, original and hard won *fails* and collapses back into the commonplace. Deviating from its etymology, it has become a term that is primarily aesthetic, so much so that when Arendt uses it in the subtitle of *Eichmann in Jerusalem: A Report on the Banality of Evil* (and does so moreover in Warhol's heyday, 1963), part of the shocked reaction can only have been to an appropriation of an aesthetic term for an ethical dimension. Eichmann's banality is his failure to be adequate to the phenomenon of evil or to the burden of ethics.

Banality in pop art is often noted, though most frequently proposed as a *mistake* in reception; people, it is suggested, mistake the apparent banality of Warhol's subjects for real banality—they have failed to see the criticism of banality—the works have been misread as endorsing what they expose. Thus Buchloh: "What has been misread as provocative banality is, in fact, the concrete realization of the paintings' reified existence, which denies the traditional expectation of an aesthetic object's legibility."[9] But the question is part of a larger one, for Warhol does nothing to help us overcome the suspicion that he is enmeshed in the "real" banal of the ready-seen object, that his banality is not even provocative. If anything, his provocation consists in affirming the popular taste for Tab, his own fondness for Campbell's soup, the glamour industry, and the "business art business." The provocation seems to be in a reversal: taking soup seriously, taking politics frivolously. In the *Mao* series, a number of portraits capture the same version of the Chairman's chubby, cheerful face, in an interesting intersection with various planes of color, daubed with paint, which were often shown mounted on *Mao Wallpaper*. This is a Mao who is only an image, an image released from the righteousness of political correct-thinking and from his role as author of the cultural revolution's atrocities—empty, evacuated, "trivialized." Warhol's tactic of evacuation is sometimes contested for, like irony, how can it be proved? So Trevor Fairbrother comments on the inclusion of *Skulls* in the book *Exposures*: "Why did he raise the spectre of death in this buyer's guide to hedonism? And why did he take time to paint this morbid subject, the antithesis of his society portraits?" (*WAW*, 93–94). This may come as a surprise to those who see his society portraits—features dissolved in bland, schematic, air-brushed blanks—*as* death's heads. Nor is death necessarily a "morbid subject" (except in a technical sense), as Warhol himself remarks (*PAW*, 110). Rather, these skulls seem as empty as his other images, skulls that are "just skulls" and not necessarily caught by the laws of signification to "stand for" death. But they are spectral, if only because of their failure to be what they are supposed to be.

But if the paintings are empty, it is an unwearying kind of emptiness, and even an emptiness that has increased as the original context of his work fades. There is a little article by Dave Hickey in the art journal *Parkett* that describes in all of its cleverness the ways in which Warhol's art is a critique of what preceded it, which was not so much abstract expressionism as the overinflated rhetoric of abstract expressionism. So in pop's strange literalism or factualism, Hickey suggests that "Rothko and Newman's quasi-religious musings about the possibilities for . . . communication and redemption in the artist's struggle" become Warhol paintings of postage stamps (communication) and S&H green stamps (redemption), Jackson Pollock's "shamanistic dance" around his canvases become Andy's "dumb Dance Diagrams," and most importantly the "connoisseurship of pain," where the artist's authenticity is guaranteed by pain, a tenet endemic to modernism, is rendered as blatant scenes of abjection, literal representations of pain: the suicide in front of Bellevue, the car crashes, race riots.[10] While this historical understanding is deeply fascinating—it catches the refreshing and debunking, puncturing pop of pop—as Hickey himself remarks, it is a content that has leached away, occasional jokes having a short half-life, "leaving Andy's pictures pleasantly meaningless" (*GEW*, 160). But can his pictures be allowed to be pleasantly meaningless?

Hickey would share Benjamin Buchloh's characterization of Warhol's work as "desublimation"; it punctures the pretensions of the heroic age of abstract expressionism, it deflates the expectation for "aesthetic legibility," but does it thereby satirize the tastes of its own consumers? Buchloh's perception of Warhol is acute, and his problem is large. To his credit, he eschews the soup-kitchen Andy along with any straightforward or simple claims about the nature of social critique in his work, and indeed in pop art, for the later works and apolitical Factory pronouncements, the editorial policy of *Interview* magazine, and the Mercedes Benz ad/art of 1986 must be held to contradict early reception of Warhol as a critic of the banal mass image of advertising. Moreover, Buchloh does justice to his cleverness and "subversive humor" (*R*, 54). For one whose thinking is heavily inflected by Frankfurt School aesthetics, the problem is what to do with a kind of art that seems to have collapsed even the most minimal speculative distance between what it is and its recuperation and absorption by the mass consumer culture on which it might seem to comment. This is what Warhol calls "the Business Art Business" that succeeds art (*PAW*, 92). What do to, when the work of art no longer has even the fifteen minutes of aesthetic critical action that Adorno claimed for it, but is instantly commodity fetish as well as art fetish?[11] The process is that of the temporal collapse of dialectics, wherein new and potentially oppositional structures do not proceed from emergent revolutionary status to power-discourse attitudinizing to hollow mimicry, but are all of these things at once, instantly. When the consumers of art become unshockable, the clever artist incorporates his own consumption in the works and in his life. And certainly even at the beginning of pop, the task of social critique had become a cliché in its own right, part of the tiresome expectation of what art should do. What Buchloh is acknowledging in Warhol is a form of cynicism, the "enlightened false consciousness" so eloquently described by Peter Sloterdijk as a kind of knowingness about ideology,[12] an ineffective knowingness that is the same thing as cynical complicity. Buchloh writes of a possibility in Warhol's early work that he thinks might have evaded cynicism: "The work's emphasis on artistic deskilling, its lack of criteria of authenticity, its rejection of originality and uniqueness—all these desubliminatory aspects were perceived as oppositional acts which could subvert the traditional division of high culture from mass culture" (*WAW*, 56). On the other hand, such a salubrious task is open to the accusation "of complying with the general agenda of desublimation at work in the culture industry at large with which [Warhol's] activities seemed to merge in an increasingly perfect fusion" (*WAW*, 59). What lies behind this contradiction is a kind of confusion between two kinds of critical function, which are in fact inseparable, but which I separate for clarity. Modern art has a function of social critique—to scandalize the sensibility of the straight world in its complacent consumption; but it also has a function of critique in relation to the history of art, to its immediate predecessors. The problem so brilliantly articulated by Buchloh is that a desublimating attitude toward "high art" is just exactly the attitude of the anaesthetizing culture industry, and not only toward art but toward most varieties of human experience. In spite of the puncturing wit of Warhol's work in relation to the history of art, its complicity with structures of consumption ultimately disqualifies it, in Buchloh's view, from having an ethical perspective. He writes:

> Warhol has unified within his constructs both the entrepreneurial worldview of the late twentieth century and phlegmatic vision of the victims of that world-view, that of consumers. The ruthless diffidence and strategically calculated air of detachment of the first, allowed to continue without ever being challenged in terms of its responsibility, combines with that of its opposites, the consumers, who can celebrate in Warhol's work their proper status of having been erased as subjects. Regulated as they are by the eternally repetitive gestures of alienated production and consumption, they are barred—as are Warhol's paintings—from access to a dimension of critical resistance. (*R*, 57)

Since this is in some sense a "true" account of the predicament of postmodernity, Warhol has, in Buchloh's view, at least the merit of having displayed that truth, but has ultimately failed ethically—missed an opportunity to resist it. His account of Warhol, insofar as he thinks Warhol *has* contributed to ethical critique, relies on some saving separations—the early work from the late, and the artist from his work—which have the side effect of making Warhol's "critique" unconscious and Andy himself a naif and a decadent at one go.

If Warhol's business art redoubling is enough to render claims of critical aims on his behalf suspect, then perhaps we might find an ethics on another front, in his avant-gardism. Here I invoke the work of Lyotard who, while he does not speak directly about Warhol, has advanced the case for the task of the avant-garde in a number of interesting and persuasive essays. Central to his theory of avant-gardism is his reworking of the notion of the sublime, a reworking that makes the Kantian and Burkean sublime more closely allied with works of art than with forces of nature; the stake in Lyotard's reworking of sublimity is as that which saves the postmodern (which he himself is instrumental in delineating as an era and a sensibility) from certain shallow (or banal) forms of itself, that is, from mere "innovation" or from empty eclecticism. To the extent that Lyotard's theory discusses the most difficult and inaccessible works of modern art, works existing in glacial isolation from the mass culture that surround them, and because of the apparent aestheticism of such works, it is not immediately obvious that such a task pertains to the ethics of the political sphere. And yet it does, not directly as an ethics of responsibility to the other but as what I will call a phenomenal ethics, or an ethics of the phenomenal.

For Lyotard, Burke's account of the sublime is more productive than Kant's for modern art, because Burke has isolated, within the sublime, a fear of privation. Burke's "major stake" is "to show that the sublime is kindled by the threat of nothing further happening."[13] Lyotard establishes the characteristic moment in Barnett Newman's art as that of the event, the "it happens" of a monumental temporality, of a "now" that is not merely a moment squeezed in between past and future, an event in the sense Heidegger provides for *Ereignis*, which is in the end more the possibility or the promise of the event than the presence of one. He further formulates this event as a question—the sublime question—which stands poised before the event, an "is it happening?" The question marks a tremulous equivocation in "the way in which *it happens* is withheld and announced" (*SA*, 198). It is on the threshold of an answer to this question that avant-garde art is poised. The "task" (*SA*, 210) of the avant-garde is not mere innovation in the unfolding of the history of art (Lyotard is very severe on mere innovation), nor to bring the reassuring evidence of something still happening fully to presence in order to assuage the fear of privation, but to witness to the beyond of the presentable. Ultimately it has the responsibility for "undoing the presumption of the mind with respect to time" (*SA*, 211). These claims work extraordinarily well for the minimalist works of a Barnett Newman (whose theological disposition is well established) as they would for the wildly, almost perfectly Kantian sublime of Walter de Maria's *Lightening Field*. I call this task of witness to the possibility of the unpresentable a phenomenal ethics in that it bears witness to the continued possibility of phenomena, or at least to a condition of liminality wherein the unpresentable phenomenon *pends*, is imminent, contiguous to the world of the already present. Imminence, the about-to-happen, rather than the immanence of real presence, characterizes the sublime. The works of the avant-gardes bear witness to the possibility of an unconcealment, of a moment on the fringe of the coming to presence of things that are not *already* present, and therefore relieve us from the kind of privation that is lurking in the term *banality*—the fear that all we will have is more of the same, recycled, a staled and wearied world attempting to delude itself with a constant parade of trashy "innovations" that cloak the radical poverty of mass consumer capitalist culture with a spurious plenitude, by producing filler for the cracks where the fear leaks in. The sublime offers a mode of reception rather than consumption, of witness rather than production. Since Kant, Lyotard writes, aesthetics has focused on the addressee rather than the sender; in his own adumbration of the sublime avant-garde, because there is neither a sublime style nor content, the artist herself has come to occupy the position of addressee, and the sender is that beyond of the unpresentable, which the artist receives in the form of a question. Lyotard's phenomenal ethics, well beyond the question of soup cans or soup kitchens, seems also to assume the singularity of the work of art, a singular moment of absolute now, as opposed to the transitory now of the continuum where anguish is papered over by the continual unspooling of images, by the sheer volume of informational white noise.

The phenomenal ethic is also political. In *The Postmodern Condition*, Lyotard, addressing the legitimation crisis of the modern state, advances a theory of the inevitable fragmentation of society into separate language games, in the wake of the failure of the unifying and universalizing metanarratives of the subject, of history, of emancipation. Performativity will be the criterion of success within language games; innovation, not consensus, is the goal, and innovation will proceed by "paralogy," the ability to invent aberrant yet valid moves in the game. His theory of art is a necessary complement to his political theory. It is, in brief, what saves the postmodern world from the vacuity of phony innovation and of eclecticism, which is "the degree zero of contemporary general culture: one listens to reggae, watches a western, eats McDonald's food for lunch and local cuisine for dinner, wears Paris perfume in Tokyo."[14] This quotation (which could almost pass for a page from Warhol's diaries) comes from the essay "Answering the Question: What is Postmodernism?", which is quite properly appended to the current American edition of *The Postmodern Condition*—properly, just because it includes a restatement of the necessary theory of avant-gardism, which saves postmodernism from the danger of empty eclecticism. The avant-garde, and hence the sublime, solves the central dilemma of Lyotard's political theory, in that it shows how to preserve difference and the new, as opposed to the endless proliferation and variation of the same (which is what we are left with by total-system theorists such as Luhman, whose work Lyotard is engaged with here). "Let us be witnesses to the unpresentable; let us activate the differences and save the honour of the name" (*PC*, 82). Lyotard's political theory of social delegitimation and the succession of innovative language games in the place of the old metanarratives is then completed and guaranteed by the "task" (read "duty"? "responsibility"?) of the avant-garde.

Well—there is a whiff of sanctity about the sublime; as Jean-Luc Nancy remarks, "The word 'sublime' always risks burdening art either with pathos or morality."[15] And perhaps so does "avant-garde." "Sublime"—oh, gee. Wow. Very well, the pragmatist might claim, Warhol is obviously not an artist of the sublime, in spite of what look like sterling avant-garde credentials, certainly if we consider the 1960s "scene" at the Factory, and in spite of an apparent congruence found in my epigram, "Andy made nothing happen," which seems to speak of both the nothing and the event—the happening. What is this nothing, if it is not, and I think it is not, the anxiety about privation that is activated only in order to be triumphed over by minimalist art? In Warhol's easy ability to paper over, we are beyond the fear of the privation to the nothing itself—which turns out to be not the worst thing that could (not) happen. But if Warhol's nothing is not sublime, and the sublime performs an ethical function, is his work then unethical? If he is not undoing the presumption of the mind with respect to time, is he doing it back up? Plainly Warhol's work is opposed to singularity; in thrall to repetition, and committed to exactly that papering over of the abyss, in the very literal form of his wallpapers; his subjects are not only ready-seens, but has-beens. I have said that Lyotard's account works very well for some artists, sublime artists,[16] particularly the 1950s' minimalists and abstract expressionists whose work forms the base text of Lyotard's theory, that is, those very artists whom Buchloh saw as the targets of Warhol's desublimation; Lyotard's commitment to this period deserves comment. Where he addresses an artist such as Duchamp whose question is not the sublime question but the question "What is art?", he rejects Duchamp's own formulation of his work as "ironism" in favor of a "negative aesthetics" that formulates the essence of such art as "the gesture"—that which marks the phenomenon of the emergence of art.[17] In Lyotard's theory, art approaches the sacrament, in which the beyond touches the phenomenal world. It is no longer the "real presence" that secures the authentic from the fake, but "the unpresentable," of which we stand on the threshold, and which saves us from those ersatz presences which clog the airways and the senses of modernity and which Warhol paints. Warhol's art is not sacramental; for his view on the real presence, we might take his *60 Last*

Suppers as a droll commentary on the "temporal ecstasies" of that Now, where the reproduction of the body and blood of Christ over and over in the monumental Now is registered as crappy copies of Leonardo's singular work of art.

If Warhol is not an artist of the sublime, and the sublime supports ethics, then perhaps he escapes from the demand of both. Ought an artist be sublime, do we here feel the same stirrings of the imperative that underlay Buchloh's account, which is, after all, the grammatical mood of ethics? Lyotard is not alone in assigning such load-bearing capacity to the limit and its beyond for the support of ethics. It is the key notion, for example, in Drucilla Cornell's *The Philosophy of the Limit*, and a position that she more recently attributes to Derrida: "Derrida's promise to the real and to the ethical is always a promise to what remains beyond to any of our current systems of symbolization."[18] Now the ability to keep promises is, as Nietzsche would have it, the basis of responsibility, but perhaps only for those with a lot of responsibility chemicals. Do those with a chemical imbalance escape ethics?

Both Buchloh and Lyotard take the trashiness of mass culture as their concern, as what needs to be corrected for. Buchloh situates his "critical resistance" in the progress of history; Lyotard his "sublime in the now" outside progressive temporality. In this, he is effacing something, for avant-gardes are produced and defined by nothing but their historical moment, by their place in the history of art, and pop certainly had such a moment. The history of art would dictate that as the claims for late abstract expressionism and minimalism became more bloated, they would need to be punctured. Thus a new "task," desublimation, will necessarily follow. Succeeding those that have sublimated what is base into gold, art will return to the base—to the urinal, for example. Thus Warhol can be seen to puncture, to pop, the pretension of his immediate forebears. That there is something if not ethical, then at least *healthy* about this particular task, the satirist's task, in its refusal of pomposity, is a position of some complexity and interest, adding as it does a form of self-reflexivity.

The task of desublimation can be perceived within the history of art as part of the self-reflective practice of health. It is an open question, whether debunking is itself an ethical task, the kind of task Sloterdijk has designated as *kynical* as opposed to exactly the kind of affirmative cynicism in Warhol's art—which is exactly what raises the question about Warhol's art: is it cynical or *kynical*? How are we to tell the difference? Part of the refreshing aspect of Warhol's work in particular is the relief from the burden of agonism in late abstract expressionism, the sense that art does not have to labor to speak a new word, an ever-more minimal and restrained word. We can see this difficulty in a simple comparison of the late 1950s' scratchings of Cy Twombly, close to the degree zero of modernism's attempt to convey the limit of "expressionism" and to witness the mere trace of the possibility of the unpresentable beyond that limit. On the contrary, pop has an explosion of image, of ready-to-hand subjects in overwhelming profusion. It is easy to find stuff! Everything can be art! This ease and profusion, the tactic of simply ignoring the privation of modern subjects for painting, tames the malevolence of the demand for the new. As Lawrence Weiner remarks, "WARHOL HELPED US TO BE ABLE TO ACCEPT THE HISTORY OF ART AS JUST THAT: THE HISTORY OF ART" (R, 443).

But it is not this task and its possible purgative function in the body artistic that interests me here, but another feature of Warhol's art that seems more particular, more characteristic. If his art is not sublime and is only partly understood as desublimation, it is more characteristically *subliminal*. The subliminal is that which evades the threshold, the *limines* itself, thereby also evading the heroics and agonisms of the limit found in the sublime, gliding by the sublime question as if it did not exist. This subliminal is not that discovered by N. F. Dixon and William Bryan Key, the apostles of subliminal seduction in ads, even though the subjects Warhol chooses are those most often associated with the subliminal message, which is supposedly below the threshold of conscious detection by the senses and which convey consumer instructions and messages about death and sex to the numbed, unresisting mind of the observer. But in Warhol there are no *hidden* messages; those *are* the messages, and nothing is hidden. Nonetheless, something slides by in Warhol's art. That "nothing" of the radical poverty of mass images seeps in subliminally as enjoyment, which was *how it was experienced in the first place*. That primal enjoyment is restored. In other words, we are allowed to enjoy what we already enjoyed subliminally but which, when raised to consciousness, could only take the anxious forms of the duties of consumerism, the nausea of mass images, the detritus of the ersatz, of banality, cliché, and staleness. In this distillation, Warhol gives us back what we already had—the pleasure of our own dumbness and vacuity, in such a way that these do not choke us with self-disgust or loathing for the world of trash. Warhol gets at the reality of the unreality of the simulacrum, frees it from the presumption of the mind with respect to some absolute now, and releases us from the tyranny of conceptions of the beyond of art where its messages are, where representation is held to be "of something"; and he leaves the nothing to happen. There is nothing behind these paintings, no more mimesis or representation than there is in abstract expressionism. He makes nothing happen without shaking it out of nothingness into a kind of present-to-consciousness. In the term *enjoyment*, I mean something rather less than *jouissance*; indeed, I mean the term exactly as it has been debased by aesthetics since Kant. Thus Jean-Luc Nancy: "The aesthetics of the beautiful transports itself into the sublime wherever it does not slide into mere enjoyment" (SO, 49). Mere enjoyment is what I feel when I look at the work of Andy Warhol.

Or perhaps when I do not look at it. The effect of a great many of Warhol's installations seems to be a performative demonstration of the impossibility of really looking at them. The Whitney installation of *Flowers*, where virtually every surface is covered with minor variations of the same flower, the *Cow Wallpaper*, especially when the electric chair paintings were hung on it, *Mao* on *Mao Wall Paper*—all seem to testify more to the evasion of the gaze than its enactment. One cannot really look at all sixty *Last Suppers*, nor every Campbell's soup can or Brillo box—nor should one. Andy's most triumphant opening was famously that at the Institute of Contemporary Art in Philadelphia in 1965, at which the paintings were removed, were not there at all. The most banal forms of his ready-seens are there *not* so that we can see them anew, freshened, enlivened, but so that we can *really* not see them, instead of merely not seeing them. Warhol's work seems to affirm just what Walter Benjamin condemns in the phenomenon of reproduction: "A man who concentrates before a work of art is absorbed by it. . . . In contrast, the distracted mass absorbs the work of art." This is indeed "reception in a state of distraction" and in a "position" that "requires no attention."[19] Reception in a state of distraction is precisely what these installations induce.

Warhol is not the only artist to distract attention from the field of the visual within that field itself. Conceptual artist Daniel Buren writes on "vulgarization" as a method:

> It is a question of drawing out from its respectable shelter of originality or rarity a work, which, in essence aims at neither respect nor honours. The cancelling out of form through repetition gives rise to the appearance, at the same moment, of profuseness and ephemerality. . . .
>
> In art, banality soon becomes extraordinary. The instances are numerous. We consider that at this time the essential risk that must be taken—a stage in our proposition—is the vulgarization of the work itself, in order to tire out every eye that stakes all on the satisfaction of a retinal (aesthetic) shock, however slight. *The visibility of this form must not attract the gaze.*[20]

"Must not attract the gaze"—what gaze is eluded here? I suggest that gaze activated by the anamorph, a notion informative in relation to Warhol because of the sense that the anamorph both is, and is not, in Warhol's product. The term is a technical one for the practice of perspectival artists in the sixteenth and seventeenth centuries that "hides" an image in an alternative perspective to the main one given by the painting, as in Holbein's *The Ambassadors*, or that hides the image in a mess of distortion, from which the image is precipitated or congealed with the help of an optical device such as a viewing hole or cylindrical mirror. In the Holbein painting, the anamorph appears as a blob or rent in the lower part of the canvas. Once the anamorph is seen as a skull, the most remarkable thing about the painting is the way in which one *did not see it in the first place*; for some reason, one can gaze at this painting in the usual contemplative immersion and not ask oneself why there is a rending blob in the lower foreground. This footnote to art history is famously reconsidered by Jacques Lacan in *Four Fundamental Concepts of Psychoanalysis*. In the strict sense, of course, there is no anamorph in Warhol's art: "If you want to know all about Andy Warhol, just look at the surface: of my paintings, my films, and me. . . . There's nothing behind it" (*R*, 457) There is no hidden image to surprise the viewer, in the same sense that there is no subliminal message—and this is most true of, for example, the camouflage paintings, which play flagrantly and "on the surface" with the very notion of the hidden.[21]

The effect of the anamorph is, according to Lacan, uncanny and phallic; it is seen over the shoulder while leaving the room.[22] It is the clearest manifestation of what he calls the "trap for the gaze" in painting, that which catches the observer in "an obvious relation with desire which, nevertheless, remains enigmatic" (*FC*, 92). The anamorph surprises us as subjects of desire; it is something that was not in the picture, suddenly appearing in the picture. The anamorph is an aspect of the malevolence of the gaze; the observing subject trapped here is the annihilated subject, the one who sees the death's head at the moment that the death's head sees her, pins her down in "the imaged embodiment of the *minus-phi* $[(-\theta)]$ of castration" (*FC*, 89). Lacan links this moment (with some reservations) to Sartre's account of the voyeur discovered at his keyhole by the activation of the gaze and the resultant feeling, which is, overwhelmingly, shame. What is seen in the classical anamorph? On the whole, the images in Balstrusaïtis' book show death and pornography as the most popular subjects. Moreover, it is the satyric pornographic—puerile, smutty, mocking. And death in its most sublime form—the crucifixion, the martyrdom of saints. It reveals the abject, what is merely "dirty," the sick little frisson, the soulless and scandalous triviality of the little itch, the dirty little secrets that we hide; or, the profound, wherein what is hidden by the chaos of surface form is the one truth, the principle that underlies the variety of imagery.

In the blankness of the screen and the insistence of the repetition, the works of Warhol seem opposed to this sudden trap, to the skewering effect of the gaze of the anamorph, without hidden depths and without the repulsive fright of the anamorph. To the shame induced by the gaze, I find rather in Warhol's work an opposite response—enjoyment, a kind of freedom from the desiring machines operating in the simulacrum, so that one can stare at Marilyn Monroe, freed from the presumption of any "real Marilyn" behind the image, without offering apologies for being caught in the tabloid rack at the supermarket. In short, I am arguing for what Lacan calls *dompte regard*, the taming of the gaze.

Since many of the subjects Warhol paints are disasters and death's heads—even the Marilyns and Jackies are among the latter, in a way—there is to some extent an adventitious connection to the effect of the anamorph. The series of

Figure 15.1 Andy Warhol. *The Six Marilyns*, 1962 (Marilyn Six-Pack). Reproduced with permission of SODRAC Inc., acting as representative for the ARS.

skull paintings (1976), the electric chair paintings (*Red Disaster, Silver Disaster, Big Electric Chair*, 1967), other disaster paintings (*Saturday Disaster* [a car crash], 1964, *Tunafish Disaster*, 1963, *Suicide* 1962, *5 Deaths 17 times in Black and White*)—these images should be "upsetting"—anamorphotic particularly in their pandering to the desire to see the gruesome scenes of abjection, which one might expect would activate the gaze as that which surprises us as subjects of shameful desires. But in Warhol's work, the anamorph has become the main subject of the painting, and in so becoming, it evades the malevolence generated by the hiddenness of the hidden. If it thus erases subjects, as Buchloh has it, it at least appears not to split them, not to generate the unhappy consciousness which "in its illusion of *seeing itself seeing itself*, finds its basis in the inside-out structure of the gaze" (*FC*, 82). One looks at *Ambulance Disaster* (1963) with its gruesome irony of an ambulance in a car crash, or *Saturday Disaster* (1964), with all of the disassociated fascination of the roadside rubberneck, and without much better visual clarity, because these works are all subject to the "bad copy" interference of the techniques of reproduction—grainy, marred, shadowy—so that it cannot be that here we finally get to see what we really wanted to have a closer look at—one still peers and pries into these paintings. And one is not trapped into shame and humiliation. If one is trapped at all, it is into vacuity and stupor. But as I argued earlier, the qualities do not confront us as our own evil appetites or as the evil appetites imputed to us by the compulsory-customary; they are themselves tamed. For Lacan, "this is the pacifying, Appollonian effect of painting. Something is given not so much to the gaze as to the eye, something that involves the abandonment, the *laying down*, of the gaze" (*FC*, 105). As counter-intuitive as it might seem to affiliate Warhol with Apollonian effects, nonetheless, his work frees us from the evil eye of modern consumer mass imagery by enabling our enjoyment of it.

Those who argue for Warhol's satirical and desublimating mission to painting, on the other hand, propose reinstituting the satyr's evil eye—an eye that catches us vacantly gazing at the disaster and reveals the poverty and banality of our response. Such a satyr's gaze is posited, for example, by Dave Hickey, who takes Warhol's work to be an attack on the ethical emptiness of connoisseurship:

> Warhol's blunt images of anonymous suicides, accident victims and instruments of brutality seem to say: "You want your pain, lady? I got your pain right here, in different colors!"
> In fact as Baldessari and I walked out of the room of electric chair paintings, leaving behind a couple of east side matrons who had been perusing the work in silence, we heard one of them say to the other, "I think I like the blue one." (*GEW*, 163)

To be an East Side matron is obviously a great burden in art appreciation, but might they this time be more right than a gosh-darn genuine artist? Or is there another gaze that ricochets back from these dumbed-up images to fix viewers in a shameful relation to their own originally solicited dumb look?[23] For that is what the satyr's gaze is, a second look that sees that the first look sees only what is apparently there; but Warhol's paintings are only about what is apparently there. They instead double back again to the original dumb look, which is part of their cleverness, and their pacification effect, where skulls are "just" skulls, death is "just" death, and the history of art is "just" the history of art. The satyr's look is thus a version of the anamorph, even if it is not in the paintings. This anamorphotic gaze, that which traps subjects (and artists) in responsibility—for that is what causes shame—is itself, I suggest, the malevolent gaze of a totalizing ethics. Ethics traps subjects in their responsibility; Warhol evades this ethical gaze, and there is relief in evading it.

A trap is sprung. The springing of that trap raises the question of the desire to be ethical, of what devious source of pleasure there is in the self-censoring submission to the gaze and to the ethical demand that tells us we ought to be ashamed. The Warhol effect is to refuse responsibility in favor of something pretty and dumb, shallow and trivial. What Warhol is best at is capturing the ephemeral and spectral substance of illusion. In the *Shadows* installations (1978), there is a strange and pleasant beauty in that sheer insubstantiality, in its endless repetition; in the *Rorschach* series (1984), we find the blobs allowed to be blobs, which *do not* invite their own effacement in psychological hermeneutics; and most brilliantly, the *Camouflage* paintings seem to debunk the whole history of illusion in art—here the device of illusion is not staged as a trick to delude but exactly not to, rather to exist in its own shadowy way, to have its own difficulty in existing registered. These are light messages from the shoals of art, shallow and ephemeral existences. His work is where he claims it is, among the leftovers, the remainders of what happens to commercial design, once it has fulfilled its message and you've bought your soup, the blank screens of the simulacrum left after the cheap libidinality of the star-making machinery has exhausted itself, the insubstantial substance of a shadow that no longer hides or veils anything.[24]

What is Andy's nothing then? A cure for anxiety, especially nightmares?

> The thing is to think of nothing, B. Look, nothing is exciting, nothing is sexy, nothing is not embarrassing. The only time I ever want to be something is outside a party so I can get in. Three out of five parties are going to be a drag, A. I always have my car there early so I can leave if they're disappointing.
>
> I could have told her that if something is disappointing I know it's not nothing because nothing is not disappointing. (*PAW*, 93)

To be excused from ethics, to evade the *gravitas* of the ethical weight—this aim can only be stated in itself as an ethical goal, at least within critical discourse. When ethics arises most strongly, the ephemeral, the light, the transitory, ubiquitous and silly, the joke itself, are abolished, their intention to be outside the ethical question obliterated, and *shown to have never really been possible* in the first place. The "decadents" sent to a concentration camp. It is of the essence of the light phenomenon to be unable to answer the charge of ethics that it has fatally scotomized the ethical question; but what about what ethics has scotomized? Can it be an ethical task to shelter the effervescent bubble of the light phenomenon lest it pop?

NOTES

1. The notion is, of course, T. S. Eliot's; for Fredric Jameson, at least, what was disassociation in modernity goes so far as to be schizophrenia in postmodernism. "Postmodernism and Consumer Society" in *The Anti-Aesthetic*, ed. Hal Foster (Seattle: Bay Press, 1983), 118–23.

2. Emmanuel Levinas, "Ethics As First Philosophy," *The Levinas Reader* (Oxford: Blackwell, 1994), 84.

3. Andy Warhol, *Philosophy of Andy Warhol (From A to B and Back Again)* (New York: Harcourt, Brace, Jovanovich, 1975), 112. He also claims to be missing some "reproductive chemicals" (111), though obviously not those that lead to the reproduction of the work of art. Hereafter cited as *PAW*.

4. Andy Warhol and Pat Hackett, *POPism* (New York: Harcourt, Brace, Jovanovich, 1980), 60.

5. Jean Baudrillard, "Machinic Snobbery," *The Perfect Crime*, trans. Chris Turner (London: Verso, 1996), 84. Stuart Morgan points out that Warhol, in his early works, "gradually departed from ideas of original creation, indeed, from the idea of a person altogether" (quoted in Simon Watney, "The Warhol Effect," in *The Work of Andy Warhol*, ed. Gary Garrels, *DIA Art Foundation Discussions in Contemporary Culture* [Seattle: Bay Press, 1989], 118). Hereafter cited as *WAW*.

6. Rainer Crone's intervention. *The Work of Andy Warhol*, 134.

7. I am indebted to Dr. Sarah Kay, Girton College, Cambridge, for the etymology of *banal*.

8. Roland Barthes, *Camera Lucida*, trans. Richard Howard (New York: Hill and Wang, 1981), 22.

9. *Andy Warhol, A Retrospective*, ed. Kynaston McShine (New York: The Museum of Modern Art, 1989), 54; hereafter cited as *R*. See also Tillie Osterwold *Pop Art* (New York: Taschen Books, 1991), 102. Hereafter cited as *PA*.

10. Dave Hickey, "Getting It Exactly Wrong: Andy's Kindergarten for Connoisseurs," *Parkett* 20 (1989): 162. Hereafter cited as *GEW*.

11. "Works are most critical when they first see the light of day; afterwards they become neutralized because, among other things, the social conditions have changed," T. Adorno, *Aesthetic Theory*, trans. C. Lenhardt (London: Routledge and Kegan Paul, 1984), 325.

12. *Critique of Cynical Reason*, trans. Michael Eldred (Minneapolis: University of Minnesota Press, 1987), 5. Sloterdijk holds this to be a modern form of unhappy consciousness, but Warhol seems happy in his cynicism.

13. The "Sublime and the Avant-garde," *The Lyotard Reader*, ed. Andrew Benjamin (Oxford: Blackwell, 1989), 200. Hereafter cited as *SA*.

14. Jean-François Lyotard, *The Postmodern Condition: A Report on Knowledge*, trans. Geoff Bennington and Brian Massumi (Minneapolis: University of Minnesota Press, 1984), 76. Hereafter cited as *PC*.

15. Jean-Luc Nancy, "The Sublime Offering," in *Of the Sublime: Presence in Question*, trans. Jeffrey S. Librett (Albany: State University of New York Press, 1993), 53. Hereafter cited as *SO*.

16. Some notable critics have indeed objected to minimalism on nearly the grounds on which Lyotard explicates it (and hence preserves it for conceptual ethics) as sublime—Clement Greenberg, for example, comments on the ability of art to *hide* behind "presence," by implication a somewhat crude event, or mere presence, which is to him where "the question of the phenomenal as opposed to the aesthetic or artistic comes in." Clement Greenberg, "Recentness of Sculpture" in *Minimal Art*, ed. G. Battcock (New York: Dutton, 1968), 185–86: "That presence as achieved through the look of non-art was likewise aesthetically extraneous, I did not yet know. . . . That sculpture could hide behind it—just as painting did—I found out only after repeated acquaintance with Minimal works of art: Judd's, Morris's." Greenberg feels that what is hiding behind "presence" is merely "Good Design." His remarks are applied to pop art as much as minimalism. Oddly, and tellingly, in these remarks, Greenberg's "presence" seems to be pretty much the same thing as Lyotard's "unpresentable."

17. Jean-François Lyotard, "Gesture and Commentary," *Iyyun, The Jerusalem Philosophical Quarterly* 42 (1993): 47–48. Reprinted in this volume.

18. Drucilla Cornell, "Rethinking the Beyond of the Real," in *Levinas and Lacan: The Missed Encounter*, ed. Sarah Harasym (Albany: State University of New York Press, 1998), 172.

19. Walter Benjamin, "The Work of Art in the Age of Mechanical Reproduction," in *Illuminations*, trans. Harry Zohn (New York: Schoken Books, 1968), 239, 240.

20. Daniel Buren, "Beware!" *Conceptual Art*, ed. Ursula Meyer (New York: E. P. Dutton, 1972), 72. (Reprinted from *Studio International* 179 [1970]). The quotation continues: "Once the dwindling form/imprint/gesture has been rendered impotent/invisible, the proposition has/will have some chance to become dazzling. The repetition of a neutral form, such as we are attempting to grasp and to put into practice, does not lay emphasis upon the work, but rather tends to efface it."

21. A Warholian anecdote: My daughter stands in the street wearing army surplus camouflage trousers—a man yells from a window: "Hey you, girl! I can't see your legs!"

22. "Begin by walking out of the room in which no doubt [the painting] has long held your attention. It is then that, turning around as you leave . . . you apprehend in this form. . . . What? A skull." Jacques Lacan, *Four Fundamental Concepts*, trans. Alan Sheridan (New York: Norton, 1977), 88. Hereafter cited as *FC*. This is not an accurate account of *The Ambassadors* as currently hung in the National Gallery.

23. "The distance between the works and their trite subject matter was too small for the viewer to see through their triviality, too small to create the tensions necessary

for the viewer to catch himself taking pleasure in superficiality, gloss and extravagance" (*PA*, 102).

24. "I always like to work on leftovers, doing the leftover things. Things that were discarded, that everybody knew were no good, I always thought had a great potential to be funny" (*PAW*, 93).

CHAPTER 16

Short Circuit:
The Story of an Exhibition
That Provoked Unforeseen Consequences

Susan Gibson Garvey

There were two photos side by side. One was of a black person and the other was of a gorilla. The text read "What's a cross between an ape and a nigger?" The answer was below the pictures, covered by a little black card. You had to reach out yourself and slide the card out of the way to get the answer, so I did. The answer was, "A mentally retarded ape." When I read this it was like being hit in the chest. I couldn't remember whether I told that particular joke in the past, but I am ashamed to say I had told plenty like it. I felt sick and embarrassed and I could feel my cheeks getting red. I looked around the gallery to see if anyone was watching. . . . I can't see myself telling a joke like that again.

> —From an essay by a white male graduate, written in response to viewing the works of Carrie Mae Weems during his class visit to the exhibition *No Laughing Matter.*

This display is insensitive, repulsive, and totally counteracts the needs of the Black student population . . . We are deeply hurt and want something done about this. This is not an issue of censorship; instead this racist depiction perpetuates hatred and restrictive stereotypes . . . The Black students of [the university] demand the termination of this exhibit.

> —From a protest letter circulated by the Black Canadian Students Association with regard to Carrie Mae Weems' works in the exhibition *No Laughing Matter.*

275

My friend Heather said it had been the most powerful anti-racist art she had ever seen. We were sitting in her kitchen, discussing the fact that I had been asked to write about Carrie Mae Weems' photographs—the ones that had caused such a ruckus in the gallery a few years ago. I was conscious of the familiar knot of anxiety gathering in my stomach, sucking me into the abyss of memory. I was reluctant to write about the incident, partly because it was painful to recall, but also because I was concerned that I might inadvertently spark a negative reaction again, especially if my recollections were misinterpreted as an exercise in self-justification. Of course, Heather was convinced that I had to write about it, as an instructive example of an excruciating moral dilemma, and I was grateful for her unwavering conviction about the value of this work, just as I had been grateful at the time for her unwavering support during the tense days of the exhibition itself. "I substituted concentration camp jokes for the black jokes, and it worked for me," she said. Heather is a Jewish writer and journalist. Carrie Mae Weems is a black activist artist. I am a white, English-born art gallery curator. So it would seem that the whole thing is about race.

It should not have been so. The exhibition *No Laughing Matter* included work by thirteen contemporary activist artists and artists' collectives, tackling a range of social issues from race and class to environmental issues, televangelism, the power of the multinational corporations, and the artist as celebrity to gay rights, feminism, and American cultural imperialism. But race has become the defining social issue at the turn of the millennium.

It is nearly a decade since the gallery hosted the exhibition. I write about it, as I said, not because I wish to provoke but because I must try to recall clearly, in the relative tranquility of the present, an important and a difficult experience. What follows is not *the* truth about what happened. It is how I personally remember it, supplemented by some documentation from the time. Others may well remember it differently.

No Laughing Matter was a brilliantly conceived exhibition, filled with surprising, challenging, and occasionally very funny works. It presented the work of well-known activist artists, such as Hans Haacke, the Guerrilla Girls and Gran Fury collectives, and feminist artists Cindy Sherman and Louise Lawler, all of whom use some form of humor to initiate a response and, it is to be hoped, to raise awareness to the point where social change might occur. They employ silly humor; serious, heavy humor; twisted humor, sarcasm, puns, paradox, and irony. The reputable New York-based nonprofit organization Independent Curators Incorporated offered the show for circulation. The exhibition's curator, Nina Felshin, had formed her thesis around the power of humor to bring forth, or provide a new perspective on, social issues. The carefully chosen participants were to present challenging works in a range of media: sculpture, painting, photography, mixed media, sound, and installation art. In the advance publicity for the exhibition, it was evident that the work would be provocative—but, as we said when we first considered presenting this exhibition, this was a *university* art gallery, and if one could not raise such issues for discussion here, then where could one? It seemed highly appropriate to the gallery's mandate to present leading artists whose works tackled pressing social issues in an arena where they would at least have a chance of being seriously considered and openly discussed.

The gallery was (and still is) a small institution in terms of budget and personnel: at that time there were just three qualified professionals: a director, a curator, and a registrar-preparator—all white women. (Regrettably, for the purposes of this narration, I must employ the oversimplification "black" and "white" in describing people.) There were just enough annual funds to fulfill our dual role as a public art gallery and as an academic support unit within the university (which has no visual arts faculty). In order to present a richer and more challenging program of exhibitions, animation, and educational activities, we were constantly obliged to seek extra funding. In the case of *No Laughing Matter*, we needed considerable extra funds for exhibition fees and transportation, and so we applied for, and got, a substantial grant from the Canada Council. It seems doubly ironic now, given what happened later, that among the first to congratulate us on obtaining these considerable funds was the university's president. Letters of congratulation came from him, from the vice president of finance, and from the vice president of academics (to whom our director reported), all commenting on the high standards and professionalism of the gallery's programming, and on our frequent success in raising extra funds. They had not yet, of course, seen the exhibition, which was now booked for the following spring.

Just as the 1970s to mid-1980s had been a time of serious attention to gender issues within cultural and educational institutions, the next decade was going to be a time of opening up in terms of ethnocentricity. The university had spent considerable effort to build a program responsive to the needs of First Nations and visible minorities. By the early 1990s, when our exhibition was scheduled, the Transition Year Program for Native and Black Students had been established, a significant law school program for students of ethnic origin was introduced, and fund-raising for a Chair of Black Studies was underway. There was a Native Counselling Center on campus, a Black Student Advisor, and an Employment Equity Officer.

In the gallery, we had become increasingly conscious of the need for inclusive programming. The gallery had organized the first solo exhibition of a black artist in the province in 1976 (*Winter Visions*, by Jim Shirley), and more recently it had held the African Worlds Program, a celebration of black visual art, poetry, song, and theatre that the gallery organized in conjunction with other departments on campus. When I joined the gallery as curator and programs officer a couple of years later, I began a project to include First Nations art in our offerings, not only in exhibitions but also as part of our regular artists' presentations, film program, and docent training. To us, then, booking the *No Laughing Matter* exhibition seemed to be a logical continuation of a programming direction that reflected a broadening and more inclusive attitude toward works by artists in a variety of minority or marginalized positions, as well as works that actively raised cross-cultural and social issues.

A few weeks before the exhibition was due to arrive, we received the pre-installation package—publicity material, artists' biographies, copies of the exhibition catalogue, and slides of the actual works. Reviewing the visuals, we saw that a range of hard-hitting work had been selected. There were cartoon-style paintings that parodied the greed of televangelism, installations showing the world as a miniature golf course (with the United States as the only hole that could be played), posters that challenged corporate irresponsibility and political connivance, and flyers by the famous Guerrilla Girls ("Do women have to be naked to get into the Metropolitan Museum?") and by AIDS activists, Gran Fury ("Men: use condoms or beat it"). Activist art is essentially confrontational and blunt. Humor softens the blow, of course, and can lull us into thinking what we are viewing is entertaining (as it often is). But knowing that people can feel offended by even the mildest forms of contemporary art, it was evident to us that there was plenty in this exhibition to offend.

The works of Carrie Mae Weems, in particular, were going to need careful contextualization. The curator had selected six works from Weems' series titled *Ain't Jokin'* for inclusion in the exhibition. They combined photographs of black people with texts from racist jokes, riddles, and folklore. In three of these works, the answer to a joke or riddle is situated below the image, hidden behind a card (as described by the student at the beginning of this story). The viewer has to decide whether they know, or want to know, the answer, and the simple act of physically reaching out to slide the card aside has the effect of implicating the viewer in the construction of a racist slur. The three other works employed folkloric stereotypes. In one, an attractive young black woman looks in the mirror at the face of a veiled white woman. The text reads "the black woman asked 'Mirror, mirror on the wall, who's the finest of them all?' The mirror says, 'Snow White, you black bitch, and don't you forget it!!!'"

Weems, a black artist active in the civil rights movement, agrees that her works will make people uncomfortable. She intends them to be read ironically, and to act as a means to combat racism—not just racism among whites, she insists (as quoted in the catalogue text), but also "the internalized racism of blacks." In other words, Weems has everyone squirming and lets nobody off the hook. In her catalogue essay, curator Nina Felshin discusses the social, cultural, and psychological variables of humor and notes the obvious fact that what is funny to one person may not be funny to the next. She goes on to say, "Weems' use of jokes . . . reminds us that humor can be and has been used in the exercise of power . . . [I]t is appropriate to ask not 'is this funny?' but rather, 'Funny to whom? And why?'" Titles like *Ain't Jokin'*, and the overall title for the exhibition *No Laughing Matter*, indicated clearly that the exhibition should be read ironically. However, a recent incident with regard to the exhibition *Out of Africa* at the Royal Ontario Museum reminded us how easy it could be for irony to be missed, and we decided to provide further contextualization.

We met with the gallery's Advisory Committee and previewed the exhibition package with them. This committee comprised people from both the university and community and included a range of professors, alumni, schoolteachers, artists, and businesspeople. There were no black representatives on the committee at that time. Would things have been different if there had been? You may think the answer is obvious, and of course for inclusive reasons alone there *should* have been black representation, but given the experience of this exhibition, I find it hard to say it would have made a significant difference in this instance. The committee firmly endorsed the exhibition, recommending that we increase our educational outreach and contact members of the black community for their comments and, if possible, support in relation to the Weems' photographs.

The animation activities that we had initially planned included opening remarks by a professor from the nearby art college who also happened to be an activist artist himself; a complementary film program that focused on activist art; a public presentation by the curator of the exhibition (whom we would fly up from New York); a panel discussion involving local activist artists from different communities and disciplines; and educational handouts for visiting school groups. We decided we would also include small didactic panels containing brief excerpts from the catalogue essay to be placed near works that might require additional explanation and have extra photocopies of artists' biographies and articles about their works available, along with copies of the exhibition catalogue on a "reading table" near the main entrance. Also, we would make sure that we ourselves were present in the gallery as often as possible to respond to visitors' questions. I should mention that being a small staff, we regularly spend time in the gallery, sometimes filling in for a front-desk volunteer who is unable to be there that day, or conducting impromptu tours. It is a good way for us to keep in touch with our audiences.

The gallery occupies the basement level of the Arts Center, so people rarely enter the gallery by accident. Descending the stairs to the main entrance of the gallery, one can view part of the exhibition through the glass walls encasing the stairwell. We decided to place notices in the stairwell and on the entrance doors that would alert the public to the exhibition's content, while not, we hoped, preempting their own responses. The notices read:

No Laughing Matter

This important exhibition of activist art is intended to draw attention to various social problems through the use of humor and irony.

The 13 artists in this show address sexism, imperialism, racism, corporate irresponsibility, the AIDS crisis, poverty, and the environment.

Visitors may find some of these works disturbing.

Our intention in hosting this exhibition is to encourage serious discussion about these issues which are "no laughing matter."

We also planned the layout of the exhibition so that the less provocative works were experienced first, building up toward the more confrontational works at the far end of the gallery. In fact, due to the complicated shape of the gallery, Weems' work was in the bay of the side gallery and not visible from the front desk area at all, something that became quite problematic later.

In response to the Advisory Committee's recommendations, our director set up a series of meetings with university and community members to preview the artworks and sent informational packages to those who had no time to meet. Some of these were members of the city's black artists collective, which included filmmakers, poets, musicians, playwrights, actors, craftspeople, and visual artists; others were members of the university community, especially those in leadership positions. People's responses ranged from excited and intrigued to angry and upset, indicating that opinion was going to be divided about this exhibition. I had recommended that we contact the Black Student Advisor, with the intention of eliciting her help in making sure that the gallery presentation was mediated positively for black students, offering opportunities for discussion on issues of race and discrimination. However, when she saw the slides of the artworks, she told us that she found Weems' work deeply offensive, and she went on to state categorically that she wanted nothing to do with the exhibition, and that the black students would not want anything to do with it either. We had been prepared for some negative responses, but this was the first indication of how profound an effect the work might have.

At the press preview for the exhibition, we asked a well-known local black poet to be present and to give her views on the work. The press reported her comments that Weems' work was "bludgeoning to look at" but it was also "empowering, healing—you can get your anger out and laugh too." The following evening, the exhibition opened to a large crowd. The guest speaker had composed a long and witty poem about the various social issues arising from the exhibition and on the purging power of humor. Several professors from the art college attended the opening and booked visits for their classes. The comments in the visitors' book were mainly thoughtful and enthusiastic.

During the first week or so, I gave a number of tours of the exhibition to groups from the art college, and also to high school students (racially mixed groups), who seemed exceptionally interested in all of the artworks. They commented that they rarely saw art that was this relevant to issues that concerned them. At first there were few black visitors from the community at large, but this was not an uncommon situation, given that the gallery's location within the university campus is in a predominantly white and wealthy part of the city. Soon, however, a contentious dialogue began to appear in the visitors' book, with people responding to each other's comments (both positive and negative) on the works in general and the Weems' works in particular.

About ten days into the exhibition, three black students from the law school came down after the gallery was closed and asked to see the exhibition. They asked specific questions regarding the contract we had signed with Independent Curators Incorporated, and whether we could alter the show by removing some of the artworks. We replied that we could not, but even if we could, we would not on principle remove works from any exhibition, not only because that would be an act of censorship but also because exhibitions like this one were carefully curated and balanced, and to remove works would alter its meaning.

As the days progressed, strongly negative comments started appearing in the visitors' book, some of them written by people who identified themselves only as "black" or "Malcolm X." The tone of these comments suggested to us that we needed to be present in the gallery full time, in order to be available to people who had questions about the works. It also suggested that we needed to keep an eye on the artworks themselves. We moved a small desk into a corner of the side gallery close to Weems' photographs, where one of us could sit and work, while still being available to visitors who wished to talk about the work. The trio of law students returned and asked us if we were expecting violence. We said no, but explained that it was our responsibility to look after the artworks. They wanted to know if we felt it was our responsibility to be sensitive to the black community's negative reaction and remove the works altogether. The irony of black law students asking a white curator to remove the works of a black female artist whose stated intent was to combat racism was not lost on any of the parties.

A few days later, a group of ten black students (not law students, but part of the general student body) came into the gallery and asked to speak with us. They told us that there had been a meeting among all of the black students on campus, and that they had taken a vote to boycott the exhibition, which they thoroughly condemned because of Weems' work. They said that they thought the work was actually promoting racism, rather than fighting it, that it perpetuated stereotypes and would give comfort to the white supremacist groups that they knew to exist in the city. They wanted to remain in the gallery to distribute a formal letter of protest to all gallery visitors. The letter was signed by the president of the Black Canadian Students Association of the university and expressed the students' outrage concerning the exhibit. It specifically named the director and me, calling us insensitive and offensive for booking this exhibition without consulting the black community, and it demanded the removal of the offending works. Our director explained that she could not remove the artworks, but that she would gladly mount their letter on a card and place it on the wall in the area where Weems' photographs were hung, so that visitors would see that the students objected to the art. We then tried to engage the students in a conversation about the works themselves, but their leader said that they were too profoundly hurt by the exhibition to discuss it further, and they left.

We mounted the letter on the wall near the didactic panel for Weems' works, and we talked about what we should do next. We felt it was vitally important to keep communications open and to embrace the students' negative responses. They had a right to their own feelings, and the work was certainly hard to take. The following day, the students returned. At the same time, a white politician (a member of the Legislative Assembly) and one of his black constituents arrived. The students said that they would be staging a sit-in as a protest and would occupy the space where Weems' works were hung. They meant to stay there until the works were removed or the show was closed. We said that they had the right to protest, but that they could not prevent others from exercising their right to view the works. We suggested that they bring some of the gallery benches into the area to sit on. They would have preferred to stand in front of the works, but we were quite firm about not interfering with other people's access. The students were very unhappy about this. The politician took me aside and started to berate me for being insensitive to the students' needs. They were hurt, he said, and did not need a discussion about other people's rights. I was surprised by his attitude and had no immediate reply. After he left, a reporter and photographer arrived and said that they were covering the student sit-in. The students were quite dignified in their protest and did not want it sensationalized. They were quite clear that they did not want to be photographed and had not called the press themselves, nor had we. So who had called them in? I asked the photographer. He identified the politician. We asked the press to leave and explained that photographing the artworks was a violation of the artists' copyright. They asked if we had any official press photos of the exhibition, and we felt obliged to give them those.

The students continued their sit-in the following day. Since they were not inclined to discuss the works with us, we felt it was time to contact Carrie Mae Weems herself and, if possible, persuade them to talk to her. In looking at our finances, we determined that we could fly her in to do a public presentation about her work, if that was the best course of action. Our director managed to track her down in California and get her on the phone. When she heard about the student sit-in, Weems exclaimed, "Why are they picketing an art gallery? Why aren't they picketing the banks and shops and companies that won't employ them or their parents simply because they're black?" We told her the students felt hurt and offended by her work. "Of course my work's offensive!" she replied, "So is racism! Let me talk to them." We asked the students if they would like to talk to Weems. No, they did not want to talk to her. She had the right to make any kind of art she wanted, they said, but it was *we*, the gallery staff, who had erred in bringing her work *here* where it was not appropriate. We relayed this to Weems and asked her if she would be available to fly up to do a public presentation. She replied that she would only come if the students themselves wanted her to come. The students said they were not interested.

In the next few days, the students were present in the gallery every day and were joined by other protesters, including a sympathetic group from the Native Counselling Center, as well as a group of law students, and, occasionally, a black law professor. (This same professor had worked closely with our director on the African Worlds program a few years earlier.) Some of the older protestors had brought along their children and asked us if we thought it was right that children should be subjected to this offensive art. We pointed out that the exhibition was not intended for young children, and that the gallery's location in the basement of the art center on the university campus made it very unlikely that children would accidentally wander in. We agreed with the protestors, that the work was indeed very hard hitting but, despite their requests, we said that we would not remove the works. The protesters sent letters to the university's President, the Senate, and the Board of Governors, asking them to close the show and censure us.

Many more professors and students and some members of the administration came down to the gallery to see what the fuss was about, and the discussions intensified, both verbally and in the written entries in the visitors' book. Reactions were highly polarized, either fiercely opposed or vigorously in favor, and although the polarization seemed to fall along racial lines, it was not entirely so. One of Weems' stated intentions was evidently playing itself out: her work must make us feel uncomfortable, she insists, as though our integrity were being called into question, "if only to make sure we have any at all." Some people found this statement arrogant and insulting, others found it clarifying and humbling. The core of the sit-in students, however, consistently refused to discuss the works with us and told us that as white people we could never understand their suffering—a statement that effectively silenced us. Some more vocal black visitors complained that we were simply using black people's pain to increase our gallery's attendance figures and enhance its profile.

The exhibition's curator flew in from New York and gave an informative slide presentation on the exhibition to a large audience. Unfortunately, despite widespread invitations, there were only two black community members present at her talk: the poet, who had all along supported the exhibition, and one of the law students, who said he was trying to understand the dynamics around the exhibition. Although we encouraged the other sit-in students to come to the presentation, they stuck to their boycott.

The exhibition controversy spread across the campus and beyond, cohering on the one hand around the question of censorship, and on the other hand around the less easily defined issue of "sensitivity." Our director kept all of our advisory committee members up to date with developments in the gallery by sending photocopies of visitors' book comments and reports on scheduled events and unusual occurrences. Copies also went to the vice president of academics and to the various community members with whom she had consulted earlier. She received a terse letter from the Black Student Advisor, stating that she had already made her feelings clear with regard to the exhibition, and that she wanted no further reports sent to her.

We received a copy of a letter that the politician had sent to the university president, complaining about the offensive nature of the artwork and the insensitive behavior of the gallery staff. We heard that high-level meetings had begun to take place in the administration with regard to complaints about the exhibition. The vice president of academics, to whom our director reported, continued to be very supportive, made several visits to the gallery, and could occasionally be seen standing in the stairwell discussing the show with visitors. But many members of the administration stayed away, and we could sense that they were starting to distance themselves from us. Our director called the president's office to ask if he would stand by the gallery and defend the artists' freedom of expression, and not ask us to close the exhibition or remove any of the artworks. She received an ambiguous answer.

The press reports came out, and news of the student protest traveled throughout the city. While the student sit-in continued sporadically, we began to receive more visits from people who would not normally come into the gallery at all, both from the university community and from the city in general. There was still plenty of discussion, pro and con, but there were more and more angry visitors arriving from the black communities in and adjacent to the city. Many simply wanted to confirm what they had heard about the "racist art." They often descended the stairs in a hurry and went straight to the front desk, demanding to know where the "racist art" was hung. They would then traverse the gallery, usually ignoring all of the other artworks, and head straight to the Weems' photographs where, of course, without a sense of context, all of their suspicions were confirmed. Expressions of outrage ensued, and usually before we could elicit discussion, they left the gallery, carrying home with them exactly the same idea about the work as that with which they had arrived. All of our carefully planned contextualizing work had been literally short-circuited.

Members of the city's Black United Front visited the gallery one day and asked what we would do if they came in and removed the offending works from the walls themselves. Our director replied by asking what they would do if we went into their office or home and started removing things. We then had a brief but civil discussion about the problem and were more or less reassured that they were not really about to take any illegal action. Nevertheless, due to the much increased volume of visitors and the heated emotions expressed, it was clear to us that we needed extra help with security.

This was a very difficult question. The recent case of the Royal Ontario Museum's *Out of Africa* exhibition had so outraged the black community that the staff had felt obliged to retreat, security was called in, and the museum was virtually turned into an armed camp. This was the last thing we wanted. We had been so careful to be present at all times in the gallery and to encourage dialogue. People in uniform in the gallery would likely disturb visitors even more and confirm the black community's suspicions that we regarded them as violent, when in fact there had been no violence at all. Nevertheless, we had a responsibility to protect the artworks from a potential threat, especially since they were not visible from the front desk. In addition, we ourselves were reaching the exhaustion point, being constantly in the gallery and virtually suspending all of our office work in the meantime. In the end, we made an agreement with campus security to have one of their members dressed in casual clothes present in the far end of the gallery at all times. They would only be identified by a small badge stating "Security," and they agreed to read all of the materials available about the exhibition to inform themselves about the artworks and the accompanying controversy. Two of the security people on the roster were black. I asked them if they had any misgivings about guarding the Weems' works, and they shrugged affably, saying that they had heard worse jokes. Given the passionate responses the works had provoked thus far, their answer surprised me. But perhaps by this stage I was losing perspective.

It was indeed getting harder and harder to come into work, to place oneself physically in the gallery, to face the continual accusations of insensitivity and racism, and to argue the same points over and over again. It was disturbing to observe the distress on the faces of some of the young people and to be unable to engage them in discussion about it. It was exhausting to repeat, over and over, the principle of freedom of expression, or to agree that, yes, the works were upsetting, but that was the point. Much repetition will drain the meaning out of anything, and my voice started to sound hollow in my own ears. I felt that there was a whole section of the community that was slipping away from us, alienated, and that there was absolutely nothing we could do about it without betraying the artist, the gallery, and our responsibilities with regard to the free and uncensored presentation of art. It was a dreadful moral dilemma. We did receive comments from a number of local artists, professors, and other visitors, who said that the exhibition was vitally important, and on no account should we give in to pressures to remove the works. But we were conscious that tensions were rising, and the university was officially distancing itself from us and any trouble we might cause.

On the evening that the panel discussion on activist art was scheduled to take place, a rumor circulated that the gallery was going to be picketed by a large crowd of protesters from both the city and the campus, and that some people were looking for trouble. I was supposed to be moderating the panel discussion that evening, and the stress was so intense that I sat at my friend Heather's kitchen table at suppertime and wept. She bolstered me with strong words of encouragement and got me to the gallery on time. There was, in fact, a large crowd of people wanting to attend the discussion, but mercifully no picketers. Among the audience were more members of the black community than had hitherto attended any of our official events in relation to the exhibition.

The panel comprised six activist artists from all disciplines, two of whom were black (one was the co-director of the Transition Year Program and a singer-songwriter; the other was the previously mentioned poet). While a whole range of activist practices was addressed—there was a gay filmmaker, a feminist performance artist, a First Nations visual artist, and the art college professor who had been our opening night speaker—the discussion turned inevitably to the problem of Weems' works. The poet was the last to speak and made an impassioned presentation regarding the right to speak and to discuss anything, about the need to face hurtful issues squarely, even if it tears us apart, and about the transformative power of pain and truth.

In the question period, a white professor, who had expressed considerable indignation when the exhibition first opened, stated that artists such as Weems were arrogant and wondered whether artists in general did not have too much freedom and whether they should not ask permission before producing work that might offend community standards. This incensed the poet, who demanded to know from whom she should seek permission. She asked the audience if we should silence anybody who dares to offend our sensibilities and declared that she would ask nobody's permission to speak the truth of what is on her mind and in her heart.

One of the points that seemed to be at issue was the fact that the exhibition originated in New York, where people are "more pushy" about things in general. Part of the Black Canadian Students Association letter of protest had read, "This exhibit has come from New York, though it may be reinforced in that city, it is utterly inappropriate for this city." Why it was considered so inappropriate for this city was not clearly stated, given that blacks in both cities suffer equally from endemic racism. The fact that Weems herself was from the States, and was active in the civil rights movement, also seemed to be a bone of contention. "Canadians are gentler people; they're more aggressive down there in the States," seemed to be the feeling.

There was also an attitude on the part of some senior-level black students and several well-meaning whites, that of course *they* knew what the irony in the artworks was all about, but that it was too much for their less-educated fellows to grasp, particularly for the black community in this city in general. An articulate black Ph.D. student took this line during the question period after the panel discussion and was roundly turned on by a feisty black woman from the city's North End, who declared that he was spouting "patronizing bull" and that she could understand the work very well by herself, thank you. She was, in fact, one of the handful of black people who came out in open support of the exhibition, much to the annoyance of those who held the opinion that there were no blacks at all who supported it.

I also remember that at one point an artist in the audience said that he was truly annoyed by the fact that he had come to hear a discussion about activist art in general and found that the discussion was hijacked by people wanting to discuss only this one issue of Weems' work. He pointed out that the exhibition had many interesting works in it, all of which had something substantial to say about social issues, and that they too had been somewhat relegated to the background because of this one overriding controversy. I agreed that this was a pity, but there was an overwhelming will among audience members themselves to focus on this one issue. There were other points raised during the discussion, but the ones I have described are those that I remember as being most significant. Others may remember different points, and I wish now that we had recorded the discussion, as it would have been useful to have an accurate record of the many important points raised.

A few days after the panel discussion, the university president finally issued his statement in the form of a letter, a copy of which arrived at the gallery. It had been sent to all chairs of departments, the Co-ordinating Committee Members for Measures to Increase Black and Native Participation, the protesting students, and the campus media. Since the statement was eventually published in the campus paper, I feel no constraint in quoting from it here:

> I personally and many others at [the university] recognize the painful difficulties that the exhibit is causing to the Black community. It is important for [people] to appreciate that the exhibit was selected by the Art Gallery alone, and that the choice and timing of this exhibition is totally within the responsibility of the Art Gallery . . . The University officially, through the Board, the Senate or the senior administration is not involved in any way in these decisions, and the exhibit, therefore, does not have any official University sanction or endorsement. Moreover, I personally do not endorse the exhibit, although it is my duty as President to uphold the right of the Art Gallery to show the exhibit and the right of members of the University who choose to view the exhibit to do so.

The president went on to praise the black community for their admirable restraint in the face of such provocation and to suggest that the gallery needed to appreciate fully the offense it has caused, perhaps by setting up a meeting between the gallery's staff and the Advisory Committee and Co-ordinating Committee Members for Measures to Increase Black and Native Participation.

So there it was. The president had held his nose and upheld the principle of freedom of expression, but he had effectively hung us out to dry. We were on our own, to sink or swim as the tides of opinion took us. To be fair, he had a very tense situation on his hands that required gracious defusing, and we were the sacrifice that had to be made. But I did resent the line about not personally endorsing the exhibit. After all, he had never set foot in the gallery, and certainly he had not seen enough of the exhibit to know whether he should endorse it or not.

Ironically, the next day there was a call from the president's office to say that he would like to come and have a private viewing of the exhibition. After hours, of course. I held my own nose and volunteered to stay behind to give him the tour. Incidentally, there were several other members of the university faculty and administration—both black and white—who felt that they could not allow themselves to be seen entering the gallery during normal hours but who phoned for private viewings after hours. It was as if the gallery were hosting some form of pornography.

The reference to timing in the president's letter was important. There had been a number of racial incidents in and around the city the summer before, and tensions had been higher than usual because of it. We had booked the exhibition two years prior to its presentation and could not have predicted these heightened tensions. However, the students' reference to our "insensitivity" in their letter of protest related in part to this fact. Was it all just a matter of bad timing? The students were of course disappointed that the president did not close the gallery. They felt as let down as we did, and the spirit went out of their protest. I felt a wave of empathy and sadness. Others had used the exhibition controversy to gain professional or social advantage, or to demonstrate their own political correctness (on either side of the issue). But the students were, in general, sincere, and if we had managed from the outset, with the help of the Black Student Advisor, to involve them more fully in the issues arising from the work, the whole situation could have been different. They could have been advocates themselves for bringing racial issues to the fore, and they might have channeled the emotional energies that Weems' works aroused in visitors into constructive debate. As it was, I felt that they had been turned against the work before even seeing it, and an opportunity to talk together had been lost in favor of protest and, ultimately, of silence.

The students would perhaps have been comforted by an article that came out a few days later, written by a leading black journalist who had spent a long time in the gallery considering the whole exhibition, and who came out firmly against the Weems' works. He also suggested that we, the staff of the gallery, had set race relations in the university back by decades and had undone all of the good work of the recent committees and appointments. This thought had also been expressed to us by a few others—that by our actions, we had destroyed the goodwill that had built up between the races. I felt that this was a harsh and wrong statement but doubted my ability to speak against it at the time. After so many weeks of stress, I doubted our ability to do more than hang in there until the exhibition closed. I felt that there were many issues that had been misrepresented, as well as a number of small betrayals, but there were few avenues left for calm consideration of these things, since the situation had become so thoroughly charged. The visitors' book was the one place where relatively untrammeled commentary continued. Someone had written appreciatively about the exhibition: "Healers have always maintained that wounds heal faster when exposed to fresh air." I hoped it was true in this case.

Eventually, it was all over. The exhibition closed on schedule without further incident and was sent to its next tour venue, with appropriate warnings to the hosting gallery concerning our recent experiences. A new show was mounted and, as we resumed our regular duties, we began the long process of assessment.

Reviewing the debates about the exhibition, the main issue within the university seemed to be artistic freedom versus censorship, while the main concern of the black community was a perceived lack of sensitivity toward them. This raises the matter of "discursive communities." The discursive community that comprised the regular gallery-going public, whether from the city or from the university, and whether black or white, was reasonably familiar with the manner in which contemporary art behaved and knew more or less that their sensibilities would be challenged by activist art and generally accepted the cleansing role of irony, paradox, and humor. The discursive community of black citizens in the region, and of many of the black students, faculty, and staff on campus, seemed to have rather different sensibilities. For a variety of historic and social reasons, they rarely visited public galleries, unless there was something specifically related to their own culture on display (which I have to say was at best infrequent), and found it hard to appreciate the irony of Weems' works in the face of their own history of pain and injustice. In fact, it seems to me that the two things that most thoroughly short-circuit the action of irony are ideological convictions and deeply hurt feelings.

I do not want to oversimplify or polarize the two discursive communities (or to insist that there *were* only two discursive communities, rather than a number of overlapping ones). It was evident throughout that there were black people who felt that the exhibition was profoundly important and who wanted no part in the call for its closure. Equally, there were members of the white community who were profoundly offended on behalf of their black neighbors, who did not appreciate the art or its ironies and who joined in the call for censure. However, in general, it appeared that Weems' work was, at least initially, read and experienced by the two communities in rather different ways. And, unfortunately, because the situation began in a confrontational rather than a cooperative way, despite efforts to provide appropriate opportunities, the two communities never really expressed and fully discussed, in a nonheated manner, their differing experiences.

Such discussions did take place, with I believe beneficial consequences, among the school and college groups who visited the gallery for guided tours, many of which were racially mixed groups. We received several packages of essays and letters from teachers and professors who wrote that their visits had prompted valuable discussions on social issues. The quotation at the beginning of this chapter was taken from one such package.

For our own part, it was clear to us that we could not in good conscience have allowed Carrie Mae Weems' art to be removed before the scheduled closing date. This principle applies to *any* work that we present in the gallery, but the dilemma was made even more excruciating due to the fact that we, as white gallery staff, had been asked by some members of the black community to take down the works of a black activist woman artist. We believed in its right to be on our walls, we appreciated its purpose and integrity, and we would stand by the exhibition in its entirety as one of the most coherent, worthwhile, and thought provoking that we had hosted to date. But we knew we now had many bridges to repair or build and a lot of outreach to do.

An important issue for the black community had been the lack of consultation with them prior to the exhibition's arrival. We were told that the consultation that we did do was irrelevant, because it occurred after the show was booked and related only to the issue of contextualizing the works. Although we had never previously specifically consulted with anyone before booking any exhibition, whatever its content (preparing our programming in the same way, and with the same professional autonomy as any faculty would prepare its course offerings), many members of the black community believed that adequate consultation would have prevented us from booking the exhibition in the first place. Whether this would have been the case or not, we certainly perceived the need to build a better relationship with culture-specific groups and to encourage more dialogue about our programs. We invited the co-directors of the Transition Year Program to sit on our Advisory Committee. One was the black singer-songwriter who had participated in our panel discussion, and the other was a First Nations filmmaker.

The question of consultation is important. While at first it seems attractive and democratic to consult widely, the process has many pitfalls, not least because we are dealing with the thorny issue of contemporary art, where community values, if agreed upon at all, tend to be conservative and suspicious of artistic motives. Despite the fact that many contemporary activist artists are motivated by sincerely held ethical positions, these are often perceived as anarchistic, or at least at odds with the majority. It continues to be important for us to consult, but I am equally convinced that we must seek members of the community who are not only representatives of minority groups but who also have an interest in, and a concern for, contemporary art to sit on our Advisory Committee.

There was also the matter of sensitivity to community—that is, the local, long-established black community in and around the city, rather than the university community (the black members of which have varied and wide-ranging origins, both local and global). It was pointed out to us that if stronger links with the local black artistic community had been established prior to the exhibition, there would perhaps have been a more solid set of relationships to call on, and more understanding. While it was not true, as some claimed, that the gallery had never exhibited art by black artists prior to the Weems' works, it was certainly evident that we had not built an adequate relationship with the local black arts community, especially with regard to actively seeking out the work of local black artists to exhibit. This was something we resolved to change. It was also pointed out to me recently that now that a number of exhibitions, both celebratory and critical, both solo and group, of black artists' works have been held in a variety of galleries around the city (including our own), a different climate pertains, in which works such as Weems' would be more welcome. I am not so sure about this. Weems' photographs essentially rely on provocation in order to work, and looking at reproductions of them today, I squirm just as painfully as I did nearly a decade ago.

One day, the black law student who had attended all of the events during the controversy came to the gallery and asked for a job working at the front desk. We did not immediately have a vacancy, but we were short of volunteers. He agreed to volunteer until a job vacancy arose, which happened quite soon after he joined us. His presence with us was a quiet confirmation that all had not been lost with the student body—in fact, we learned through various channels that other black students had thought that the exhibition was in fact worthwhile but, in the interests of solidarity with their colleagues, they had felt it prudent to keep quiet at the time. Our new front desk worker was a reminder to us that we needed a more inclusive program for minority student groups. We initiated an affirmative action plan in which we would give hiring preference to students of First Nations ancestry and visible minorities. This plan has been actively in effect for nearly eight years, and as a result we have had the benefit of a wide range of students working within the gallery setting as receptionists and docents, as well as contract gallery assistants, funded through our programming grant, who provide us and our visitors with a variety of thoughtful perspectives on our public programming.

The university president, the Black Student Advisor, the vice president of academics, most of the students, and many others involved in this story have since moved on to new situations elsewhere. The gallery survived another serious threat of closure (due to financial exigencies this time, rather than calls for censorship) and has continued to obtain public funding for its programs. We have indeed organized exhibitions by local black artists since the controversy, as well as a number of other culture-specific exhibitions, lectures, artists' presentations, and film series. We continue to seek ways to maintain the gallery as a space for free and open discussion of aesthetic and ethical issues.

As for Carrie Mae Weems, the year after her work was presented in our gallery, she held a major solo retrospective at the National Museum of Women in the Arts in Washington, D.C., which went on tour across North America. When I first heard this, I had to admit that at first I felt somewhat resentful. We had all, on both sides of the issue, suffered much on account of her work—and there she was, sailing on unscathed to new heights in her career! And then of course I had to laugh at myself. I spend a great deal of my professional life defending the right of artists to create any work, *any* work, according to their conscience—whether or not we choose to exhibit it. And, anyway, was Weems herself unscathed? Surely this work came from deep communal experiences and memories of unspeakable damage. Her photo-series *Ain't Jokin'* had brought our gallery to the brink of disaster and pushed many of us personally to the limits of emotional endurance. But of course *everyone* involved in this controversy had had their limits tested in a way that was a slim but poignant echo of the suffering of all of the victims of colonialism and slavery whose lived experience prompts work of this kind. I am driven to conclude that there are many things that are unforgivable, but making and exhibiting art that tests our conscience is not one of them.

CHAPTER 17

Other Tongues:
Language and Hybridity in
Recent Canadian Video Art

Marusya Bociurkiw

How do you tame a wild tongue . . . ?

—Gloria Anzaldúa, *Borderlands/La Frontera*[1]

Ghosts of language—of mother tongue, indigenous voice, colonial speech—haunt the remembered and unremembered narratives of Canadian history. The changing of names at the ports of Ellis Island or Halifax; the play of immigration across fields of power; the body of the foreigner lost in the accidents of collection and classification that create a sutured story of the past; the signifiers of the Canadian imaginary: snow; unity against the elements; a hardy, enterprising whiteness.[2] How were all those different, wild, unofficial tongues tamed? Or were they?

Language is a useful tool with which to carve out a cross-section of Canadian video practice grappling with difference. This chapter will describe some aesthetic strategies of the postcolonial in the works of six Canadian video artists. These artists—Ruth Cuthand, Nelson Henricks, Philip Napier, Elizabeth Mackenzie, Shani Mootoo, and Cathy Sisler—represent an emergent generation of video artists with a particular approach to cultural politics. Eschewing the epistemological shoals of the autobiographical, these works move beyond essentialist codes to address language as a fluid, ever-changing metaphor for hybridity. Identity politics is often represented within the framework of the confessional where, following Foucault, power accrues to the confessor. In these videos, identity is remade into an uncertainty, a shifting location without a fixed, autobiographical first person.

The stark, low-budget production values of the works (graininess, economy of camera movement, a single layer of sound) create another, parallel language, a revolution that cannot be televised. Video art originated in the 1970s in reaction both to television and to modernism, rebelliously situated in opposition to the European beaux arts tradition that had heretofore been central to Canadian art practice. Utopian in its rejection of mainstream production values, grotesque in its opposition to classical aesthetics in cinema, video art has always, to borrow from Bakhtin, appeared unfinished, transgressing its own limits, enjoining its audience to "look at the world with different eyes, not dimmed by 'normal,' that is, commonplace ideas and judgements."[3] Over twenty-five years since its inception, video art remains, outside of the video community, an abnormality, an unknown art form displaced by its mainstream connotations—the video store, the music video, or America's funniest home movies. Scholar and video artist Janine Marchessault describes video as encompassing "the fragmentary dispersal of postmodernity."[4] From the military installation to the department store, video is everywhere; those traces of ubiquitousness are reflected back in the narratives of video art that function like a hall of mirrors, transmitting a culture's stories back to itself in a manner resistant to the cinematic apparati of identification.

Given such a narrow preexisting discursive space, it can be difficult to challenge this medium's markers of East/West, French/English, us/them, and to carve out a space in-between. The exhibition and criticism of Canadian video art have been, at times, marked by binaryism, in which video histories are too carefully and unevenly separated out, subaltern identities forming a narrow sidebar. Curator/critic Monika Kin Gagnon, in her essay "How to Search for Signs of (East) Asian Life in the Video World," describes an official history of Canadian video art that "only cautiously gives voice to cultural difference within a designated space of discussion, rather than allowing [discovery of] tropes as intrinsic." She describes Canadian video art about marginalized cultural identities as being a relatively recent project, and she writes of being unable to locate "politicized identifications" among Canadian video artists before 1985 (*MM*, 95).

> Even the smallest unit of language, a sound, is politically charged. By altering the way we represent the sounds of our language, we transgress.
>
> —Wendy Waring, *Work in Progress*

English Lesson, by Vancouver-based, Trinidadian-Irish artist Shani Mootoo, was produced in 1991. The oldest video in this grouping, it gives us a sense of first voice, both of the video maker's own oeuvre (this is her second video) and of the beginnings of a radical politics of difference within theoretical discourse and art practice emerging in the late 1980s. Heated debates within feminist communities and communities of color about cultural appropriation and colonization of language form a context for this work. Its premise turns on a simple reversal of power relations—in this case, an immigrant teaching an (assumed) white Canadian viewer how to speak West Indian patois. The setting is a crowded, bohemian, urban kitchen; the "teacher," a Trinidadian man, uses a wooden spoon for a pointer, and the format apes that of an instructional film, the kind we used to have to watch in French class. *English Lesson*, at a scant three minutes, makes efficient use of an imaginary, utopian device that has been used early on in many a radical politic, from Charlotte Perkins Gilman's nineteenth-century novel *Herland* to Lisa Steele and Kim Tomczak's 1984 video *Working the Double Shift*. The oppressor takes on the role of the oppressed, and we are asked to see the workings of colonization through the oppressor's eyes. Perhaps even more striking than the premise itself (which can be reductive) is the disruption of cinematic-looking relations that occurs. As Ann E. Kaplan asks, "What happens when the look is returned—when black people own the look and startle whites into knowledge of their whiteness?"[5]

What happens when official languages are displaced—when colonial address is returned with a different, subaltern language? Implicit in the text of *English Lesson*, and within several other videos in this collection, is a sense of the English language as colonizer: stealer of dreams, swallower of history.

> Who is to say that robbing a people of its language is less violent than war?
> —Ray Gwyn Smith, "Moorland is Cold Country,"
> unpublished manuscript, quoted in Anzaldùal, *BLF*

Sovereign, a twelve-minute video by Philip Napier, locates this general notion in the specific: a lyrical, poetic examination of the genealogy of Irish and Canadian place-names—and the military forces that replaced Irish and First Nations place-names with British ones. A series of vignettes is sutured together with the haunting incantation of Belfast and Vancouver street names and a repetition of luminous images: Vancouver bus signs, an Irish coin embossed with a British sovereign, X rays of a human skeleton and mouth. The imagistic use of the body in this work evokes both the corporeal reality of war—the anguished toll of names and bodies—as well as the metaphor of language as tongue. Napier does not let us forget that the physiological and psychological mechanisms that create speech are located in the body: the brain, vocal chords, tongue, teeth, mouth—a human ability both fragile and complex, passed on through ties of kinship and blood. But this is not the fetishized cinematic body as we know it, folding the gaze back into the Symbolic. Napier's disavowal of a unified "I," of a body recognizably his, results in a deflecting of the voyeuristic gaze.

Who speaks? What speaks? The question is implied, and the function named, but the individual never reigns, and the subject slips away without naturalizing its voice. S/he who speaks, speaks to the tale as s/he begins telling and retelling it. S/he does not speak about it.

—Trinh-T. Minh-ha, *Over There*

This disavowal of a unified colonial gaze allows for a retelling of the tale of language acquisition and loss. As those of us who have experienced the erosion or loss of our mother tongues know: to intervene in this process is to create wounds that are generations deep. Says Anzaldúa: "So, if you really want to hurt me, talk about my language. Ethnic identity is twin skin to linguistic identity—I am my language" (*BLF*, 55). Napier writes a history that painfully yet elegantly acknowledges the phantom limb of forgotten language: "It is not what they built, it is what they knocked down . . . not the streets, it is the streets that no longer exist."

[S]tumbling through tangled mazes in mind and mouth, the language crippled inside, phantom limb asserting absence.

—Lydia Kwa, *West Coast Line*

It is a commonplace, even if relatively recent, notion that language can be physical as well as textual. "Body language" is a concept that took root in the 1970s, amid a confluence of pop-psychology and industrial forces whose original purpose was to provide new methods of measurement and evaluation in the workplace. The body as unconscious signifier of language—"closed," "angry," "open"—the body as wild tongue, loose lips in need of control, language as a site of power—a standardized North American corporate tool whose roots exist in the corpus, the body. Cathy Sisler's work is about the grotesque body that lacks this corporate alliance, this fluency in body language and social skills, yet carries itself with dignity and crazy wisdom. What stories do the face, the legs, and the arms tell when the story is in an aberrant (lesbian) foreign language?

This video's images, like its sound track, are minimalist and jazz driven. We see Sisler walking along the street in slow motion, riffing movement with a ragged, shambling gait. The poetic, beatlike voice-over speaks of her own history of addiction, interspersed with information on the phenomenology of staggering. Reenacting the gestures of her past drug addictions, Sisler intervenes into the repetition of earlier traumas through parody. Sisler's "body language"—eccentric, peculiar, funny—appears in counterpoint to dictionary definitions of various words (appearing on the screen) such as "stagger" and "deviance." Sisler's body, with no official definition, operates in code, creating a privileged language for those—lesbian, recovered alcoholic, fat, inconsistent—in the know.

This sexual dialect has a quality of improvisation. It is urban. Unsettling. Undoing . . . understanding words of sex in relation to my body.

—Camille Roy

While Sisler's work has been the subject of several eloquent critical texts (most notably, Nicole Gingras'), the lesbian "dialect" in her work is never remarked upon. And yet Sisler's work speaks movingly of the lesbian body in public space, simultaneously spectacular and invisible. Aberrance and deviance—concepts used frequently in her work—are labels that have, historically, been used to describe lesbians and gays under the rubric of sexology. Sisler's video persona—with her flapping, oversized men's overcoat, wild hair, and inappropriate body movements—seems to embrace a utopian, Bakhtinian madness, "a gay parody of official reason, of the narrow seriousness with 'official' truth. It is a festive madness" (*RHW*, 39). Her carnivalesque reversals of the body—private, furtive gestures in public space, a tenderness and crazy wisdom accruing to her largesse—parody the autobiographical. Sisler performs her body rather than presenting it, skillfully resisting ontological claims. The lesbian is a trace identity, made visible by repetition, made invisible by the culture. Her aberrant body language is risky, perhaps even dangerous, her appreciation of the margins ambivalent: "I remember how to stagger: I remember how not to stagger; I have control over my legs." To survive, she has become multilingual; to do more than survive, she maintains allegiance to her stagger, her "othernesses." She remembers.

Memory lies at the core of cultural survival. The remembering of language is linked to the remembering of history, and of culture: songs, stories, the wisdom of elders. If the language is lost, then only nonlanguage-based cultural artifacts survive. This can lead to a cultural identity based on ethnic food and dance, the meat and potatoes of official multiculturalism. *Word for Word* is a deceptively simple work that expresses a primal need to remember ancestral languages. In it, Ruth Cuthand and Elizabeth MacKenzie—its Cree and French/Scottish directors—utter phrases in their mother tongues, while a crawling text provides English translation, complete with grammatical errors. The visual and textual images are of everyday domestic life—food, pets, family photos—locating language, within North American lifestyles, that provides a fragile home for difference. The languages that result are piecemeal, raising questions about how languages change and develop across generations. Are Cuthand's and MacKenzie's utterances just bad grammar, or are they a kind of patois, an authentic daughter tongue, formed by the erosions of place and time?

The video also touches upon some interesting parallels and differences between the status of First Nations and French languages. French, given official status in Canada in the 1960s, has become a language of power in Québec. Outside of Québec, however, francophone communities are dwindling and are sometimes the object of right-wing, anti-French campaigns. The Cree Nation, one of the larger Indian Nations in Canada, lays ancestral claim to most of Québec's land, while its language receives little government support. Indeed, many aboriginal languages face extinction, diminished by the residential school system and racist government policies. The collaborative, even-handed nature of this video implies a certain universality. The video reveals that MacKenzie's daughter is able to go to French immersion class. In the video, MacKenzie expresses her hope to have a conversation in French with her daughter some day, "the conversation I couldn't have with my mother." But some languages will survive, while others, orphaned by colonialism, may disappear. As Franco-Métis film/videomaker Marjorie Beaucage asserts, "We are all related, but we are not the same."[6]

> I carry two tongues inside my mouth, or maybe it is just one, with two tips.
>
> —Carmen Rodríguez, *West Coast Line*

Window, by Montrealer Nelson Henricks, also provides translation from one language to another, but in this case the switch from French to English and back again is rapid-fire, staccato, almost disorienting—the way, in Québec, living between two languages can be. The images in this video consist entirely of the view from Henrick's front window, over the period of a year: a dappling of green leaves, red and yellow foliage, the tracing of black branches against a wintry white sky. Television "snow" is intercut into the window images. On the sound track, English and French rub frictively against each other, making sparks, creating static. The view from Henrick's window is a microcosm of this tension, *dans différent temps*: fierce weather and the heat of language on the streets. The phrases in the video speak of longing and desire: "to know you . . . I return . . . many times . . . to see you." Whether Henricks is speaking of love for a city, Montreal, or love for another, it is clear that this love is both molded and ruptured by language. While media portrayals present a unitary image of anglophone Québecers oppressed by the French language, this video illustrates a mode of coexistence in which rootlessness, hybridity, and living in-between become a kind of home. In this work, neither language is dominant; the two languages collide and blur, becoming like Rodríguez' single tongue with two tips. Sexual or linguistic, this double tongue refuses nationalisms; it will not be tamed into a unitary, essential identity. Embedded within this triumphant refusal is, however, a sense of loss, what Said has called nationalism's "essential association with exile."[7]

> History is harvested and collected, to be assembled, made to speak remembered, re-read and rewritten, and language comes alive in transit, in interpretation.
>
> —Iain Chambers, *Migrancy, Culture, Identity*

The search for a subaltern language in these works mirrors the search for a post-colonial cinematic language of difference in contemporary video art. Video's scant twenty-five-year history means that sites of cultural difference are not yet fully realized. Too often, as video artists Karen Lefkovitz and Shashwati Taluk-dar have pointed out, artists with politicized identifications become "cultural brokers,"[8] explaining, negotiating, and finally negating difference. As struggles for global capital play across the fields of public and private culture, the desire for expression, creativity, transcendence, or social change is reterritorialized. Deviation from the regime of normalcy (of the body, or of the body politic) becomes a threat to investment opportunity and, concomitantly, national identity. Ursula Franklin has written, "Whatever cannot be merely bought or sold, whatever cannot be expressed in terms of money and gain/loss transactions stands in the way of 'the market' and is Enemy territory, to be occupied, transformed, and conquered."[9] Video art provides a marginal public space, liminally located within this enemy territory. Its implicit resistance to market forces can be a hospitable site for language that challenges globalization's colonizing urge. In this new language, the director moves beyond the role of ethnography's native informant. Travel, exile, and homelessness are dominant modes of being; the exile represents a model of knowledge that crosses borders, breaks "barriers of thought and experience."[10] Official, national history is replaced by memory, a kind of counter-memory that is almost apparitional. The languages that result are never whole, never stable. Chambers calls it "a language always shadowed by loss, an elsewhere, a ghost: the unconscious, an 'other' text, an 'other' voice, an 'other' world; a language that is powerfully affected by the foreign tongue." And all of those different, wild, unofficial tongues that were never tamed.

NOTES

1. Gloria Anzaldúa, *Borderlands/La Frontera* (San Francisco: Spinsters/Aunt Lute, 1987). Hereafter cited in the text as *BLF*.

2. In his book *White*, Richard Dyer writes about how mythical notions about mountainous origins of whiteness bring with them notions of enterprise, purity, and discipline: "Such notions . . . can still be found in, for instance, nineteenth and early twentieth-century notions of Canadian identity, where the experience of the cold North is claimed to have molded in the settler people a distinct white national character" (London: Routledge, 1997), 21.

3. Mikhail Bakhtin, *Rabelais and His World*, trans. Helen Isowlsky (Bloomington: Indiana University Press, 1968). Hereafter cited in the text as *RHW*.

4. Janine Marchessault, "Preface," *Mirror Machine: Video in the Age of Identity*, ed. Janine Marchessault (Toronto/Montreal: YYZ Books and CRCCII, 1995), 8. Hereafter cited as *MM*.

5. Ann E. Kaplan, *Looking for the Other: Feminism, Film, and the Imperial Gaze* (New York: Routledge, 1997), 4.

6. Marjorie Beaucage, "Aboriginal Voices: Entitlement through Storytelling" (*MM*, 214).

7. Edward Said, "Reflections on Exile," *Out There: Marginalization and Contemporary Cultures*, Ferguson, Gever, Minh-ha, eds. (New York: New Museum, 1991).

8. Karen Lefkovitz and Sashwati Talukdar, "Tell me your story, baby: Personal narrative, resistance, or capitulation." Unpublished conference paper presented at Console-ing Passions: Feminism Television & Video, May 1997.

9. Ursula Franklin, "The New Deadly Face of War Is Economic Globalization," *CCPA Monitor*, vol. 5, no. 8 (February 1999).

10. Trinh T. Minh-ha, "Cotton and Iron," *Out There: Marginalization and Contemporary Cultures*, ed. Ferguson, Gever, and Minh-ha (New York: New Museum, 1991).

CONTRIBUTORS

Marusya Bociurkiw is a long-time activist in Canadian cultural and feminist communities. She is the author of *The Woman Who Loved Airports* and has published articles and reviews in arts and feminist publications. In recent years her narrative writings have been anthologized in *Fireweed*, *Dykewords*, *Queer Looks*, and *The Journey Prize Anthology*. She has produced and directed over a dozen videos and films, including *Unspoken Territory*, *Night Visions*, and *Bodies in Trouble*.

Stephen Boos is Associate Professor of Humanities and Social Sciences, teaching in the Foundation Year Programme at the University of King's College in Halifax, Canada. He has written papers and articles on Hegel's aesthetics, contemporary critiques of epistemology, and theories of imagination.

Tina Chanter is Associate Professor in the Department of Philosophy at the University of Memphis, Tennessee. She is the author of *Ethics of Eros: Irigaray's Rewriting of the Philosophers* and numerous essays on Derrida, Hegel, Heidegger, Kristeva, Kofman, Merleau-Ponty, Lacan, and Levinas. Her forthcoming books are *The Time of Death: Levinas with Heidegger and Derrida* and edited collections *Rethinking Sex and Gender* and *Feminist Interpretations of Levinas*.

Alex Colville is an internationally known Canadian artist and the 1982 recipient of the Order of Canada. His work has been exhibited in solo exhibits in Germany, England, Canada, Japan, and China and has been represented in numerous public and private collections, including the National Gallery of Canada, the Art Gallery of Ontario, the Museum of Modern Art in New York, the Musée Nationale d'Art Moderne in Paris, and the Museum Boymans-van Beuningen in Rotterdam.

Drucilla Cornell, one of the most influential feminist thinkers today, is professor of women's studies, political science, and law at Rutgers University. She is the author of, among others, *The Philosophy of the Limit*, *Deconstruction and the Possibility of Justice*, *Transformations: Recollective Imagination and Sexual Difference*, *The*

Imaginary Domain: Abortion, Pornography, and Sexual Harassment, At the Heart of Freedom, Beyond Accommodation: Ethical Feminism, Deconstruction, and the Law, and *Freedom, Identity, and Rights.*

Terry Eagleton, a prominent Marxist literary critic, is the Warton Professor of English Literature at St. Catherine's College, Oxford University. Among his many publications are *Walter Benjamin, Marxism and Literary Criticism, The Ideology of the Aesthetic, Ideology: An Introduction, Literary Theory, The Illusions of Postmodernism, Saint Oscar and Other Plays, Criticism and Ideology: A Study in Marxist Literary Theory, Marx: The Great Philosophers,* and most recently *The Idea of Culture* and *The Truth about the Irish.*

Elizabeth Edwards is Associate Professor of Humanities and Social Sciences at the University of King's College in Halifax, Canada. She teaches in the Contemporary Studies Programme, the Foundation Year Programme, and in the Department of English at Dalhousie University. By training a scholar in Middle English, she is the author of *The Genesis of Narrative in Malory's Morte d'Arthur.*

Rodolphe Gasché is Eugenio Donato Professor of Comparative Literature at the State University of New York at Buffalo. His books include *Die hybride Wissenschaft, System und Metaphorik in der Philosophie von Georges Bataille, The Tain of the Mirror: Derrida and the Philosophy of Reflection, Inventions of Difference: On Jacques Derrida, The Wild Card of Reading: On Paul de Man,* and *Of Minimal Things: Studies on the Notion of Relation.* Currently , he is working on a book-length study on Kant's aesthetics.

Susan Gibson Garvey is an artist, a curator, a teacher, and a writer who has lived and worked in Nova Scotia, Canada, for the past twenty-five years. Her artworks have been exhibited in solo and group exhibitions in England and across Canada and are represented in private and public Canadian collections. She has curated over thirty-five exhibitions and published essays, reviews, and articles in various Canadian journals and exhibition catalogues. She is currently director of the Dalhousie Art Gallery in Halifax, Nova Scotia.

Dorota Glowacka is Associate Professor in the Contemporary Studies Programme at the University of King's College in Halifax, Canada. She has published articles and reviews in the area of American, Polish, and French literature, continental theory, and Holocaust literature. Her current work focuses on representations of the Holocaust in literature and art in the context of contemporary philosophical debates. She is working on a book *The Shattered Word: Writing of the Fragment and the Holocaust Testimony.*

Richard Kearney is Professor in the Philosophy Department at University College in Dublin and Visiting Professor at Boston College. He is the author of numerous books, including *The Wake of Imagination*, *The Poetics of Imagining*, *The Poetics of Modernity*, and *Questioning Ethics*, co-edited with Mark Dooley.

Victor Li is Associate Professor of English at Dalhousie University. He has published articles on modernism, postmodernism, and postcolonial theory in journals such as *Ariel*, *boundary 2*, *Criticism*, *English Studies in Canada*, *Cultural Critique*, *Genre*, and *Prose Studies*. He is currently working on a study of neo-primitivism in contemporary theoretical discourses.

Jean-François Lyotard, prominent literary critic and theoretician of the postmodern, was Professor of Philosophy at the Université de Paris VIII and Professor of French and Italian at the University of Califronia at Irvine. Some of his best-known works include *Discourse, Figure*, *Libidinal Economy*, *Postmodern Condition*, *Just Gaming*, *The Differend*, *Heidegger and "the jews," Hyphen*, and essays collected in *The Lyotard Reader* and *Political Writings*. Professor Lyotard died in 1998.

David MacFadyen is Associate Professor of Russian at Dalhousie University in Halifax, Canada. He is the author of *Joseph Brodsky and the Baroque*, *Joseph Brodsky and the Soviet Muse*, and *Personality and the Soviet Popular Song after 1955*. His recent books (under review) are *Estrada!? Grand Narratives and the Russian Popular Song after Perestroika* and *Songs for Fat People: Affect, Emotion, and Apoliticism in the Soviet Popular Song, 1917–1955*.

Martin Rumscheidt is Professor of Historical and Systematic Theology at the Atlantic School of Theology in Halifax, Nova Scotia. A native German, he studied in Germany, Switzerland, and Canada. He is the author of numerous publications on Karl Barth and Dietrich Bonhoeffer and on the Holocaust and the churches in countries under Communist governments. With Barbara Rumscheidt, he has translated a number of books and articles in theology and biblical studies.

Marjorie Stone is Associate Professor of English at Dalhousie University in Halifax, Canada, and former president of the Association of Canadian College and University Teachers of English. She is the author of *Elizabeth Barrett Browning* and numerous essays in collections and journals, such as *Victorian Studies*, *Victorian Poetry*, *Victorian Literature*, and others. She has recently co-edited *Literary Couplings: Writing Couples and Collaborators in Historical Context*.

Krzysztof Ziarek is Associate Professor of English at the University of Notre Dame. He is the author of *Inflected Language: Toward a Hermeneutics of Nearness: Heidegger, Levinas, Stevens, Celan* and *The Historicity of Experience: Modernity, the Avant-Garde, and the Event,* and the editor of *Future Crossings: Literature between Philosophy and Cultural Studies.*

INDEX

Abortion: feminist ethics and, 149–151

Abstract expressionism, 260–261

Aesthetic, the, 15: autonomy of, 1, 2, 9, 23, 188–189, 220, 255; ethics and, 16, 22–23, 51–53, 62–64, 120–121; as non-conceptual, 20, 22–23, 50, 58, 60, 77–78, 81–82; reason and, 16–17, 21, 22, 50, 56–58

Aesthetics, 16–17, 222, 231–232, 251: as emancipatory, 21, 173; of feeling, 5, 52–53, 80–81; feminist, 6–7, 150; formalist, 220, 221; history of, 1–2, 15–17, 78; knowledge and, 15–16, 18, 60, 221–222; materialist, 220, 221; negative, 80–81; philosophy and, 15–17; politics and, 21, 246–247; Soviet, 9; as unethical, 103

Adorno, Theodor, 79, 89: *Aesthetic Theory*, 219–222, 227; on art, 2, 8, 219, 222–223, 227

Affect: *see* Feeling

Agnon, Shmuel Yosef, 87

Alterity, 5 (*see also* Difference): ethical relation and, 196, 234; Holocaust testimony and, 97, 99, 102–103; representation and, 3, 100–102

Améry, Jean, 124

Anamorph, 267–268, 270, 271

Antisemitism, 125–126; Christianity and, 126–127

Appadurai, Arjun, 205–206

Ardon, Mordechai: *A Doll of Auschwitz, The Road of Numbers, The Shadows* [triptych], 99, 101

Arendt, Hannah: *Eichmann in Jerusalem*, 259

Aristotle, 1

Arnold, Matthew, 144–145

Art, 65–66, 74–75, 219–220, 228–230: abstract, 232–233; activist, 276, 286–287; autobiographical, 293; classical, 24; exhibition of, 9–10, 277–279, 289–291; experience of, 9, 80–81; gesture of, 74, 77, 79–80; history of, 265–266; knowledge and, 224, 227; me-

chanical reproduction and, 258, 264, 267, 270; philosophy and, 1, 23–24, 74, 75–76; politics and, 21, 189, 233–234, 253; pop, 9, 255–257, 259, 260, 265, 271–272; power and, 233–234; racism and, 276, 278–279, 283, 289; self-consciousness of, 26; singularity of, 75, 76; social role of, 8, 219–221, 231–233; subliminal, 266; time and, 223, 253; video, 10, 293–294, 299; as work, 223–224

Art criticism: demand for, 74–75; inadequacy of, 76–77, 79, 81

Auschwitz, 6, 124–125 (*see also* Holocaust, the)

Avant-garde, 2, 81, 93, 196, 262–264

Banality, 9, 122, 256, 258–259, 266–267, 270: ethics and, 259, 271–272

Barber, Benjamin, 38, 47n

Barrett Browning, Elizabeth, 136, 140–141: *Aurora Leigh*, 141; "Hiram Powers' *Greek Slave*," 132, 134; "Runaway Slave at Pilgrim's Point," 134, 136, 138, 143–145

Barthes, Roland, 81, 85, 258

Baumgarten, A.G.: *Aesthetica*, 1, 15

Beaudrillard, Jean, 257

Beauty, 16, 18–19, 21, 49, 54, 60, 231, 251: of art distinguished from nature, 65–66, 68; judgement of, 19–20, 49–50; moral goodness and, 50–53, 68–69; natural, 69–70

Beckett, Samuel, 232–233

Benhabib, Seyla, 38–39

Benjamin, Walter, 78, 267

Black (African-American): identity, 137–138, 177; women, 177–178; writing, 176–177

Blackstone, William, 251

Blanchot, Maurice, 91

Body, the, 22, 35, 295, 297: female, 39, 41, 143, 164–165, 171–172; maternal, 172–173

Böll, Heinrich, 119–121, 128

Bonhoeffer, Dietrich, 126